T0286140

GOA, 1961

Celebrating 35 Years of
Penguin Random House India

ADVANCE PRAISE FOR THE BOOK

'Of the several books I have read on the subject, this is the first that treats the issue from every conceivable angle—from a brief history of Goa to that of revolts against the colonial power, to the many non-violent steps taken by India, including diplomacy, an economic blockade, satyagraha, third-party intervention, backstage diplomacy and, finally, Op. Vijay. Every aspect has been deftly handled in the fewest of words. Being of Goan origin, I learnt much about Goa and its rich history. This is a book that every Goan—whether in Goa or in the diaspora—must read'—**Air Marshal Yeshwant Rao Rane, PVSM, AVSM, VSM, ADC, veteran, fighter pilot, retired as air officer commanding-in-chief, Southern Air Command**

'This book is highly recommended to all those who take serious interest in the business of war-making, covering strategies and tactics involved at diplomatic, political, social and military levels leading to a successful military operation and its aftermath, in its entirety'— **Vice Admiral Sunil K. Damle, PVSM, AVSM, NM (G), VSM, veteran, carrier-borne naval fighter aviator, retired as flag officer commanding-in-chief, Southern Naval Command**

'*Goa, 1961* is a unique compilation of what really happened during India's Operation Vijay. The author, through diligent research, has skilfully put together a gripping account of how the Indian armed forces took Goa back from the Portuguese. Written in an easy and lucid style, this book provides a valuable historical account of the war and is a must-read for every Indian citizen'—**Major General Ian Cardozo, AVSM, SM, veteran, Gorkha Regiment, and author**

'This book is an eye-opener. It has revealed details of not only the military action in 1961 but the entire history of Goa since the Portuguese arrived in the subcontinent more than 600 years ago. The freedom movement in Goa started well before it did in India, a fact unknown to most of us. A well-researched book that should be read by every Indian, especially those living or having roots in Goa'—**Major General V.K. Singh, veteran, Signals, and author**

'This is a most comprehensive, no-holds-barred and accurate account of the Indian political and military action against Portugal in 1961. It highlights the overwhelming Indian military action against Portuguese forces, due to poor intelligence inputs'—**Commodore Gilbert Menezes, VSM, veteran, pioneer submariner**

GOA, 1961

The Complete Story of Nationalism and Integration

VALMIKI FALEIRO

VINTAGE

An imprint of Penguin Random House

VINTAGE

USA | Canada | UK | Ireland | Australia
New Zealand | India | South Africa | China | Singapore

Vintage is part of the Penguin Random House group of companies
whose addresses can be found at global.penguinrandomhouse.com

Published by Penguin Random House India Pvt. Ltd
4th Floor, Capital Tower 1, MG Road,
Gurugram 122 002, Haryana, India

Penguin
Random House
India

First published in Vintage by Penguin Random House India 2023

Copyright © Valmiki Faleiro 2023

ISBN 9780670097920

Typeset in Bembo Text by MAP Systems, Bengaluru, India
Printed at Thomson Press India Ltd, New Delhi

www.penguin.co.in

To the Goan
who held his head high,
from the mid-seventeenth century to 1961

CONTENTS

PREFACE

Goa was a 'pimple' on the face of the Indian empire. Sometimes called 'a carbuncle' by the Indian leadership overseas, led by the indefatigable V.K. Krishna Menon, famous for his friendship with Pandit Nehru, Lord Mountbatten and Indira Gandhi.

The liberation of Goa in 1961 was engineered by the indomitable will of defence minister V.K. Krishna Menon, who once, as India's ambassador to the United Nations, delivered a mesmerizing nine-hour-long speech. What Vasco da Gama had started in 1498, from his entry into Calicut, was ended in 1961 by this Calicut native. It was the beginning of the cultural upheaval in the tiny Portuguese state.

The conquest was decisive and brief, as Valmiki Faleiro has testified in this book, backed by the most meticulous research on the military operation commanded by Major General K.P. Candeth.

Gen. Candeth was the son of M.A. Candeth, a history professor at Presidency College, who admitted Menon into his college. Menon obviously had implicit confidence in the commanding general. Candeth was appointed the military lieutenant governor on 20 December 1961 and held that office until 6 June 1962.

Pandit Nehru and his soulmate Krishna Menon had always extended support for decades to movements in Spain, South Africa, Angola, Mozambique, Cuba and some states like Portugal, for which Menon became a legend.

Mahatma Gandhi led the fight for Indian independence from within. London was the centre of the universe in those days, and Krishna Menon led that global struggle externally from there.

Menon had powerful backing from Harold Laski, Stafford Cripps, R. Palme Dutt, Bhicoo Batlivala (Inner Temple 1932),

Wilfred Roberts, MP, Reginald Sorenson, MP, George Strauss, MP, and S.A. Wickremasinghe.

When the Constituent Assembly was drafting India's Constitution, Menon also gave the first draft of the Preamble, which was incorporated by Pandit Nehru and Dr Ambedkar almost verbatim and passed in 1946.

Earlier, it was Krishna Menon, K.M. Panikkar, V.P. Menon, K.P.S. Menon and Shankara Menon—all Kerala stalwarts—who got international support for Panditji's close friend Sheikh Mohammad Abdullah, who wisely opted to join the Indian side with Maharaja Hari Singh. This was confirmed by the Sher-e-Kashmir Sheikh Abdullah himself in 1978 in Srinagar, when I was a state guest.

It was Krishna Menon and his team of London-based barristers, Rajni Patel, Siddharth Shankar Ray with Annie Besant, R. Palme Dutt, Madame Blavatsky, Anna Pallak, Feroze Gandhi, P.N. Haksar, Stafford Cripps, E.M. Forster, Paul Robeson, Michael Foote and the pre-eminently brilliant Harold Laski, who gave the liberation of Goa the momentum and ballast to integrate this tiny piece of Europe back into India. These dignitaries had publicly endorsed the anti-colonial stands of Nehru and Menon.

Menon told Nehru: 'Goa has to come home!' (This is a direct quote from Rajni Patel.) I knew many of those stalwarts. Barrister Rajni Patel, who successfully coordinated Menon's poll campaign in 1957 and 1962, had several conversations on Goa with me at his eleventh-floor Cuffe Castle apartment at Cuffe Parade, Bombay.

In 1962, one of Menon's successful platforms was the heavily publicized 'Liberation of Goa'. Menon presented the prime minister with a fait accompli *after* Operation Vijay had begun. The operation was over in a day with the surrender of the Portuguese forces.

Thus, Menon diligently heeded the advice of Ram Manohar Lohia, Jayaprakash Narayan and George Fernandes (who told me so himself).

Author Jairam Ramesh has paid just and brilliant tribute to Menon in his mammoth book *A Chequered Brilliance*.

The liberation was a swift surgical manoeuvre. In the final analysis, Portugal had to submit to India's overwhelming might, as detailed by Faleiro in this book. The operation comprised some of the finest military officers, many with Goan backgrounds.

Personal interactions recalled with Portuguese prime minister Mario Soares, with Goan freedom fighters Lambert Mascarenhas, Purushottam Kakodkar, Dionisio Ribeiro and with Indian proponents like Rajni Patel, Siddharth Shankar Ray and Sheikh Abdulla gave me an insight into the ideological background that obliterated what was once called a 'pimple on the face of Mother India'.

Rajni Patel repeatedly cautioned Krishna Menon to discard the use of the word 'pimple'.

'What word should I use?' asked Menon.

Replied Rajni Bhai: 'Since you are canvassing in English use "anachronism", then explain what it means.'

'Out of touch and out of place.' Simple!

Yes, Nehru had a mental block about liberating Goa. He had promised the great White powers that he would not take Goa. But Menon convinced him that he could not have a separate yardstick for this Portuguese territory from his public stand in Spain and apartheid-loving countries.

Although Maj. Gen. Candeth was the first Indian face of the liberated territory, certain upper-crust Goan families harboured animosity towards the general. They said he regularly plonked his boots on to the highly polished mahogany tables in Cabo Raj Niwas, the governor-general's residence. This might have been true, as I saw the furniture during Lieutenant Governor S.K. Banerjee's time!

A Goan footnote: Russi Karanjia, editor of the noted tabloid *Blitz*, was a conduit to convey advice on Goa, Spain and Cuba to Krishna Menon, as he told me himself in my weekly editorial meetings for a column that Margao's professor D.M. Silveira and I wrote for *Blitz*.

Four years in Goa, from 1972, influenced this alien in his own land. I found it had more sweetness than light! Now it has evolved.

Goa was an emotion, not economics to the Portuguese, says Faleiro. It still is for me.

So, who is the author of this book, *Goa, 1961*? Faleiro was admitted to Vidya Vikas Mandal's Commerce College at Margao by me in 1974. It was an honour and service to the cause of Goan history!

This unique institution fulfilled the dreams of its founders, Prof. Ganesh M. Daivajna and Prof. H.M. Gaunekar, and teaching staff, like Prof. G.G. Kondli, Prof. Joan Rebello, and principal S.V. Deshpande.

It has produced great students: Aleixo Sequeira, Valmiki Faleiro, Sanjay Hegde, Shekhar Raiturkar, Savio Mascarenhas, Jacinto Moniz, Blasco Faleiro (the author's late younger brother), S.V. Raman and Leslie Rodrigues, contributor to the *Global Goan*.

Valmiki Faleiro is primarily a military historian and is now an authority on the liberation of Estado Português da **Índia**, Goa's erstwhile name, in 1961.

He was my star student from 1974 to 1976 in VVM College, Margao, and a devoted student of English; and he became widely read, devouring all kinds of books.

He left an indelible impression then, which has only evolved positively over the last forty years. He is dogged with details because details provide authenticity to research. On occasion, we must locate the basic truth, sifting it from the mass of facts.

'Mayor of Margao', as one often calls him, is loyal to his findings and never camouflages the truth. His love for Goa and for India has won the respect of all Goan thinkers, cutting across political and religious hues, which is a tall order and a respectable achievement.

First-hand witnesses to the Goa operation are now difficult to find. But the superior research single-handedly done by Valmiki Faleiro would have been saluted by my great historian friend Dr George Moraes, a Goan heading the history department of Bombay University, who was deeply immersed in Goan history.

Please note: this is Faleiro's magnum opus. Military history must record Goa's debt to him.

When I was there in 1974, Portuguese foreign minister (later prime minister) Mario Soares visited Goa to fly the flag of socialism in an erstwhile outpost. I accompanied him to the Goa Museum and mentioned to him that there was a life-size portrait of the dictator António Salazar which he would not want to miss.

He responded: 'I do not want to see that face again. He deprived many of us of our freedom during his brutal dictatorship.'

Faleiro, your tome will be treasured!

Biji George Koshy
Independent corporate director

PROLOGUE

Thanks to Covid, I began catching up on long-pending tasks. One of them was revising the text of my first book, *Patriotism in Action: Goans in India's Defence Services*, first published in 2010 by Goa, 1556, for a final edition. The list of 400 Goan-origin commissioned officers in the three arms of the defence services of India in the first edition had grown to more than twice the number.

That book had a chapter called 'The Wars'—all the wars fought by India, from the 1947–48 J&K operations to the continuing war (narco-terrorism, dubbed the 'heroin-Kalashnikov culture' by the Pakistani media), without which the reader may not have understood the contribution of Goan-origin officers in the armed forces in the pages that followed.

A part of this chapter on India's wars was the use of force to oust the Portuguese from Goa in 1961. The quick thirty-six-hour cakewalk was covered in a mere five lines in the 2010 edition. When revision of the text began in the monsoon of 2021, I realized we were in the sixtieth year of the 1961 event. Being of interest to the primary target reader, i.e., the Goan, wherever in the world she/he may be, I decided to do an in-depth study of the subject and write a more exhaustive account of this military event, minor albeit one fraught with grave international ramifications in that era of the heightened Cold War between the world's two major power blocks.

Consulting about 150 sources—printed, online and a few oral testimonies—across languages (primarily English and Portuguese) and geographical origin (Goan, Indian, Portuguese and other western), I ended up with much more material than I had bargained for … and certainly too much for a book otherwise devoted to listing Goan-origin military officers who served the motherland.

That is when the decision came to produce this *Goa, 1961* story as a standalone book.

It is my cherished hope that you will enjoy reading this book to the end as much as I enjoyed researching and writing it.

1

THE BACKGROUND

1510: Goa Turns Portuguese

Portugal, although puny with a population of just over a million and nothing noteworthy about her ocean-going traditions, was the first European nation to chart a sea route to Asia. The fall of Constantinople (now Istanbul) to the Ottoman Turks on 29 May 1453 made Portugal feel the need to open a new battlefront with the Ottoman Empire by joining forces with the mythical Rei Preste João (King Prester John of Abyssinia, today's Ethiopia), for which naval power was a prerequisite. Until then, Portugal only had half-decked sailboats and sailors who were unable to navigate out of sight of land and into the oceans.

A far-sighted Portuguese prince, Dom Henrique, better known as Henry the Navigator, invested some of his own wealth and that of the Templars into shipbuilding and navigation. He launched a maritime school at Sagres on Portugal's southwestern cape of São Vicente facing the Atlantic. (Modern historians call Sagres a myth. In 1960, the Portuguese in Goa built a monument—a sextant with a mariner's globe—to commemorate 500 years of the Sagres School for Navigation at Campal in Panjim. Portugal's vessel to commemorate the fifteenth-century voyages of discovery was named *Sagres*—she docked at Mormugao, Goa, in the mid-1990s amidst howls of protest by local freedom fighters.) At Sagres, or some such place, Portuguese sailors were trained in cosmology, cartography, math, medicine and shipbuilding by hired Arabs, Jews, Genoese and Moroccans.

Henry the Navigator sponsored annual maritime expeditions to explore and map the west coast of Africa, to establish provisioning points en route and to constantly modify and improve the sturdiness of his sail ships. He died in 1460. After a lull of two decades, his nephew, King João II (1481–95), picked up the threads in 1480.

In 1487–88, Bartolomeu Dias made the historic rounding of the much-feared Cape of Torments, where Adamastor, the tempestuous sea devil, was believed to swallow sail ships and turn white men black. With Portugal's maritime conquest, the Cape of Torments became the Cape of Good Hope. It was then that King João II conceived the *Plano da Índia*, a plan entailing the search for a sea route to India. The fall of Constantinople to the Ottomans had closed the land route to Asia and the trade of spices, silks and other Asian merchandise was now a monopoly in the hands of seafaring Arabs and Venetian merchants, who profiteered at the cost of Europe. Portugal would soon emerge a European leader in maritime discovery—and of the lucrative Asian trade!

The Portuguese were the first to arrive in India. Discoverer Vasco da Gama dropped anchor near Calicut in May 1498, long before the Mughals stepped into India. Calicut was, coincidentally, the hometown of India's future defence minister, Vengalil Krishnan Kurup Krishna Menon—the principal backstage actor in the 1961 Operation Vijay, which evicted the Portuguese after more than four-and-a-half centuries in India.*

The Portuguese discovery of a sea route to India was an epoch-defining moment in the history of mankind. It would open the gates to an 'Age of Discoveries', lead to lands hitherto unknown to the European world—in Africa, Asia, Australia and, accidentally, the Americas—and spur a commercial revolution, the initial indicators of globalization and a world economy. It was to change the world's history, economics and politics. It had an underbelly too: it would lead to colonialism and spur slavery.

---

* Called Operation Vijay-1 after Kargil 1999 was also named Operation Vijay, necessitating the use of numerals 1 and 2 to distinguish one from the other.

Interestingly, Portugal's prideful narrative of the 'Age of Discoveries' makes no mention of the burgeoning and highly profitable African slave trade that continued well into the nineteenth century. Film-maker and journalist Ana Naomi de Sousa writes:

> Until now, there has never been a single explicit reference, memorial or monument in Portugal's public space to its pioneering role in the transatlantic slave trade, nor any acknowledgement of the millions of lives that were stolen between the 15th and 19th centuries. There is also a deafening silence on the cruelty and brutality that the Portuguese inflicted to achieve the domination of their trading posts and colonies.[*]

When it arrived at the shores of south-west India, Portugal was barely out of the late Middle Ages and on the threshold of the Early Renaissance. Lisbon, established circa 1200 BC, was the oldest European capital city—older than Madrid, Rome, Paris and London. The Indian civilization was far more ancient, second only to Mesopotamia and Egypt, older than the civilizations of Maya/ Mexico, China and Andes (Aztec, Inca); and all of those, much older than Europe.

The Portuguese set up spice-trading bases in Cochin (Kochi) and Cannanore (Kannur) on the Malabar coast. They raked in such giddy profits that the envious European royalty nicknamed their king, Manuel I, The Fortunate. Their Asian capital, initially in Cochin, was shifted to Goa in 1530, fifteen years after he died, thanks to Afonso de Albuquerque, the Portuguese governor in India from 1509 to 1515. Albuquerque had conquered the *Cidade de Goa* (City of Goa) in 1510, and it appeared as though he had fallen in love with the place because he wanted it to be Portugal's Asian capital.

---

[*] Ana Naomi de Sousa, 'How Portugal silenced "centuries of violence and trauma"', Aljazeera, 10 March 2021, https://www.aljazeera.com/ amp/features/2021/3/10/how-portugal-silenced-centuries-of-vio- lence-and-trauma

Cochin was eminently suitable to be the capital of Portugal's littoral empire in the east. It had the best and most naturally protected harbour on the Malabar coast. It provided fine hardwood and its shipyards built worthy vessels that enabled the Portuguese to sail in Asia and on the Cape route. Carracks and galleons built here would earn a reputation as the most seaworthy of the Carreira da Índia (vessels of the Portuguese on the India–Portugal searoute). A series of lagoons and creeks connected Cochin's port to the pepper-producing districts. Expectedly, therefore, Cochin emerged as a major entrepôt after the Portuguese dug in, and a large *casado* community (Portuguese men married to native women) settled there. Owing to its proximity to important trade points like the Coromandel, Orissa, Bengal, Pegu (Burma), Siam (Thailand), Malacca (Melaka), China and the Far East, Cochin was better located than Goa for trade—and thereby as the principal base in India.

In 1510, together with the city of Goa, Albuquerque conquered the island taluka of Tiswadi (*Ilha de Goa*) with its neighbouring islands of Chorao, Divar and Jua (*Santo Estevam*). The talukas of Bardez, Salcete and Ponda were also captured but were soon retaken by Bijapuri reinforcements. A see-saw contest between the Adil Shahis of Bijapur and the Portuguese in Tiswadi followed over the next forty-two years for Bardez and Salcete, which finally came into the definitive possession of the Portuguese in 1543.

The three talukas of Bardez, Tiswadi and Salcete (Mormugao was detached from Salcete as a separate taluka only at the fag end of the nineteenth century) were called the 'Old Conquests'. All were coastal talukas abutting the sea. The vast majority of the population in these three talukas was converted to Christianity by the early 17th century—those who resisted conversion were persecuted in a variety of ways: their properties were confiscated and they were evicted. With their gods, idols and faith, such Goans (many converted ones too, escaping the rigours of the Inquisition) resettled in areas beyond Portuguese control (in the remaining talukas of what is today Goa, in the Deccan areas from Kolhapur to Belgaum, and in coastal Karnataka and Kerala).[1]

Force and coercion, although prominently employed in the conversion of natives, were not the only reasons for the natives embracing a new faith. The Switzerland-based, Goan-origin, retired, chemical engineer and author Bernardo Elvino de Sousa, has skilfully adopted a case-study approach, indicating a varied and complex set of reasons for religious conversion in Goa through specific cases of individual and group conversions.[*]

More than 250 years later, in the second half of the 18th century, the Portuguese acquired the rest of Goa's talukas—Canacona, Quepem, Sanguem, Ponda, Bicholim (known earlier as Sanquelim), Sattari and Pernem—and these were collectively called the 'New Conquests'. Save Pernem at the northern end and Canacona at the southern extremity of Goa (and a very tiny part of Quepem), which abutted the sea, all the New Conquest talukas lay in the hinterland. The 'New Conquests' surrounded the 'Old Conquests' and served as a buffer against attacks over land. The Portuguese did not follow a policy of proselytization in the New Conquests, which remained predominantly Hindu.

However, there was an odd aspect to the Old and New Conquests. The seven New Conquest talukas accounted for 80 per cent of Goa's geographical area but housed only 27 per cent of its population, mostly Hindu. Most of the major Hindu temples like those of Mangesh, Mahalsa, Shantadurga, Kapileshwar and Ramnath had been shifted to the New Conquest taluka of Ponda (a non-Portuguese area then) at the height of religious persecution in the 16th–17th centuries. (There is a common misconception that the temple of Lord Naguesh at Bandora in Ponda taluka may have been shifted from Nagoa in Salcete taluka. This is not so. The Naguesh temple is the only temple originally from Ponda

---

[*] Bernardo Elvino de Sousa, *The Denaming of Goans: Case Studies of Conversions in Medieval Goa,* Pothi, 2022.

taluka which predated the Portuguese and is mentioned in the copper plates of Vim'n Mantri, circa 1350 CE.) The bulk of Goa's mineral-ore wealth was in the New Conquest talukas of Sanguem, Quepem and Bicholim.

The three Old Conquest talukas were only 20 per cent of Goa's landmass but had 62 per cent of the population, mostly Christian. (The remaining 11 per cent of the population was in Daman and Diu.) There was more agricultural production in the Old Conquest talukas than in the largely undeveloped New Conquest talukas. This was thanks to coastal *khazan* fields, the most productive in Goa. Situated along riverbanks, these low-lying fields were protected by bunds and sluicegates, and were rotated for pisciculture and salt production in the fair season (brackish tidal river water flow into and out of the khazans was regulated by sluice gates) and for salt-resistant varieties of rice cultivation with fresh monsoon waters. River waters also deposited fertile silt from the Western Ghats into the khazans. All major towns, the capital city (and later, the port, rail, air connectivity and tourism draws) were centred in the Old Conquests.

Consequently, Goa was about 65 per cent Christian in the early nineteenth century. The bulk of both Christian Goa and Hindu Goa was poor. The Dutch blockades in the first half of the seventeenth century emasculated the Portuguese in Goa. Goa was left to languish. Subsistence living was the norm in the predominantly agrarian society. There were hardly any educational facilities and, in any case, hardly any local jobs.

In this bleak scenario, two British gunboats—*Arrogant* and *Suffolk*—arrived under the command of Commodore Rainier with troops that occupied the Cabo and Aguada forts in 1799. It was the era of Napoleonic wars in Europe. The British told the surprised Portuguese governor that the French in Pondicherry were conspiring with Tipu Sultan to attack Goa.

On 6 September 1799, Colonel William Clarke arrived with three infantry and artillery battalions (1100 British troops, later shored up to 3000 troops) and occupied, besides the forts at Cabo and Aguada, those at Gaspar Dias (Miramar), Dona Paula, Reis Magos and Mormugao. Col Clarke told the Portuguese governor that Napoleon had ordered twenty-six warships and fourteen frigates at Brest to set sail and capture Goa.

The Portuguese said they could deal with the French threats themselves. It hardly mattered. The British stayed on for fourteen years, intermittently, until 1813, when the plan of two brothers with the British East India Company—Richard Wellesley and the future Duke of Wellington, Arthur Wellesley—to occupy Goa was called off after the Lisbon–London talks.

During this time, the British noticed that the Goan Christian natives dressed and ate like their own, were hardworking and honest, and that coastal Goans were given to sailing in country craft. The British hired 3300 Goans for the Royal Navy and more from the celebrated 'Goan ABC'—ayahs, butlers and cooks.[2]

Directors of the British shipping company, Calcutta and Burma Steam Navigation Company (that changed to British India [BI] Steam Navigation Company in 1862), aka Mackinnon Mackenzie, soon followed suit. The company would recruit thousands of Goans for its ships, heralding the institution called the Goan *tarvotti* (seaman). More were later recruited by the Peninsular and Oriental (P&O) company. Most of the recruitment was of Christians from the Old Conquests.

The great Goan emigration had begun. This was not restricted only to the depressed classes. Middle-class families began migrating to British India for jobs for themselves and a better education for their children.

However, when they first arrived in India, the Portuguese dominated maritime trade between Asia and Europe for about a century (the sixteenth) initially from Cochin and then from Goa from 1530. Goa then became the prosperous chief entrepôt of Asian spices, silks and other merchandise headed for Europe. Portugal monopolized the Asia–Europe trade with a littoral empire of strategic forts along the sea routes from Far East Asia to northwest Africa and thence to Europe.

The Spanish king's donning of the Portuguese crown in the late 16th century heralded Portugal's decline. The Dutch, at war with Spain, viewed all Portuguese possessions in Asia as Spanish and pursued them relentlessly. The Dutch practically dismantled Portugal's littoral empire in Asia and frequently imposed maritime blockades on Goa right through the first half of the 17th century. The Portuguese in Asia were in no position to contend with the competition that arrived from other European powers around the same time.

Yet, the tottering Portuguese survived them all—the Danes, the Dutch, the British and the French. Portugal, in fact, held the world's first and longest colonial empire, capturing Ceuta (next to Morocco on the north coast of Africa) in 1415 and withdrawing from Timor (now Timor Leste, in Indonesia) in 2002—almost 600 years. They were in India for 463 years, from 1498 to 1961.

Political Timeline

Portugal's political timeline relevant to Goa can be simplified into four broad eras:

1. **Absolute monarchy**: Absolute monarchy from Goa's conquest in 1510 to 1821. The king ruled Portugal and the colonies at his whim;

2. **Strife**: A revolution that began in the city of Porto in 1820 overthrew the monarchy and established a parliament (*Côrtes*) in 1821 with a constitutional monarch who would now exercise only a dignifying influence over his dominions. Portugal's king and the royal family had earlier, in 1807, fled to the then colony of Brazil with British naval help in view of the French invasion of Portugal. The last of the French troops were expelled from Portugal in 1812. Portugal's king ruled from Brazil from

1807 to 1821, when he returned to Portugal. The period between 1821 until 1834 witnessed a power struggle in Portugal between democracy under a constitutional monarchy on the one hand and absolute monarchy on the other. Its repercussions naturally echoed in Goa. The king's older son, heir to the Lisbon throne, ruled Brazil democratically and backed democracy in Portugal while the younger son, Miguel, sought a return to absolute monarchy. Meanwhile, the first ever elections in Goa (for three seats in the *Côrtes*, won by Dr Bernardo Peres da Silva, Constancio Roque da Costa, both Goan, and Dr António José da Lima Leitão, a Portuguese surgeon in Goa who stoutly defended constitutional monarchy) were held in Goa in January 1822;

3. **Constitutional monarchy**: Constitutional monarchy upto 1910. Regular elections were held in Goa from 1822 until 1894, oftentimes rigged by the incumbent governor-general in favour of the political party back home, to which he owed his position. Elections were suspended in Goa after 1894 because of the turmoil they produced (representatives were thereafter nominated based on experience and seniority); and,

4. **Republic/dictatorship**: The republican era from 1910, followed by dictatorship between 1928 and 1961. Regular elections were held in Goa during the republican era. Under dictatorship, elections were held only from 1945 to 1961, but under the charade of a single-party system.

Elections throughout the period (from 1822 to 1961) were not by universal franchise but by a qualified electorate that amounted to less than 4 per cent of Goa's population. Only the educated and landlords who paid a minimum specified amount of tax were qualified to vote. More ethnic Portuguese residents in Goa than natives were elected during the 139-year period. These elections were marked by rivalries, insults, disorder, crime and arguments right from the governor down to the drunken voter, as was observed by the popular Orientalist Joaquim Heliodoro da Cunha Rivara, an ethnic Portuguese appointed the *secretário-geral* or chief secretary of Goa in 1855.[*]

Twentieth-century Goa was of no practical use, economic or strategic, to Portugal. It was an annual burden of some 7 million escudos, as Portugal's prime minister, António de Oliveira Salazar, disclosed in a national broadcast on 30 November 1954. But Goa held a special place in the national pride of Portugal—a 'point of honour'.

When it was taken over by the Spanish crown in the last quarter of the 16th century, Portugal's national poet (now world poet) Luis Vaz de Camões rekindled Luso pride, recalling the glory of Portugal's Age of Discoveries in his epic *Os Lusíadas* (The Lusiads, sons of Lusus, meaning the Lusitanians/Portuguese). Goa was the surviving soul of that glory.

In 1899, Portugal's minister of overseas said in parliament that Goa was a *padrão glorioso* (glorious memorial) of Portuguese dominions.[†] (In the Age of Discoveries, Portuguese explorers planted a tall and distinctly hewn stone pillar, called *padrão*, to mark a new place of discovery. Such stones were shown on route charts and were of much help to future navigators coming that way.)

Portugal declared that her conquerors did not encounter 'savage people' in Goa, as they had in many parts of Africa and Asia.[‡]

Goa of the 20th century was only a dear jewel, Portugal's Pearl of the East—a 'memorial of Portuguese discoveries'—of a once glorious empire. In 1955, Egas Moniz, the Portuguese neurologist who won the Nobel Prize in 1949 for his contribution to psychosurgery and psychiatry, wrote that Goa was '*o mais alto*

---

[*] *Boletim do Instituto Vasco da Gama,* 1953, pp. 46–47.

[†] *Diário da Câmara dos Srs. Deputados,* or parliament proceedings, vol. 3, 20 March 1899, p. 32.

[‡] Ibid.

padrão da gloriosa história náutica de Portugal' (the highest standard of Portugal's glorious nautical history).[*]

To Portugal, Goa in the mid-twentieth century was an emotion, not economics. Portugal had lost vast lands in central and southern Africa to the British. Whatever little pride the Portuguese were left with—and Goa, though worthless, was the jewel of that remnant imperial glory—had to be saved.

To India too, Goa was of mere symbolic value, a tiny speck, 0.1 per cent area of India's landmass, on her western seaboard. Perspectives changed post-1947 when India rose to become a world leader against colonialism, after intervening with USA and the Netherlands in 1949 on granting independence to Indonesia. India led campaigns against racism in South Africa and against Portugal's colonialism in Asia and Africa. Colonial Goa undermined India's role of leadership in the anti-colonial movement at the UN and the world at large.

It was ironic that Goa, rooted in nationalism since the earliest years of Portuguese occupation as we shall see later, was dependent on India to sort out the issue of colonial domination and, from 1930, repression.

The Indian National Congress (INC) had been founded in December 1885. In July 1886, Goan Catholics in Bombay founded the nationalist journal, *O Anglo-Lusitano*. Local political parties formed after the 1820 revolution (which replaced absolute monarchy with constitutional monarchy in Portugal, and introduced the conduct of the first parliamentary polls in Goa in January 1822)— Patuléa, a party of liberals (aka Partido Popular that morphed into the Partido Ultramarino in 1864) and the Chafarica of the conservatives (that morphed into the Partido Indiano, also in 1864)—had been

---

[*] In 'A acção do General Norton de Matos em Angola', *Seara Nova,* July–November 1955, as mentioned by Filipa Alexandra Carvalho Sousa Lopes in her thesis, *As vozes da oposiçã oao Estado Novo e a Questão de Goa,* p. 161 (available at: https://repositorio-aberto.up.pt/bit-stream/10216/108453/2/226681.pdf).

alternatively pro- and anti-establishment, depending on the direction of the winds blowing in Portugal.

At a rally in Margao on 14 November 1912, the local Partido Indiano leader, Roque Correia Afonso, floated the idea of a forum on the lines of the INC. The suggestion was supported by the popular journals *O Debate* (founded in 1911 by Luís de Menezes Bragança) and *Bharat* (founded in 1913 by H.P. Hegdó Dessai of Quepem). Dr Miguel de Loyola Furtado, editor of *A Índia Portuguesa*, backed the idea of such a forum but wanted it to be named after Afonso de Albuquerque.

By the end of the first quarter of the 20th century, Portugal was in a deep economic recession. It had migrated from one financial crisis to another. At this grim juncture, the famed professor economist of the University of Coimbra, Dr António de Oliveira Salazar, was made finance minister in 1926. Salazar managed to bring about a degree of economic stability. By 1928, he assumed the powers of a dictator.

By this time, Indian nationalism had gained strength in British India. The same year, 1928, a Paris-trained engineer, Tristão de Bragança Cunha, who was from Cuelim, Cansaulim, formed the Goa National Congress (GNC) in Margao, to spread the national fervour in Goa. He was destined for the title Father of Goan Nationalism.

The INC invited the GNC to its Calcutta session and recognized the GNC as an associate. The freedom movement in British India would now cover Goa. (The GNC was known as the Goa Congress Committee after its shifting to Bombay.)

Amid growing nationalism among Goans, Salazar promulgated the infamous Acto Colonial on 8 July 1930 (Law No. 18570). The Colonial Act downgraded Goa's status as a province of Portugal to that of its colony. From being full citizens, meaning equal to ethnic Luso citizens of mainland Portugal, Goans were now their subjects. Goan civil servants were methodically replaced by whites to 'renationalize' Goa.

Civil liberties ceased. Political parties, rallies and speeches were banned. Gatherings of any kind (even birthday parties) needed state approval. Censorship was clamped on all printing material. Any printed word—even an invitation card to a wedding, a house-warming party, a child's baptismal or a thread-ceremony party, a folkplay handbill ... anything and everything, even those meant exclusively for private circulation—had to mandatorily carry the imprimatur *Visado pela Censura* (approved by the censors) before being printed. A reign of repression—typical of a dictatorship—was let loose.

Whoever dared raise a whimper of protest was dealt with harshly under amended laws. The Acto Colonial and racial discrimination would prove counter-productive: it intensified nationalism, even among elite Goans in Goa and those studying in Portugal who until then had steered clear of politics.

Despite the environment of a police state, T.B. Cunha's GNC managed to galvanize a large section of Goans in the fight for freedom. But in 1934, the INC, together with its own branches in London and New York, disassociated itself from the GNC on the grounds that it functioned from alien land.

GNC shifted to 21 Dalal Street, Bombay, in 1936 to dodge the 'alien land' embargo, but the INC was unimpressed. Goa was excluded from India's freedom movement.

Local embers for liberty died down. Given the atmosphere of repression, the scene shifted from Goa to Bombay and Belgaum. In 1938, GNC leaders met INC president, Subhas Chandra Bose, but to no avail.

Goa Forgotten and Forlorn ... a Land without Opportunity

Goa languished like a forgotten backwater. Without educational facilities beyond a lone *liceu* (higher secondary school) and a medical/pharma/nursing school and without local jobs, more than half of Goa's working population migrated to British India, British Africa and the British Middle East, or worked aboard ships on the seven seas. The exodus that had begun in the nineteenth century now ran full steam ahead.

According to Dr Remy Dias, reader in history and researcher, 3.21 lakh Goans emigrated in just thirty years, from 1880 to 1910.[*] By the second quarter of the twentieth century, Bombay alone housed over 1.5 lakh Goans. This is out of a population of less than half million. (The 1960 census figure was 5,89,997.)[†]

Dr Themistocles D'Silva, a chemical engineer who spent over twenty years with Union Carbide in the US (his first post-retirement book was *The Black Box of Bhopal: A Closer Look at the World's Deadliest Industrial Disaster* [Victoria: Trafford Publishing, 2006], writing on his native village of Arossim in Goa points out that opening of a new railway line (in 1888, connecting Goa to the rail network of British India) catalyzed Goan migration.[‡]

When taking over as external affairs minister of the interim Government of India on 2 September 1946, Jawaharlal Nehru decried the deplorable economic conditions in Goa.

Edila de Andrade Gaitonde, the Azores, Portugal-born wife of surgeon-freedom fighter Dr P.D. Gaitonde from Palolem, Canacona, said the Portuguese only chanted '*Goa é nossa*' (Goa is ours) and did nothing more.[§]

Dr Nishtha Desai observed in her masterly book *Liberation vs Armed Aggression*: 'The fact was that Goa's potential was never harnessed for the benefit of Portugal or for the benefit of the people of Goa'.[¶] She had hit the bull's-eye.

---

[*] Pius Malekandathil and Remy Dias (eds), 'Goa in the 20th Century: History & Culture', *Some Aspects of the Consumption History of Estado da India: 1900–50,* Institute Menezes Braganza, Goa, 2008, p. 104.

[†] *Censo do Estado da India Portuguesa - 1960* (Census of 1960 of the Portuguese State of India).

[‡] Themistocles D'Silva, *Beyond the Beach: The Village of Arossim, Goa, in Historical Perspective*, Goa, 1556, 2011, p. 20.

[§] *Visão História,* vol. 14, 2011, p. 70.

[¶] Nishtha Desai, 2011, p. 30.

Following the Dutch onslaught of the 17th century, the once monopoly Portuguese trade in Asian merchandise ground to a trickle. The Portuguese could have exploited Goa's natural resources to build a prosperous Goa but lacked the foresight. With better opportunities now available in British India, a substantial slice of Goa emigrated.

The bulk of Goan-origin commissioned officers in India's armed forces came from émigrés settled in places like Agra, Ahmedabad, Ahmednagar, Ajmer, Amravati, Bangalore, Baroda, Belgaum (city and district), Bellary, Bhopal, Bhusaval, Bombay, Calcutta, Delhi, Hyderabad, Jabalpur, Kanpur, Karachi, Kolhapur (city and district), Lonavala, Madras, Mysore, Nagpur, Poona and Sholapur—even Burma. Goans in Goa could not join the British Indian forces until 1947 or the Indian armed forces until 1961. They could only join the Portuguese military (and dream of rising to Tenente Coronel or Lieutenant Colonel; all higher executive ranks were held exclusively by Whites).

Out-migration was far more accentuated among Goan Catholics than among Goan Hindus. Indo-Aryan Hindus were considered contaminated if they travelled beyond three hilltops in ancient times and crossed the sea in medieval times. If they did so, such persons had to undergo elaborate 'purification' ceremonies in the local temple. Goa's population of 2.52 lakh in 1810 (61.3 per cent of it in the Old Conquests and 27.3 per cent in the New Conquests, and the rest in Daman and Diu), rose to 2.73 lakh in 1820 (61.1 per cent in Old Conquests and 28.8per cent in New Conquests), according to Paulo Teodoro de Matos of the ISCTE–Instituto Universitário de Lisboa.[*] Portuguese Census figures placed Goa's population in 1850 at 3.84 lakh.[†]

---

[*] Paulo Teodoro de Matos, 'The Population of the Portuguese Estado da Índia, 1750–1820: Sources and Demographic Trends', *The Making of the Luso-Asian World*, edited by Laura Jarnagin, ISEAS Publishing, Singapore, 2011, p. 162.

[†] *Censo do Estado da India Portuguesa—1850* (Census of 1850 of the Portuguese State of India).

According to Paulo de Matos and Jan Lucassen of Amsterdam, 90 per cent of the emigrants were Goan Christian, only 7 per cent were Goan Hindu. The official report of a fifteen-member enquiry committee appointed in 1930 by the colonial administration to report on the state of more than a lakh emigrants from Goa (about 60,000 'Portuguese citizens' were counted in Bombay, Karachi, Calcutta and Rangoon alone—Goans who 'nationalized themselves as British subjects or descended from naturalized parents' were not counted) living in British India (*Comissão de Inquérito a Situação dos Emigrantes Indo-Portuguesesna India Britânica*) stated that only about 7500 were Hindu, the rest were all Christian.[*]

Of Goa's population of 3.84 lakh in 1850, 64 per cent was Catholic and 36 per cent was Hindu. Thanks to emigration, the situation reversed by 1961: Goan Catholics dwindled to 38 per cent and Goan Hindus comprised 60 per cent of the 5.90 lakh population.

The few whose hearts still beat for Portugal seem to forget one basic truth: that, save a few bright sparks, it was Portuguese lethargy and lack of foresight to create a self-sufficient society which largely caused the Goan Catholics to disperse all over the world—like the Biblical lost tribes. For higher and professional education, Goans had to depend on Belgaum, Dharwar, Poona, Bombay, Bangalore, Madras, New Delhi, Calcutta, Karachi, etc.; for jobs and a decent living, they had to rely on India (and the world at large).

With the bulk of Goa's working population now in British India and abroad, the local economy was almost entirely dependent on their remittances to their families back home. Goa was reduced to a 'money-order economy'.

The sun is about to set and a darkness that is frightening will soon submerge the village ... Most of the houses around here are deserted, their inmates having long ago gone away to places

[*] Souza, 1973, pp. 149–150.

where they can earn a living, and live as free beings ... But
I know one thing ...when the foreign oppressor is driven away,
these houses will open again and be peopled, the fields will yield
bountifully, this village and others like it will be full of life again,
and Goa, this land of my forefathers, which now lies sorrowing,
will smile and be gay once more ...

These are the concluding lines of *Sorrowing Lies My Land*, a 1955
novel by Padmashri and Gomant Vibhushan Lambert Mascarenhas,
freedom fighter, journalist and editor, who vowed not to marry
until Goa was free, a promise that he kept.

In real life, Mascarenhas's lament rings true sixty-two years later,
but with a twist. Goa is free, democracy and civil liberties prevail,
elected Goan politicos steer Goa's destiny, yet Goans continue to
abandon hearth and field. Once verdant fields have turned deserted
again—cracked and dry in summer, slushy and weedy in the rains—
as (someone said): Goans 'flee from their liberators, on passports of
the country from which they were liberated', to seek a living that
liberation promised but did not deliver. From 38 per cent in 1960,
Goa's Catholic population plummeted to 25 per cent in the 2011
Census of India and is estimated at 20 per cent today—thanks largely
to Portuguese passports, which is actually a ticket to the European
Union. This phenomenon is not restricted to the Goan Catholic
alone. The emigration bug has bitten the Goan Hindu too, so much
so that today, the Goan is reckoned to be a minority in his own land.

Dying Embers Come Alive

Goa's nationalist movement had begun with a rally in Margao on
14 November 1912. Leaders like Adv. Roque Correia Afonso, Luís
de Menezes Bragança, H.P. Hegde Desai and Dr Miguel de Loyola
Furtado surged with the founding of the Goa National Congress
in 1928 by T.B. Cunha. The movement died down after the 1930
Colonial Act reduced Goa to a police state and the Indian National

Congress disassociated itself from the GNC. A spark was needed to resuscitate it.

The firebrand Indian nationalist, Gandhian and socialist Ram Manohar Lohia had been imprisoned in Lahore Fort jail from May 1944. He was shifted to Poona and released on 11 April 1946. He had a friend in nearby Bombay, whom he decided to visit.

. When Lohia studied for a master's and a doctorate in economics in Germany,[*] Dr Julião de Menezes (1909–80) of Assolna, Goa, pursued an MD in dermatology at Berlin University. Both were friends, had a socialist bent of mind and were student activists in Europe.

After Menezes completed his studies in Germany and returned to Goa, he established a youth club called Club Juvenile. It was more a cover for nationalistic activities. In 1938, the Piazza Cross in front of the Assolna church was found demolished. The police immediately suspected the hand of Menezes and his Clube Juvenile in the vandalism. The club was banned and its office sealed. Before Menezes could be arrested, he shifted to Bombay. He launched the *Gomantak Praja Mandal* in 1939 in Bombay.

Lohia had been enfeebled by the incarceration and Menezes suggested he recuperate in Goa.

On 10 June 1946, both arrived in Assolna, where Dr Menezes's ancestral house was. They were due to return to Bombay on 19 June. Latter-day freedom fighter Evágrio Jorge splashed news of the duo's arrival in the local daily *O Heraldo* of 12 June, and a stream of young nationalists turned sleepy Assolna into a hushed Mecca, seeking advice from Lohia.

Among them were Dr António Sequeira, Prof. Dionísio Ribeiro, Evágrio Jorge, Adv. José Inácio Francisco ('Fanchu')

---

[*] Rahul Ramagundam, in his biography *The Life and Times of George Fernandes*, Penguin Random House, Gurugram, 2022, says that after Lohia returned from Humboldt University in Germany, he was called 'Doctor Saheb' but 'truth be told, he never submitted a printed copy of his thesis to the university and therefore was never awarded a degree', p. 58.

Xavier Cândido de Loyola, Purushottam Kakodkar, Vasant Kare and Vicente João de Figueiredo.*

Meeting young men at Mormugao and Panjim between 15 and 17 June, Lohia and Menezes spread word that they would defy the ban on public meetings and address Goans in Margao on 18 June. The duo returned to Margao on 17 June, where they met nationalists at Damodar Vidyalaya. Suspecting Portuguese plans to thwart the meeting, they did not return to Assolna but checked into Hotel Republica at Francisco Luis Gomes Road (Old Station Road) in Margao—to give the police waiting at Assolna the slip.

The police then instructed all Salcete taxis to report at the Margao police station with their passengers before proceeding to their destination. The police surrounded the venue the next day. Nevertheless, small groups of people waited around in expectation.

Lohia and Menezes hoodwinked the police and arrived at the venue in a horse carriage. Policemen encircling the ground refused to let them in.

'Move aside,' thundered Lohia. The sheer force of his personality overawed the constables.

Three persons stepped forward to garland Lohia and Menezes. The Portuguese police chief of Margao (some reports say he was the taluka administrator), Capitão Fortunato Miranda, pointed a revolver at Lohia. Lohia placed his hand on the captain's shoulder, asked him to calm down, pushed him aside and proceeded to the spot to address the people gathered.

From almost nowhere, a big crowd—including women—suddenly converged at the open ground from all directions, like bees to a hive. Litterateur and freedom fighter Ravindra Kelekar recalled that the crowd was estimated between 600 and 700—the largest political gathering in Goa until then.†

---

* Evagrio Jorge, *Goa's Awakening: Reminiscences of the 1946 Civil Desobedience* [sic] *Movement,* p. 10.

† Interview with the author.

Capt. Miranda ordered Lohia to not speak, saying he was a foreigner. Lohia said that he was an Indian, that Goa was a part and parcel of India and insisted that he was going to speak to his people. Miranda repeated that Lohia should not speak. Lohia defied him and said he would speak, and dared Miranda to arrest him if he had the guts.

An enraged Miranda whipped out his revolver again and held it to Lohia. Lohia smiled, and in no uncertain terms told Miranda that he would speak and asked Miranda to put the stupid gun away because it did not scare him. Lohia then brushed aside the hand holding the weapon. Miranda was taken aback but did not allow Lohia to speak beyond a few opening sentences. He told Lohia he was under arrest.

Holstering the revolver, Miranda beckoned a group of policemen and had Lohia and Menezes physically lifted and whisked away to the *quartel* (police station). A baton charge dispersed the crowd.

However, the crowd regrouped and marched to the police station, demanding the release of the duo. The situation threatened to get out of hand. The police requested Lohia and Menezes to ask the crowd to leave.

Lohia spoke to the people gathered outside:

> 'Gomantak[*] is part of Hindustan, and Portugal rules over it as the British do in the rest of the country. This is an accident, a bad dream, and it will pass. The state of Hindustan will come. Our people are creating it ... I am not asking you today to overthrow Portuguese rule. That will come in its own time ... People of Gomantak, think freely, speak freely, write freely ...'

He exhorted the crowd, before asking them to go home but to continue the struggle for civil liberties.[†]

---

[*] Gomantak is an old name of Goa.

[†] *Goa Gazetteers* Department, Government of Goa, *Who's Who of Freedom Fighters,* vol. 2, 1990, pp. xi–xiv, gives the text of Lohia's full

The venue of the meeting has since been named Lohia Maidan and 18 June is observed as Goa Revolution Day (Kranti Divas).[3] Lohia and Menezes were shifted to Panjim the same day. The following night, Lohia was put on a train at Vasco and, under heavy police guard, was seen off at the border in Castle Rock. Lohia, who returned with advance notice three months later, was held in jail for ten days, but by then had already rekindled the fervour for civil liberties and freedom in Goa. He was to leave the Congress party in 1948.

Menezes was released in Panjim. He took a taxi home. The driver was German, a survivor of the four Axis spy ships—three German *(Ehrenfels, Drachenfels* and *Braunfels)* and one Italian *(Anfora)*—destroyed at Mormugao on 9 March 1943 by the British during World War II (the story was written by James Leasor in a book titled *Boarding Party,** the last action by veterans of the Calcutta Light Horse sent in a ramshackle, rusted barge called *Phoebe* to Mormugao harbour, some with a glass eye and most with dentures, later made into a film called *The Sea Wolves* starring Gregory Peck, Roger Moore and David Niven). The cabbie was thrilled that his passenger had studied in his fatherland. Menezes escaped to Bombay soon after and continued with nationalistic activities in the metropolis through his *Gomantak Praja Mandal.*

Unanswered Questions

Two things remain uncertain:
     There was a third person, a local nationalist, who went to Hotel Republica to escort Lohia and Menezes to the meeting venue. This third person arranged the horse carriage when Portuguese police turned back a taxi that was to carry Lohia and Menezes to the venue. Who was this third person?

---

speech.
* Houghton Mifflin Harcourt, 1978.

Most accounts mention the name of Laxmidas Borkar (later editor of *Navaprabha*, a Marathi daily in Goa) as the person who escorted Lohia and Menezes to the meeting venue. However, the Goa Gazetteers book, *Who's Who of Freedom Fighters—Goa, Daman & Diu Vol. 1*, states that it was Gopal ('Sadanand') Narayan Virginkar, a freedom fighter and businessman from Margao, who escorted the two men to the venue.* The identity of the person is not clear.

The second doubt: Was Portuguese Capitão Fortunato Miranda, who twice pointed a revolver at Lohia, the police chief of Margao or was he the Salcete taluka administrator? The answer is ambivalent again. Most accounts say he was the police chief of the town, but others like P.P. Shirodkar say he was the Salcete taluka administrator.†

Flame Burns Bright

Tristão de Bragança Cunha followed up the Lohia encounter with a public meeting the same month at the same venue (30 June 1946). At this meeting, the Portuguese police publicly beat Cunha to humiliate him. Poet Bakibab Borkar, who was present at the meeting, recited *Dotor bos, uthun cholunk lag* (doctor, sit down, arise and march).‡

Cunha marched into history—he became the first Goan to be deported (aboard the *Lourenço Marques*) and jailed at the Peniche Fort jail in Portugal in 1946. He would be followed by Adv. José Inácio Loyola (convicted as a 'state threat' for writing an article on civil liberties in Goa in Bombay's *Free Press Journal* of 22 September 1946). Freedom fighters Dr Ram Hegde and Laxmikant V. Bhembre (aboard the *Bartolomeu Dias*) and Purushottam Kakodkar were also jailed in Peniche in December 1946.

---

* P. 374.

† P.P. Shirodkar, *Goa's Struggle for Freedom*, South Asia Books, Gurugram, 1988, p. 35.

‡ See https://www.artandculture.goa.gov.in/art-culture/konkani-literature-of-goa and *The Global Goan*, vol. 2, issue 10, October 2021, pp. 51–53.

Peniche, a coastal town situated a few kilometres north of Lisbon, had an ancient fort built by invading Muslim Berbers on a rocky peninsula, long before Portugal was born as a nation in the year 1143. The fort was used by Salazar as a jail for political prisoners. Surgeon Pundalik D. Gaitonde, a nationalist at heart, married an Azorean (Portuguese) musician, Edila de Andrade. They spent their honeymoon in Peniche. Their first lunch there was hosted by the five Goan freedom fighters in the visitors' room of the fort jail.

Edila Gaitonde wrote that conditions in the jail were poor, in her book *As Maçãs Azuis: Portugal e Goa 1948–1961* (The Blue Apples).[*] After shifting to Goa, Edila would assuage her mother back in Lisbon, writing that Goa was an exotic place. Even the apples were big and blue. (They hailed from an Azorean island, where the hedges were of blue hortensia, the yonder sea blue and the sky blue. The family had shifted to Lisbon so that Edila could pursue higher studies in music. This is where Edila met Dr Gaitonde by chance and it was love at first sight.) After some years in Goa, Edila's mother wrote from Lisbon, 'Tell me, daughter, are the apples in your orchard still blue?'[†]

It was at this lunch in jail that a female French journalist, after interviewing T.B. Cunha, suddenly turned and asked Dr Gaitonde, 'What made you choose this place for your Honeymoon?'

The surgeon promptly replied, 'Homage to sacrifice.'

In December 1947, P.P. Shirodkar, Vinayak N. Mayenkar, Guilherme D'Souza Ticló, Nilkanth M. Karapurkar, Narayan Naik, Mukund Kamat Dhakankar and Jaywant Kunde were exiled and jailed in Angola. All were granted amnesty in 1950.[‡]

Goan nationalists met in Londa on 17–18 August 1946 and formed the National Congress Goa (hereafter, NCG), integrating

---

[*] Portugal: *Editorial Tágide*, 2011, pp. 9 and 18–20.

[†] Ibid., p. 23.

[‡] Filipa Lopes, *As vozes da oposição ao estado novo e a questão de Goa (1950–1961)*, p. 99.

Dr Ram Hegde's Gomantak Congress and Purushottam Kakodkar's Goa Congress. It was led by Dr Ram Hegde (prior to his exile) and had Laxmanrao Sardesai, Balkrishna Borkar, Narayan Prabhu Bhembre, Venkatesh Vaidya and Vasant Kare as executive members.

Several Goan nationalist organizations had sprung up before: Shamrao Madkaikar's Gomantakiya Tarun Sangh (1938) and Purushottam Kakodkar's Goa Seva Sangh (1945), both formed in Margao, and T.B. Cunha's Goan Youth League (1945) formed in Bombay. There was also the Goa Ashram. The nationalistic flame, lit by T.B. Cunha in 1928 and resuscitated by Lohia in 1946, was bearing fruit. Among the largest of this plethora of organizations was the NCG.

However, there was no unanimity among members of the NCG. A hot-blooded 'young Turk' section of NCG felt that peaceful means would not impress the Portuguese and advocated violent means. The NCG thus split in 1947 into two factions. The militant and underground section continued to be based at Londa. The one advocating peaceful methods moved from Londa to Belgaum and finally to Bombay.

Eventually, the NCG went on to spawn four distinct groupings: Vishwanath Lawande's Azad Gomantak Dal (1947), Goan People's Party (1949, George Vaz, Divakar Kakodkar, Berta de Menezes Bragança), United Front of Goans (1950, Francisco Mascarenhas and Vaman Desai) and the Goa Liberation Front, all started in Bombay.*

Goa Action Committee was formed in 1953 in Bombay at the instance of T.B. Cunha to coordinate efforts of diverse groups (essentially NCG, United Front of Goans and the Goan People's Party, which were working at cross purposes).

---

* Divakar Kakodkar was arrested later the same year, 1949, and after two years in Aguada and Lisbon, was exiled to the West African island in the central Atlantic, Cabo Verde, where he was held for seven years.

The Goa Liberation Council (Prof. Aloysius Soares, Dr Ulbaldo Mascarenhas, Dr Arthur de Sa, Prof. Francisco Correia Afonso, Prof. Armando Menezes, Prof. L.N. Velingkar, L.J. de Souza, J.N. Heredia, J.M. Pinto, Dr Rogaciano Moraes, Vincent Raymond and Nicolau Menezes) was formed in Bombay in June 1954. It launched a fortnightly, *Goan Tribune,* to highlight Portuguese atrocities in Goa, and distributed the journal both among Indian political leaders and those of western countries.

Prof. Soares's manifesto—signed by the renowned Goan-origin gynaecologist Dr V.N. Shirodkar and eminent editor Frank Moraes—demanding self-determination for Goans was submitted to Salazar. Nothing happened. Prof. Soares's 'Open Letter' to Salazar, debunking the latter's assertion that Goa was wholly Catholic and that the Hindu Indian state wanted to grab Goa against the wishes of the local people, was reproduced and quoted widely all over the world.

A number of periodicals, in English, Portuguese, Konkani and Marathi were launched by Goans in Bombay. Besides the *O Anglo-Lusitano* (1886, *O Patriota* was started earlier in 1858 but was not regarded as a nationalist publication), journals like *Amchem Gõi, Porjecho Avaz, Resurge Goa, Azad Goa, Free Goa, Goan Tribune* and *Dipagraha* kept the flame of nationalism burning.

Back in 1942, Goa's president of the National Union, Salazar's single-party system, Sócrates da Costa of Margao, had cautioned that the vast majority of Goan Hindus and Goan Catholics were almost entirely (*'quasi na totalidade'*) anti-Portuguese.

The Goan National Union was formed by J.M. Souza in Bombay in 1954. There were now more than fifteen organizations, six of them militant, fighting for Goa's freedom.[*]

Nationalism was also secretly alive in Goa, a police state. In Margao, PIDE (Polícia Internacional e de Defesa do Estado, the Portuguese secret police) reported that the Abade Faria Road

---

[*] A full list has been provided in Annexures.

residence of Adv. Francisco Paula Ribeiro was the venue of regular meetings of nationalists who stood for restoration of civil liberties, autonomy for Goa and eventual dismantling of Portugal's colonialism in Goa. Another PIDE report said freedom fighter Adv. Tovar Dias hosted in his house nationalists Narayan Virgincar, Adv. Atmaram Poi Palondicar and Anant Palondikar.

With India gaining independence, Salazar knew that Portuguese colonial rule would be endangered in Goa. Mahatma Gandhi declared in *The Harijan* of 30 June 1946 that Goa could not remain under Portuguese rule:

> ...he [Lohia] has thereby rendered a service to the cause of civil liberty and especially to the Goans. The little Portuguese settlement, which merely exists on the sufferance of the British Government, can ill afford to ape its bad manners. In free India, Goa cannot be allowed to exist as a separate entity in opposition to the laws of the Free State.[*]

T.B. Cunha sloganeered it as,

> A Free Goa in a Free India.

Gandhi also said:

> I would venture to advise the Portuguese Government of Goa to recognize the signs of the times and come to honourable terms with its inhabitants rather than function on any treaty that might exist between them and the British Government.[†]

---

[*] *Harijan,* 30 June 1946.

[†] P.N. Khera, *Operation Vijay: The Liberation of Goa and Other Portuguese Colonies in India (1961),* Historical Section, Ministry of Defence, Government of India, 1974, pp. 30–31.

In the letter dated 2 August 1946 to the governor-general of Portuguese India, the Mahatma wrote:

> That the Indians in Goa have been speechless is proof not of the innocence or the philanthropic nature of the Portuguese Government but of the rule of terror.[*]

The Indian National Congress, during its Working Committee Meeting in Wardha on 12 August 1946, resolved:

> Goa has always been and must inevitably continue to be a part of India ...What its future status will be in a free India can only be determined in consultation with the people of Goa and not by any external authority.[†]

Gandhi again wrote in the *Harijan*:

> It is ridiculous to write Portugal as the motherland of Indians in Goa. Their motherland is as much India as mine. Goa is outside British India but it is within geographical India as a whole.[‡]

---

[*]   Ibid., p. 31.

[†]   R.P. Rao, *Portuguese Rule in India*, Asia Publishing House, Bombay, 1963, p. 69.

[‡]   *Harijan,* 8 September 1946.

2

INDIA'S DIPLOMACY

Diplomacy Begins

After the Interim Government of India took office on 2 September 1946, it appointed Mirza Rashid Ali Baig—the prince of a small kingdom near Delhi—as India's first consul general in Panjim. On 15 August 1947 while India rejoiced, M.R.A. Baig hoisted the national tricolour at the consulate (with Portugal's flag also flying at full mast, a Portuguese pre-condition*). That evening, Baig threw a party that was jam-packed. According to the consul's son, author Murad Ali Baig, then an eight-year-old (who now has a house in Goa), the consul was 'told that the entire Portuguese police, army and navy personnel had locked themselves inside their barracks fearing an uprising and a naval vessel had left the port'. Seeing a historic opportunity, M.R.A. Baig urgently cabled Prime Minister Nehru to declare Goa independent. The reply was that such a hasty step 'would not look good to the world and that Portugal would eventually have to recognize the "historic inevitability" of leaving the colony.'†

After the British left in 1947, India grappled with the fallout of Partition, communal strife, a refugee crisis, food shortages and to cap it all, the 1947–48 invasion of Jammu and Kashmir by Pakistan. Towards the end of the J&K operations, the Congress Party adopted a resolution in Jaipur on 18 December 1948 on the

---

* https://www.incrediblegoa.org/feature/august-15-1947-when-goa-was-still-under-the-portuguese-rule/

† Article titled 'Goa on 15th August 1947'.

need to integrate the surviving remnants of colonial rule in India. This was reiterated at Nasik and Calcutta in 1952.

The French, with four small enclaves (Pondicherry and Karaikal on the Tamil coast, Yanam on the Andhra coast and Mahe on the Kerala coast—Chandernagar north of Calcutta had merged with India in June 1949), negotiated with India, secured some guarantees for the people of their possessions and gracefully left after signing a bilateral treaty with India on 28 May 1956. India expected Portugal to follow suit. That did not happen.

The land-locked state of Hyderabad, which had signed a one-year standstill/status quo agreement with India, desperately needed a seaport to realize the Nizam's secret dream. Once the richest man in the world—he famously used the famous Rs 438-crore Jacob diamond that he had found in his father's shoe as a paperweight—the Nizam offered to buy Goa. The Portuguese spurned the offer and said it could neither cede nor lease (*não alienava nem arrendava*) and reportedly made a counterproposal that negotiations similar to those between South Africa and Portugal (on a similar question) could be arranged.[*]

Dr P.D. Gaitonde also quotes a special adviser to Portugal's Permanent Mission at the United Nations who spoke of a plan to smuggle in arms, ammunition and other war material from Alexandria to Indian princely states (to resist accession to the Union of India) in vessels of a dummy shipping company registered under the Panamian flag via Goa. The Nizam and his friends were all for the idea negotiated by private individuals in London.[†] Portugal's Ambassador in London, Palmella, scotched rumours of Portugal's talks with the Nizam through Sir Alexander Rogers acting on behalf of the Nizam.[‡] Portuguese foreign minister, Caeiro da Mata,

---

[*] P.D. Gaitonde, *The Liberation of Goa: A Participant's View of History*, Rajhauns Sankalpana, Goa (first published in 1987 by C. Hurst & Co. Ltd, London), 2016, p. 45.

[†] Ibid., pp. 46–48.

[‡] Ibid., pp. 51–52.

categorically told India's high commissioner to London, Krishna Menon, in Paris on 24 July 1948, that Portugal had no direct or indirect contact with the Nizam.[*]

The Goan Political Conference held in Bombay on 21 and 22 June 1947 denounced the move of the Nizam to buy Goa.[†] Gandhi said the Indian Union would not allow such a transaction.[‡] The *National Standard* of Bombay wrote:

> The [Goan Political] Conference has also warned the Portuguese government and the colonial authorities against entering into any negotiations with the Nizam's government in the transference in any manner of any strip of land to His Exalted Highness.[§]

Although infuriated by the Nizam's actions in 1948, Nehru later only made a passing reference to it.[¶] In the words of army commander Lt Gen. Eric A. Vas, a Goan with origins in Saligao:

> When the partition of India took place ... Indian princes [were] bound by special treaty relations with the British Crown, which exercised its domain over them under the Doctrine of Paramountcy. This doctrine ... conceded no independent status to any prince. The Indian successor Government could not be expected to accept a position which its predecessor had rejected for good reason.
>
> A month before the partition, Lord Mountbatten, the last Viceroy of undivided India, addressing the princes for the last time in his capacity as the Crown Representative had advised them that practical considerations left them only with the choice

---

[*] Ibid., p. 54.

[†] B.G. Kunte (ed.), *Goa Freedom Struggle vis-à-vis Maharashtra*, p. 98.

[‡] Ibid., pp. 110–11.

[§] Edition dated 23 June 1947.

[¶] *Hindustan Overseas Times,* 2 September 1954, p. 12.

of accession either to India or Pakistan subject, among other considerations, to the factor of geographical contiguity.*

In other words, Indian princes were to join whichever nation abutted their territory and only in case both India and Pakistan adjoined their land (e.g., J&K) would they be free to join either country—and that in no circumstance would Britain confer dominion status on any princely state. Hyderabad, a Hindu-majority state, was fully within India. Yet its Muslim ruler asked India for one year's time and then plotted to buy Goa, have his own seaport and join Pakistan as the third wing of that country. Nehru was incensed at this transparent betrayal of trust.

The Portuguese occupation of Goa was a double insult for Indian nationalism. Portugal called her possessions in India 'Estado da Índia' (State of India), thereby implying two Indias on the world map. Author Emil Lengyel notes in the book *Krishna Menon*:

> ... that was another insult, indicating that there were two Indias on this globe, only one of which had for its capital New Delhi. The 'other India' had for its capital the city of Pangim ... These very names were bound to affront Indian sensibilities... Goa was the last remaining reminder of the past humiliation of the subcontinent. There, hated colonialism still conducted itself in the spirit of olden days, ruffling Indian patriotic sentiment. And Portugal itself, ruled by its apparently perennial Prime Minister, Dr Antonio de Oliveira Salazar, was in every way the social, political and economic antithesis of democratic, socialist India.

> Salazar's Portugal was also considered particularly obnoxious for another reason. Indians were familiar with Africa, the 'Dark Continent', and they knew that it was darkest wherever Portugal ruled. It was an anomaly and an abomination to have a slice of

---

* PVSM Vas, A. Eric, *Without Baggage: A Personal Account of the Jammu & Kashmir Operations, October 1947—January 1949,* Natraj Publishers, Dehradun, 2003, p. 7.

Portugal right in the core-land of progressive-minded India. But what was New Delhi to do? It was dedicated to the policy of non-violence.[*]

(An aside: Portugal always, or at least since 1635, called its colony in India a 'state'—Estado Português da *Índia* or Estado da *Índia* Oriental or just Estado da *Índia*—the Portuguese State of India. From the nineteenth century, when Portugal came under a more liberal constitutional monarchy, Goa continued to be called a state not because of Lisbon or Goa, but because of the Vatican. In 1886, the Vatican had bestowed a perpetual honorific, 'Patriarch of the East Indies', on its archbishop in Goa and it was quite unthinkable to have a patriarch perched in a mere colony!)[†]

On 27 February 1948, India requested Portugal to open negotiations to decide the future of Portuguese enclaves in India. Prime Minister Nehru asserted that these enclaves were a part of India. On 12 March 1948, Portugal turned down India's request for negotiations.

Following intense backstage diplomacy in London (where V.K. Krishna Menon was India's first High Commissioner), New Delhi and Lisbon agreed on 15 July 1948 to exchange diplomatic representatives.

On 12 August 1948, following a meeting in Paris between Krishna Menon and the Portuguese foreign minister, José Caeiro da Mata (he spelt his surname with a double 't' with an orthographic scent of the ancient), a simultaneous announcement was made that India and Portugal had decided to establish diplomatic ties at the legation level.

---

[*] Emil Lengyel, *Krishna Menon*, Walker and Company, New York, 1962, pp. 202–04.

[†] Author's interview with Antonio Palhinha Machado.

After the ceasefire in J&K (1–2 January 1949), India established diplomatic relations with Portugal at the legation level. Vasco Vieira Garin presented his credentials to Governor-General Chakravarti Rajagopalachari in New Delhi on 27 January 1949, and Parakat Atchyuta Menon submitted his credentials to President Field Marshal Oscar Carmona in Lisbon on 19 August 1949.

On 27 February 1950, India formally requested Portugal to start negotiations on the future of the tiny Portuguese colonies in India. These comprised Goa—wedged between Maharashtra and Karnataka—and the overland pockets of Daman and Diu in coastal Gujarat.

Daman included hinterland areas of Dadra and Nagar Haveli, which were at some distance inside Gujarat. The Peshwas had given a *jagir* (revenue grant) vide treaties of 4 May 1779 and 11 January 1780 over seventy-two villages of Nagar Haveli to the Portuguese as compensation for the burning of the ship *Sant'Ana* by Janoji Dhulap in 1773. The deal was that the Portuguese would recover the cost of the vessel from revenue of the villages and then return Nagar Haveli to the Marathas. Infighting and turmoil at the Peshwa court in Pune, until their final ouster in the 1818 Third Anglo–Maratha War, ensured that Nagar Haveli remained with the Portuguese. The Portuguese purchased nearby Dadra in 1785.

India regarded the enclaves of Goa, Daman and Diu as historically, geographically, ethnically, culturally, linguistically and legally one with the rest of India. All Goans settled in India prior to 1945 were treated as Indian citizens and registered as voters in their place of domicile. Goans from Goa were allowed free entry into India, without passports or visas, prior to Nehru's imposition of the 1954 economic blockade. Ethnic Portuguese, when entering India by land, sea or air, had to produce passports and visas. Indians entering Goa, however, were subjected to strict restrictions.

On 15 June 1950, Portuguese Foreign Minister José Caeiro da Mata said the negotiations proposed by India were ...

only to define how the Portuguese State of India would be
integrated into the Indian Union

... and rejected the request.

Portugal asserted, despite the Colonial Act being in force, that
these enclaves were not colonies but were 'a part of the Portuguese
Nation', as integral as its province of Algarve—meaning, integral parts
of mainland Portugal as 'overseas provinces'—albeit across the Atlantic
and the Indian Oceans, and that their transfer was non-negotiable.

Other than the emotion Portugal attached to Goa, there might
have been a practical reason for Portugal to hold on steadfastly to
Goa: if Portugal were to lose Goa, it could open the floodgates
to vacate the African colonies of Angola, Mozambique, Cabinda
(Congo), Cabo Verde, Portuguese Guinea (now Guinea-Bissau),
São Tomé and Príncipe, and in Asia, Macao and Portuguese Timor
(now Timor Leste). Unlike tiny Goa, which was actually a burden,
Angola—and to some extent Mozambique—contributed positively
to Portugal's exchequer.

On 1 October 1951, Nehru told Parliament[*] that whatever
justification such islands of foreign authority like Goa had to India
in the days when India herself was a subject country had disappeared
with the coming of independence to India.

Portugal reiterated that India had no right to Goa because India
did not exist when Goa came under the Portuguese (in 1510, India
was a conglomerate of principalities and kingdoms).

Salazar later famously told his parliament:

For the Indian Union to claim to turn the clock of history back
to the 15th century, to come forward now and make out that she
already existed potentially at that time, or to set herself up as the

---

[*] Quotes from Parliament debates (Lok Sabha and Rajya Sabha) are not
   individually referenced, as the debates are freely accessible public records. Interested readers may refer to debates from authentic sources,
   like the website of the Indian parliament library: https://eparlib.nic.in/
   handle/123456789/7

rightful heir of those whom we found holding sway there, is the
fancy of static dreamers; it is not for the dynamic shapers of history
that the men who received an empire from England want to be.[*]

While many in Portugal felt that the country should abandon
colonialism in Asia and Africa (where Portugal had colonies), they
were up against a dictator. The few who publicly voiced their
opinion (opposition leaders, socialists and university teachers), were
promptly put behind bars by the PIDE. Future premier and later
president of Portugal, Mario Soares, was among them. However,
there were some who felt otherwise and held a low opinion of
Goans. For instance, Portuguese lawyer António Neves Anacleto
once said:

... [Goans] are for our race what the woodworm is to wood.[†]

Yet, Portugal wanted to hold on to the woodworm.

On 11 June 1951, by a constitutional amendment (Law
No. 2048), Salazar reverted Goa from a colony to an 'overseas
province' of mainland Portugal. We know of corporations across
nations (multinationals)—but here was a nation across continents, a
'multicontinental' nation! The legal stratagem of redesignating Goa
as a phoney 'overseas province' of metropolitan Portugal fooled
none. Goa was a colony, pure and simple.

In the wake of World War II, most nations were opposed to
colonialism ('non-self-governing territories') and favoured freedom
from foreign rule. The world had changed. Salazar had not.

Salazar decided he knew the world without stepping out of
Portugal. Unlike modern heads of state and government, Salazar did
not travel. The furthest he went was in 1942 to adjoining Spain, just

---

[*] Salazar, *The Case for Goa,* Secretariado Nacional da Informação, Lisbon,
     1954, p. 8.
[†] Thesis of Filipa Alexandra Carvalho Sousa Lopes, *As Vozes da Oposição
     ao Estado Novo e a Questão de Goa (1950–1961),* University of Porto, p.
     177.

once—the distance between Lisbon and Seville and Merida in Spain was half the distance between Goa and Mumbai. He strongly feared aircraft and ships: when Transportes Aéreos Portugueses—TAP, the Portuguese airline—bought its first aircraft and coaxed Salazar to pose in it for good publicity, he had the airplane thoroughly inspected and verified that its fuel tanks were dry, and only then entered the plane parked at a far corner of the airport, put on the seat belt and flashbulbs popped.[*] Like the sixteenth-century historian João de Barros, who chronicled *As Décadas da Ásia* in 1552 without ever visiting Asia, Salazar thought he understood Goa, India and the world sitting in Lisbon.

Dialogue of the Deaf

On 14 January 1953, India served another *aide-memoire,* calling for a 'direct transfer' of the territories, declaring (at paragraph six) the Government of India's ...

> ... desire to maintain the cultural identity and other rights, including language, laws and customs of the inhabitants of these territories, and make no changes in such and like matters except with their consent.[†]

Portugal declared she could not discuss the question, let alone accept the solution offered by India.[‡]

Diplomacy was leading nowhere. Portugal was deaf to India's pleas to see reason and quit Goa gracefully. India was deaf to Portugal's fantastical claim that Goa was a part of mainland Portugal ('overseas province') and not a colony—despite the Colonial Act being in force.

---

[*]   Author's interview with Antonio Palhinha Machado.
[†]   *Vinte Anos de Defesa,* vol. I, pp. 279–83.
[‡]   Ibid., pp. 219–21.

Salazar re-labelled the colony of Goa as an 'overseas province' of Portugal not just to bamboozle India but also to gain UN entry—colonial powers were anathema to the United Nations—and, possibly, with an eye on NATO help, should the contingency occur.

Portugal finally joined the UN, with India's support, on 14 December 1955—and within eight days, as a UN member, filed the 'Rights of Passage' case against India before the International Court of Justice at The Hague. India had barred the passage of Portuguese military personnel from Daman over Indian territory to Dadra and Nagar Haveli in October 1953. (The verdict of The Hague, though ambiguous, was welcomed by both parties as a victory. The Soviet judge said that Portugal 'never had and has not any right of passage over Indian territory to these regions and between each of them'. The Greek judge held that 'Since the right of passage assumes the continuance of the administration of the enclaves by the Portuguese, the establishment of a new power in the enclaves must be regarded as having ipso facto put an end to the right of passage'.)

With this move of calling Goa an 'overseas province' of Portugal, Salazar may have figured out that Nehru would cease asking for a part of Portugal, albeit an 'overseas' part located within the Indian subcontinent.

As for NATO intervention, it was out of the question, irrespective of whether Goa was a colony or an overseas part of Portugal. NATO's Article V clearly stipulated 'armed attack against one or more of them [the NATO Parties] in Europe or North America' and Article VI specified 'armed attack ... on the territory of any of the Parties in Europe or North America ... or under the jurisdiction of any of the Parties in the North Atlantic area north of the Tropic of Cancer'.

The operative words were 'north of the Tropic of Cancer'. Goa clearly fell outside the NATO ambit. John Foster Dulles, the US Secretary of State stated:

That part of the world is definitely outside the North Atlantic
Treaty area ... Dr Paulo Cunha, the Portuguese Foreign
Minister, had also admitted at about the same time that the
NATO framework applied only to the North Atlantic zone and
was unlikely to be extended.[*]

Portugal could not expect any military help from NATO in the
event India attacked Goa. Portugal would later appeal to NATO
under Article IV, which said:

The Parties will consult together whenever, in the opinion of
any of them, the territorial integrity, political independence or
security of any of the Parties is threatened.

In other words, only 'consultation' not 'armed intervention'.

Gen. Carlos de Azeredo (a descendant of the famous Távoras,
whose last marquis, Francisco de Assis Távora, was the forty-fifth
viceroy in Goa, 1750–54), was a Portuguese military officer who
arrived in Goa in 1954, when he was twenty-three years old, was
repatriated in 1956, and sent back to Goa in January 1961 when a
captain. He wrote a book, *Trabalhos e Dias de Um Soldado do Império*,[†]
and was also interviewed for an article where he accurately dubbed
the Indo–Portuguese talks as a '*dialogue of the deaf*' (emphasis added).[‡]

India's note of 14 January 1953 was followed up with notes
later that year on 1 May and 21 May. Portugal refused to come to
the negotiating table. India then served its final note on 26 May
and closed its legation in Lisbon on 11 June. Portugal, however,
continued with its legation in New Delhi.

---

[*] P.N, Khera, Ministry of Defence, Government of India, 1974, p. 50.

[†] Carlos de Azeredo, *Work and Days of a Soldier of the Empire*, Livraria
Civilização Editora, Lisbon, 2004.

[‡] *Passagem para a Índia* (A Passage to India, published in *O Expresso* of
8 December 2001, https://web.archive.org/web/20011209004006/
http://semanal.expresso.pt/revista/artigos/interior.asp?edi-
cao=1519&id_artigo=ES44188).

The same year, the UN General Assembly held that 'overseas provinces' anywhere in the world were colonies, and a plebiscite under UN supervision would decide the fate of such 'overseas provinces'.

Meanwhile, things had been heating up in Goa after Lohia's call of 18 June 1946. Demonstrations on Indian national days with the Indian flag borne aloft, cries of the nationalistic salutation, *Jai Hind* (which meant 'Victory to India!' until 1947 and thereafter, 'Long Live, India!' or 'Salute to India!'), distribution of pamphlets and other banned literature, secret meetings, sabotage, detentions, tortures, arrests, jail terms and exile started to become commonplace. The *Economist* of London described Goa as:

> ... the only place where Indians actually live under a police state.[*]

On 18 June 1954, nationalists unfurled the Indian tricolour in Goa. Over twenty groups of people were arrested. The Government of India warned it could no longer continue to remain a silent spectator of the repressive policy followed by the Portuguese authorities, meaning, India would act.

But the Government of India did the diametric opposite: it remained a mere vocal spectator. Goans began taking matters into their own hands.

India's 'Policy of Peace'

India had barred the passage of Portuguese military personnel through Indian territory to Dadra and Nagar Haveli in October 1953. On 22 July 1954, thirty-five volunteers of the militant United Front of Goans (led by Francisco Mascarenhas, J.M. D'Souza and Vaman Desai) occupied Dadra, which was being defended by thirty-two Portuguese policemen. Portugal later claimed that a battalion of the Maratha Light Infantry had encircled Dadra.

---

[*] *The Economist*, 1 May 1954.

Volunteers of the militant Azad Gomantak Dal (led by
Vishwanath Lawande) and others, including Prabhakar Sinari of
Ribandar and Cristovam Gabriel Paulo das Angustias Furtado of
Chinchinim) and the Goan People's Party (led by George Vaz) along
with volunteers of the RSS, freed Nagar Haveli by 2 August 1954.

Again, there were Portuguese claims of Indian armed
involvement (1200 Indian reserve police with eleven jeeps). Morarji
Desai, at the time chief minister of Bombay State, which surrounded
Dadra and Nagar Haveli, wrote in his *The Story of My Life* that
he did post some state reserve police personnel—who from their
appearance and training resembled military forces—around Dadra
and Nagar Haveli before the Goan nationalists struck (they had met
him and sought his help).*

Elated by these developments, Goan nationalists in Bombay
decided to launch a *satyagraha* ('force of truth' movement devised
by Gandhi that had been used quite effectively against the British
in India) in Goa from 15 August 1954, India's Independence Day.

The Government of India felt Indian participation in
this peaceful form of protest would be construed as India's
interference in the 'internal' affairs of Portugal and invite western
condemnation. Also, Nehru possibly feared that if Indians
were allowed to cross the international border and participate
in the satyagraha in Goa, Pakistan in turn would send armed
'satyagrahis' into Kashmir—just as it had sent thinly disguised
army regulars commanding trained and armed Pathan tribals
into Kashmir in 1947.

Thus, India declared it would not allow Indian participation
in the satyagraha. Nehru did allow Goans living in India to cross
the border into Goa, but without arms. (We shall return to the 15
August 1954 Satyagraha later.) India also did not integrate Dadra
and Nagar Haveli into the Indian Union. This would be done only
seven years later, on 11 August 1961.

---

* Morarji Desai, *The Story of My Life*, Macmillan (vols I and II), 1974;
   S. Chand & Co. (vol. III), 1979.

Nehru's biographer, the Goan-origin editor of the *Times of Ceylon* and later of the *Times of India,* Frank Moraes, noted:

> For most of his life Prime Minister Nehru had resisted the idea that non-violence should be projected to the plane of defence against external aggression.[*]

But Nehru had evidently begun doing it now. He was assuming the robes of a world pacifist. Nehru told the Lok Sabha on 25 August 1954:

> The policy that we have pursued ... [is] one of non-violence.

A year later, on 26 July 1955, he again told Parliament,

> We have always been clear that we will not use force except for defence, that we will not provoke or wage war or adopt any aggressive tactics leading to war.

To Nehru, the minuscule foreign presence in an area of 0.1 per cent of the country was like a 'pimple on the face of Mother India'. Lohia retorted:

> It was a pimple that disfigured the face of India more than that other pimple of Kashmir.[†]

The brotherhood of Indian socialists within the Congress Party and outside—like Jayaprakash Narayan, Minoo Masani, Yusuf Meherally, Asoka Mehta, Ram Manohar Lohia, George Fernandes and barristers Krishna Menon, Siddharth Shankar Ray and Rajni Patel—regarded Portugal-held Goa not as a 'pimple' but as an anachronism that needed to be corrected.

---

[*] Frank Moraes, *Jawaharlal Nehru: A Biography,* The MacMillan Company, New York, 1956, pp. 291–92.

[†] Ram Manohar Lohia, *Bombay Chronicle,* 15 July 1945.

India preached non-violence to the world and Prime Minister Nehru, forever conscious of his world image and his internationalist aspirations, pledged India would not attack Goa. He said:

> There must be peaceful methods. This is essential. We rule out non-peaceful methods entirely.

Nehru was a key organizer of the Bandung Conference held from 18–24 April 1955 in Indonesia to forge Asian-African solidarity between twenty-nine nations representing 54 per cent of the world's people. The conference roused a major part of the world to the anachronism of colonialism. The UN was clearly against colonialism. Major European colonial powers like France and England were shedding their colonies. But the oldest of them all, Portugal, now under a dictator, was paying no heed. The Bandung Conference was to have a direct bearing on the anti-colonial movement. It also strengthened the anti-apartheid movement. And it was to eventually lead to the creation of the Non-Aligned Movement. On 15 August 1955, Nehru told the nation from the ramparts of the Red Fort:

> I declare here and now that we shall not send our Army [into Goa]. We will solve this problem peacefully. Let everybody understand this clearly. India has decided not to use force.[*]

In widely quoted words, Nehru told the Uttar Pradesh Congress Committee at Sitapur on 21 August 1955:

> Opposed as we are to colonialism everywhere, it is impossible for us to tolerate the continuance of colonial rule in a small part of India. It is not that we covet Goa. That little bit of territory makes no difference to this great country. But even a

---

[*] *Times of India*, 16 August 1955.

small enclave under foreign rule does make a difference, and it is a constant reproach to the self-respect and national interest of India. To take Goa by force would be easy ... (but) police action would be contrary to the policy of the Government as well as to the dignity of India. We have assured Goans that it is for them to establish their own future.

Goans of most shades of opinion were happy about Nehru's utterances. Those who stood for Goa's integration with India welcomed Nehru's commitment towards freeing Goa from colonial rule. Those who wanted autonomy to be devolved upon Goa were aware that their tiny voice would not move an intransigent Salazar, and Nehru's words were gratifying. Those of the militant persuasion were, however, unhappy that Nehru kept reiterating India's policy of non-violence and peaceful negotiations. Their fears would turn valid. This oft-repeated policy of solving all international disputes by peaceful means would backfire against India when it finally decided to use force in 1961. Later that year, on 6 September, Nehru told the Rajya Sabha:

I wish to remove from the mind of each and every person the idea that we have decided to compel or force the people of Goa to join the Union of India.

Again, on 17 September, he reiterated in Parliament:

We rule out non-peaceful methods. Even police action will lay Indians open to the charge of being deceitful hypocrites. Peaceful methods ... [are] not only a sound policy, but the only possible policy.

In July the following year, President Gamal Abdel Nasser of Egypt nationalized the Suez Canal. Fearing that the passage of their ships would be imperilled, Britain and France (largely owning the Suez

Canal Company that built and operated the canal until then) para-dropped troops together with those of Israel at Port Said in October–November. The USA and USSR brought pressure and had the invading troops withdrawn. Contrasting the position of Britain and France towards Egypt in Suez with the position of India towards Goa, Nehru once again declared:

> India will never deviate from her policy of peace.

Nehru's Unflinching View on Goa

Goans were not unanimous on the approach to Goa's future. There were diverse schools of thought. Most wanted integration with India but some wanted autonomy—with Goa as an overseas state of Portugal and others with Goa as a quasi-nation aligned to a Portuguese Commonwealth (like India as a nation aligned to the British Commonwealth). Nehru was aware of these diverse views. As leader of the country, he possibly felt he had to placate all divergent views so as to carry all together. Nehru told a gathering in Bombay on 4 June 1956:

> If the people of Goa … deliberately wish to retain their separate identity, I am not going to bring them by processes of compulsion or coercion into the Indian Union … I merely say that my national interest involves the removal of the Portuguese from Goa and not the use of any coercion in bringing about the union of Goa with India … I want to make it perfectly clear that I have no desire to force Goa to join India against the wishes of the people of Goa … But the point is we feel that Goa's individuality should remain. Whenever the time comes for any changes, internal or other, it will be for the people of Goa acting freely to decide upon them.[*]

---

[*] Jamie Trinidad, *Self-Determination in Disputed Colonial Territories*, Cambridge University Press, 2018, p. 189.

Goans were thrilled to hear this. Nehru's consistent and unwavering assertions clearly comprised of two distinct parts:

1. Portugal as a colonial occupier needed to be removed from Goa, Daman and Diu; and,
2. Goans would be allowed to 'establish their own future' and 'acting freely [without compulsion or coercion], to decide' the question of joining India (i.e., self-determination).

Liberating the territories of the Portuguese yoke was one thing. An overwhelming majority of Goans would readily welcome it. But, annexing the territories without consulting the affected people was quite another. Goans would not cheer being 'liberated' without knowing the nature of the replacement regime.

It must be said, however, that a large section of Goans—Hindu and Catholic—favoured Goa's integration with India, but as Nehru said on 4 June 1956 in Bombay:

... whenever the time comes.

To sense the mood, Goan members to the Portuguese Parliament, *Cónego* (Canon) Castilho Noronha and Sócrates da Costa, invited twenty-two Goans to a private meet on 10 July 1955. The process of selecting the twenty-two was entirely arbitrary—the invitees were either rich businessmen or big landlords or known public figures. Eighteen attended, while the viscount Rauraji Deshprabhu of Pernem, medical doctor and owner of Goa's then most famous private printing press, Dr Jaime Rangel of Bastora, baron Vasantrao Dempo of Santa Cruz and eminent medical doctor Dr António Dias of Jua/Margao did not.

At this meet, Adv. A.X. Gomes Pereira and Dr Álvaro de Loyola Furtado favoured integration with India. Dr António Colaço affirmed that:

... the majority of Goans are in favour of integration with India,

... although personally he was not for immediate integration but after a reasonable period, when the atmosphere was less oppressive and the issue could be discussed openly.[*]

Nehru, meanwhile, continued with diplomacy in 1956. He had told Parliament before (referring to the Goa question):

> We deal with national and international issues and we have often to be very patient. It is this reputation we have built in the world ... [that] we do not act in haste, we give mature consideration to problems. Because we try to function as a mature nation and have not taken hasty decisions or hasty actions. Therefore, the world pays attention to what we say.

Meanwhile, in Portugal ...

Opposition leaders in Portugal, including Cunha Leal, Quintão Meireles and Nuno Rodrigues dos Santos, as well as African writers and poets (some of them born and bred in Portugal) like Agostinho Neto, Hermínio Marvão, Ângelo Veloso, Cecília Alves and Hernâni Cidade, urged Salazar to enter into negotiations with India and find a peaceful solution to Goa. Not all, however, went scot-free. Communist leader Alvaro Cunhal was held in Peniche jail (from where he and other political detainees would escape in January 1960).

Earlier in August 1954, Portuguese professor Rui Luis Gomes and four others were arrested, tried and sentenced to serve time for trying to publish an article urging the Portuguese government to negotiate with India and ascertain the wishes of the local people by holding a plebiscite in Goa. The five had to suffer imprisonment with jail terms ranging from nine to nineteen months.

Salazar steadfastly refused to talk and refused to vacate the last vestige of European colonialism in India. At first, he condescendingly declared that Goa was the:

---

[*] Lopes, *As Vozes da Oposição ao Estado Novo e a Questão de Goa (1950–1961)*, pp. 233–34.

... light of the West in the Orient.

Later, the furthest he was willing to go reflected in his 1956 suggestion:

> ... invoke the principle of self-determination, and let the people decide by plebiscite whether they want to continue with Portugal or join India.

He quickly withdrew from the idea when—as per Gen. Francisco Costa Gomes, the second post-revolution president of Portugal (1974–76, after Gen. António de Spinola)—he was told that not more than 10 per cent of Goans would vote for continuance of the Portuguese in Goa.

Gen. Costa Gomes, when a lieutenant colonel, was Portugal's undersecretary of war. He visited Goa in December 1960 and recommended a reduction of troops because Goa could not be defended militarily against India. He informed Salazar that force levels in Goa were irrelevant because:

> ... even Portugal's entire army would not be able to resist, for more than five hours, an invasion by the elite Indian troops who had fought in World War II.*

This quote appears in a book by Portuguese cavalry officer João Aranha. Aranha was an armour captain with 7 Cavalry in Portugal. He arrived in Goa by the ship *Niassa* on 7 May 1957 and, after working in South Goa, was seconded to the PEI (Polícia do Estado da Índia) at the Panjim police headquarters. In 1961, he headed the police in North Goa. In the book, Aranha describes his days in Goa, the madness of Salazar's policy towards Goa, the absurdity of 'total sacrifice' (or fight to the last man) and his days in captivity.

---

* João Aranha, *Enquanto se esperam as naus do reino ...,* Esfera do Caos, Lisbon, 2008, p. 90 and footnote no. 22 on the same page.

Aranha was a prisoner of war (POW) held at police headquarters in Panjim, transferred to the Altinho camp, then to the Ponda camp and finally to the Aguada camp until repatriated in May 1962.

The idea of a plebiscite or referendum in Goa was first proposed by Marcello Mathias, Portugal's ambassador to France and later foreign minister, 1959–61.[*] Salazar's council of ministers rejected it because they thought it would set a bad precedent for Angola and Mozambique. Salazar concealed the real reason for his objection to a referendum in Goa (viz. that the vote would go overwhelmingly against him). Instead, he publicly dubbed a referendum as tantamount to 'an abandonment' of Goa.[†] Marcello Mathias felt that it was:

> ... better to abandon with honour than to abandon beaten, crushed, with dead, wounded and prisoners in the hands of the Indian Union. And if we win the referendum while not having guarantees that the Indian Union will respect this result, our position will be much stronger internationally.[‡]

At a US State Department meeting in Washington on 30 November 1955, Secretary of State John Foster Dulles asked Portugal's foreign minister, Paulo Cunha, whether any thought had been given to a referendum in Goa. Cunha replied that a referendum was politically impossible because every Portuguese constitution had contained a provision against the alienation of Portuguese territory. Portugal's ambassador to the US, Luis Esteves Fernandes, told Dulles that Nehru recently said that even if a referendum was held in Goa and was favourable to Portugal, India would not accept the result.[§]

---

[*] *Visão História*, vol. 14, 2011, pp. 64–65.

[†] Lopes, *As Vozes da Oposição ao Estado Novo e a Questão de Goa (1950-1961)*, p. 253.

[‡] *Visão História*, vol. 14, 2011, pp. 64–65.

[§] https://history.state.gov/historicaldocuments/frus1955-57v27/d148

Although it vaguely referred to 'the popular feeling in these territories was for union with the new and free Republic of India', India never officially proposed a plebiscite in Goa. Portugal's diplomat in New Delhi, in a letter to Lisbon dated 23 March 1950, said that the ambassadors of Brazil and the United States were of the opinion that even a mere suggestion of a plebiscite on Portugal's part would scare away the Indians.* In frequent public utterances, Nehru obliquely referred to ascertaining the wishes of Goans but never proposed a plebiscite.

Salazar never countenanced the other option: that Portugal withdraw and let Goa remain an autonomous region—as Nehru had implicitly said in Bombay on 4 June 1956.

The first call for autonomy for Goa was made way back in 1910 by journalist and liberal Luis de Menezes Bragança when Portugal became a republic. Bragança quit the Council of Government in protest of the 1930 Colonial Act, and again demanded autonomy for Goa.

The clamour for autonomy intensified after 1946, as Goans, led by the redoubtable scientist, Dr Froilano de Melo, later elected to the Portugal Parliament as an MP from Goa, pitched for it.

In 1947, Portugal asked a few leading Goans, probably thirty in number, what they wanted. Twenty-three sent back a memo demanding autonomy.

Salazar effected a few reforms in 1943 and 1954, but these were far from the local call for autonomy—a case of too little too late. (It is said that Dr Froilano de Melo took self-exile in Brazil after Salazar refused to heed his pleas for autonomy for Goa.)

Nothing, of course, came out of these local demands for autonomy. Salazar was not willing to alter his stand on imperialism. His regime, Estado Novo, needed to 'civilize' Goans. Goa needed to be ruled with an iron fist.

---

* P.D. Gaitonde, *The Liberation of Goa: A Participant's View of History*, Rajhauns Sankalpana, Goa (first published in 1987 by C. Hurst & Co. Ltd., London), 2016, p. 65.

Salazar was a devout Catholic, abidingly loyal to the Vatican, more papal than the pope. His deep faith was often scoffed at. However, the Vatican's criticism of his actions did not affect him.

Msgr Lino Lozza, papal delegate at the third assembly of the World Council of Churches held in New Delhi from 19 November to 5 December 1961, stated that the Vatican did not approve of the activities of Salazar in Angola and Goa, which he said were 'inconsistent with the Gospel'. Almost 200 churches sent their representatives for the New Delhi assembly. The Vatican deputed a team of five.* Msgr Lozza added that

> ... the Roman Catholic Church identifies with the urge of the dependent people for self-determination.†

The devout Roman Catholic Portuguese dictator wouldn't be moved one bit.

Autonomy for Goa

António Anastácio Bruto da Costa (1902–84) was a leading—and fearless—advocate from Margao. Six foot plus, with an athletic build and a booming voice, Costa vented against Portuguese colonialism as well as Indian nationalism. He was for Goa as an autonomous quasi-nation aligned to a Portuguese Commonwealth. Nationalists favouring integration with India denounced him as a fifth columnist; Portugal loyalists berated him as a traitor; and PIDE secret reports labelled him as 'an active element against the Portuguese regime'.

Costa stood for probity at all levels of Goa's administration especially the gubernatorial, restoration of civil liberties and complete autonomy for Goa as a quasi-nation aligned to a

---

*   For a full report of the third assembly proceedings, see: https://archive.org/stream/newdelhireportth009987mbp/newdelhireport-th009987mbp_djvu.txt
†   *Times of India*, 24 November 1961.

Portuguese Commonwealth. His essays on these three subjects were blacked out by the censors.

Cdr Fernando de Quintanilha Mendonça e Dias was one of Goa's notoriously corrupt governors (1948–52). Not a *tanga* (anna) left the state treasury without an underhand percentage paid to the governor. Even that was small change for him. Three chartered seaplanes of Belgium's Sabena Airways ferrying bribes of the Goan mine-owner cartel for the governor—mostly in gold—landed one fine day in Goa, two in the River Mandovi near his office, one in the Dona Paula Bay near his residence. Offloaded in canoes, the gold was stored at the river front Customs House (free of duties, of course!) for onward smuggling into India.

The Portuguese minister for overseas, Commodore Manuel Maria Sarmento Rodrigues, was due to visit Goa from 20 April to 12 May 1952, the first such minister to do so. He came on the inaugural run of the Lisbon–Timor passenger ship *Índia* (the same ocean liner that, nine years later, in December 1961, would be hastily converted into an evacuee ship). Costa and Dr António Colaço of Margao convened a meet in Margao on 29 March, preparatory to the visit of the overseas minister. A memorandum calling for civil liberties and complete autonomy was signed by seventy-four prominent citizens, both Hindu and Catholic. This was called 'The Group of Margao'.

Governor Quintanilha Dias did his best to prevent his long-standing critic Costa from meeting the visiting minister. However, the overseas minister himself granted Costa an appointment. On the evening of 2 May, Costa received a letter from Fernando de Fonseca, head of office of the governor-general, communicating the appointment for 3 May 1952 at 7 p.m. at the Palácio do Cabo.[*] The memorandum of The Group of Margao was handed over to the visiting minister by Costa and Colaço at this meeting.

---

[*] Mário Bruto da Costa, *Goa: A Terceira corrente*, self-published, Goa, 2013, p. 43.

The governor, concealed behind a partition screen, eavesdropped on the conversation and thus overhead the fearless Costa speaking of the governor's misdemeanours in Goa. When Costa and Colaço rose to seek leave of the minister at the end of the hour-and-a-half meeting, Quintanilha quickly left the room and waited outside.

Inviting Costa to an adjacent room saying that he wished to speak, Quintanilha told Costa, 'I will not tolerate insinuations against my honour.'

Costa replied, 'I am not accustomed to insinuate. I make affirmations, based on hard evidence. If the facts speak against your honourability, whose fault is it?'

The governor raised his hand first. Costa's spectacles fell to the floor. With a serious vision impairment, eyeglasses were a necessity for Costa.

Blinded by fury, Costa twice punched and floored the Portuguese naval commander and pinning him down with a bended knee, reduced this supine governor of the once mighty Estado Português da Índia to a punching bag. Two younger Portuguese men— Quintanilha's son-in-law and the chief secretary, Pamplona Corte Real—who tried to intervene were tossed against the wooden wall panelling with a single sweep of the Goan advocate's arm.

As Costa later explained to the overseas minister by letter dated 5 March 1952:

> ... I, for myself, given my education, was incapable of offending
> anyone in my own house, and much less, people who had come
> at my invitation or that of my guests ...*

When the overseas minister changed, Governor Quintanilha Dias recommended that Costa be exiled to Angola. Lisbon ignored the plea and replaced Quintanilha the same year.

Costa was later prevented from seeking medical help in Bombay that might have saved his eyesight. When, finally and too late, he

---

* Ibid., p. 45.

was allowed to proceed to Spain, the police chief of Goa, Joaquim Pinto Brás, in a confidential letter of 10 November 1959, informed the PIDE chief in Lisbon that:

> Advocate António Anastácio Bruto da Costa, resident of Margao, flew today to Karachi, bound for Barcelona, to undergo an eye operation. I would like to inform that the said Bruto da Costa is an active element against the current Portuguese political regime, and takes every opportunity to propagate his political ideas.[*]

Costa met Salazar in August 1947 in Lisbon, requesting him to restore civil liberties, repeal the offensive Acto Colonial and grant complete autonomy for Goa aligned to a Portuguese commonwealth. He even drafted a constitution for the State of Goa, along the lines of the Government of India Act of 1935, mandating universal adult franchise. (Less than 4 per cent of Goans were entitled to vote in those days—only those paying a minimum amount of tax and those who were qualified professionally or educated up to a certain level of formal education were entitled to vote. This was later amended to include heads of households, whether literate or taxpayers or not.)

Autonomy entailed amending the Portuguese Constitution, and Salazar would have none of it.

On the Colonial Act, the fearless advocate told Salazar, 'Your Excellency made us objects of possession.'

Salazar disclosed that he himself had drafted the law.

'In that case,' Costa retorted, 'the offence is even more serious!' The indomitable advocate told friends on his return, 'Salazar turned red, but kept mum.'

Only once, addressing his National Assembly on 30 November 1954, did Salazar speak of making Goa a sovereign state with the same international guarantees as any world state. He was evidently not serious about the idea and was possibly trying to buy time. Nothing more was heard of his idea of Goa being made a sovereign state.

---

[*] Ibid., p. 268.

Nationalists like advocates Pandurang Mulgaokar and Gopal Apa Kamat associated with a 1947–48 move of Loutulim's Vicente João de Figueiredo for autonomy, but with Goa as an overseas state of Portugal. This would bestow a 'special status' to Goa of the kind granted to the state of Jammu and Kashmir in 1947, except that Goa's arrangement with Portugal would be permanent (unlike J&K where the 'special status' was envisioned to last until the state adopted its own constitution). Laxmikant Bhembre was also a part of this initially, but soon left. Advocates Mulgaokar and Kamat from North Goa, litterateur Ravindra Kelekar from Central Goa and many others from South Goa were consistent adherents of the cause of autonomy for Goa. Figueiredo and Adv. Fanchu Loyola launched a daily, *A Vôz da Índia*, in May 1946 to further the demand. (The newspaper was later sold to a Goan group of ten Hindus and ten Catholics.)

As mentioned earlier, advocate Bruto da Costa had demanded complete autonomy for Goa as a quasi-nation aligned to a Portuguese commonwealth. His Group of Margao issued an appeal favouring the Opposition candidate, former air force chief Gen. Humberto Delgado, in Portugal's 1958 presidential election. (Portugal's Opposition favoured an end to colonialism in the post-World War II era, like France and Britain. Gen. Delgado would later be liquidated by Portugal's secret police, PIDE, in Spain.) The appeal in favour of Gen. Delgado was signed by Goan Hindus as well as Catholics.

It is clear that Goans had divergent opinions about their future: integration with India, continuance under Portugal but with autonomy; complete autonomy or a quasi-nation only aligned to a Portuguese Commonwealth; and a few—the tiniest group—for status quo. But no approach was based on caste or religious grounds—Brahmins on one side and the other castes on the other; or Hindus on one side and Catholics on the other—as is often erroneously believed. The adherents of each school of thought were a mix of both Catholic and Hindu, irrespective of caste.

(Post-1961, this boiled down to those who strove to maintain Goa's separate identity within the Union of India—largely the erstwhile autonomy camp; and those who strove to smother that identity by merging Goa with the gigantic neighbour, Maharashtra—largely the erstwhile integration camp. However, there were exceptions in either camp as, for instance, a large section of Goan Catholics—and some Goan Hindus like Shabu Dessai of Cuncolim—who stood for integration with India pre-1961 but were dead against merger into Maharashtra.)

Even in early 1961, freedom fighters Pandurang Mulgaokar, Gopal Apa Kamat and Shankar Sardesai argued for autonomy for Goa under Portuguese sovereignty.[*] Again, in early 1961, Purushottam Kakodkar, the Congress veteran who had served an exile sentence of a decade in Portugal (1946–56), also thought the idea of autonomy was worth pursuing and went to Lisbon for talks on this proposal.[†] (Freedom fighter P.P. Shirodkar, free Goa's first elected Legislative Assembly speaker and author of the book under reference, was a staunch champion of Goa's post-1961 merger into Maharashtra.)

This approach of autonomy under Portuguese sovereignty was called the 'moderate' school of thought. Historian Sarto Esteves says:

> Among others who subscribed to this approach in one way or the other were José Inácio de Loyola, Paolo Ribeiro, Gopinath Kurade, Vicente João Figueiredo, AX Gomes Pereira, António Sequeira and Francisco Xavier Furtado. Their approach and attitude towards freedom for Goa was to a great extent

---

[*] Suresh Kanekar, *Goa's Liberation and Thereafter: Chronicles of a Fragmented Life*, Goa, 1556, 2011, p. 35.

[†] P.P. Shirodkar, *My Life in Exile*, translated into English by Lt Col Dr. Pravinkumar P. Shirodkar, Pradnya-Darshan Prakashan, Goa, 2012, p. 238, and Goa Gazetteer, *Who's Who of Freedom Fighters*, vol. 1, Goa Gazetteer Department, Government of the Union Territory of Goa, Daman and Diu, 1986, p. 149.

conditioned by the censored press and the police rule that was prevalent in Goa.[*]

As long back as 26 June 1946, Gandhi had written in *The Harijan* that Goa had no future as an autonomous entity in an independent India. Gandhi was clearly against any notions of autonomy and strongly felt that Goa should be a part of India since it was within the Indian sub-continent. Goans opposed to this said that, by that logic, Pakistan, Bangladesh, Nepal and Sri Lanka also ought to have been part of India.

India, meanwhile, rejected the offer by USA and UK to mediate a peaceful Portuguese exit from Goa. Instead of mediating, India asked them to exert pressure on Portugal to quit Goa. The diplomatic deadlock between New Delhi and Lisbon continued.

Goans were never part of the debate, says Philip Bravo in the abstract of his paper, 'The Case of Goa: History, Rhetoric and Nationalism'.[†]

> [In] the fruitless diplomatic contest between New Delhi and Lisbon ... the arguments used by each government to defend its right to Goa provide an interesting case study of how history can be used in an attempt to define a 'people'. Few Goans were persuaded to make a stand on either side of this debate... Goans seem to have been indifferent to this problem. A mass nationalist movement that represented either the Portuguese or Indian position did not exist in Goa... [Quoting M.N. Pearson, The Portuguese in India].[‡] In 1961, following the Indian 'liberation' of Goa and celebrations throughout India, journalists noted an unusual lack of enthusiasm among Goans.

[*] Sarto Esteves, *Politics and Political Leadership in Goa*, Sterling Publishers, New Delhi, 1986, p. 48.

[†] Philip Bravo, *The Case of Goa, Past Imperfect*, vol. 7, Alberta (Canada), 1998, pp. 125–154, https://journals.library.ualberta.ca/pi/index.php/pi/article/view/1400

[‡] M.N. Pearson, *The Portuguese in India*, Cambridge University Press, New York, 1987, pp. 160–61.

It was not as if Goans were entirely apathetic. Besides, based outside Goa, given that Goa was a repressive police state, Goan organizations fought for freedom by means either peaceful or violent. These were, alphabetically: Azad Gomantak Dal, Goa Action Committee, Goa Liberation Army, Goa Liberation Council, Goa Liberation Front, Goan National Conference, Goan National Union, Goan Political Convention/Goan League, Goan People's Party, Goa Vimochan Sahayak Samiti, Goan Youth League, National Congress (Goa), Quit Goa Organization, Rancour Patriotica and United Front of Goans.

Of the above, only the Goan League (a.k.a. Goan Political Convention) was based overseas, in London. It was founded at a convention of Goans at Earl's Court London. Chaired by the Goan medico Dr H.C. Denis, it had Goan advocate João Francisco Caraciolo Cabral, who held a Portuguese passport, as secretary. When Portuguese authorities complained to Britain that a Portuguese passport-holder was indulging in politics detrimental to Portugal, Cabral stepped down and Anthony P. Remedios—the famed chartered civil engineer with origins in São Matias, Divar, then a British colonial passport holder—held the post for three years until his return to India in 1959. Nehru later observed:

> The story of Goa's fight for freedom is one that all of us should remember... What is worth remembering is that this small territory produced a relatively large number of men and women who have sacrificed much in this struggle.*

The significance of Goa to both the contending parties explains what Philip Bravo describes as 'Salazar's recalcitrance and Nehru's procrastination'†. One headed a nation that gained independence by non-violence; the other was a dictator who championed 'peaceful' methods.

---

* Goa Gazetteer, *Who's Who of Freedom Fighters,* 1986, back cover.

† Philip Bravo, *The Case of Goa: Rhetoric and Nationalism* in *Past Imperfect,* vol. 7, 1998, p. 134.

Two ground realities obtained at the time: one, India's diplomacy with Portugal over Goa had failed. Two, Salazar stubbornly refused to consider via media options about Goa's future that were offered by the USA, the UK and by Goans themselves (unacceptable to Salazar since all options entailed the complete withdrawal of Portugal from Goa).

The Economic Blockade

Left with barely any negotiated options in the face of Portugal's protracted intransigence, India clamped an 'economic blockade' on Goa, Daman and Diu—partially from April 1953 and fully by 15 August 1954. This was done after the Goan Catholic political leadership in Bombay prevailed upon Nehru to enforce the measure, in the hope that the Portuguese regime would buckle and withdraw from Goa under pressure of rebellious natives who would be adversely impacted by the blockade.

Economically, Goa's umbilical cord was attached to India rather than to Portugal. Goa's trade with Portugal was 7.67 per cent, while that with India was over 60 per cent. Goa's exports to India consisted, chiefly, of betel nuts, coconuts and salt. Imports from India were of foodgrain, vegetable, fruit, soap, coal, textile, cotton thread, tea and tobacco.

Only one-third of the currency circulating in Goa was Portuguese. The rest was Indian. Attempts between 1942 and 1952 to flush out Indian currency failed.[*]

P.N. Khera, author of India's official account of Operation Vijay quoting Rao, p. 59, states that:

> In 1951, remittances from India amounted to Rs. 680 lakhs, whereas, those from Portugal totalled only Rs. 41 lakhs.[†]

---

[*] P.N. Khera, *Operation Vijay*, 1961.

[†] Ibid., p. 7.

Author Arthur Rubinoff (quoting none) later wrote:

> The Indian government claimed that in 1951 remittances
> from India to Goa totalled 68 million rupees ... In comparison
> remittances from Portugal to Goa totalled only 4.1 million rupees.[*]

In 1951, telegram traffic between Goa and Portugal was 7000, while
between Goa and India it was 1,52,000.[†] A large number of Goans
(estimated at half of Goa's working population) had established and
made a living in India; about 1.5 lakh of them in Bombay and the
rest spread all over metropolitan India. Corresponding numbers in
Portugal were negligible.

Author K.N. Menon pronounced:

> In Bombay city alone there are 10,000 Goan domestics, and
> more than 3000 tailors, while music shops and bands are their
> monopoly. There are thousands of Goans in clerical posts in
> industrial towns in India, and a very large number of Goans
> occupying high positions as doctors, lawyers and professors.
> Their remittances to Goa estimated at fifty million rupees a year
> enable the middle class keep up a reasonable standard of living,
> provide money for education, and make good the trade deficit.[‡]

In 1954 alone, 23,616 Goans migrated to India.[§] The number of
migrations to Portugal during the corresponding period, though not
known, could at best be a few dozen. This is because the bulk of
Goa went to mainland India while only a few went to Portugal.

---

[*] Arthur G. Rubinoff, *India's Use of Force in Goa*, Popular Prakashan,
Bombay, 1971, p. 34, footnote 10.

[†] Khera, *Operation Vijay*.

[‡] As quoted by historian Teresa Albuquerque in *The Anglo-Portuguese
Treaty of 1878—Impact on Goa*, September 1990, https://www.mail-
archive.com/goanet@lists.goanet.org/msg98414.html

[§] *Rajya Sabha Debates*, vol. 10, column 1696, 2 September 1955.

With the economic blockade, the flow of people and goods by road, rail and sea was stopped, communication lines were cut, the accounts that Goan residents held in Indian banks were frozen and money transfers from India to Goa suspended. This was all done to induce the native population to rebel against the Portuguese.

Nothing of the kind happened, even though poorer locals, especially from the Catholic segment, dependent on remittances from close relatives working in India's metros, were hit hard. Later, in 1960, Goan freedom fighters Purushottam Kakodkar and Adv. Pandurang Mulgaokar met Nehru and asked for the withdrawal of the sanctions particularly on remittances. Dr P.D. Gaitonde said:

> From the Goan point of view, this [the closure of the Indian legation in Lisbon and, by implication, the economic blockade] represented a sort of defeat; it meant that India was unable to solve the Goa problem diplomatically.[*]

He coined the phrase 'the graveyard of Indian diplomacy'.[†] Had Indian diplomacy succeeded there would've been no need for an 'economic blockade'. T.B. Cunha rued:

> The weakness and the indecision of the Indian Government has secured to the Portuguese Dictatorship an unexpected diplomatic triumph.[‡]

The perceived 'failure' of Indian diplomacy that led to the continuance of status quo in Goa was viewed as a diplomatic victory for Portugal.

But one cannot blame diplomacy: it can succeed only when the negotiating parties desire a solution, and here was Salazarian Portugal

---

[*] Gaitonde, *The Liberation of Goa*, p. 75.

[†] Ibid., p. 114.

[‡] T.B. Cunha, 'Salazar Faces Internal Dissention but His Goa Victory Saves Him', *Free Goa*, 25 May 1958, vol. 5, no. 14, pp. 1–2.

refusing to come to the negotiating table in the first place. Portugal saw no problem; hence there was no question of a negotiated solution. Rightly or wrongly, however, the Indian government was blamed for weakness and indecision.

As pressures of the economic blockade began to show, the Portuguese began imports into Goa: rice from Burma, wheat flour from Australia, vegetables from Pakistan, apples from Japan, frozen beef from South Africa and Argentina, caviar from Russia, potatoes from the Netherlands, oranges from Israel, tea from Ceylon, sugar from Cuba and Mozambique, wine from Portugal, champagne from France, cigars and cigarillos from South America, cigarettes and tobacco from the western world, cotton yarn from Pakistan, cement from Japan, steel from Belgium.

The Junta de Comércio Externo (foreign trade board) constructed huge foodgrain storage godowns to build buffer stocks on the Cortalim riverfront.

Goan Hindu traders imported Indian goods via Aden, Singapore and South Africa to blunt the effect of the economic blockade. The Union Ministry of External Affairs and Bombay Police gathered intelligence on such Goan traders who colluded with the Portuguese. The documents are yet to be declassified.[*]

Mining, Ahoy!

Starved of money remittances that were flowing from Goans working in India, the colonial masters had to shore up revenues. One key was mining Goa's rich reserves of iron and manganese ore. The first mining manifest had been issued in 1905. The French company Compagnie de Mines de Fer de Goa (or 'Companhia das Minas e Ferro de Goa', as the Portuguese called it) sought to develop mining in Goa in 1911. The Italians and the Japanese were to later develop an interest in the mineral wealth of Goa.

---

[*] Khera, *Operation Vijay*.

It is said that the Portuguese were aware of Goa's mineral ore wealth as far back as the 18th century but were reluctant to begin exploiting it lest it drew the covetous eyes of the British in India. The first private mining concession was granted in 1929. The production of iron and manganese ore was stepped up from 1955. By 1960, some 800 private concessions were issued to just about anybody who asked for them.

Extraction was manual throughout, but with the pressures of the economic blockade, mining was mechanized with foreign capital. Ore handling and loading into ships at Mormugao port was also modernized.

When Mormugao found it difficult to handle an annual 2,50,000 lakh tonnes of ore, the colonial administration invited the Sandhur Mining Company, which raised 2.5 million pounds and modernized Berth Nos. 5 and 6, providing cranes and other handling equipment. This made it possible for six large ships to simultaneously berth at the port.

In 1959, Goa-based Chowgule Mining Company erected a mechanical ore-handling plant at Mormugao, the first of its kind in Asia. Chowgule, a dairy-keeping family from Belgaum, emerged as a major player in mining in Goa, together with Damodar Mangalji, a Gujarati who was close to the Portuguese governor-general, Cdr Fernando de Quintanilha Mendonça e Dias, from their days in Angola.

Mine owners actively abetted the colonial rulers in offsetting the effects of India's economic blockade. (Interestingly, the only Goan Catholic mining major was Cipriano Souza of Dempo-Souza fame. The firm soon morphed into a single-family-owned Dempo Mining Corporation.)

There was good demand for Goan mineral ore, especially from Japan (40 per cent), West Germany (30 per cent) and USA (manganese ore). By the end of March 1961, Goa was annually exporting 6 million tonnes of ore, which, according to the *Economic Weekly*:

...compared very favourably with, perhaps equalled or exceeded the exports from India.*

Revenues zoomed from Rs 12 million to Rs 30 million. Goa found new prosperity. The pivotal role of mining in blunting the effects of India's economic blockade is confirmed by the figures of the colonial administration. Mineral ore exports accounted for a gargantuan 96 per cent of Goa's export revenues. Mining operations were, however, described as 'haphazard, unscientific and wasteful' by S.C. Talukdar, writing in the *Economic and Political Weekly* (vol. XIV, no. 23) in 1962.

While the colonial regime egged on compliant mine owners to produce more and stymie the effects of India's economic blockade, Goan freedom fighters of the underground variety, including Goan Catholics, disrupted mining operations with attacks and blasts. The colonial regime deployed armed policemen and began protecting mines. More Portuguese policemen would have died in raids on mines than raids on police stations. (It is ironic that Goan Catholics—not the mine owners and not the importers/traders who colluded with the Portuguese to offset the effects of India's economic blockade— were, and still are, regarded as 'pro-Portuguese, un-Indian and anti-national'.)

Prosperous Goa, Thank You, India

The economic blockade produced unexpected results.

Instead of the anticipated economic depression, there was an economic boom in Goa. In marked contrast to neighbouring Indian states, high-wage jobs and luxury goods from the developed world suddenly became easily available to Goans. Goa enjoyed a period of prosperity unseen either in Goa before or in India now.[4]

For the first time, Portugal drafted a six-year Economic Development Plan for Goa. A provision of 20 million escudos was

---

* *Economic Weekly*, vol. XIII, nos 51 & 52, 23 December 1961.

made for the construction of airports in Goa, Daman and Diu in the first development plan for 1953–58. Under architects sent from Portugal, airfields were quickly constructed in Goa, Daman and Diu in 1955–57 by the Obras Públicas (public works department).

At the time, Goa had only a *kutcha* airstrip inaugurated by Governor-General João José Carlos Craveiro Lopes, whose son and aide-de-camp was an avid aviator, at the Sada plateau in Vasco da Gama in 1930, to receive the first flight from Lisbon to Goa. After three aborted attempts, the inaugural trip in a de Havilland Gipsy Moth named *Marão*, took nineteen days to cover the air distance from Lisbon to Goa via Spain, Italy, Algeria, Tunisia, Cairo, Gaza, Baghdad, Karachi, Diu and Bombay, with halts en route, including an eight-day halt at Gaza. A local soap manufacturer, Krishna Keni of Caranzalem, named his soap bar *Sabão Mãrao*.

A Goa-based civilian airline, Transportes Aéreos da Índia Portuguesa (TAIP), began operations with two de Havilland quad-engine Herons, each carrying fourteen passengers with a flying range of 608 nautical miles. Goan expatriate Gabriel de Figueiredo, in a well-researched paper titled *Dabolim and TAIP*, mentions that these aircraft were replaced by two twin-engine Vickers Vikings carrying twenty-seven passengers over 1477 nautical miles, and later by two McDonnell Douglas DC-4 Skymasters. The fleet was later expanded with McDonnell Douglas DC-6B.

For the record, TAIP was the first civilian airline from India whose airhostesses wore the sari as uniform. Patsy Almeida Cardoso, who worked as a TAIP airhostess, recalled how, every time a flight landed in Lisbon, its airport staff would say, *Já chegaram as pombinhas brancas de India* ('The white doves of India have arrived', referring to the white saris that the Goan airhostesses wore in summer).[*] TAIP flew to Colombo, Daman, Diu, Karachi, Aden and Jeddah

---

[*] Mentioned in Gabriel de Figueiredo's essay, published online and available at http://www.colaco.net. Colaco.net shut after the Nassau-based Goan paediatrician–founder Dr Jose Colaco died around 2016.

and Lisbon via Damascus, Beirut and Malta, then a British colony. The seven-year economic blockade led to three unwitting results:

1. It demonstrated to India that Goa was not economically dependent on it and could survive on its own.
2. Imports of western merchandise—especially luxuries like silks, fountain pens, watches, liquor, silver, gold and precious stones—led to cross-border smuggling by locals who posed as 'freedom fighters', thereby successfully avoiding interception and harassment by border policemen on the Indian side.

In fact, Goa's first elected chief minister, D.B. Bandodkar, called freedom fighters *blackists*, meaning smugglers, to the protests of genuine freedom fighters. Brig. (later lieutenant general and corps commander) Sagat Singh had an interesting account of an attempt by a sub-unit of his 50 Para Brigade to capture the Sanquelim Bridge intact where Goan smugglers helped with maps and ground guidance (follows below).

In August 1953, Dr P.D. Gaitonde told Nehru:

… of the gold smuggling between Goa and the surrounding territories and mentioned some of the ingenious methods used for this purpose. He [Nehru] was very surprised when I told him that I had once had to operate on a patient who had swallowed three gold chains which resulted in symptoms of obstruction. He was so impressed with the story that he recounted it to a cabinet meeting that took place soon afterwards.*

Wife Edila, in her book *As Maçãs Azuis,* writes on p. 74 that the three gold chains weighed half a kilogram, adding blithely that it was the first and last tumour of gold her cancer-surgeon husband extracted from a stomach … *Foi o primeiro e ultimo tumor de ouro que*

---

* Gaitonde, 2016, pp. 76–77.

Lica teve de estrair de um estômago. In the English version of the book, Edila writes that the three chains weighed 14 ounces and

> That was the first and only gold tumour that Lica [as she affectionately called her husband, Pundolica, aka Pundalik] ever extracted from a stomach![*]

Indian border police did not notice that Goan 'farmers' took large herds of cattle with swollen rectums for grazing across the border, and returned to Portuguese Goa a day or so later with the animal posteriors now in perfectly normal disposition.

In just three months, the Indian customs department seized contraband valued at Rs 25 lakh (of the value of 1954, when gold was Rs 5 per gram as against Rs 5,000 of today's value). The customs department believed it had detected/seized only about 10 per cent of the goods smuggled from Goa into India.[†]

The Consul General of India in Panjim pointed out that one-third of Goa's economy survived on contraband smuggled into India. Of the Rs 9 crore imports, only Rs 3 crore worth goods were utilized in Goa; the rest was smuggled into India, he said.[‡]

Silk imported into Goa was to the tune of Rs 5,68,000 in 1948. By 1957, this increased to a whopping Rs 10 million.[§] It was not as if Goans had suddenly discarded cottons and begun the exclusive use of silk!

In 1956, Rs 5 crore worth of gold was 'officially' imported into Goa; of course, there was also gold 'unofficially' being imported by businessmen, like one who held both a TAIP ticket-selling monopoly

---

[*] Edila Gaitonde, *In Search of Tomorrow*, Rajhauns Vitaran, Goa, 2010 (first published in 1987 by Allied Publishers), p. 70.

[†] Rubinoff, 1971, p. 34.

[‡] Khera, *Operation Vijay*, 1974.

[§] Gerald Pereira, *Resources and Potentialities of Goa*, 1958, https://medium.com/@larapereiranaik/resources-potentialities-of-goa-during-the-portuguese-regime-c1c6797424be

in Goa, Daman, Diu and Karachi and a diplomatic passport,* and
by Goan mine owners to bribe the Goa governor-general, ferried,
as seen, in three chartered Sabena Airways seaplanes. Most of this
gold, of either description (official and otherwise), was smuggled
into India.

The third unwitting result: locals masquerading as 'freedom
fighters', who clandestinely carried contraband across the border and
fed lies about the Portuguese military disposition existing in Goa to
Indian intelligence gathering. This would boomerang in intelligence
reports and, consequently, on the war mobilization.

At various points of time, some of the stringent economic
measures were relaxed, as for instance on remittances and travel to
and from Goa. India finally lifted the trade embargo of Portuguese
Goa on 1 April 1961. Nehru emphasized that this was not an
abandonment of economic sanctions but only a variation to help
poorer Goans. Under the new terms, only betel nut would be
imported, and medicines, cloth, books, tea and leather goods would
be exported to Goa.

---

* Teotónio Souza, *Portuguese Literary and Cultural Studies 17/18*,
  University of Massachusetts, Dartmouth, 2010, p. 158.

3

THE TIDE TURNS

The Run-up Begins

The last phase of Goa's anti-colonial movement started on the seventh anniversary of India's independence, 15 August 1954. It wasn't just the significance of that day; there was another reason as well.

As mentioned earlier, thirty-five volunteers of the United Front of Goans, led by Francisco Mascarenhas, J.M. D'Souza and Vaman Desai, captured Dadra on 22 July 1954 while those of the Azad Gomantak Dal, led by Vishwanath Lawande, Prabhakar Sinari and Cristovam Gabriel Paulo das Angustias Furtado, Goan People's Party led by George Vaz, and RSS activists, began occupying Nagar Haveli and fully occupied it by 2 August 1954.

Of the five policemen defending Dadra, four—Deputy Chief Aniceto do Rosário and constables António Joaquim Francisco Fernandes, Clemente Francisco Pereira and Mamod Can (Muhammad Khan)—perished. The first was a native of Diu, the next two were from Daman and the fourth was from Goa.

Capt. Virgílio Fidalgo and Lt Falcão, both European Portuguese, were in charge of defending Nagar Haveli with 150 policemen. All fled south and surrendered to Indian Special Reserve Police at Udva on 11 August 1954.

Local Portuguese sources claimed that Dadra and Nagar Haveli were freed by armed action of the State Reserve Police of the erstwhile Bombay State. Portugal claimed that Indian Army regulars from the Maratha Light Infantry were involved in the action. (Recall that Morarji Desai wrote that he had posted some state reserve police personnel who resembled army troops.) It was Portugal's first loss of territory in India.

Elated at the success, Gandhian Goan freedom fighters in Bombay announced the launch of the satyagraha movement from 15 August 1954. Arrangements were made to stage an impressive march on Goa with the help of Indian volunteers mobilized by Opposition parties like the Praja Socialist Party. Two days before the event, Nehru declared that he would not permit Indian participation in the march (if he did, he feared that Pakistan would send satyagrahis into Jammu and Kashmir). Nehru also said that only unarmed Goans would be allowed to cross the border into Goa.

Disappointed but not defeated, Peter Alvares, a prominent Goan member of the Praja Socialist Party, assembled three modest *satyagrahi* batches of about fifteen volunteers each, all Goan, who marched from Siroda to Tiracol, from Banda to Patradevi and from Majali to Polem on 15 August 1954. The leader of each group carried the Indian tricolour.

Alfred Afonso led one group that entered the Tiracol fort. The Portuguese garrison-in-charge, José António Álvares, a Goan from Chinchinim, ordered his men to abandon the fort and run away. Álvares was tried and sentenced to three-and-a-half years' imprisonment. Afonso planted the Indian flag, and it flew there even the next day.

Mark Fernandes led the second group from Banda to Patradevi.

Anthony D'Souza led the third group from Majali–Karwar to the Polem border post.

All the satyagrahis were arrested. Forty-six were sentenced to imprisonment, with terms ranging from one to eight years. Only Anthony D'Souza got twenty-eight years' rigorous imprisonment. He was a seminarian who had set out to become a Catholic priest, but went to Kashi to study the Vedas. He did not become a Hindu priest either. He became a freedom fighter and ended up as a minister—not in a church—but in the Goa Cabinet (1967–70).

On 18 February 1955, Bala Raya Mapari of Assonora, belonging to the Azad Gomantak Dal, was tortured to death by the police in the lock-up of the Mapusa police station. He became the first martyr of the last phase of the freedom struggle.

Meanwhile, in Portugal, through most of the 1950s, various democratic, socialist and communist leaders, youth organizations and university students, pleaded for freedom in Goa. They urged Salazar to negotiate with India and quit Goa. Since the press was censored, they did this through illicit pamphlets. Dozens of such leaders were hunted down by the PIDE, tried for 'conspiracy against the security of the state through illicit and secret association' and jailed.* Bombay's *Free Goa* lamented that:

> ... strangely enough the Indian information services and in consequence, the Indian press remain silent about these important facts which closely concern India ... they [also] keep mum about events which are favourable to India and deserve to be known by the Indian public as well as in foreign countries.†

In New Delhi, an All-Party Parliamentary Committee for Goa was formed on 5 May 1955 to mobilize opinion in India in support of freeing Goa from colonial rule. Many satyagrahis and Indian Opposition members of Parliament entered Goa in small groups. The satyagrahis were sent back and, in a most embarrassing situation for India, the parliamentarians were arrested and jailed.

Among the prominent Indian leaders detained at Aguada Jail were Madhu Limaye of Ram Manohar Lohia's Socialist Party, Jagannathrao Joshi of the Jana Sangh (forerunner of today's ruling BJP), Rajaram Patil of the Communist Party of India, Nanasaheb Goray and Shirubhau Limaye of the Praja Socialist Party, V.G. Deshpande of the Hindu Maha Sabha and Tridib Kumar Chaudhary

---

* Sousa Lopes, 2017, p. 222.

† 'Democrats in Portugal are Jailed for Pleading for Goa's Freedom', 25 July 1957.

from Calcutta, who was an MP of the Revolutionary Socialist (Marxist-Leninist) Party.

They were released on amnesty in February 1957, which, according to the Indian Navy's official account of the operations, came 'at the intervention of the Pope'.[*] Dr P.D. Gaitonde says that, while Indian prisoners held by the Portuguese in Goa were released following Nehru–Eisenhower talks in Washington in late December 1956, India sought the Vatican's intervention in the release of both Indian and Goan prisoners.[†]

Goan hospitality is legendary, even in the adversity of a prison. At Aguada, Goan political detainees entertained the state guests from India with English news from Aguada Radio. The 'radio' was hosted by college student Suresh Kanekar who, to the chagrin of his family (his father was the postmaster at Mapusa), interrupted his studies in Poona to join the freedom movement, was jailed, but eventually resumed his studies and capped them with a PhD in USA, where he is settled.

Kanekar sat by a kitchen window of his block and read out loud to the Indian leaders in the opposite block an impromptu English translation of news from the local Portuguese language newspapers. Cellmates who knew English stood listening, so that it appeared to any lurking soldier that the lad was reading to them. In the opposite block, the Indian leaders were all ears.

> My cellmates were very kind to me in getting to me all the newspapers I needed, and there were plenty of them. Ernesto Costa Frias was particularly helpful. On his own initiative, he would collect the various newspapers and make sure that I got them well ahead of the broadcast, so that I had time to read the newspapers and determine what to select for transmission and what to ignore. Gradually I learnt that Madhu [Limaye] was

---

[*] 'Liberation of Goa, Daman and Diu', https://www.indiannavy.nic.in/sites/default/themes/indiannavy/images/pdf/chapter12.pdf, p. 28.

[†] P.D. Gaitonde, 2016, pp. 121–22.

not interested in how many people were killed in Algeria or Cyprus or Egypt, but rather in the significant diplomatic and political happenings around the world, and I selected my news accordingly.[*]

The Congress Party, meanwhile, seemed to realize that it was losing ground to the Opposition parties. Nehru began to be supportive of the satyagraha movement. By 25 July 1955, trains had stopped plying between Goa and India. On 8 August, India shut down the Portuguese legation in New Delhi.

Nehru said he was taking this 'drastic action to prove that the Congress Party was as against the Portuguese rule as any other group in India'. Clamouring for more effective action, dock workers in Bombay, Calcutta and Madras refused to handle any ship of any line that had anything to do with Portuguese Goa. Indian textile mill and railway workers struck work. All in support of the big day: 15 August 1955.

The Goa Vimochan Sahayak Samiti was formed on 14 May that year, under the presidentship of Bal Gangadhar (Lokmanya) Tilak's grandson, Jayantrao Tilak, editor of Poona's daily *Kesari*. The samiti was formed for the purpose of launching a 'final march' on Goa on 15 August 1955. Dr P.D. Gaitonde recalled that Samiti members would say that,

> ... this satyagraha [of 15 August 1955 was not just against the Portuguese administration but it] was also against the Government of India inasmuch as they [the Samiti's members] wanted the government to take police action ...[†]

At a smaller protest at Kiranpani–Pernem on 25 June, police had beat a satyagrahi, Amirchand Gupta, to death. Undaunted, Indian

---

[*]   Suresh Kanekar, *Goa's Liberation and Thereafter: Chronicles of a Fragmented Life,* Goa, 1556, 2011, p. 66.

[†]   Gaitonde, 2016, p. 111.

Opposition parties, including the Praja Socialist Party, Kisan Mazdoor Sabha, Hindu Mahasabha and Communist Party of India, mobilized around 4000 volunteers for the 15 August march on Goa. On 14 August, police shot dead Krishna Shet and Yeshwant Shirodkar, both members of the Azad Gomantak Dal, at Pomburpa.

Slaying the Satyagrahis: 15 August 1955

The Portuguese, perhaps fearing an invasion, invited some forty international journalists to witness the march. Among them were three American journalists, Arthur Bonner of Columbia Broadcasting System, John Hlavacek of United Press of America (ex-NBC) and Homer Alexander Jack, an American Unitarian clergyman, writer and civil rights activist.

Three main groups of Indian satyagrahis assembled at the borders of Goa on 15 August. They tried to enter Goa from the frontier posts of Patradevi in the north, Polem in the south and Caranzol in the east. Fewer dispersed numbers attempted to enter from various other points, including railway tunnels in the ghats.

Troops deployed inside the Goa borders were only European Portuguese, not African Portuguese. The Europeans feared giving guns to the Africans near the border, lest the Africans desert and run away with the guns, or worse, turn the guns on their European superiors, fire and then flee.

At Patradevi, ten armed Portuguese soldiers faced 1500 unarmed satyagrahis. Their five-step orders seemed ambivalent—start with oral warnings, continue with oral warnings firmly, fire three shots in the air, fire on the ground in front of the invaders and finally, in extreme cases, shoot to kill. Less violent measures at crowd control do not appear to have been considered at all.

Disregarding the five-step drill, Portuguese soldiers at Patradevi opened fire into the crowd without any warning. American journalists Arthur Bonner and John Hlavacek witnessed the incident.

Among the first to fall with a shot in her right arm was a young widow, Sahodara Rai Sagar of Madhya Pradesh (later an elected

MP for three terms). Seeing her fall and perhaps presuming that she was dead, a CPI volunteer, twenty-five-year-old Karnal Singh Benipal, a Sikh from Isru village of Punjab, who had got married just three months before, tore open his shirt and dared the soldiers to shoot him instead of a woman. The soldiers promptly obliged him—in his chest.

In a remote Pernem village, Homer Jack saw fifty unarmed satyagrahis huddled in a moss-covered temple, sitting silently around a comrade who lay on the stone floor, dead. Another was wounded in the hand. Panna Lal Yadav, the dead man, was a thirty-two-year-old Harijan from Rajasthan. He had a wife and four children. He was a member of the Praja Socialist Party and a municipal councillor of Ramganjmandi.

Jack learned that the group had crossed the border and arrived at the village at 5 a.m. Planting the Indian flag atop the temple, they began to shout slogans to awaken the villagers. Four Portuguese soldiers appeared. They fired in the air. The demonstrators did not move, but continued sloganeering. A soldier then struck a satyagrahi with the butt of his gun, moved back and fired into the ground, and then fired at Panna Lal Yadav.

He fired like a hunter hunts animals.[*]

At another place in Pernem, two Indian satyagrahis were wounded allegedly because they tried to wrest a submachine gun from a soldier. The gun went off and the two satyagrahis fell, seriously wounded. Almost twelve hours later, they were put in the back of a military truck and taken to hospital. They were declared dead on arrival.[†]

---

[*] Homer Alexander Jack, *Callous Mentality of Portuguese: American Reporter's Impressions*, Information Service of India, New Delhi, 1955.

[†] For more on the 15 August 1955 Satyagraha, see *Inside Goa* by Dr Homer A. Jack.

Caranzol and Tunnel No. 10 past Castlerock were also scenes of firing, as eight armed soldiers faced more than 1000 unarmed demonstrators. There were 1249 satyagrahis in Daman and 81 in Diu.

In all, twenty-two died, 225 were injured and twenty went missing. But for the presence of foreign journalists, the toll could have been much higher.

'Don't shoot, they are unarmed!' Arthur Bonner and John Hlavacek had shouted to the soldiers at Patradevi. Cameras slung over their shoulders, the journalists hoisted the dead and carried them to the Indian side. On his way back, Homer Jack observed that, 'half of the 69 admitted at the civil hospital in Belgaum had bullet wounds'.

The following day, Nehru told Parliament that the Portuguese firing on Indian satyagrahis was

... brutal and uncivilised in the extreme.

Portugal lodged a formal protest with India, accusing the government of allowing thousands of its nationals to invade Portuguese territory and violate its sovereignty. Portugal claimed that force had been used as a last resort to repulse the intruders.

It was clear, however, that firing was used not as the last option but at first opportunity. Tear-gas and cane charges, which should have sufficed for crowd control given that the demonstrators were unarmed, were evidently not even considered.

Nehru under Attack

The killing of unarmed Indian satyagrahis sparked an immediate backlash in India. Strikes and *hartals* (closure of shops, offices and transport in protest and grief) across Indian cities followed in the wake. This resulted in more deaths and injuries as 'hoodlums who had never heard of Goa' took to the streets.

In Bombay and Calcutta, mobs attacked the Portuguese, British and Pakistani consulates. India was roundly condemned by the western media for allowing the violence on Indian soil, in clear-cut violation of each one of the five lofty principles of Panchsheel—the cornerstones of peaceful co-existence adopted by India in 1954 for the conduct of international relations. Nehru apologized and offered recompense.

Portugal responded by holding the Indian Union responsible for this new and extraordinary form of settling international disputes by peaceful methods.

Portuguese soldiers had shot and killed Indian satyagrahis, yet it was the Indian prime minister who came under attack. Nehru was attacked from all sides—from the western world for the assault on diplomatic offices, and from India for the lack of support to satyagrahis.

His chief minister in Bombay, Morarji Desai, a professed proponent of patience with the Portuguese, dispersed protestors marching to Mantralaya, demanding action against the Portuguese in Goa. The protestors were met with police-cane charges and teargassing. Small mercy they were not shot and killed like those at the Goa borders. Morarji would do that with protestors demanding a separate state of Maharashtra a year later in 1956 at Bombay's Flora Fountain, since renamed Hutatma Chowk or martyrs' square. At the time, the Bombay State comprised today's states of Maharashtra and Gujarat (bifurcated in 1960).

If force was to be used in Goa, the time was now. The killing of unarmed satyagrahis had triggered worldwide outrage. A retaliatory Indian invasion could be justified. Portugal had brought in about 9000 African troops, to make it a total of 12,000 soldiers in Goa. One destroyer (NRP *Afonso de Albuquerque* that the Portuguese media called a cruiser, a larger warship) and three frigates (NRP *Bartolomeu Dias*, NRP *Gonçalves Zarco* and NRP *João de Lisboa*) also sailed in. The numbers were inconsequential to India. Goa could have been taken in a matter of hours, as Portugal's undersecretary for war was to later observe.

But Nehru abhorred violence. He stood for 'peaceful methods'—mindful of his world image as a pacifist and a champion of solving international disputes by non-violent means. In a way, he was not to blame. Educated in England, he hailed from peace-loving traditions. India's religions Hinduism, Buddhism and Jainism eschewed violence even towards animals. Moreover, he was heir to the legacy of Gandhi.

Nehru forthwith stopped Indian participation in satyagrahas. On 19 August 1955, he snapped diplomatic relations and told Portugal to close its Consulate General in Bombay and the Honorary Consulates in Calcutta and Madras by 1 September 1955. He withdrew Vincent Coelho, India's consul general in Panjim (Vincent Coelho—and his wife Mary—were of Goan ancestors who resettled in Mangalore to escape the rigours of inquisitorial persecution of converted natives; he had earlier served on the staff of Prime Minister Nehru). Egypt would look after India's interests in Goa and Brazil would look after Portugal's interests in India.

The prime minister also sealed India's borders with the Portuguese enclaves. Travel between Goa and the rest of India was now practically impossible as the then prevailing 'permit system' for travel was stopped.

At the All India Congress Committee meeting in New Delhi on 4 September, the chief ministers of Bombay State and West Bengal, Morarji Desai and Dr B.C. Roy, successfully moved a resolution that it would be 'inappropriate' in the circumstances for Indian nationals to enter Goa in the name of satyagraha or otherwise.[*]

The Portuguese ambassador in London informed his foreign ministry that this was a notable success for Portugal. The resolution was roundly criticized by all Indian Opposition parties. Nine political leaders said the unilateral declaration of policy by the Congress Party could not be accepted as the national policy. They said:

---

[*] Gaitonde, 2016, pp. 114–15.

... the brave people of Goa, who have been fighting against fascist
dictatorship, will feel suddenly let down by the ruling party.[*]

Dr P.D. Gaitonde has an interesting take on the reason for India's
inertia on freeing Goa. In April 1961 (or thereabouts), Dr Gaitonde
was at a meeting with officials of the US State Department. He was
asked, 'What is the policy of the Government of India? Why are
they so inactive? We are not even aware of any diplomatic pressure
anywhere ... After all, India should be more interested than other
countries. Why is she silent? Is she benefitting from Goa, as China
does from Macau?' Dr Gaitonde then writes,

> ... I wonder whether the totally passive attitude of the Congress
> was not linked to the Gujarati businessmen who were then
> prospering in Mozambique ... It was clear that the Indian Embassy
> in the United States was deliberately seeking to dissociate itself
> from any anti-colonial movement, particularly regarding Goa—
> almost a case of Yogic detachment.[†]

Nehru said it was for Goans to fight for their own liberation. The
communist organ *New Age* shot back, stating,

> When Kashmir was attacked it was not left to the Kashmiris to
> defend themselves.[‡]

Militant Goan freedom activists took Nehru seriously. The Goa
Liberation Army was formed on 30 September 1955 at a meeting
in Belgaum. The command of six consisted of Augusto Alvares,
Balkrishna Bhonsle, Urselino Almeida, Shivaji Desai, Jaysingrao
Rane and Madhavrao Rane. The militant Azad Gomantak
Dal, founded earlier by Vishwanath Lawande on 27 April 1947,

---

[*] Ibid., p. 115.

[†] Ibid., pp. 156–57.

[‡] *New Age*, 28 August 1955, p. 1.

and its dissenting offshoot, the Rancour Patriótica, led in action by Prabhakar Sinari (later an IPS officer), featured in the armed struggle. The United Front of Goans (Francisco Mascarenhas, J.M. D'Souza and Vaman Desai), Goan Peoples' Party (George Vaz and Divakar Kakodkar) and Quit Goa Organization (Janardhan Shinkre) also adopted violent means. Portuguese authorities reported eighty-six violent acts within Goa in the first seven months of 1956.

Independent of one another, the outfits executed some daring raids on mines and Portuguese armed stations. Between 1955 and 1959, the colonial regime recorded 179 assaults, 152 sabotages and scores of unsuccessful attempts to sabotage, resulting in the death of 30 Portuguese and 73 Goan military/police personnel.[*]

In about two years starting from 1955, the colonial regime imprisoned about 3000 Goans, including notables like advocate and former president of Salcete municipality Álvaro Pinto Furtado of Panjim/Chinchinim, advocate and former additional public prosecutor Ariosto Tovar Dias of Margao/Chinchinim, businessman Frank de Sequeira of Panjim/Moira, editor of *Diário de Goa* and former president of Salcete municipality Álvaro da Costa of Margao/Colva, and businessman Ilidio da Costa of Panjim/Betim. None were connected with the armed struggle but were non-violent nationalists. (Three thousand was a large number for a largely peaceful resident population of about 3 lakh.)

Although Nehru sent an official note to friendly countries following the 15 August 1955 massacre, requesting their support to India on the Goa problem, he did not wish to internationalize it. But given the nature of the issues and the players involved, it was but inevitable that the 'case of (tiny) Goa' would snowball into an international issue between 1955 and 1961. The world became divided into two camps: the Warsaw Pact group of the USSR and East European countries together with Afro-Asiatic countries

---

[*] Gen. Carlos de Azeredo, 'Passagem para a Índia', *O Expresso*, 8 December 2001.

supported India over Goa, while NATO and Western countries generally sided with Portugal (even though some professed to be anti-colonialism).

In November 1955, Marshal Bulganin and Nikita Khrushchev visited India, and the Soviet leaders commented on the Goa issue. US Secretary of State John Foster Dulles and Portugal's foreign minister, Paulo Cunha, referred to their comments as Soviet attempts to whip up prejudice and hate. Nehru's nightmare had begun to unfold. On 30 December, Portugal's ambassador in Paris, Marcello Mathias, wrote to Salazar that as Goa turned into an international problem, Portugal could liberate itself from the Luso–Indian dialogue. Internationalizing Goa clearly favoured Portugal.

Nehru stuck to his (non-violent) guns that the case of Goa should be sorted out only by diplomatic means. Backstage diplomacy between India and Portugal intensified. India's UN delegation chief and a personal friend of Nehru, Belthi Shah Gilani, visited Lisbon to find a solution. While Nehru felt that Portugal was unwilling to talk and negotiate a peaceful settlement, Gilani was convinced that a midway solution could be found between the positions of India and Portugal. He continued the dialogue until 1958, telling Portugal that a solution was possible as long as Nehru's patience lasted. Once it was exhausted, Nehru might, in exasperation, decide to use force.

The former Portuguese legation envoy, Vasco Garin, also tried hard to bring about a solution, and sought Salazar's permission to reopen formal or informal talks with India. Salazar agreed, but with an impossibly steep caveat: talk but don't compromise Portugal's position that Goa was an overseas province and an integral part of Portugal.

By end 1956, focus on the 'case of Goa' panned to the UN. India vehemently contended that Goa was a colonial issue. The USSR, as well as African, West Asian and some socialist countries, supported India at the UN. The western world did not.

Goa Evades Solution

Western countries tried and failed to move an intransigent Portugal. But they kept pressurizing India to not resort to force in Goa. Meanwhile, disquiet continued in various forms in Goa.

On 17 February 1957, the Goa Liberation Army militant freedom fighters Camilo Pereira and Suresh Kerkar were shot dead by police while trying to blow up a pipeline supplying water to the Portuguese garrison at Ponda. (In all, GLA lost seven men in its short but impactful life, particularly when attacking mines.)

In New Delhi in June 1957, perhaps to assuage the growing criticism of his stand, Nehru for the first time met eleven Goan leaders from a cross-section of the Goa freedom movement. They were (alphabetically): Prof. Armando Menezes, Evagrio George, Adv. Gerald Pereira, J.N. Heredia, Luis Gracias, Nicolau Menezes, Peter Alvares, Dr Pundalik Gaitonde, Purushottam Kakodkar, Dr Ram Hegde and Vishwanath Lawande. At the time, 360 Goans languished in Portuguese jails—350 in Goa, 8 in Portuguese Africa and 2 in Lisbon. Nehru expressed 'full sympathy' with the plight of Goan prisoners.* Nehru told the Rajya Sabha in September 1957,

> Portugal and her NATO allies should no longer be in any doubt about India's firm policy towards Goa. India has tried all possible means, short of war, to settle the problem of Goa. But Portugal seems determined to perpetuate colonialism ...

However, these words rang empty as they were backed by no action. Wrote Air Vice Marshal Arjun Subramaniam (veteran), in his tome *India's Wars: A Military History 1947–1971*,

> The procrastination of the Government of India after such aggressive pronouncements by its PM reveals Nehru's reluctance

---

* *Free Goa*, 10 June 1957, vol. 4, no. 15, p. 7.

to use force, even if it was against the last vestiges of colonialism in India.[*]

By the November 1957 general elections, Portugal's national Opposition—consisting, broadly, of two streams of republicans (led by Vasco da Gama Fernandes and António Sérgio, respectively), monarchists (Vieira de Almeida), Catholics (Francisco Lino Neto) and a mix of democrats, liberals, socialists and communists (Abranches Ferrão, Cal Brandão, Cruz Ferreira, Arlindo Vicente, Mário Soares, Cunha Leal and Alvaro Cunhal)—more or less crystallized its position on Goa on the basis of a writing by António Sérgio (a European Portuguese, born and raised in Daman):

1. Illegitimate and forced that it was, the Salazar regime was not competent to deal with the Goa question on behalf of the Portuguese people;
2. The regime's imposition of the Colonial Act and racial discrimination is what started the disquiet in Goa; and,
3. The best solution would be a UN-supervised plebiscite with the UN enforcing its result.[†]

While some freedom—for propaganda reasons—existed in Portugal during the pre-poll period, there was no such window in Goa where, bereft of Opposition candidates, both the 'official' candidates—Msgr Castilho Serpa do Rosário Noronha and Puruxotoma Ramnatha Quenim—were elected by the 3.3 per cent of the population entitled to vote.

By April 1958, the pioneer Goa National Congress, formed in 1928 by T.B. Cunha, ended its active role, urging the Government of India to seek a peaceful solution and faded into oblivion. T.B. Cunha passed away on 26 September 1958. Loknayak Jaiprakash

---

[*] Arjun Subramaniam, *India's Wars: A Military History 1947–1971*, Harper Collins, Noida, 2016, p. 490.

[†] Sousa Lopes, 2017, p. 263.

Narayan was a pallbearer. The Government of India issued a postage stamp in his honour, and later unveiled his portrait in the Central Hall of Parliament. The World Peace Council at Stockholm decorated him with a gold medal posthumously in 1959.

In 1960, all Bombay-based Goan organizations working towards Goa's freedom met for a three-day convention. In one voice, they called for immediate action by India against the Portuguese in Goa. Rev. Dr H.O. Mascarenhas was nominated to proceed to Delhi and place the plea before the Indian prime minister. On 25 November 1960—the day of the Portuguese conquest of Goa in 1510—Afro-Asian countries observed 'Goa Day', demanding the immediate withdrawal of Portugal from her colonies.

India did three things in 1960. They indicated a gradual hardening of attitude towards the Portuguese in India.

1. First, it took the 'case of Goa' to the UN and, as it had done in 1956, argued that Goa was a colony. Portugal maintained that this was its internal matter, and nobody had the right to raise it at the world body. On 15 December 1960, the UN General Assembly, by sixty-eight votes to six, adopted Resolution No. 1542 (XV) declaring Goa and other Portuguese possessions in Asia and Africa to be 'non-self-governing territories' (meaning, colonies), rejecting Portugal's contention that they were 'overseas provinces'. The six that voted against the resolution were Portugal, South Africa, Belgium, Brazil, France and Spain. There were seventeen abstentions, including by the USA and the UK. The UN mandated Portugal to file information on the colonies with the UN secretary general. It also directed Portugal to allow the people of the colonies to exercise the right of self-determination.
2. Two, India finally deputed an administrator to Dadra and Nagar Haveli, something it had refrained from doing since the territories were freed of colonial rule in 1954.

3.   And three, it appointed IPS officer Gopal ('Gopi') Krishna
     Handoo, an Inspector General of Police of the Jammu and
     Kashmir cadre, to head the organization of border guards,
     the Central Reserve Police (there was no Border Security
     Force then). Together with the out-of-turn-promoted Lt
     Gen. B.M. Kaul and Intelligence Bureau chief B.N. Mullik,
     Handoo would become defence minister Krishna Menon's
     triumphant trio—or unholy triumvirate, depending from
     which side one views them.

Handoo's appointment heated things up for the Portuguese in Goa.
He trained, armed and infiltrated saboteurs across the border into Goa
in waves, sporadically but relentlessly. There was a stark difference
between Goan and Indian saboteurs: while Goans carefully selected
targets to hit the Portuguese where it hurt the most (armed stations
and economic interests like mines), Indian guerrillas were far less
discriminatory. Wrote Gen. Carlos de Azeredo:

> The most evolved guerilla warfare which our [Portuguese] armed
> forces encountered was in Goa. I know what I'm talking about,
> because I also fought in Angola and in Guiné. In 1961 alone,
> until December, around 80 policemen died. Major part of Azad
> Gomantak Dal was not Goan. Many had fought in the British
> Army under General Montgomery against the Germans.[*]

But Portugal had a worthy terror counterpart in Goa: PIDE, the
dreaded secret services police—and its most notorious torturer:
Agente Casimiro Monteiro, who had also fought under General
Montgomery against the Germans.

Nehru was anxious that Goa not turn into a Cold War issue
between the two power blocks. He again requested NATO countries
friendly to Portugal—the USA and the UK—to exert pressure on

---

[*] 'Passagem para a Índia', *O Expresso*, 8 December 2001.

Portugal to quit Goa. Both tried to persuade Portugal to withdraw peacefully ... but failed.

The UK was aware of Portugal's help to Hitler's Germany during World War II—supplying Germany with wolfram, an important raw material for war—and hiding behind a veil of neutrality when the UK sought the use of Portuguese ports and airfields during the Battle of the Atlantic in 1943. They were also aware of Salazar's proximity to Mussolini. Salazar had allowed Goa to be used by the Axis powers: he sheltered four German and Italian spy ships—three German and one Italian—at Mormugao. Spying on British shipping, German U-boats rained havoc on British ships. As seen, the spy ships were destroyed by British veterans at Mormugao. Moreover, the UK was caught between a British Commonwealth partner, India, and an ages-old 'ally', Portugal, that she was pledged to defend.

The USA was against colonialism. But Portugal being a NATO member, the US offered Salazar another option, which, if accepted, would have changed the course of Goa's history (for the fourth time, if one may add: the first being the Indo-Aryan migration to Goa, the second being the Muslim invasions from the early 14th century, and the third being the Portuguese conquest in the early 16th century).

The USA urged Salazar to withdraw and let Goa rule itself as an autonomous region, *à la* Hong Kong, on US funding.

Salazar abhorred American capitalism. He refused to budge. There was no chance of Portugal changing her stance. USA President John F. Kennedy led, from 20 January 1961, a Democratic Party dispensation that was favourably disposed towards India, unlike the Republican government that preceded it. Yet Kennedy wrote to Nehru hoping that war would be avoided, and asked his ambassador in India, Prof. John Kenneth Galbraith, to discuss the issue with the Indian prime minister.

On 26 January 1961—India's Republic Day—a 'Goa Gate' was erected at Bombay's major traffic junction opposite Metro cinema, the entrance to the Goan hub of Dhobitalao. The arch was 10 metres tall and well lit—with the legend, *'Remember Goa is not yet free'*.

Agente Casimiro Monteiro

As mentioned earlier, Portugal had an able terror counterpart in Goa: PIDE. It was set up in Goa by Governor-General Brig. Paulo Bénard Guedes (1952–58). Guedes also brought his wife, Maria José Borges, a colourful and famous personage. Her visits to churches and homes in Goa inspired a feeling not of privilege but of trepidation: she gracefully plundered antiques and artefacts, and sold them for giddy sums in Europe.

PIDE was created in Portugal in 1945 as an autonomous secret police force under the Ministry of Home by law no. 39,749 of 9 August 1954, PIDE was reorganized and vested with overriding powers. It became an extra-constitutional monster. Portugal's minister for justice, Manuel Gonçalves Cavaleiro Ferreira, resigned in protest over the law two days before its enactment.

In Goa, PIDE bypassed every authority, including the local governor—it had a radio transmitter in Panjim and communicated with Lisbon without the knowledge of the governor. PIDE agents wielded unrestrained power and committed excesses with human rights violations and extortion—both on suspects, often innocent, and political prisoners. PIDE's most notorious torturer of political suspects was a *mestiço* (Luso-Indian), Casimiro Emérito Rosa Teles Jordão Monteiro, aka Agente Monteiro.

The Goan advocate-notary Fernando Jorge Colaço, in his book *December 18–19, 1961: Before, During and After (Memoir of a Twentieth-Century Voyager)*, says Casimiro Monteiro

> … would boast that his mother was a good Brahmin lady from Curtorim.

It was, of course, a lie (his lineage is mentioned below). Monteiro was fluent in Portuguese, English and Konkani. He was a mercenary who fought for the dictator Francisco Franco in the Spanish Civil War, then for the Blue Division of Nazi Germany against the USSR and, as a commando, under General Montgomery against the Germans. He later killed a goldsmith in London. Describing him as 'human only in the form', Adv. Colaço says that, in Goa, Monteiro lived in Santa Cruz/Kalapur and operated from police HQ. He would roam the territory in a jeep, mostly after 10 p.m., with a group of guards, picking up suspects and sadistically torturing them. He even committed three or four murders and used to 'beat' every woman arrested.* Freedom fighter Dr Suresh Kanekar says:

> If there was one person who, more than any other, fiercely battled the freedom movement, it was the *mestizo* Casimiro Monteiro … He [Casimiro Monteiro] used a variety of crude methods of torture and harassment to gather information about the armed movement … Occasionally, innocent people were tortured into giving false confessions, and a few died under the inhuman treatment received …
>
> A poignantly tragic case was that of a woman from Mapusa Shrimati Diukar [who was a nurse with surgeon-freedom fighter Dr P.D. Gaitonde] … After she was arrested and put in police custody in Panaji, Casimiro Monteiro apparently had his way with her … Mitra Kakodkar [later Mitra Bir, wife of legislator Madhav Bir] … was felled by Monteiro to the ground unconscious with a mighty slap one day because she tried to warn Diukar against his machinations. I heard about this from Mitra herself.[†]

On 18 September 1956, at about 9 p.m., masked men of the Azad Gomantak Dal killed policeman Jerónimo Barreto at Ardhafond in Canacona. The next morning, policemen swooped down on the nearby Partagal Vaishnavite Matha and arrested thirty priests and students suspected of having helped the assassins. Monteiro

---

[*] Fernando Jorge Colaço, *December 18–19, 1961: Before, During and After (Memoir of a 20th-Century Voyager),* jointly published by Goa,1556, Saligao and Golden Heart Emporium, Margao, 2017, pp. 28–30.

[†] Suresh Kanekar, *Goa's Liberation and Thereafter: Chronicles of a Fragmented Life,* Goa, 1556, 2011, p. 60.

interrogated them. Two died the same evening—head *pujari* Parashuram Acharya and *bhatt* Keshav Tengse—and their bodies were hurriedly cremated under police guard.

Fifteen of the accused, led by Parashuram's father, Srinivas Dharma Acharya—who was allegedly tortured by Monteiro—were arraigned (one in absentia). They were charged with being 'terrorists' and killing the cop. Four of the five judges at the Tribunal Militar Territorial (military court in Panjim) were army officers.

Brainy, brawny and brave, Adv. António Bruto da Costa of Margao was a pacifist at heart. At a time when few would dare, he led the solemn cortège, carried the urn and delivered a stirring oration when Gandhi's ashes were immersed at Colva in 1948. When provoked, as mentioned earlier, he had punched the daylights out of the governor, Commander Quintanilha Dias.

Now, in 1956, he defended 'terrorist' Srinivas Acharya and eleven other accused, while Adv. Vinaica Sinai Coissoro (Vinayak Shenvi Kaissare) defended the remaining two. Condemning terrorism in all its forms, Bruto da Costa pointedly referred to:

> … extortion of confessions, false statements, specious denunciations and unjust accusations, made in the shadow of a true and elevated judicial regime, which is the bulwark of all well-organized societies, by misguided, impatient, violent *agentes*, easily prone to untold abuses and barbarities that are still in vogue in countries that pride themselves on being civilized.[*]

Bruto da Costa told the miffed court that

> dogs imported from Germany need smell to follow the trail of a criminal, but the police's nose is superior to that of dogs. Nobody had recognized the perpetrators, but the police had smelled them at Partagal Matha from thin air![†]

---

[*] Adv. Mário Bruto da Costa, *A Terceira corrente*, self-published, Goa, 2013, p. 206.

[†] Ibid, p. 209.

At the start of the trial, the Portuguese police chief of Goa, Captain Joaquim Pinto Brás, the mayor of Tiswadi (Presidente da Camara Municipal de Tissuari), who changed the name of the riverfront park opposite Collectorate from Parque Carmelina Quintanilha Dias to Parque Salazar and placed a bust of Salazar in it, the Goan Dr Constâncio Mascarenhas and the editor of *Heraldo*, Álvaro de Santa Rita Vaz, again a Goan, hosted a banquet in honour of Casimiro Monteiro during which they sang his praises. During the trial, Bruto da Costa made mincemeat of the feared agente.

The Supreme Military Court in Lisbon annulled the case and ordered a reinvestigation. At the retrial, all the accused were acquitted.[*]

On 17 May 2005, the first death anniversary of freedom fighter Felicio Cardoso, Goa's inimitable and multilingual (Konkani, French, English, Marathi, Hindi and Portuguese) poet-laureate, Dr Manohar Rai SarDessai said that every wannabe Goan politician should first undergo a month's solitary confinement at Aguada Jail and taste some strokes of Agente Monteiro as Felicio Cardoso had done.[†] Of medium height and build, Felicio Cardoso, a high school teacher by profession, was indeed a giant of a man, a dauntless freedom fighter and an upright and fearless journalist-editor who had been a victim of Casimiro Monteiro.

Another Goan freedom fighter, Mário Rodrigues of Cavelossim, was an airman with the Indian Air Force in Bangalore. Influenced by the 1946 Naval Mutiny in Bombay, he left the IAF and joined the Azad Gomantak Dal in 1947 and became an underground freedom fighter. Rodrigues was determined to get Casimiro Monteiro. He roamed with a fully loaded handgun for the purpose. The firearm

---

[*] For more on the court proceedings of that sensational case, see *Goa: A Terceira corrente (Discursos, artigos, cartas e defesas forenses de António A. Bruto da Costa*, by Adv. Mário Bruto da Costa, 2013, pp. 204–215.

[†] Xavier Cota, *Tribute to Felicio Cardoso: The Unassuming Giant*, http://konknnifelicio.blogspot.com/2016/07/tribute-to-felicio-cardoso-unassuming_31.html?m=1

did not fit into his trouser pocket, so Rodrigues would tuck it in his
waistband with his bush shirt over it.

Rodrigues often paid nightly visits to his friend, Nuno Rosario
da Silva, whose father Raimundo Domingos da Silva ran two shops
in Margao's old market. In one shop, Domingos made coffins (Casa
Domingos, AgenciaFunerária), and Rosario hired out BSA and
Zundap 50 cc mopeds from the other. A good part of Rosario's
clientele was Portuguese troops who, during their evening break,
hired the bikes to go to Chandravaddo, a tribal area, for some fun.
While the soldiers frolicked at the nearby hilltops, one of Rosario's
friends punctured tyres of their bikes parked on the road, fetching
Rosario some extra income.

Possibly to get information on Portuguese military personnel,
freedom fighter Rodrigues befriended and often paid nightly visits
to Rosario, who slept in the coffin shop to make it a 24 × 7 service.
One night, when Rodrigues was with Rosario at the coffin shop,
they heard a PIDE *ronda* (armed surveillance patrol) approaching.
Rosario told Rodrigues that his presence there would get him in
trouble and quickly hid the freedom fighter with his handgun in
a coffin until the danger subsided. Rodrigues never succeeded in
consigning Casimiro Monteiro to a coffin.

While in Goa, Monteiro tried to build a personal fortune.
He was allegedly involved in contraband gold. He built the only
cinema hall in Ponda. He also tried to extort money from certain
rich families. The son of a leading hardware merchant died at his
hands. Some wealthy businessmen enjoyed fail safe insurance against
the high-handedness of colonial officialdom thanks to their idle
and bored wives back home. Knowledgeable sources of the time
(the mid-20th century) say that high-society Goan women were
invariably enamoured by the Portuguese military officer's uniform.
Hardly surprising that offspring at times resembled Europeans.
A Portuguese-language ditty was popular in Panjim at the time:

   Se todo o cabrão trouxer na ponta do corno um lampião,

Ó minha mãe, ó minha mãe, que grande seria a iluminação!
(If every cuckold donned a lantern at the end of his horn,
Oh mother! Oh mother! How bright would the streets be!)

Consenting husbands/cheating wives and Portuguese Casanovas were one thing. PIDE and Casimiro Monteiro were quite another—they were above even the highest-ranking military officer in Goa serving as the governor-general. There was no sure-fire insurance from the PIDE and Casimiro Monteiro!

To trace the genealogy of Casimiro Monteiro, one needs to go back to the 19th century when a Portuguese-Brazilian, Francisco Xavier Alvares Castro Roso (pronounced Rôzo), fleeing the long arm of the law for an alleged major crime, bought a ship, packed it with merchandise and sailed for Goa. He sold the merchandise and the ship, and settled in Ponda. Roso and his wife, Maria Natalia de Jesus Lourenço, had four daughters. One married an Antao from Chandor, the second a Menezes from Raia, the third an Amaral from Ponda (all three Goan), and the youngest—Maria Florencia da Piedade de Araujo Alvares Castro Roso—married José Teles Jordão Monteiro, a Ponda-based Portuguese second sergeant.

The Teles Jordão Monteiros hailed from Guarda in Portugal. José was born in Chaves-Portugal circa 1875. When transferred from Ponda, he shifted with his wife to Panjim. It was here that Casimiro, their fourth son, and Anibal, also a PIDE agent but an ethical man, were born; Casimiro, on 20 December 1920.* Roso was changed to 'Rosa' in Casimiro Monteiro's name. He was legally wedded to a Scotswoman, the daughter of a butcher whom he worked for when in England.

Casimiro enlisted in the Portuguese Army, which he deserted, and fled to Italy, joining the Foreign Legion. Around 1950, he returned to Portugal. He joined the PIDE and eventually arrived in Goa.

---

* Part genealogy is borrowed from Dr Jorge Forjaz and Dr José Francisco de Noronha in *Luso-Descendentes da Índia Portuguesa*, vol. 3, Fundação Oriente, pp. 873–80.

The downfall of the state terrorist came after he was seriously wounded in an operation. Monteiro and forty armed secret-service guards took on two Azad Gomantak Dal activists, Bapu Gawas and Bala Desai, at Hali-Chandel in Pernem. The Goan duo fought valiantly, killing five and injuring Monteiro before they were shot dead. Monteiro went to Portugal for medical treatment.

The families of some military officials' local paramours who had fallen victim to Monteiro and a former PIDE colleague in Goa complained about Monteiro's misdeeds to the Goa governor-general, and presented material stolen by Monteiro in London. Monteiro was accused of fifty crimes in Goa alone. Colonel Miguel Mota Carmo of the GNR (the paramilitary Guarda Nacional Republicana or the National Guard of the Republic, created during Portugal's first Republic, 1910–26) conducted the inquiry. After examining evidence of various crimes—torture, murders, extortion and rape of women committed in Goa—Monteiro was arrested and incarcerated at the Trafaria military prison in Portugal.

However, he was later reinstated and continued his activities, especially in liquidating political opponents of the ruling regime, both in Portugal and Portuguese Africa.

Author Dalila Cabrita Mateus tells us that Casimiro Monteiro was recruited by Hermes Oliveira, an official in Portugal's ministry of overseas, for the post-1961 Operation Nemasté meant to organize armed resistance to the Indian Union and liquidate the opponents of Portugal. Monteiro arrived in Goa and carried out several acts of terrorism using bombs. He also executed Goans who had collaborated with India. He managed to get a Goan freedom fighter to a meeting near the Daman border, under the pretence of wanting to convince him to take control of erstwhile Portuguese territories as governor. The Goan was overpowered, gagged and tied to the back of a horse, but was released on orders from Lisbon.*

---

* Mateus, *A PIDE/DGS na guerra colonial (1961-1974),* Terramar Editores, Distribuidores & Livreiros, Lisbon, 2004, pp 172–74.

On 20 June 1964, when some bombs went off in Goa, it was said to be the handiwork of Casimiro Monteiro and a Goan settled in Portugal.

After Operation Nemasté, Monteiro returned to Portugal in November 1964 and, although he was not qualified, became a PIDE brigade leader. He routinely bumped off opponents of the regime. He travelled with Rosa Casaco to Paris, tailing the former Portuguese Air Force chief, Gen. Humberto Delgado (who had crossed swords with Salazar in the 1958 presidential election, taken political asylum in Brazil in 1959 and later moved to Europe). Casimiro Monteiro shot Gen. Delgado and strangled his Brazilian secretary, both to death, on 13 February 1965 near Badajoz in Spain. He went to Tanzania in February 1969 and was allegedly behind the assassination of Eduardo Mondlane, the Mozambican freedom struggle leader and president of the Mozambican Liberation Front, Frelimo. In the wake of Portugal's Carnation Revolution in 1974, Monteiro fled to political asylum in South Africa and, destitute and almost blind, died unsung at Richards Bay in Natal on 25 January 1993.

'Lord High Everything'

While Nehru continued to reiterate that India would not use force, his defence minister, Krishna Menon, with G.K. Handoo of the Central Reserve Police, B.N. Mullik of the Intelligence Bureau, and Lt Gen. Brij Mohan Kaul, chief of staff at army HQ (promoted out of turn, but who would soon quit after the China debacle in 1962), actively planned to take Goa by force behind Nehru's back.*

Putnam Welles Hangen, former chief of bureau of *New York Times* who switched to TV and was now with the National Broadcasting Corporation in New Delhi, wrote that the plan was to

---

* *The Dirty Game Played by V.K. Krishna Menon Against Goa*, https://portugueseindia.wordpress.com/2011/07/09/the-dirty-game-played-by-v-k-krishna-menon-against-goa/

... send a party of Indian border police into Goa, some of whom would allow themselves to be captured by the Portuguese. The rest were to fall back and give the alarm. Under the pretext of rescuing the captured border guards, a small Indian force would move in and engage the Portuguese. The main body of Indian troops would then quickly overrun Goa ...[*]

This was actually surprising because all along Krishna Menon had projected himself in the mould of Gandhi and Nehru: as a man of peace and goodwill. At international levels—whether in meetings with foreign leaders or on the floor of the United Nations—Menon championed the cause of resolving all disputes by peaceful means and without the use of force. His biographer, Jairam Ramesh, says that Menon was

... masterminding a military operation [in Goa] that he had, ironically, been ruling out for well over five years at least at the UN.[†]

As late as 1961, shortly after John Fitzgerald Kennedy was sworn in as the 35th President of the United States of America on 20 January 1961, Menon, in his foreword to Kennedy's biography written by journalist Ramesh Sanghvi, reiterated a 'warless world'. Menon would turn out to the prime force behind India's armed action against the Portuguese in Goa.

Nehru got wind of Menon's scheming in late November 1961.[‡] He summoned Menon and his henchmen and rebuked them for plotting direct action in Goa without his permission. Menon's pressure persisted, nonetheless. Hangen says,

---

[*] Ibid.

[†] Jairam Ramesh, *A Chequered Brilliance*, Penguin Viking, Gurugram, 2019, p. 546.

[‡] Welles Hangen, *The Dirty Game Played by V.K. Krishna Menon Against Goa*, https://portugueseindia.wordpress.com/2011/07/09/the-dirty-game-played-by-v-k-krishna-menon-against-goa/

With the help of hand-picked lieutenants like G.K. Handoo, a
top security officer, he [Menon] stepped up subversion against
the Portuguese in Goa. The Indian border police under Handoo's
direction recruited, trained, and equipped saboteurs, who were
slipped across the border into Goa. Fabricated stories about
Portuguese 'border provocations' were fed to the Indian press.[*]

India had cultivated an image that she firmly stood for settlement
of all international disputes by peaceful or non-violent means. This
precluded India from using force in Goa. When the Dutch used
force in Indonesia in 1947, India's delegate told the UN,

> Can any country be allowed to indulge in aggression of this type
> and refuse arbitration? ... If any power can act as it chooses in
> such matters then there is no purpose left for the United Nations.
> It will have no prestige or authority and [is] bound to fade away.[†]

The US delegate to the United Nations Security Council (UNSC)
would slam India with the same words on 18 December 1961.

India had already used force in Kashmir, Travancore, Junagarh
and Hyderabad. But, Goa was a different kettle of fish: this was a
West European nation that it had to contend with in the days of
the Cold War between the world's two superpower blocs. Journalist
Sridhar Telkar once commented:

> Nehru alone dictated India's foreign policy.[‡]

Prof. Norman D. Palmer of the University of Pennsylvania (and
chairman, Friends of India Committee in USA) famously wrote,

> To the extent that the decisions are made by Nehru himself, it
> is difficult to determine whether he is acting as Prime Minister

---

[*] Ibid.

[†] UN records.

[‡] Telkar's Feature Service, 1962, p. 124.

or as Party Leader or as Lord High Everything. He wears many
hats and sits on many seats, but whatever hat he wears or seat he
occupies, he is India's supreme decision maker.[*]

For fourteen long years, Nehru had made multiple attempts to
resolve the 'Goa case' peacefully and by legal means—employing, as
already seen, diplomacy, satyagraha, economic blockade, informal
diplomacy, third-party intervention, the United Nations and
cross-border saboteurs. Nothing moved Salazar. Nehru personally
abhorred dictators, but he was on the horns of a dilemma. Would
he continue talking to a deaf dictator, or would he take the option
of abandoning his long-professed policy for settling international
disputes by non-violent means and expose himself to the charge of
hypocrisy?

Salazar exploited Nehru's situation. Salazar knew that it was not
possible to defend Goa militarily but was convinced that Nehru
would not risk his world reputation—for so little gain—by attacking
Goa. What Salazar did not know was that Nehru's pacifism was
limited by political compulsions and an upcoming general election.
Until then, India had deployed peacekeeping troops in the Congo
and Gaza, but shied away from sending them to Goa.

Jurist, diplomat and Union minister Mohammadali Carim
Chagla questioned this, adding that Goa was a simple question
complicated by politicians who could be trusted to complicate any
issue.[†] (Justice Chagla had upheld 'the right of Goans to ventilate
their domestic grievances freely in British India', in a Bombay High
Court verdict of September 1945.)

Nehru's detractors at home chorused that as long as Nehru was
prime minister of India, Goa was safe for Portugal.

However, Paul Gore-Booth, who was Britain's high
commissioner in India from 1960, felt that Nehru's

---

[*] Norman D. Palmer, *The Indian Political System*, Houghton Mifflin
Company, Boston, 1961, p. 190.

[†] Parliament debates.

... decisions are ... less his own than they used to be ... he is certainly more vulnerable to over-persuasion by men of determination, in particular Krishna Menon ...*

The Tide Turns

On 4 February 1961, African nationalists in Luanda, Angola, killed white Portuguese policemen in a shootout. When the bodies were taken for burial, there was another shootout at the cemetery. By July the same year, civil unrest mushroomed into a widespread revolt against the Portuguese authority. Portugal let loose waves of state terror, repression, imprisonments and killings in Angola.

Nehru said that the civil unrest in Angola was the most terrible thing happening in the world at the time. Liberia took the matter to the UNSC. For the first time, the USA, with a Democrat president, John F. Kennedy, from earlier that year, attacked the Portuguese colonial policy at the UNSC.

The Casablanca Conference, held between 18 and 20 April 1961, brought leaders from Afro-Asiatic colonies of Portugal together. With five of the fourteen primary delegates being Goan (George Vaz and Aquino de Bragança for Goan People's Party, Dr P.D. Gaitonde for National Congress-Goa, Caetano Lobo for Goan Liberation Council and Adv. João Cabral for Goan League), the conference was regarded as the handiwork of India. With reference to Goa, the conference observed that:†

a) The people of Goa, Daman and Diu are ethnically, culturally and traditionally Indian;
b) Goa, Daman and Diu are within India, separated only by artificial political barriers;
c) Goa, Daman and Diu are economically linked to India; and,
d) The people of Goa, Daman and Diu were always averse to Portuguese occupation

---

* British Foreign Office DO No. 196/127 of 25 August 1962.

† Lopes, *As vozes da opposicao,* p. 307.

And it declared—rather undecidedly—that these people aspired to unite their destinies with India. The qualification 'undecidedly' is because no referendum or plebiscite was held, thanks largely to Salazar, to ascertain the wishes of Goans.

São João Batista de Ajudá was a micro, 4-acre Portuguese possession in Africa. The tiny area, part of the kingdom of Dahomey, was occupied by Portugal in the 17th century. France seized the rest of the kingdom in 1904. The French made Dahomey a self-governing colony in 1958 and granted full independence on 1 August 1960. São João Batista de Ajudá continued with Portugal. (Note the parallels between Dahomey–India and São João Batista de Ajudá–Portuguese Goa upto this point.)

The Republic of Dahomey asked Portugal to quit São João Batista de Ajudá before 31 July 1961, the day before their first independence anniversary. Portugal did not. On 31 July 1961, the forces of Dahomey (now known as Benin) stormed and captured São João Batista de Ajudá. The retreating Portuguese troops reduced São João Batista de Ajudá to a pile of ashes on the express instructions of their supreme commander Salazar. After some mild noises, Portugal silently accepted the loss.

Nehru's attitude to the Goa question soon turned.

In a symbolic change of stance, on 12 June 1961, India got the Varishta Panchayat of 'Free Dadra and Nagar Haveli' to seek merger with India. On 11 August 1961, K.G. Badlani, IAS, as 'prime minister of Dadra and Nagar Haveli' for just one day, signed the instrument of accession. India integrated Dadra and Nagar Haveli by the Tenth Amendment of the Constitution passed by the Lok Sabha on 14 August and by the Rajya Sabha on 16 August the same year.

Parliament debate over the Tenth Amendment of the Constitution panned to Goa. Pandit Nehru told the Rajya Sabha on 16 August 1961 (in response to Communist leader Bhupesh Gupta):

... the time may come when we may even decide to send our army there.

The ageing Nehru then quipped,

I have no intention of passing away before Goa is liberated.

The year 1961 did not bode well for Portugal's dictator, Salazar. Other than trouble in Angola and the loss of São João Batista de Ajudá in Dahomey/Benin, the loss of Portuguese steamship *Santa Maria* (pirated by political rebels when on the Madeira–Rio de Janeiro run) made international headlines; his defence minister Julio Botelho Moniz attempted a coup, his undersecretary of state for the army, Lt Col Jaime Filipe da Fonseca, died in another failed assault and, on 10 November 1961, Herminio da Palma Inácio hijacked a TAP Super Constellation and airdropped thousands of leaflets all over Lisbon, urging citizens to revolt against the dictatorship.[*] December would be even worse for the dictator—in faraway Goa.

Towards the end of August 1961, the military brass was told to prepare for action. One of India's adept soldier-writers who, when a brigadier, was director of military operations at army HQ at the time, Maj. Gen. D.K. ('Monty') Palit, quoted from a note recorded on 4 September 1961 by Lieutenant General J.N. Chaudhuri, general officer commanding-in-chief, Southern Command, then officiating as army chief in New Delhi, which stated:

On the afternoon of 30 Aug '61, while travelling back [from the National Defence College] in a car with the Defence Minister, the DM [defence minister] mentioned GOA. He said that the PM had now agreed to a plan for the use of troops in or against Portuguese possessions in India might be committed to paper. Later that afternoon in his office ... the DM again said that a plan as above could be prepared but it should be kept at a very high and top secret level ...[†]

---

[*] Joaquim Correia, *Once Upon a Time in Goa*, Goa, 1556 and GPR Associates, 2022, p. 58.

[†] D.K. Palit, *Musings and Memories, Vol. II,* Palit & Palit in association with Lancer Publishers & Distributors, New Delhi, 2004, p. 416.

Maj. Gen. D.K. Palit starts the description of the follow-up by
the officiating army chief as follows:

> In a setting reminiscent of a comic opera ... so it was with
> some curiosity that I received an urgent summons from him
> [the officiating Chief of Army Staff, Lt Gen. Chaudhuri] one
> morning. When I arrived at the office of the Chief's Military
> Assistant, I found Brigadier Jangu Satarawala (DSD) and Brigadier
> Bim Batra (DMI) also [there] ... After the Military Assistant had
> ushered us into the presence and had sat us down, Chaudhuri
> dismissed him, adding that he did not wish to be disturbed for the
> next half-hour, 'unless, there is a call from the Prime Minister, of
> course,' he added grandiloquently, glancing meaningfully in our
> direction ... he [Lt Gen. Chaudhuri] began by warning us that he
> was going to entrust us with a matter of the greatest import and
> the highest security grading. 'So far only the Defence Minister,
> Harish Sarin, and I are privy to this secret,' he said ... He then
> turned to me and said that I was to prepare a directive to the
> Southern Command requiring it to submit an appreciation of
> the situation and an outline plan for the liberation of the three
> enclaves of Goa, Daman and Diu. He wanted the directive within
> twenty-four hours and added that as officiating Chief he would
> sign it himself.'*

But, as Maj. Gen. Palit observed, Lt Gen. Chaudhuri's

> ... signing an Army HQ directive to himself as Southern
> Commander ...

would not be proper.† The directive for a war plan would come
later. The tide had turned.

---

*   Ibid., pp. 412–13.

†   Ibid., p. 416.

The revered Sikh Guru Gobind Singh had epitomized in a Persian verse 250 years before:

Chu Kar az Hameh Heel-te Darguzasht
Halal ast burdan b-Shamshir Dast
(When a problem defies all other means of solution,
it is just and proper to take the sword in hand)

Nehru had come under great strain with India's February 1962 general elections looming on the horizon. He was under pressure of public opinion to demonstrate that he could deal firmly with foreign intruders. (India was already facing major border problems on her north-western and north-eastern borders. For a sense of the situation, recall Pakistan's capture of large areas in J&K on the north-western border in 1947–48 and China's incursion into J&K's Aksai Chin in Ladakh on the north-eastern border in 1952–57.)

S. Mulgaonkar, the Goan-origin editor of the *Hindustan Times,* then the largest circulated daily in New Delhi, wrote that India's failure to deal with foreign intruders would considerably weaken the Congress's prospects in the ensuing elections. Nehru knew that it was true.

China was too powerful to be accosted over Aksai Chin. To take on Pakistan in Kashmir meant an all-out war. Nehru must have felt compelled to choose a soft target like Goa—consistently being championed by his defence minister Krishna Menon. After all, every Indian Opposition party, except the Swatantra, had made Goa an election issue in their poll manifestos. A quick military victory in Goa would 'keep the people happy' and divert public attention from Red China's aggression at the northern borders. Paragraph 4 of the US Central Intelligence Agency's 'Special National Intelligence Estimate Number 31-61' dated 13 December 1961 read:

He [Nehru] will also be conscious of the favourable effect vigorous action [in Goa] is likely to have on the Congress Party's position in February's elections'.[*]

Maj. Gen. Palit wrote:

A colleague in Army HQ once described the Goa episode as light relief from the gloom and foreboding of the general strategic scene ... In a way, the comment was apt; the involvement in the south did indeed offer respite from the continuing crises in the north. Activities set in motion by the decision to liberate Goa, however hectic and pressing, were untainted by concern about national security.[†]

In other words, the borders in the north—with China and Pakistan—were serious issues, while Goa was not even a military threat to India. But as Paragraph 3 of the CIA 'Special National Intelligence Estimate No. 31-61' said:

Probably the most important factor militating against an invasion is what we believe to be Nehru's longstanding conviction that the acquisition of Goa is not so essential to India's national interests as to justify its seizure by military force.[‡]

Krishna Menon, however, was gaining influence under Nehru, the ageing monarch. The CIA report No. 31-61 of 13 December 1961 observed:

Krishna Menon, who needs public support in a tough re-election contest and who has strong anti-Western inclinations, is using his

---

[*] The CIA's Special National Intelligence Estimate No. 31-61, dated 13 December 1961, was declassified and approved for release on 26 March 2014.

[†] Palit, *Musings and Memories*, vol. 2, 2004, p. 411.

[‡] CIA report no. 31–61 of 13 December 1961.

position as Defense Minister and his considerable personal influence with Nehru to try to swing the balance in favour of action.[*]

If not for Menon, the mastermind of the military action in Goa in 1961, it is doubtful that Nehru would have even ordered it. This was echoed by journalist Sridhar Telkar, who said that,

Krishna Menon influenced Nehru's decision to invade Goa.[†]

The US political establishment too considered Goa's liberation a result of pressure from Krishna Menon.[‡]

It was rumoured at the cocktail-party circuits in Delhi at the time that Menon, now with sufficient power and influence in the army, threatened Nehru to engineer a military coup when the latter hesitated over Goa (although he was perhaps aware that in such an attempt at naked seizure of power, he was not wholly assured of success).[§]

---

[*] Ibid.

[†] *Goa Yesterday and Today*, Telkar's Feature Service, Bombay, 1962, p. 124.

[‡] Jairam Ramesh, *A Chequered Brilliance: The Many Lives of V.K. Krishna Menon*, Penguin Viking, Gurugram, 2019, p. 546.

[§] Ibid., p. 553.

4

MAJESTIC MENON

Majestic Menon

Krishna Menon had worked hard for the cause of India's freedom when he stationed himself in Britain from 1924 through the decades up to Independence. He was a barrister-at-law but went on to acquire additional qualifications, for instance at the London School of Economics (where he was a 'perennial student' and was to come within the orbit of Prof. Harold Joseph Laski), just to be able to continue propagating the India story on British soil—by way of lobbying, organizing meetings, giving speeches, writing books, pamphlets and newspaper articles. He was practically an ascetic who lived off tea, buns and frequent illness.

As secretary of the Commonwealth of India League (later known as the India League), he almost single-handedly crusaded the cause and roped in British notables like Bertrand Russell, Aldous Huxley and a number of Labour Party MPs. He publicized the stands of the Indian National Congress and Indian socialists and helped shape public opinion in Britain in favour of freedom for India. Despite the legitimate commitment and toil, a long shadow followed him.

Krishna Menon was suspected to be a 'closet Communist'.

British intelligence and police agencies put him under surveillance and kept a tab on his regular meetings with top leaders of the Communist Party of Great Britain.[*]

---

[*] Ramesh, *A Chequered Brilliance*, p. 43.

By 1939, Scotland Yard was convinced that Krishna Menon was
a communist in all but name.[*]

Sardar Vallabhbhai Patel, the deputy prime minister, saw Menon as
a communist sympathizer, according to notes left behind by Louis
Mountbatten, the first governor-general of India (until June 1948),
after a meeting with Patel on 14 February 1948. On 5 December
1948, Menon, who was now India's first high commissioner to
Britain, told T.G. Sanjeevi Pillai, director of India's Intelligence
Bureau who was deputed to London to explore cooperation with the
British security service, that the Government of India's action against
Indian communists was altogether untenable. He told Pillai that the
Government of India could use the Intelligence Bureau to round up
black-marketers and agents of corruption instead of hounding and
harassing the communists.[†]

Communists—particularly in the then provinces of Hyderabad,
Madras and West Bengal—had rejected the independence of
India as a sham, denounced Gandhi and Nehru and indulged in
rampant murders, arson and looting.[‡] Government of India cracked
down on them, something that Menon regarded as 'altogether
unsupportable'.

Earlier, Krishna Menon had been a member of the China
Campaign Committee in Britain and promoted Edgar Snow's *Red
Star over China* which proved very influential in moulding world
opinion in favour of Mao Tse Tung and the Chinese communists.[§]

After Japan invaded China for a second time on 7 July 1937,
India sent a medical team with ambulances, X-ray sets, disinfecting
apparatus, cars and many cases of medicine. Krishna Menon received
a letter from a top Chinese leader, which read in part:

Dear Friend:
… The Indian medical unit, which you have been instrumental
in sending, has arrived with us in Yenan and have begun their

---

[*] Ibid., p. 199.

[†] Ibid., pp. 339–40.

[‡] Ibid., p. 342.

[§] Ibid., p.153.

work energetically ... In the name of the members of the 8th
Route Army we wish to thank you for your help and hope that
you will continue your good work and constantly help us in all
ways possible so as to help in driving out the Japanese imperialists
from China.
Yours sincerely,
Mao Tse Tung[*]

Krishna Menon's Labour Party ticket for Britain's 1940 parliament
elections was cancelled because he was charged with being a
communist.[†] After parting ways with the Congress, Menon would win
the 1969 and 1971 parliament elections as a CPM candidate in Kerala.[‡]
Menon's one-time friend, Minoo Masani described him in 1956 as

... a violent anti anti-Communist without being a
Communist himself.[§]

Menon had the uncanny ability of turning friends into foes. He
could be quite acerbic in his replies to critics. One day, when
delivering a talk at the University of Wisconsin, a woman was
critical of India's position on Korea and of Menon. (Communist
North Korea had invaded South Korea in 1950 and Menon, as
part of India's UN delegation, had greatly helped bring about the
Korean Armistice Agreement in 1953.)

As she sat down after her comments, Krishna Menon replied,
'Madam, you have one great gift that I do not have on this subject
and that is the gift of ignorance!'[¶]

[*] Ibid., p. 179.
[†] Ibid., pp. 196–97.
[‡] Ibid., p. 656.
[§] Ibid., p. 53.
[¶] Ibid., p. 411.

Proponent for Military Action in Goa

When high commissioner in London, Menon championed restraint on the part of India and constantly advised Nehru against declaring war on Pakistan in their 1947 invasion of Jammu and Kashmir or taking any military action in Hyderabad. The long-standing champion of restraint and peace would change his tune when it came to Goa.

A military action in Goa, rather than in Pakistan-occupied-Kashmir or the more recent China-occupied-Ladakh, suited Menon. He was supportive of Red China, beholden to its leadership; he painted Pakistan as India's No. 1 enemy, playing down the threat from China. Says his biographer Jairam Ramesh:

> It is clear that Krishna Menon saw Pakistan as a greater threat to India than China.[*]

Pakistan could be handled, as the fourteen-day war a decade later in 1971 would demonstrate. China was the mightier, more ominous enemy, but it did not suit Menon to try to wrest illegally occupied territory in Ladakh from that neighbour. Goa, on the other hand, was not even a military threat to India but, compared to China or Pakistan, was chickenfeed.

Menon had the powerful backing of the brotherhood of socialists worldwide, led by Prof. Harold Laski, to end the last of the colonial traces in India as its defence minister. He was also egged on towards the same end by Indian brother barristers like Siddhartha Shankar Ray and Rajni Patel, and socialists like Jayaprakash Narayan and Ram Manohar Lohia at home.[†] It appears that Menon was raring to go at Goa from much earlier.

---

[*]   Ibid., p. 506.

[†]   The Congress Socialist Party of Jayaprakash Narayan and Ram Manohar Lohia born in 1934 was 'incubated not in Patna or Bombay, not even in Nasik Jail, as history books faithfully report, but at Allahabad, in Nehru's

As far back as 1958, Yona Loyola-Nazareth says that her father, Adv. Fanchu Loyola, returned to Bombay from a meeting with Nehru in New Delhi 'quite defeated and disconsolate' and crying 'we have lost Goa'. He was convinced that with Krishna Menon at the helm, a military takeover of Goa was imminent.[*] Yona's father stood for the autonomy of Goa, not its integration with India.

Facing a difficult re-election in February 1962, Menon became the chief proponent of invading Goa before the general elections. He needed to bolster his electoral prospects by demonstrating to the voters that he had freed Goa from the clutches of a foreign power. Jairam Ramesh says that,

> Krishna Menon's critics were to link Operation Vijay to his need for a 'big bang' success a few weeks prior to the elections ...[†]

Menon was preparing to recontest from the North Bombay constituency but faced stiff party resistance for being pro-communist. Ramakrishna Bajaj, the well-known Bombay industrialist whose father, Jamnalal Bajaj, was called the fifth son of Mahatma Gandhi, wrote to Nehru opposing Menon's candidature. There was a virtual campaign to deny Menon a Congress party ticket, orchestrated by Maharashtra Congress heavyweight S.K. Patil. Party opposition to Menon's re-nomination was firmly put down by Nehru.

Two stalwarts came out openly against Menon. Chakravarti Rajagopalachari ('Rajaji') said on 8 February 1962:

Anand Bhavan home', writes Rahul Ramagundam in *The Life and Times of George Fernandes*, Penguin Random House, Gurugram, 2022, p. 58.

[*] *Goa's Foremost Nationalist: José Inácio Cândido de Loyola: The Man and His Writings*, XCHR Studies Series No. 9, New Delhi, Concept Publishing, 2000.

[†] Ramesh, *A Chequered Brilliance*, p. 546.

If Mr. Menon succeeds, it would be one point to Indian
Communists and two points to world Communists ... Kripalani
[his electoral opponent Acharya J.B. Kripalani, a former Congress
president] dramatically announced on 12 February 1962 that he
would withdraw from the contest if Krishna Menon openly
condemned the Communist Party and declared that he was not
a communist.[*]

(Menon became the Congress candidate in North Bombay, where
he faced Kripalani who was backed by the Swatantra Party, Jan
Sangh and the Praja Socialist Party. The Goa victory punctured
Opposition's sails and Menon, with the support of the communists,
trounced Kripalani by a 2:1 margin.)

'The Second Most Powerful Man in India'

Defence Minister Vengalil Krishnan (Kurup) Krishna Menon bore
interesting credentials. He was an articulate debater who, like Che
Guevara, could talk continuously for hours on end. His marathon,
eight-hour-long speech on the Kashmir issue at the UNSC on 23
January 1957 (which spilled over to the next day, with the dramatic
finale of Menon either fainting or feigning a faint) is regarded as
the world's longest speech. Menon's verbal and intellectual prowess
evidently impressed Nehru. Jairam Ramesh quotes from a letter
dated 19 July 1951 which Nehru wrote to his finance minister,
C.D. Deshmukh, providing a candid assessment of Menon:

> ... In some ways Krishna Menon is a person of remarkable ability
> and capacity. From a purely intellectual point of view, I cannot
> remember having met any person with a keener intellect. He

---

[*] Ibid., p. 561.

is a man of high integrity and his whole life has been one of simplicity and sacrifice.*

Nehru and Menon had been close friends since the 1930s. Nehru would confide more in Menon than in his own sister, Vijayalakshmi, or daughter, Indira. Jairam Ramesh writes,

> Annie Besant had 'discovered him' sometime in 1917 or 1918. [Prof. Harold] Laski had mentored him in the late 1920s and 1930s. Nehru would now become his patron saint for almost three decades.†

Those who were well acquainted with Menon attested to his personal integrity. Yet there were flummoxing cases. These happened when he was India's high commissioner in London (1947–52). In 1948, he bought 4275 cases of Scotch whiskey for the Indian Armed Forces at a price much higher than could be justified. Jeeps were urgently needed in the 1947–48 J&K Ops. The US and the UK governments had banned the supply of jeeps to India and Pakistan because of the Indo–Pak war.‡ Menon chose a little-known UK firm, Anti-Mistantes, for the supply of 2000 refurbished jeeps at the price of new jeeps available in the US. Menon advanced £1,43,000 to the firm, which had a paid-up capital of £605. The firm, floated by one of his friends, supplied 155 unserviceable jeeps and then filed for bankruptcy.

The whiskey and jeep scandals created a furore in the Constituent Assembly and agitated the Public Accounts Committee. The commotion was no more than water off a duck's back. Nehru defended Menon in Parliament saying that,

---

*   Ibid., p. 371.

†   Ibid., p. 116.

‡   Ibid., p. 672.

... the only scandal about this matter is the [repeated] use of the word 'scandal' all the time.*

A top British intelligence official, Percy Sillitoe, had cautioned his prime minister on 7 May 1951 that the Indian High Commission in London represented a security risk. Sillitoe said in writing that the

... suspicion that has attached to Menon in regard to the placing of Government of India's contracts ... [with] his close associate ... a black market operator called [Robert] Cleminson, who also has a history connected with arms deals, etc.[†]

Recommendations of the M.A. Ayyangar Inquiry into the 'scandal' were ignored. In 1951, Menon again contracted for 1007 jeeps with another little-known UK firm, Sir James Marshall Cornwall & Partners (Menon told Nehru in a telegram on 31 May 1951 that the chairman of the company was 'General Sir James Marshall Cornwall, KCB, CBE, DSO, MC' who was also a military adviser to the Foreign Office),[‡] at higher than the previous price, and again paid a substantial advance. The firm delivered forty-nine jeeps.

The Government of India filed a claim to recover £2,54,498 from the firm. Menon waived the entire claim after Nehru made him India's fourth defence minister on 17 April 1957. (Menon was brought into the cabinet as minister without portfolio on 14 February 1956; he might have been inducted at least two years before—after the passing of Nehru's soulmate Rafi Ahmed Kidwai in 1954—but Maulana Abdul Kalam Azad was stoutly opposed to Menon's inclusion and threatened to resign if that happened; Azad finally yielded at Nehru's insistence in 1956 and Menon was sworn in as minister.) The 'jeeps scandal' refused to die down and lasted

---

* Ibid., p. 365.

[†] Ibid., p. 366.

[‡] Ibid., p. 370.

some seven years in parliament, causing considerable pain to Nehru, chief defender of his defence minister.

But once inducted in the cabinet, Menon became what many said, 'the second most powerful man in India'.

He would soon become the chief architect of India's most humiliating defeat at the hands of China in 1962. As defence minister, Menon lorded over a realm of which he only had a rudimentary idea. But he did it with a flourish as one with an inherited fiefdom would.

Foreseeing the threat from China, one of India's most respected generals, army chief Gen. K.S. Thimayya (1957–61) repeatedly asked for army upgrades. Even a simple plea to replace World War I vintage .303 single action Lee-Enfield rifles with modern Belgian FN4 rifles was dismissed because Menon did not want NATO weapons in India.

Gen. Thimayya pleaded for redeployment of troops on the China border. The pleas were ignored. But, as the editor-author Frank Moraes once wrote, Menon

... suffers neither fools nor wise men gladly.[*]

According to Maj. Gen. Ian Cardozo (veteran), Menon wanted then Maj. Gen. Sam Manekshaw to criticize army chief Gen. K.S. Thimayya. Maj. Gen. Manekshaw refused. Menon instituted a frivolous inquiry against him and held up his promotion for eighteen months.[†] (Menon then got Lt Gen. P.N. Thapar to level thirteen charges against Gen. Thimayya and five charges against Lt Gen. S.P.P. Thorat, widely seen as the next Chief of Staff, in a letter dated 23 April 1961 that Gen. Thapar thinly disguised was

---

[*] As quoted by Lt Gen. Stanley Menezes, *Fidelity and Honour: The Indian Army from the Seventeenth to the Twenty-First Century*, Oxford University Press, 1999, p. 476.

[†] Major General Ian Cardozo, *1971: Stories of Grit and Glory from the Indo-Pak War*, Penguin Random House India (Ebury Press), Gurugram, Preamble.

being written under instructions. Gen. Thapar became army chief in May 1961.)

Menon promoted Maj. Gen. B.M. Kaul to lieutenant general over the heads of twelve senior officers. Gen. Thimayya, aged fifty-three, resigned on 31 August 1959. Nehru asked him to continue, and after a drab holding on, he officially retired on 8 May 1961, prophetically telling his men in a valedictory address,

I hope I am not leaving you as cannon fodder for the Chinese.[*]

Lt Gen. Kaul, made chief of general staff, was Menon's henchman plotting military action in Goa. After Goa, Kaul—who was 'dʳ tined to outsmart himself'—was put in charge of defence against China in the North-East Frontier Agency (NEFA). Experienced voices on China strategy, like Gen. Thimayya, Lt Gen. S.P.P. Thorat, Lt Gen. Daulet Singh, Lt Gen. Umrao Singh and Brig. (later lieutenant general) Premindra Bhagat, were paid a deaf ear.

In his post-retirement autobiography, *From Reveille to Retreat*, Lt Gen. S.P.P. Thorat wrote:

> When I met Mr. Menon in Delhi [in 1959, when Lt Gen. Thorat was GOC-in-C Eastern Command], I opened the subject [of defence against China] with him. In his usual sarcastic style he said that there would be no war between India and China, and in the most unlikely event of there being one, he was quite capable of fighting it himself on the diplomatic level.[†] (Maj. Gen. Palit also writes about this in *War in High Himalaya: The Indian Army in Crisis, 1962.*)[‡]

---

[*] http://www.indiandefencereview.com/spotlights/the-panchsheel-agreement/2/

[†] New Delhi, Allied Publishers, 1986.

[‡] New Delhi, Lancer International, 1991, p. 55.

Besides other bungling, Menon punished Lt Col (later lieutenant general and army commander) Eric Vas from Saligao, Goa, for exposing the pathetic state of affairs on the China border via the famous 'chapati letter' that rocked Parliament in late 1961.

Shortages were galore at the China border—boots, warm clothing, arms and ammunition—and the future army commander decided to register his protest in an offbeat way. Commanding 1/9 Gorkha Rifles, the first Indian Army unit deployed on the China border at NEFA—a task until then performed by the para-military Assam Rifles, a force under the Ministry of External Affairs that was neither trained nor equipped for the role—the prolific future author of hundreds of authoritative articles and a string of books, addressed a letter to his superiors written on a dry chapati when even writing paper was exhausted without replenishment.[*]

Another Goan, Maj. (later lieutenant general and army commander) Walter Anthony Gustavo Pinto from Santa Cruz/Kalapur, Goa ordered on a long-range patrol to the McMahon Line along the Subansiri River valley in 1951, exposed the woeful lack of cartographic data on India's border with China.[5] Despite his recorded observations, the government took no steps to remedy the lacunae.[†] The devastating China attack starting on 20 October 1962 nailed Nehru's foolhardiness, Menon's culpability and Kaul's ineptitude.[6] All of Krishna Menon's victims were reinstated after his resignation was accepted on 31 October 1962.

Gen. Manekshaw went on to become one of India's most popular army chiefs. Air Chief Marshal P.C. Lal was the resolute IAF chief during the Bangladesh War. Lt Gen. Eric Vas almost became the first Goan-origin chief of the Indian Army in 1981.

---

[*] Col Anil Athale in 'Unsung Heroes VII: The Thinking General: The Chapati Truth' and *A Tribute to Lt Gen Eric Vas, 15 May 1923–18 Aug. 2009*, https://www.sify.com/news/unsung-heroes-vii-the-thinking-general-imagegallery-0-national-jj4uwKbjihbsi.html

[†] Walter Anthony Gustavo Pinto, *Bash on Regardless: A Record of a Life in War and Peace,* Repro India Ltd, Navi Mumbai, 2011, pp. 31–35.

(That honour would go to Gen. Sunith F. Rodrigues, who became the first Goan COAS in 1990.)

A foreign diplomat titled V.K. Menon with a sobriquet twisted from the snake 'boa constrictor', *Goa Constrictor*.[*] The highly respected British academic, Hugh Tinker, when reviewing the UK-based Indian journalist T.J.S. George's biography of Menon, said Menon was

... commonly regarded as a near relation to Lucifer.[†]

Jairam Ramesh observed:

He [Krishna Menon] has been referred to at various times as Rasputin, Mephistopheles, Lucifer, Svengali, Evil Genius, The World's Most Hated Diplomat, Sombre Porcupine, The Formula Man and other colourful images.[‡]

The world had been rather unkind to the unfortunate man whose sanity was seriously doubted in diplomatic channels, particularly of the USA and the UK. Jairam Ramesh quotes from the correspondence between two British diplomats:

... the UK high commissioner in India, Paul Gore-Booth, wrote to Seville Garner of the Commonwealth Relations Office in London on what he called 'the case of Krishna Menon'. Gore-Booth sent Garner a note prepared by one of his colleagues, John Banks:

From late 1960, however, Menon's psychological difficulties, in which there was now a physical element as well, began to intervene in his work. He asked, I was told, repeatedly that the Prime Minister should relieve him of his office ...

---

[*] Emil Lengyel, *Krishna Menon*, Walker, New York, 1962, p. 207.

[†] Ramesh, *A Chequered Brilliance*, p. 625.

[‡] Ibid., p. xiii.

> In October 1960 Mrs. [Indira] Gandhi consulted a
> psychiatrist in London about Krishna Menon's case showing
> him the reports of Menon's doctors. The psychiatrist is said to
> have commented that a man in his condition should not on any
> account be holding any position of great responsibility ...*

It appears that Krishna Menon suffered from some mental disorder
from 1952. In the very opening chapter of his book, Jairam Ramesh
says that, among his seven siblings, Menon was 'extremely close'
to an elder sister, Janaki Amma, his constant emotional support.†
Menon, a rationalist, had a curious belief in astrology. Under
'extreme depression' Menon apparently wrote to Janaki Amma to
consult an astrologer with his horoscope. On 16 June 1952, Janaki
wrote back:

> I got a good astrologer from Feroke [part of Calicut]. He says
> that during this period [15-4-52 to 6-7-52] you will be mentally
> agitated and although there is no danger of your being unbalanced
> mentally or even getting irritated outwardly still there is no
> chance of your being highly mentally worried.‡

It is known that Menon was dependent on protracted mind
medication. But whether this had any influence on India's decision
to use force in Goa is a matter of conjecture.

What we know for sure is that during the 1–6 September
1961 Belgrade Conference (the first summit of the Non-Aligned
Movement championed by Nehru, Josip Broz Tito of Yugoslavia
and Gamal Abdel Nasser of Egypt), Nehru, the most preeminent
persona attending, came under pressure from the twenty-four
member nations, particularly the newly created African states, to use

---

* Ibid., pp. 601–02.

† Ibid., p. 8.

‡ Ibid., p. 9.

force in Goa, soon. According to Goan freedom fighter Dr Pundalik Gaitonde, Nehru

    ... was the target of violent and angry criticism.[*]

Urging Nehru not to lose his 'anti-colonial fire', African leaders told him that whatever was happening in Goa affected the revolution in Portuguese Africa. They told Nehru

    ... to act and not just talk.[†]

On 7 October 1961, army HQ wrote 'Top Secret' letter No. 46715/GS/MO to Lt Gen. J.N. Chaudhuri, GOC-in-C Southern Command, instructing him to take a scrutiny of the military situation in Goa with the aim to occupy it militarily. In other words, to prepare a war plan.

Lt Gen. Chaudhuri had led the 'police action' in Hyderabad when he was a major general. Learning of the Nizam's attempts to 'buy' Goa from the Portuguese to have a seaport of his own and join Pakistan as the third wing of that country, India's Deputy Prime Minister and Home Minister Vallabhbhai Patel launched Operation Polo on 13 September 1948. A division (35,000 troops) under Gen. Chaudhuri was sent in with bloodied results that left 40,000 dead, mostly civilians. On the morning of 17 September, Gen. Chaudhuri shook hands, lit cigarettes and quietly talked with Maj. Gen. Syed Ahmed El Edroos, the Arab commander-in-chief of the Hyderabad Army, and Hyderabad became a part of India.[‡]

---

[*] P.D. Gaitonde, *The Liberation of Goa: A Participant's View of History*, Rajhauns Sankalpana Goa (first published in 1987 by C. Hurst & Co. Ltd., London), 2016, p. 140.

[†] Ibid., 2016, p. 162.

[‡] See: https://twitter.com/indiahistorypic/status/1571180529613164544?lang=en;https://military-history.fandom.com/wiki/Syed_Ahmed_El_Edroos; https://en.bharatpedia.org/wiki/Syed_Ahmed_El_Edroos

The Die Is Cast: The New Delhi Seminar

Between 20–23 October 1961, India hosted a seminar on colonialism at the Constitution Club in New Delhi. The seminar was seen as an exercise by India to mobilize world opinion for armed action in Goa.

The idea of the seminar was put forth to Nehru by Dr P.D. Gaitonde.[*] In Goa in 1948, Dr Gaitonde was surgeon-director of the Hospital (Asilo) dos Milagres in Mapusa. He was famous for his excellent skills in surgery. On 15 February 1954, at a farewell dinner to Portuguese judge Semedo, the Goan advocate Santa Rita Colaço, a great admirer of Salazar and of the Portuguese empire, in his speech said that Goa was Portuguese. Dr Gaitonde loudly interrupted, 'Protesto!' (I protest!). That single word got him behind bars two days later. He was deported to Portugal aboard the *Índia* and jailed for a year. He became a high-profile freedom fighter and 17 February was since observed as 'Gaitonde Day'. (Incidentally, Dr Gaitonde was close friends with judge Semedo and the Goa high court justice Gonçalves Pereira, also Portuguese, who, together with their families, vacationed in Kashmir in the early 1950s and together called on Sheikh Abdullah, then chief minister of Jammu and Kashmir, at his official residence.)

Dr Gaitonde's arrest and exile hardened Nehru's attitude towards Portugal. India lodged a formal protest with Portugal's legation in New Delhi.[†] Following his release in 1955, Dr Gaitonde settled in New Delhi and founded the cancer department at Irwin Hospital, where he worked as senior surgeon. Post-1961, he was one of the two Goans—the other being Dr António Colaço of Margao—nominated to the Lok Sabha in August 1962.

---

[*] Gaitonde, 2016, pp.159, 163.

[†] Full text of the Government of India protest is provided by Dr P.D. Gaitonde himself, in his book *The Liberation of Goa: A Participant's View of History,* Rajhauns Sankalpana (first published in 1987 by C. Hurst & Co. Ltd, London), 2016, pp. 79–80.

Prominent international champions of freedom, leaders of subjugated Portuguese colonies (Angola, Mozambique, Portuguese Guinea, Cabo Verde, São Tomé and Principe, Macao, Timor and Goa, Daman and Diu), and representatives of other nations like Burma, Ceylon, Congo, Ethiopia, Indonesia, Iraq, Morocco, Nigeria, Sudan, UAE and Yugoslavia were invited to the four-day seminar in New Delhi. Its official sponsor was the Indian Council for Africa, which had catalogued Portuguese repression in Africa.

At the inaugural of the seminar on 20 October 1961, Prime Minister Jawaharlal Nehru declared that at no time had India renounced recourse to a military solution against the Portuguese in Goa. He did not disclose that India had decided on a military solution almost two months before (late August).

The invitee British Labour leader, Anthony Wedgewood Benn, urged that a resolution be adopted declaring Portuguese colonialism a threat to peace and calling upon Portugal to begin negotiations for self-determination within a specified time. Benn said Goa was the key to freedom of all territories under the subjugation of Portugal.

Dr Gaitonde called for 'direct action against the Portuguese occupation in Goa' and cited the example of São João Batista de Ajudá in Dahomey (now Benin).* Dr Gaitonde urged African and Asian countries to sever diplomatic and trade ties with Portugal.

Angolan leader J. Ferreira Viana said India's failure to liberate Goa had retarded liberations all across the world. What had begun as a condemnation of Portuguese colonialism turned into an attack on India's policy on Goa.

The Africans told Nehru that they did not understand metaphysics—Nehru's pet branch of philosophy—or pious resolutions. They were struggling bloodily with the Portuguese. They wanted India to evict the Portuguese from Goa. Once Goa fell, Portuguese colonialism in Africa would collapse, they told Nehru.

---

* Gaitonde, *The Liberation of Goa: A Participant's View of History*, p. 164.

Kenneth Kaunda (chair, Northern Rhodesia), Mgilo Sivai (Tanganyika), Mbiyu Koinange (Pan-African Freedom Movement), Abdel Karim-el-Khatib (Morocco), Thomas Khanja (Congo), Augustine Sinando (Southern Rhodesia), J. Savimbi (Angola), Alfredo Pereira (Portuguese Guinea), Marcelino dos Santos and Adelino Gwanbe (Mozambique), Manuel Sertório (Portuguese Opposition in exile), Berta de Menezes Bragança and Adv. João Cabral (Goa) in one voice urged Nehru to use force in Goa.

At the end of the four-day seminar, on 23 October, Nehru declared at a mammoth public meeting at Chowpatty beach in Bombay:

> We have to think afresh now because of the happenings in Goa, particularly in the last few months, cases of torture have come to our notice and the terror that is spread there by the Portuguese. When I say afresh, I mean that we have been forced into thinking afresh by the Portuguese to adopt other means to solve this problem. When and how we do it cannot be forecast now. But I have no doubt that we will do it, that Goa will soon be free.[*]

The die was cast.

On 24 October 1961, while the plan for the invasion was being prepared, the prime minister, who was in Bombay en route to the USA, sent for the GOC-in-C Southern Command, Lieutenant General J.N. Chaudhuri, and asked him for the time it would take to occupy Goa. General Chaudhuri gave a figure of three days in the event of Portuguese resistance and a considerably shorter period in the event of no resistance or of qualified resistance.

> On 28 October 1961, while both were returning to Poona after the Armoured Corps Conference in Ahmednagar, Lieutenant General B.M. Kaul, the Chief of General Staff and [Lieutenant] General Chaudhuri discussed the appreciation and outline plan. It was tentatively agreed that HQ 17 Infantry Division with

---

[*] Khera, *Operation Vijay*, 1974, p. 39.

one or two brigades and 50 (Independent) Parachute Brigade
would be made available for the operations against Goa. These
formations would come from Western and Eastern Commands.
For operations against Daman and Diu, troops from within
Southern Command would be used.[*]

Acting on the 7 October 1961 instructions of army HQ, Lt Gen.
Chaudhuri submitted his 'Appreciation of Situation' (invasion plan)
to army HQ on 10 November 1961. Its full text is reproduced
by Shrikant Y. Ramani in his book *Operation Vijay: The Ultimate
Solution*.[†]

The previous day, 9 November 1961, in a speech over national
radio, Salazar reaffirmed his policy of maintaining the multicontinental unity of the Portuguese nation, confirming, in his
words, that,

> ... the rearguard is to be defended, just like the front in Africa
> or India.[‡]

Excuse to Attack

India had decided to use force to evict the Portuguese from Goa,
Daman and Diu towards end of August 1961. In early October
1961, the Indian Army's Southern Command began preparing a
plan for the invasion. By 10 November 1961, the plan was ready.
Only niceties remained for the Government of India to order the
armed forces to mobilize. A suitable excuse to attack had to be either
found or fabricated—and India's defence minister was a resourceful

---

[*] V.K. Singh, *History of the Corps of Signals*, vol. 3, Chapter 3 ('The
Liberation of Goa', 1961), Corps of Signals, Army Headquarters, New
Delhi.

[†] Shrikant Y. Ramani, *Operation Vijay: The Ultimate Solution*, Broadway
Book Centre, Goa, 2008, pp. 55–83 and P.N. Khera, 1974, Appendix
I, pp. 145–65.

[‡] Lopes, 2017, p. 344.

wizard at the latter. The 15 August 1955 slaughter of satyagrahis had spent squandered.

On one side of the line of contention was a dictator from a small and impoverished nation on the western extremity of Europe who believed, until about this time, that Nehru would never invade Goa. On the other was the prime minister of the world's second largest democracy—once the world's most prosperous but now an impoverished nation that produced the concept of *ahimsa* or non-violence towards all living creatures; a man who saw himself as a world pacifist, but was willing, upon the urging of his defence minister, to throw his staunch beliefs overboard for the expediency of domestic general elections. (Incidentally, Nehru and Salazar were born in the same year: 1889.)

When Portugal contended that Nehru had renounced the use of force to end Portuguese rule in Goa at the United Nations Trusteeship Committee meet in New York on 6 November 1961, India's defence minister Krishna Menon declared:

> My country has at no time abjured the use of force in international affairs ... India will not hesitate to use force if provoked.[*]

A 'provocation'—the key word—had to be found, or, as said, fabricated.

Midday 17 November 1961, the Bombay Steam Navigation Company's 1949 Belfast-built Indian passenger ship SS *Sabarmati*, navigating from north to south, was headed to take a halt at Karwar en route to Cochin, just south of the defence minister's hometown.

Portuguese corporal Fernando Carvalho Ferreira fired at the ship from atop the Anjediva Island—a fact that was not reported to the superiors in Goa. There were denials initially, and then, after a local inquiry, Lisbon admitted to the incident, but said the ship had sailed too close to Anjediva in Portuguese–Goan territorial waters

---

[*] Andrew Jon Rotter, *Comrades at Odds: The United States and India, 1947–1964,* Cornell University Press, 2000, p. 185.

and failed to respond to internationally accepted SOP (standard operating procedure) for identification of ships. The corporal said he only fired a warning shot at the civilian vessel, after which she sped off. Considering the angle of the trajectory of the warning shot, the local inquiry concluded that it could have not hit the ship.

On the eve of 25 November,[*] between 10 p.m. and 2 a.m., a group of fishermen from Karwar in about twenty boats made repeated forays towards Anjediva from various directions. Portuguese defenders, placed on alert for possible enemy attempts to disembark an assault party in the wake of the SS *Sabarmati* episode, fired three shots towards the boats. Atmaram Kochrekar, an alleged smuggler, died the following day from gunshot injuries. The Portuguese claimed Kochrekar was found smuggling and had been shot dead by Indian police.

The relatively minor incidents, suspectedly orchestrated, used as the *causa proxima* or closest cause for a *casus belli* or event that justifies war would cast a taint on the pristinely legitimate anti-colonial cause championed by Nehru on the world stage.

A fantastic and at times self-contradictory press campaign, choreographed by the Indian defence minister, followed. Krishna Menon proclaimed that Portugal was provoking India to attack Goa. Between 4 and 11 December 1961, India reported five incidents of Portuguese patrols crossing into Indian territory, firing and even searching a house in India.

India also alleged that Goans from the northern border village of Tiracol were forcibly evicted from their homes by Portuguese troops who wanted to occupy their houses. When the affected Goans crossed into the neighbouring village in India and were welcomed by the villagers there, Portuguese troops crossed the international border and fired from machine guns and detonated bombs to frighten the villagers. The intruders retreated only when Indian police arrived and fired back, wounding a Portuguese soldier.

---

[*] Goa was taken by the Portuguese on 25 November 1510.

Wrote the renowned Indian editor-author, D.R. Mankekar, in the *Goa Action*:

> One explanation as to why the Government [of India] would sponsor such a campaign of obvious pretense, places the blame on the Defence Minister who directed it ...[*]

It was plainly implausible that a minuscule Portuguese force (actually 3300 mainly raw recruits, soldiers only in name and uniform, and hopelessly ill-equipped) would deliberately provoke a gigantic and better-armed neighbour. Twenty-five lakh Indian soldiers, fighting in practically every theatre of World War II, had demonstrated that they were among the best and bravest in the world.

The tell-tale signature of Defence Minister Krishna Menon's creative deviousness was writ large over the SS *Sabarmati* and Karwar fishermen episodes, and the press campaign unleashed from New Delhi. Brig. (later major general) Palit, director military operations at army HQ at the time, later wrote,

> I am not certain how much ... reported about Goa was true intelligence and how much tendentious fabrication. It is even possible that the whole scheme was cooked up between Krishna Menon, Bijji Kaul and the Intelligence Bureau to make out a feasible *casus belli*.[†]

India deployed two naval vessels—destroyer INS *Rajput* and anti-submarine corvette INS *Kirpan*—at Karwar from 28 November 'to protect fishermen'. The following day, the Government of India issued definitive instructions to the Armed Forces. India described the *Sabarmati* and Karwar fishermen incidents as 'tension exploded', and used them to precipitate military action. A warning order was sent to the Indian Armed Forces, stating,

---

[*] Bombay, Popular Book Depot, 1962, p. 22.

[†] Major General D.K. Palit, VrC, *Musings and Memories, Vol. II,* Palit & Palit in association with Lancer Publishers & Distributors, New Delhi, 2004, p. 420.

As a result of Portuguese hostile action against our nationals, the Government proposes taking certain steps in the area of Angediv Island.*

On the same day (28 November), Prime Minister Nehru received a report from R.B. Kakodkar. The latter had just completed a 'study tour' of Goa and found that the time was ripe for use of force in Goa. Nehru replied to Kakodkar on the same day and sent both Kakodkar's report and his own reply to Defence Minister Menon.

Krishna Menon held a meeting with the three service chiefs on 29 November. He wanted immediate mobilization and concentration of forces for action in Goa. The service top brass said it needed fourteen days to do that, a proposal that was accepted by the defence minister.†

On 30 November, the Indian Navy launched Operation Chutney, putting frigates INS *Betwa* and INS *Beas* on linear patrol seven nautical miles (13 km) off Goa from 1 December to report shipping and air movements in and out of Goa and retaliate with necessary force if engaged by the enemy. Other naval warships were placed on operational standby alert.

Plans Firm Up

The order sent out on 29 November put HQ Southern Command under Lt Gen. J.N. Chaudhuri in charge of the action called 'Operation Vijay'.

India's 17 Infantry Division would be the Special Task Force for Operation Vijay. Its GOC, Maj. Gen. M.M. Khanna, MVC, was due to proceed for a course at the UK's Royal College of Defence Studies. Defence Minister Krishna Menon quickly approved Brig. K.P. ('Unni') Candeth, who was at the Directorate of Artillery at army HQ, to be promoted to major general and appointed GOC 17

---

* Khera, 1974, p. 112.
† Ramesh, Penguin Viking, 2019, p. 548.

Infantry Division. And thereby hangs a story ... Jairam Ramesh writes
in his biography of V.K. Krishna Menon:

> After completing school in Calicut, Krishna Menon came to Madras
> in mid-1915 to study at the famed Presidency College. He was
> admitted thanks to his father's friend M.A. Candeth, who was then a
> professor of history at the college. Candeth had been a contemporary
> of Nehru at Cambridge. Forty-six years later, in December 1961,
> one of Candeth's sons would lead the Indian Army in liberating
> Goa from the Portuguese rule, an operation masterminded by the
> then defence minister of India—Krishna Menon.[*]

The Task Force would be deployed less a brigade (with one
operational brigade and one reserve brigade), but another brigade
would fill in. On the same day, Brig. D.K. Palit left a message for
Brig. Sagat Singh, commander 50 Independent Parachute Brigade
at Agra, to rush to Delhi.

> Sagat commandeered a Dakota of the Paratroopers' Training
> School, and was in Palit's office in less than an hour.[†]

It was here that Brig. Sagat Singh learnt about the operation for the
liberation of Goa. There was a conference in the office of the chief
of general staff, General Kaul, where the plans were finalized. The
Warning Order for the operation was issued as a flash signal under
the signature of Lt Gen. B.M. Kaul, chief of general staff, at 1530
hours on 29 November in the form of a 'Personal For' signal from
the chief of army staff to the army commanders, with copies being
endorsed to Maj. Gen. M.M. Khanna and Brig. Sagat Singh.

Portugal was aware of India's naval deployment as well as
plans for ground attack. Portuguese brigadier António Leitão and
the Goa Governor-general Maj. Gen. Manuel António Vassalo e

---

[*] Ibid., p. 18.
[†] *History of the Corps of Signals*, vol. 3, Chapter 3.

Silva himself pleaded with Lisbon for reinforcements: armaments, munitions, transporters and communication equipment. The little that was there was old and obsolete.

To Salazar, there was no war, hence no need of reinforcements.

The Portuguese military command in Goa could only improvise the Plano Sentinela (sentry plan). The plan was to first delay entry of the enemy at the borders, with the use of guerrilla tactics if necessary. When aggression could no longer be resisted at the borders, the bridges were to be blown up and the enemy held back on the opposite bank of the rivers. The essence of the plan was to delay enemy advance. Finally, when it was no longer possible to resist, defenders were to resort to a gradual fallback to the Mormugao peninsula, the last redoubt, and once there, defend it at all costs—until UN intervention arrived.

Portuguese cavalry captain (later general) Carlos de Azeredo, posted in Goa at the time, said the sentry plan

> was totally unrealistic and unachievable ... [for the plan to work], portable communication equipment was necessary. There was none available.[*]

Alluding to the 17 November event at Anjediva Island, Nehru said on 1 December:

> We cannot tolerate such acts. We will take the necessary steps at the right time.[†]

Krishna Menon assured a Goan delegation from Bombay that

> ... force would be used if necessary to liberate Goa at the right time.[‡]

---

[*] *Passagem para a Índia*, *O Expresso*, 8 December 2001.

[†] Khera, 1974, p. 44.

[‡] Ibid., p. 44.

As we now know, India had already decided to use force in August 1961 and the order for armed mobilization was issued on 29 November the same year.

On the same day (1 December), India approved the ground assault plan. It would be a two-pronged attack. 17 Infantry Division less a brigade under GOC Maj. Gen. K.P. Candeth would be the main Task Force to enter Goa from the east and capture Panjim, Vasco da Gama, Margao and other key objectives. (Maj. Gen. Candeth would be issued with detailed operational instructions—Instruction No. 2—by the GOC-in-C Southern Command Lt Gen. J.N. Chaudhuri on 7 December 1961. The same has been reproduced by P.N. Khera in his book *Operation Vijay.*[*])

A subsidiary thrust from the north was assigned to the 50 Independent Parachute Brigade under Brig. Sagat Singh, in order to divide Portuguese forces.

It was the first time that all three arms of India's defence services—land, water and air—would be used in an operation.

On 2 December, troops began to move to the concentration area (pre-commencement of war position), Belgaum. All were in place by 9 December. The D-Day was to be 14 December.

Meanwhile, on 3 December, the BBC reported Portugal saying that India planned an invasion of Goa. Police oppression mounted in Goa. Foreign media correspondents converged on Goa. Freedom fighter Vinayak Kaissare, a well-known advocate from Panjim, was arrested for expressing nationalistic sentiments to the mediamen. Freedom fighter and future labour leader George Vaz cabled Nehru on the searches, arrests and torture of freedom fighters in Goa. Freedom fighter Thomas Dias was arrested and severely tortured— this was reported in the 4 December edition of *Hindustan Times*. They were among the forty Goans and ten Portuguese soldiers arrested, the latter for objecting to the suicidal resistance plan.[†] On 5

---

[*]   Ibid., Appendix II, pp. 166–69.

[†]   Ibid., pp. 54–55.

December, *Hindustan Times* front-paged the headline, 'Indian Army Build-up on Goa Border—No Action is Planned'.

Red China and Justifying an Attack

On 6 December, Portugal asked Britain to intervene in the situation. As mentioned earlier, Britain was aware of Portugal's dubious role in assisting the Axis powers and denying the same to the Allied powers (hiding behind a veil of neutrality) during World War II. Britain was also caught between a Commonwealth partner (India) and an ages-old ally she was pledged to help (Portugal). Britain made some diplomatic noises, played neutral and effectively did nothing.

When in India, the British were wary of China next only to Tsarist Russia. Britain suspected that Russia might make a dash across her interests in the subcontinent for the warm waters of the Indian Ocean. China came second as a potential enemy. Britain ensured that Tibet remained independent, as a buffer between British India and China.

The world's most populous country, China, was a monarchy and, after a revolution in 1912, became republican. Following another revolution in 1949, China turned communist and swallowed Tibet. China began asking India to open border negotiations, refusing to recognize the borders delineated by 'British imperialists' with monarchical China that were tacitly accepted by republican China. Beset by his own problems, Nehru paid no heed to the requests.

From 1952 to 1957, China built a road from Sinkiang (now Xinjiang) to Lhasa in Tibet. A length of 160 km of this road was in Indian land at Aksai Chin. India protested that China took no 'permission' to build the road within India and said the Chinese workers who entered India to construct the road and those now using it did not apply for Indian visas.

Chairman Mao Tse-tung (now Mao Zedong) and Premier Chou En-lai (now Zhou Enlai) were astute and practical men. China saw some Indian political leaders as *éminences grises* and some senior

Indian army officers as *chair-borne soldiers,* and decided to teach them 'a lesson'. Under a deceptive sheen of bonhomie (*Hindi-Chini bhai-bhai*), China secretly began preparations from 1959 to attack India.

Now, in 1961, Portugal turned to China. An article in the magazine *Visão História* quoted the then Portuguese minister for overseas, Adriano Moreira, saying that Portugal offered Goa's Dabolim airport and Mormugao seaport to China in the hope of deterring India's plans of aggression.* The go-between was Ho Yin, father of latter-day Macao president, Edmund Ho. The Chinese premier Chou En-lai said that the proposal interested him, but that there was a lot of time, since Nehru would not attack Goa and whistle his world image as a pacifist down the river.

Chou En-lai was wrong. India invaded Goa within eight days. (China would invade India in ten months, but that is another story. Western media said that China was emboldened to attack India by India's use of force in Goa.)

On 7 December, three days before Portugal approached China, Nehru told Parliament that, after fourteen years of experience, he was confident that peaceful negotiations would not bring results as far as Portugal was concerned. On the same day, Krishna Menon told the Lok Sabha:

> Reports have been pouring in for the last two weeks of intensified firing activity, oppression and terrorism in Goa, of heavy reinforcements of Portuguese armed forces ...There was a report of 2,500 troops having been deployed along the Goa border ... also a report of a fleet of two Portuguese frigates standing guard ... 3,000 more troops from African and other places have also arrived ... It was also reported that dawn-to-dusk curfew had been imposed ... The Portuguese armed forces are thus poised near the border at various points to overawe and intimidate both the residents of Goa and those living in the border villages on the Indian side. Hit-and-run raids across the border already seem to

---

* Vol. 14, 2011, pp. 36–37.

have started. A raid in a village near Sawantwadi was reported
two days ago.*

Save the continuing police oppression within Goa, all were lies.
Nothing of the kind mentioned by Menon was actually happening
on the ground: no troop reinforcements, no frigates and no
curfew. Salazar had been told, as early as 1954, that it was militarily
impossible to defend Goa. Defence Minister Gen. Júlio Botelho
Moniz told Salazar that a sustained campaign against decolonization
would create for the army

... a suicide mission in which we could not succeed.†

Later in 1960, as seen, Portugal's under secretary of war, Lt Col
(later general) Francisco Costa Gomes, who visited Goa to assess
military needs, informed Salazar that even Portugal's entire army
would not be able to resist, 'for more than five hours', an invasion
by experienced Indian troops.

Following The Hague's verdict of 12 April 1960 in the Dadra
and Nagar Haveli 'Rights of Passage' case, Salazar, like Chou En-lai,
believed that India would not attack Goa. Salazar reduced troops in
Goa (from 12,000 in 1955 to 3300 in 1960) three times from 1958.

The last reduction of troops in 1960 followed the visit and
recommendations of Lt Col Gomes and was done on the basis
that Goa was militarily indefensible. It left 3300 ill-trained troops
in Goa. They were deployed in three more or less battalion-sized
formations, each head quartered at Old Goa (*Agrupamento D. João de
Castro*), Mormugao (*Agrupamento Vasco da Gama*) and Aquem Baixo
near Margao (*Agrupamento Afonso de Albuquerque*).

The trained and experienced troops were shifted to Angola and
Timor. What remained in Goa was a ragtag band of men, soldiers

---

* Record of parliament debates.

† Porch Douglas, *The Portuguese Armed Forces and the Revolution*, Routledge,
  Oxfordshire, 1977.

only in name and uniform. Squadron Leader (later air marshal) S. Raghavendran, staff officer to the AOC-in-C Air Vice Marshal Erlic Pinto during Operation Vijay, commented in a *Bharat-Rakshak* article,

> I have never seen such a set of troops looking so miserable in my life. Short, not particularly well built and certainly very unsoldierlike.*

Worse, those remaining in Goa were armed pathetically. There was no artillery, no armour and no air defence.

Of the four warships in Goa, three frigates—NRP *Bartolomeu Dias,* NRP *Gonçalves Zarco* and NRP *João de Lisboa*—had been shifted out, but Indian intelligence reported there were four warships and three 'S' Class submarines in Goa. Only the ageing destroyer NRP *Afonso de Albuquerque* remained in Goa. There were three small patrol vessels, each armed with a 20-mm Oerlikon gun: *Sírius* in Goa, *Antares* in Daman and *Vega* in Diu (while the *Sírius* was scuttled undercontroversial circumstances by its Portuguese commander in Goa, the *Vega* was sunk in action in Diu). There were no other men-of-war, surface or underwater.

The only other surface vessels in Goa were merchant ships, Japanese carriers coming for mineral ore, motor launches, ferryboats, some sailboats and plenty of canoes.

The governor declared Emergency on 14 December 1961, only after Indian troops surrounded Goa.

That such a tiny, inexperienced and badly equipped Portuguese force could even think of launching raids across the border or threaten to bomb Indian cities—as also reported by Indian newspapers, on cue from Krishna Menon—was fanciful, to say the least. Later on, at the end of the invasion, the special correspondent of *The Times* would state in a despatch from Panjim:

---

* *Eye Witness to the Liberation of Goa,* https://www.bharat-rakshak.com/ IAF/history/1961goa/raghavendran/

The number of actual Portuguese soldiers captured belies the
Indian propaganda which before the invasion spoke of 'massive
reinforcement' of the garrison. Much else of the propaganda
which preceded the assault can now be seen to have been baseless.*

An article in the *Guardian* stated:

Portugal's 12,000 troops have shrunk to a quarter of that number.
Negro troops from Mozambique have vanished. A satyagrahi
tortured to death last month has turned up alive and well ... The
pity is that these trivialities masked and discredited India's real
case ...†

* 20 December 1961.
† 27 December 1961.

5

MOBILIZING THE WAR MACHINE

Troops Begin Moving In

Indian troop mobilization began from 2 December 1961. The 50 Independent Parachute Brigade was shifted from Agra, Hyderabad and Madras to Belgaum. The 63 and 48 Infantry Brigades of 17 Infantry Division were moved from Ambala to Belgaum. (50 Para and 63 Infantry were the two operational brigades, while 48 Infantry was the reserve brigade. The third brigade of 17 Division, 64 Infantry, was left behind at Kasauli.)[*7]

The two brigades of 17 Infantry Division entrained from six railway stations in or near Ambala. 50 Para Brigade's 1 Para Punjab Battalion entrained at Agra. 2 Para Maratha Battalion, which had earlier been moved to Begumpet in Hyderabad for exercises in an initially proposed airborne op (that was later dropped) was moved by rail from Hyderabad to Belgaum. Short of a battalion, 50 Para was allotted 2 Sikh Light Infantry, a regular infantry battalion on garrison duties in Madras that was moved by rail to Belgaum.

Rail traffic in northern, western and southern India was disrupted as more than 100 passenger trains were diverted to transport the personnel of the brigades. Each brigade had its own HQ, infantry, artillery, armour, engineers, signals, supply corps, ordnance, medical, liaison and provost. Besides passenger trains, scores of goods trains were requisitioned for military use to shift

---

[*] Major General V.K. Singh, *History of the Corps of Signals, Volume III,* which covers all military operations in India during the period 1947–72.

material from various points across India to Belgaum. According to the *New Statesman* of 15 December,

> Stranded passengers were more upset with the Indian Railways than with the alleged Portuguese atrocities in Goa.

Nehru complained that the very ones who wanted him to take military action in Goa were now incensed about the inconvenience. Diversion of goods trains for military purpose so affected life that steel mills in Ahmedabad shut down for the lack of coal.

Tactical HQ for Operation Vijay was set up at the MES Inspection Bungalow in Belgaum. All ground forces reached the concentration area, Belgaum, by 9 December. Supplies, ammunition, fuel and bridging equipment were moved from various locations by 12 December. The D-Day was, as mentioned earlier, 14 December. On 10 December, Nehru told Parliament:

> Continuance of Goa under Portuguese rule is an impossibility.[*]

The following day, he told the Rajya Sabha:

> India's patience is certainly exhausted.[†]

On that same day, Salazar formally invoked the Anglo–Portuguese alliance (the Treaty of Windsor of 14 October 1899), asking Britain to comply with her obligations and 'frustrate the imminent aggression against Goa'—an impossibility again. (Britain had told Portugal in 1954 that its aid could only be diplomatic and not military since India was a British Commonwealth nation. Moreover, at that point of time, Britain was busy dismantling her own colonies in East Africa—beginning with Tanganyika/Tanzania on 9 December

---

[*] Record of Parliament debates.

[†] Ibid.

1961.) Portugal, as seen, also contacted China on 10 December 1961. On 11 December, Nehru declared in the Rajya Sabha that,

> Our patience is certainly exhausted. We still hope that the Portuguese, either by themselves or by the advice of their friends ... will accept the natural culmination of all this, which is their withdrawal from Goa. The Government of India believe that it is never too late to take the right step and hope that, in accordance with the immutable principles of humanity and the irreversible processes of history, the Government of Portugal will leave their Indian colonies forthwith and remove their persistent irritants against international peace. The people of India are determined to ensure that their independence is complete and that there are no longer any vestiges of colonial rule on their territory.

That same day, land forces were ordered to advance from Belgaum to the assembly points near the Goa border, and HQ 17 Division issued operations order No. 1/61 dated 11 December 1961.[*] Portugal drew attention of the UNSC to India's build-up of troops, and border violations by Indian land and air forces. India replied that Portugal had reinforced her land and sea forces, and therefore India had to strengthen her border and coastal defence.

The Portuguese passenger ship *Índia,* otherwise on the Lisbon–Timor run with halts in Portuguese Africa and Goa, was hurriedly converted into an evacuee ship and sent specifically to evacuate the gold and other securities pawned by Goans with the Banco Nacional Ultramarino (national overseas bank) and other liquid assets of the bank such as foreign exchange. The ship arrived at Mormugao from Lisbon on 9 December. Governor-general Vassalo e Silva detained the ship at Mormugao to enable Portuguese civilians, especially women and children, to embark on the vessel. The ship finally set sail for Lisbon on 12 December. With a carrying capacity of 380 pax, the ship sailed with 650, some say with 700 (women and

---

[*]   Khera, 1974, pp. 173–81.

children alone numbered around 400). The vessel it seems was so packed, its passengers occupied even the toilets.

Governor-General Vassalo e Silva's decision to evacuate civilians was criticized by the Government of Lisbon because evacuation of the families,

... could indicate the fear of an invasion, with possible disturbance of public order ...

as noted by Portuguese cavalry (armour) officer João Aranha, who showed what he thought of that statement by saying:

No comments!*

Tactical HQ Southern Command at Belgaum began full operations from 13 December, the eve of D-day. COAS Gen. Pran Nath Thapar, GOC-in-C Southern Command Lt Gen. J.N. Chaudhuri, GOC 17 Infantry Division Maj. Gen. K.P. Candeth, staff officers and heads of arms and services converged at Belgaum.

They were joined by AOC-in-C of the then unified Air Ops Command, Air Vice Marshal Erlic Pinto (a Goan-origin officer from Porvorim) from Poona to make it a combined HQ of the Army and IAF at Belgaum, Chief Civic Administrator R.C.V.P. Noronha, a Goan-origin ICS Officer of the Madhya Pradesh Cadre, Special Adviser G.K. Handoo, a Kashmiri Pandit IPS Officer of the J&K Cadre who was the CRP chief, B.N. Mullik, director of the Intelligence Bureau and the Goa IGP-designate, N.R. Nagoo, IPS.

On 13 December, George Vaz, Divakar Kakodkar, António Furtado and Berta Menezes Bragança for the Goan People's Party addressed an Open Letter to the Goa governor from Belgaum. It recalled that the regime had, over the previous thirty-one years, deprived Goans of their fundamental freedoms and subjected

---

* João Aranha, *Enquanto se esperam as naus do reino ...*, 2008, p. 42 and footnote no. 28 on the same page.

protestors to long prison sentences and deportation, and for the past fourteen years ignored India's calls for peaceful negotiations. So for the last time,

> we ask you to choose between going as a friend or a foe. Whichever path you choose, quit you must and you shall—with all your bag and baggage: your army, your PIDE, your tortures, your arbitrariness, your rule by decrees, your mercenaries and even your Goan traitors and stooges if they will go with you. The hour has sounded. Quit India! Jai Hind!*

On 14 December, Prof. Aloysius Soares, Prof. Francisco Correia Afonso, Prof. L.N. Velingkar, J.N. Heredia, J.M. Pinto, L.J. de Souza and Nicolau Menezes for Goa Liberation Council wrote from Bombay that Goans recalled that the people of Portugal were also fighting for freedom and justice against the common enemy—Portuguese fascism. The liberation of 451 years of Portuguese domination will

> inflict the final defeat on Salazarism ... Regards the future, people of Goa would solidly defend the Portuguese people in their struggle against the cruel dictatorship of Salazar that has crushed and destroyed the best intellectual, moral, and political minds of Portugal in prisons and concentration camps. The struggle of Goan people was not against the Portuguese people but against colonialism and fascism. May our Victory be your Victory!†

For reasons that we will come to later, the D–Day of 14 December was twice postponed. On 15 December, the acting secretary general of the UN, U. Thant, wrote to both India and Portugal urging them to ensure that there was no threat to peace and to negotiate a peaceful settlement in accordance with the principles of the

---

* Lopes, 2017, p. 345.

† Ibid., pp. 345–46.

Charter of United Nations. Portugal replied that it had proposed neutral international observers to monitor the border situation, but that India did not accept the proposal. India blamed 'Portuguese aggressiveness along the Indian frontiers', which led to this serious situation. 'It is hardly possible to negotiate on the basis of the [UN] Charter with a Government which takes its stand on 16th-century concepts of colonial conquest by force,' said India.*

The same day, Gen. Pran Nath Thapar with Lt Gen. (later general and COAS) P.P. Kumaramangalam, Adjutant General (the man who, recognizing the potential of Brig. Sagat Singh, a non-paratrooper, had given him command of a Para Brigade), and Lt Gen. J.N. Chaudhuri visited the 50 Para Brigade at Sawantwadi. There, Brig. Sagat Singh presented his battle plan. The army commander thought the brigadier's time frames were 'too optimistic'. According to military historian Maj. Gen. V.K. Singh, Brig. Sagat Singh then gave his timings in writing, having kept a reserve of four hours. The party left after wishing the brigade good luck.†

Back at Tactical HQ in Belgaum, the army commander discussed his reservations about Brig. Sagat Singh's battle plan. However, Chief of Staff Maj. Gen. (later lieutenant general and corps commander) Patrick O. Dunn and Air Vice Marshal Erlic W. Pinto, who knew the brigadier well, were supportive of it, and Brig. Sagat Singh was reluctantly allowed to proceed with his plan.‡

The GOC-in-C Lt Gen. Chaudhuri was so apprehensive about the brigadier's timeline that he placed three bets on the eve of ops that Brig. Sagat Singh would not meet the deadlines—and lost all three bets and Rs 500 to Air Vice Marshal Pinto.§

Brig. Sagat Singh was so confident not only of his timings but also that he would be the first to enter Panjim that he promised his

---

* Record of UN debates.

† V.K. Singh, *History of the Corps of Signals*, vol. 3, Chapter 3.

‡ Ibid.

§ https://www.sify.com/news/remembering-lt-gen-sagat-singh-on-his-birth-centenary-news-columns-thprpwhjbhbdg.html friend Brig. Palit a drink at Hotel Mandovi—and Brig. Palit did fly down to Goa later to honour his end of the deal.[*]

That was the Indian Army mobilization—a comparatively huge force against a diminutive, ill-trained and ill-armed enemy.

Mobilization: Navy and Air Force

India assembled three naval task forces for Operation Vijay. The carrier group was led by the newly acquired aircraft carrier INS *Vikrant,* bearing twenty-one Sea Hawk combat and Alizé anti-submarine aircraft. The carrier group had the Indian Navy's flagship, cruiser INS *Delhi* (later joined action in Diu), destroyer INS *Rajput* and three frigates, INS *Kirpan,* INS *Khukri* and INS *Kuthar,* with anti-submarine, torpedo and anti-aircraft capabilities.[†] Patrolling some 80 km seaward off Goa, the carrier group was deployed to fend off possible external intervention (by NATO and/or Pakistan).

Pakistan seemed intent to fish in troubled waters. There were frequent exchanges between Pakistan and Portugal in the mid-1950s when an air agreement was concluded. Pakistan's baggage declaration forms referred to Goa as 'Portuguese Pakistan'. On 14 December 1961, a seven-man Pakistan military delegation arrived in Daman and a few days earlier the Pakistani naval ship, PNS *Zulfiquar* was sighted in the Arabian Sea in a south-easterly direction from Karachi.

The main surface action assault group comprised five warships, of which two, cruiser INS *Mysore* and frigate INS *Trishul,* headed for Anjediva. The remaining three frigates—INS *Betwa* (lead ship), INS *Beas* and INS *Cauvery* (since renamed *Kaveri*)—were billed to engage the three Portuguese frigates and three S-class submarines believed to be at Mormugao. Two frigates of the carrier group were held in reserve to assist this three-warship assault group.

---

[*] Randhir Sinh, *A Talent for War,* Vij Books India Pvt. Ltd, New Delhi, 2013, second reprint 2015, p. 54 and footnote 31.

[†] Details of major warships deployed (displacement, speed, main and secondary armaments, horsepower, etc.) are provided by Khera, 1974, at Appendix XIX, p. 214.

However, other than an ageing destroyer, NRP *Afonso de Albuquerque,* there were no frigates or submarines and the two Indian reserve frigates were not used. There were claims, though, that the enemy destroyer disabled two Indian frigates of the assault group and that the two reserve frigates of the carrier group had taken their place. Lt Cdr John Eric Gomes of Margao, Goa (now in Defence Colony, Porvorim) was aboard the INS *Cauvery* during battle. He rubbishes the claim.[*]

(Lt Cdr Gomes was also part of the landing at Mormugao, and later led Christians in the Indian naval Task Force for the midnight Christmas Mass at St Andrew's Church, Vasco da Gama. After mass, the Goan Catholics invited the Indian naval party to their homes for cake and coffee.)

Cruiser INS *Mysore,* one of the two warships tasked to storm Anjediva Island, doubled up as the command ship for the surface action group at Anjediva and Mormugao.

The third task group was the minesweeping flotilla. It had INS *Karwar,* INS *Cannanore,* INS *Kakinada* and INS *Bimilipatan.* The support vessel was INS *Dharini.* The oil tanker of the fleet was INS *Shakti.*[8]

The HQ for naval operations of Operation Vijay was set up at the Maritime Operations Room, Bombay.

The Indian Air Force was led by Air Chief Marshal Aspy Merwan Engineer, DFC, one of the famous four flying Parsi brothers of the IAF. He was a bold and adventurous early Indian aviator—a peer of J.R.D. Tata, Subroto Mukerjee, Biju Patnaik and Karachi-based Edmundo Sequeira (the Goan civilian pilot with roots in Moira, after (Flight) Lt Shrikrishna Wellingkar—from Veling, Goa—the pioneer Goan aviator who was among the first five Indians to fly. Wellingkar flew for the Royal Air Force in World War I and died in France). Air Chief Marshal Engineer was a pilot at the age of seventeen in 1930 and became the second CAS (chief of air staff, 1960–64) upon

---

[*]   Interview with the author.

the sudden demise of Air Chief Marshal Subroto Mukerjee, OBE, on 8 November 1960.

Air operations in Goa, Daman and Diu were under the command of Air Vice Marshal Erlic Pinto, AOC-in-C of the then unified Operational Command of the IAF responsible for the conduct of air ops throughout India. Air Vice Marshal Pinto won a bet that he would drink a Portuguese beer at the main square in Panjim, but only partially. As P.N. Khera wrote,

> The Army Commander [Lt General J.N. Chaudhuri] and Air Vice Marshal Pinto had taken a bet the day before that they would drink a Portuguese beer in the main square of Panjim the day after the attack went in. Alas for them, when they got to the square, all shops were closed and no bottle of beer was available.[*]

From 2 December 1961, the IAF moved two squadrons each of the newly acquired Canberra jet bombers (16 Squadron and 35 Squadron) and Hawker Hunter fighter aircraft (37 Squadron and 17 Squadron less one Section), Vampire NF54 Night Fighters (101 Squadron), four Vampires (45 Squadron), four Mystére fighters, some Toofanis (Marcel-Dassault MD-450 Ouragan jet fighters), some B-24 Liberator bomber aircraft of 6 Squadron (still in service!), two IL-14 aircraft (of 1 Comm. Flight) besides some of the 1958-acquired Gnat fighters to the Poona Air Base. (Additionally, four aircraft of 1 Squadron, two of 12 Squadron, four Hunters of 20 Squadron and one or two Mi-4 helicopters of 109 Squadron were readied at Bombay.)

Four Hawker Hunter fighter aircraft (one Section of 17 Squadron), three Vampires (of 108 Squadron), two Harvard aircraft (of 122 Squadron), 3 AOP Flight, three Mi-4 helicopters (of 109 HU Squadron) and two Otter helicopters (of 2 Comm. Flight) were moved to the Air Station at Sambra, Belgaum, in addition to the de Havilland Vampires (45 Squadron) already based there.

---

[*] Khera, *Operation Vijay*, 1974, p. 85.

P.N. Khera in *Operation Vijay*, 1974, mentions that Packet, Dakota, Super Constellation-G and Antonov AN-12 transport aircraft were also used in the operations.*

It may be noted that the number of squadrons need not reflect the air power deployed.

An IAF fighter squadron (a squadron is the basic air force unit) comprised four sections of four aircraft each, or a total of sixteen aircraft. A bomber squadron had a total of twelve aircraft plus three in reserve, according to bomber pilot Group Captain Conrad Dalton, a Pune-based veteran (of Siolim, Goa, founder of the Canberra Bomber Association India). In practice, due to shortages, squadrons often did not have the full complement of aircraft.

2 Tactical Air Centre Western Air Command in Poona was assigned for the air ops. HQ for IAF air ops for Operation Vijay was later shifted from Poona to Belgaum.

Counting the 21 Sea Hawk strike interceptors and Alizé anti-submarine warfare squadrons of naval aviation borne by the aircraft carrier, it was indeed a very formidable mobilization of air power pitted against a literally non-existent enemy air force—although it was believed, wrongly again, that the Portuguese had transonic and supersonic fighters, transport aircraft fitted to carry bombs and an ultra-modern air defence in Goa.

Additional land, naval and air resources were deployed for Daman and Diu. Daman, being lightly defended by two companies and one patrol boat, was allotted a single battalion, the Jangi Paltan ('fighting battalion'), 1 Maratha Light Infantry under Lt Col S.J.S. Bhonsale, with light artillery and air support from Bombay.

Diu was defended by a similar force as Daman but had a well-built sea fort. One battalion+ (20 Rajput under Lt Col Bhupinder Singh and 'C' company of 4 Madras under Maj. P.W. Curtis) under Brig. Jaswant Singh (of the 112 Infantry Brigade) with artillery, cruiser INS *Delhi* (shifted from the carrier group in Goa) and air support

---

* Ibid., 1974, Appendix XXI, pp. 236–37.

from Jamnagar were allotted for Diu. Forces allotted to Daman and Diu would operate directly under HQ Southern Command, as would the decoy/deceptive feint into South Goa by 'B' Company of the 4 Rajput Battalion called the '20 Infantry Brigade' (more on that plucky force later).

Balance of Power

India mobilized a relatively large military force—land, sea and air—to physically oust a minuscule and ill-armed Portuguese military presence from Goa, Daman and Diu. Let us take a peek at just how imbalanced the comparative strength of the two sides actually was.

In terms of ground forces mobilized by India, the disproportion or numerical superiority was about 10:1 (30,000+ Indian troops versus the Portuguese garrison of 3000+), as estimated in most diplomatic reports. Portuguese troop numbers are dicey because police officers were drawn from the army; also used like a paramilitary were armed personnel of the customs and police; it is, however, generally accepted that the Portuguese had around 3300 troops, all ranks put together, in Goa, Daman and Diu. Some exaggerated reports put India's mobilization figure at 45,000 infantry. One patently false report declared the ratio was 30:1, stating that three 'divisions' were used, when in fact two brigades were used and the third was held in reserve (three brigades equal one division).

In terms of naval power, India deployed seventeen warships—a carrier group comprising one aircraft carrier with one cruiser, one destroyer and three anti-submarine, torpedo and anti-aircraft frigates as escort ships patrolling the Arabian Sea some 80 km off Goa, one cruiser and one frigate for the assault in Anjediva, three frigates for the assault at Mormugao, four minesweepers, one support vessel and one oil tanker for refuelling the fleet—against a lone and ageing Portuguese destroyer and a small patrol boat.

In terms of air power, there was no basis for comparison. India deployed a huge force of fighters, bombers, reconnaissance, air observation, communications, transports and helicopters in Poona,

Belgaum and Bombay, plus naval aviation's air combat Sea Hawk and recce/anti-submarine Alizé aircraft aboard the INS *Vikrant* against a non-existent enemy air force. Portugal had no military aircraft in Goa.

In terms of equipment, the disproportion varied from department to department. There was no artillery worth the name in Goa. Some ageing 6x105 mm Portuguese howitzers faced a towed field artillery regiment and a heavy mortar mountain battery with air observation support (although towed artillery was meaningless on Goa's then narrow roads).

The Portuguese in Goa had no modern infantry weapons, save a few mortars, LMGs and MMGs (light and medium automatics or machine guns).

Perhaps the only area where there was some semblance of parity was in infantry rifles: while Portuguese troops used German Mausers of 1904 vintage, the 5-shot British Lee-Enfield and the Austria-Hungarian Kropatschek rifles of pre-World War I vintage, Indian troops used Lee-Enfield rifles of 1917 vintage (instead of the recommended modern Belgian FN4 rifles, because India's defence minister Krishna Menon, as mentioned earlier, did not want NATO arms in India).

India had all it took in excess, while the Portuguese were hopelessly ill-equipped. India's AMX tanks and Stuart armoured vehicles were pitted against a handful of Portuguese 1942-vintage armoured reconnaissance vehicles that were no longer armoured at the bottom ... their worn-out bottom iron plates had been replaced with wooden planks of *bacalhau* (dried cod) crates. It typified the pathetic state of the Forças Armadas do Estado da Índia (armed forces of the Portuguese State of India).

The Portuguese magazine *Visão História* wryly commented that the Portuguese equipment, only for the reason of being deployed in Goa, was not in a museum.*

***

** *Visão História*, vol. 14, 2011, p. 42.*

In *A Queda da Índia Portuguesa: Uma Crónica da Invasão e do Cativeiro*, Col Carlos Alexandre de Morais—although mentioning an exaggerated number of Indian troops deployed (45,000 operational and 25,000 reserve)—tellingly stated that the Indian side was,

> ... using combat vehicles of the latest model, artillery, paratroopers, amphibious units, engineering support, modern aviation, etc.

while all that the Portuguese side, in the three districts [of Goa, Daman and Diu] had was,

> ... around 3,500 disadvantaged men ill-equipped with arms and ammunition, without armoured cars and anti-tank weapons, without air support and, practically, without artillery.[*]

The description Maj. Gen. Dinesh Merchant (Madras Regiment, veteran) gave was:

> It was like using a sledgehammer to kill a fly.[†]

Indeed. To say that it was merely a case of inequality of the contending forces would be an understatement. The strength of the contenders was hardly comparable. The Indian side had far, far more than necessary. The Portuguese side had next to nothing.

The obvious question was: Why then did India mobilize such a large war machine?

Faulty Intelligence

India's mobilization of this relatively large war machine could have led to a massacre in Goa—as happened during Operation Polo

---

[*] Carlos Alexandre de Morais, *A Queda da Índia Portuguesa: Uma Crónica da Invasão e do Cativeiro*, Editorial Estampa, 1995, p. 70.

[†] Interview with the author.

in Hyderabad in 1948, although for different reasons. Mercifully, it turned out to be a virtually bloodless walkover. But what had warranted the large mobilization?

The simple answer: faulty intelligence.

G.K. Handoo, IPS, was director of Intelligence sent by the ministry. As the in-charge of CRP border guards, he had done a formidable job enlisting Indian veterans and Goan freedom fighters, training and arming them to carry out raids and sabotage operations in Goa—fomenting hell for the Portuguese in 1960–61. He evidently went overboard.

Handoo was a powerful man. He annoyed the military brass in Belgaum in the run-up to the invasion. It has been recorded and is widely believed that he almost wept when the army left him behind in Belgaum and accepted the Portuguese surrender in Goa without him in centre stage. Handoo saw himself as the key factor in Defence Minister Krishna Menon's plan to quickly seize Goa.

As seen, a spinoff of India's economic blockade was rampant cross-border smuggling of foreign merchandise. Goan smugglers and goondas, masquerading as freedom fighters, provided exaggerated and false information to Indian intelligence of the Portuguese military disposition in Goa. Perhaps this was to curry favour with Handoo's border cops, so they could ply their trade without difficulty.

The Indian Army evidently had a poor opinion of such freedom fighters—in his 'Appreciation of Situation' dated 10 November 1961, GOC-in-C Southern Command Lt Gen. Chaudhuri wrote,

> This speed [of ops] ... will ensure the least disruption to law
> and order in Portuguese territory by so called nationalist elements
> or goondas.[*]

Handoo relied on the inputs of these Goan smugglers and goondas (and may have added some of his own). This was the basis of the

---

[*] Shrikant Y. Ramani, *Operation Vijay: The Ultimate Solution*, Broadway Book Centre, Goa, 2008, p. 72.

dubious intelligence reports churned out by Handoo. The Armed
Forces had no option but to draw up their plans based on these
'intelligence reports'. Lt Gen. Chaudhuri had also said in his
'Appreciation of Situation':

> I consider that all nationalist and subversive movements [that
> Handoo trained, armed and encouraged] should be discouraged
> from independent action of any nature and, in fact should be
> prevented from entering Goa while military operations are on.[*]

The cross-border 'moles' fed false stories of a massive Portuguese
military build-up. They spoke of troop reinforcements in Goa when
there actually were reductions over the previous few years—from
12,000 to 3300 troops. Expecting more or less a brigade strength
Portuguese force in Goa, India mobilized two brigades (a main
one from the east and a diversionary one from the north—with
a deceptive feint from the south by B Company of the 4 Rajput
Battalion, shored up with Reserve Police personnel to display
numbers to the enemy, and dubbed the '20 Infantry Brigade', and a
reserve brigade under Brig. Gurbux Singh, brother of editor-author
Khushwant Singh, following on the main thrust line from the east).

These 'moles' also told the Indian intelligence about the
abundance of tanks in Goa (when there were none). Armour was
mobilized accordingly. After the ops, when the moles were asked
to produce visual evidence of the Portuguese tanks, they promptly
returned with photos of water tankers! This was disclosed by Lt
Gen. Chaudhuri himself when he delivered a lecture on Operation
Vijay at the National Defence Academy.[†]

There was just one medium-sized destroyer in Goa, the NRP
Afonso de Albuquerque (that the Portuguese media called a cruiser,
larger than a destroyer). Goan smugglers told Indian intelligence

---

[*] Ibid., p. 75.

[†] Interview with Maj. Gen. Anil Raikar, a Goan-origin veteran of the
Sikh LI Regiment, who was then a cadet at Pune's NDA.

that the enemy had much more—an extra three frigates and three S-class submarines, and that NATO naval forces had already begun arriving at Mormugao, via Karachi. That was the genesis of the false apprehension that was created in India's Intelligence establishment that NATO and Pakistan would intervene militarily to support Portugal in the conflict.

The Portuguese did not have the capability to reach within gun range of Banda, the southernmost coastal township of Maharashtra closest to Goa, but Goan smugglers led Handoo's Intelligence team to believe that the Portuguese were planning to target Bombay. Transport aircraft had been modified to carry bombs, they claimed (when there were no military transport aircraft based in Goa). The claims would be laughable had they not been taken seriously. (P.N. Khera in his book *Operation Vijay* lists the precise number of prisoners, vehicles and arms seized from the Portuguese in Goa;[*] in another appendix, he gives details of military equipment seized from the Portuguese defenders separately in Goa, in Daman and in Diu;[†] in comparison, the claims are truly ludicrous!)

There was not a single aircraft of the Força Aérea Portuguesa (Portuguese air force) in Goa. Handoo's intelligence-gathering men were told that there were transonic jet fighters like USA-made F-86 Sabres, a section (four aircraft) of France-made Fouga Magister and some interceptor F-104 Star fighters. Portugal did have Star fighters in its air force but none were shifted to Goa. The only aircraft present in Goa were a couple of civilian (passenger) planes of the local airline, TAIP.

There was no worthwhile air-defence infrastructure in Goa. Yet, the moles spoke of an ultra-modern AA battery at Dabolim, perhaps referring to some 1948 vintage, light and largely ineffective, 20-mm, anti-aircraft guns. These obsolete guns were looked after by an untrained Companhia de Caçadores No. 7 (C.Cac. 7

---

[*] Khera, *Operation Vijay*, 1974, Appendix XI at pp. 195–96.

[†] Ibid., Appendix XXIII, pp. 239–41.

or Company of Hunters No. 7). Gunners to man these archaic anti-aircraft guns were smuggled in just a day before the invasion, disguised as footballers on the last TAIP flight—to no avail: the guns were obsolete and without adequate ammunition anyway.

On 8 December, a four-engine DC-4 Skymaster of the local civilian airline TAIP flew over the INS *Vikrant* and her carrier group, at a height of 5000 feet. It was about the best offensive air action that could be mounted by the Portuguese in Goa.

India had no satellite imagery at the time and the imaginary images painted by Goan cross-border smugglers were accepted at face value. They set off alarm bells in Delhi. Prime Minister Nehru told Parliament on 11 December 1961:

> In Goa itself the Portuguese have added largely to their armed forces, have brought along some ships, and have got some aircraft ... And—what is really extraordinary—they have been functioning in a most provocative manner, deliberately or for other reasons, as if they wanted us to take steps against them.[*]

This suited India's defence minister Krishna Menon, and Handoo was part of the grand endeavour. The fabricated prospect of NATO and Pakistan military intervention imparted urgency to the invasion, which in any case Menon wanted before the forthcoming February 1962 general elections.

IAF and carrier-borne naval aircraft undertook probing flights from early December, to draw out Portuguese air fangs and opposition—when there were none. These baiting flights continued until D-day. From heights just beyond the range of modern ack-ack guns, the IAF flew at sequentially lower altitudes. There was no evidence of anti-aircraft fire. Only on the eve of the invasion, 17 December, did IAF's Squadron Leader Ian Steele Loughran ('Locky'), CO of 37 Squadron

---

[*] Record of Parliament debates.

('Black Panthers'), flying a low tactical recce over Dabolim in a Vampire NF54, come under five rounds of Portuguese small arms (not ack–ack) fire. He took evasive action and escaped over the sea unharmed.

Seahawks and Alizés took off from the deck of INS *Vikrant* on combat patrols from early December, dawn to dusk. Lt Cdr (later admiral and CNS) R.H. Tahiliani, then the CO of the carrier-borne air squadron INAS 300 of Sea Hawks in 1961, recalled:

> ... we flew whole day waiting for Portuguese aircraft to come out. As it turned out the Portuguese had no aircraft in Goa although our faulty intelligence had led us to believe that there were some Sabers there.[*]

Maj. Gen. Randhir Sinh wrote,

> ... the estimated strength of the Portuguese armed forces and their capability seems to have been misinterpreted ... the Indian Intelligence agencies may not have been aware that Portugal had cut down its military strength in Goa in 1960.[†]

Air Vice Marshal Arjun Subramaniam summed it up in his book, *India's Wars: A Military History 1947–1971*:

> Intelligence gathering about Portuguese force levels was terribly inaccurate ... There were ridiculous inputs about the presence of Portuguese fighter jets in Goa and the possibility of Pakistan supporting Portugal militarily in the conflict.[‡]

---

[*] *White Tigers on the Prowl* (commemorative book of the golden jubilee of Indian Naval Air Squadron 300), INAS 300, INS *Hansa*, Goa, 2010. p. 16.

[†] Randhir Sinh, *A Talent for War*, 2013, p. 48.

[‡] Arjun Subramaniam, *India's Wars: A Military History 1947–1971*, 2016, p. 192.

Capt. Gerald Fernandes (2 Mechanised Infantry, veteran) of Morjim, Goa, added a twist to the tail:

> Overwhelming force directed towards attaining an objective is kindness in battle. Makes for swift outcomes to the victorious and provides alibi to the overwhelmed!*

Goa's *Nakli* Freedom Fighters

Faulty intelligence was just one of the factors that led the Indian defence services to train a howitzer at a sparrow. The Portuguese strength was not known with certainty, the operation had to be completed quickly to avoid foreign or UN interference, and in any case it would be disastrous to underrate the enemy. An overwhelming force was concentrated against the Portuguese to accomplish the task speedily and with assurance. India mobilized a far larger than warranted force,

> ... which no professional army in the world likes to do.†

The deployment and baiting operations for over a fortnight also resulted in a substantial economic loss to India.

Handoo was responsible, but there were no repercussions—in fact, he was to become Nehru's chief trouble-shooter in Goa.

Maj. Gen. Palit candidly assessed:

> The strength of the Portuguese forces was negligible; at no time had they posed a military threat to India. Indeed the entire course of the operation amounted to little more than large-scale military manoeuvres ... this episode was just comic relief [from the actual pressure at India's northern borders with China and Pakistan].‡

---

* Interview with author.
† Maj. Gen. Anil Raikar (V, Sikh Light Infantry Regiment) in an interview with the author.
‡ Palit, *Musings and Memories Vol. II*, 2004, p. 411.

On the flip side, the wrong Intelligence inputs may have benefitted Goa in a roundabout way. As a result of the misinformation, India mobilized an overwhelming force and in the face of a mighty enemy, the Portuguese garrison surrendered without a fight, avoiding a tragedy—for themselves and for Goans who, caught in the crossfire, would be counted as collateral victims.[9] The misinformation was courtesy Goan cross-border smugglers who posed as 'freedom fighters'.

This is not to suggest that all of Goa's freedom fighters were smugglers, as Goa's first chief minister, Dayanand Bandodkar, evidently thought. (There were fake freedom fighters who were actually smugglers, no doubt; and smuggling continued post-1961; there was no gold and foreign merchandise, but in prohibition-prone neighbouring India, Goa's feni and IMFL liquor ensured the tribe of smugglers increased.) Goa produced a large number of genuine freedom fighters who suffered detention and police brutality, served prison sentences, at times in exile in Portugal/Africa, and in some cases, death.[10]

Many genuine nationalists did not register themselves as freedom fighters. And some genuine and famous freedom fighters, like Dr P.D. Gaitonde, Dr Ram Hegde and Adv. José Inácio ('Fanchu') Loyola, left Goa after seeing the fruits of Goa's freedom. Quite a few of those who stayed back, notably Lambert Mascarenhas and Prabhakar Sinari, lamented the post-1961 fallout. Others, like Roque Santan Fernandes, later an elected MLA, stayed back—but their families left, many on Portuguese passports!

Some registered 'freedom fighters' had nothing to do with nationalism or the freedom movement. Some were plain smugglers, a few were in jail on 19 December 1961 for entirely unrelated offences, and fewer still were innocent fun-seekers who fell unwitting victim to Portuguese police paranoia.

A man was in jail for some offence on 19 December 1961. It was his lucky charm. He became a registered freedom fighter. He never stopped receiving his monthly pension and began wearing a Gandhi *topi*. He was short on temper and once flung a sandal at a judge in an open courtroom at Quepem, Goa. He was fond of venting his powerful oratory with loud and long speeches at Margao's Lohia Maidan—in front of audiences that literally didn't exist. Street idlers knew how to unnerve him with catcalls from the adjoining streets. In the midst of a fiery speech, he would leave whatever he was haranguing about and respond to the catcalls—with a shower of chaste expletives let loose in the choicest Konkani—over the public address system.

Some economically challenged but genuine freedom fighters, particularly of the underground variety, had to eke out a living even when hiding from the Portuguese police and PIDE. A retired Goan IAF fighter pilot relates how he accosted one such from the same Salcete village who tried to make off with his sister's gold chain after she alighted from the last bus home.[*] Remember there was no electricity or street lighting in villages then. The enraged pilot, on home leave, almost choked the freedom fighter with his own shirt collar outside the latter's house the same night.

The image of freedom fighters in local lore, however, was one of 'chicken thieves'.

A well-known Margao-based freedom fighter had given his best years for the cause. He was beyond the age of acquiring gainful skills. He would explode when street urchins taunted him with catcalls of *kombiepak* (chicken feather). This had to do with his taking a post-1961 rehabilitation package to start a poultry unit. A visiting audit team saw no signs of the poultry. When quizzed, the freedom fighter explained that all the birds had died of disease.

'Then where are the feathers?' the accountant smarties pressed.

Our Alec replied, 'When hens die, they don't leave their feathers behind.' What was left behind was the chicken-feather taunt, and its permanent rile.

Another Salcetan was the butt of jokes. Post lunch, while the land slumbered, it seems our hero was habituated to tell his wife

---

[*]   Interview with author.

that he was going for a walk. Walk he did, in search of fun. One day, he spotted comely Jakin (Joaquina) bent over her paddy crop. Crouching at the edge of the quiet 'bund' bordering the paddies, he beckoned, 'Jakin, Jakin!' A passing Portuguese police party, not conversant with the local idiom, heard that as *Jai Hind, Jai Hind!* The poor fun-seeker was bundled into the jeep and into jail. On 19 December 1961, he emerged as a triumphant freedom fighter.

Dr Dhillon Desai of Palolem, Canacona relates the story of another 'freedom fighter' from Canacona who earned a *tamrapatra*—a bronze plaque awarded by the Central government to freedom fighters since 1972—and lifelong pension. He was a freedom-seeker of a different kind: he was a fun-seeker. A few days before 19 December 1961, this politically innocent hero went to the Barcem temple area, near Padi village, for a night of fun. When returning pre-dawn, jittery Portuguese soldiers detained him on suspicion at the Pissonem Check Post. Soon, he was liberated from custody—and thenceforth proudly swaggered around as a registered Goan freedom fighter!

Olavio Fernandes of St Cruz/Kalapur, an agriculture graduate with the state Agriculture Department, once spruced up the Raj Bhavan gardens for the governor's Liberation Day tea party. He met a state guest, improbably young to be a freedom fighter. And out came the story.

The 'freedom fighter' was eight years old when his father, a freedom activist, had to hide from the Portuguese police somewhere in the woods of Taleigao. His mother sent him with food for the father, telling the boy to bring back the food containers. He was waiting for the empty containers when the police raided the hideout. While the father escaped, the boy and three other men were picked up and incarcerated in the Panjim police lock-up. The mother got the boy released within two days. Soon, post-1961, the boy was registered as a freedom fighter!

Miguel Mascarenhas of Sanguem, a former journalist and higher secondary school lecturer, tells of another 'freedom fighter' who was mistaken for a freedom fighter and arrested, a story reminiscent of the Marathi drama *Karaila Gelo Ek Ani Zale Baltach* (I Went to Do One Thing, the Outcome Was Another).

Two neighbours in Sanguem were forever at loggerheads. The wife of one had a brainwave. She told her husband to denounce the neighbour as a *Jaihn* (Goans generally could not pronounce *Jai Hind*, connoting a freedom fighter). The Portuguese police promptly arrested the innocent neighbour for being a freedom fighter. 19 December 1961 soon arrived. The man was released and was registered as a freedom fighter for having been incarcerated on charges of being a 'freedom fighter'. To the chagrin of the denouncing neighbour, the 'Jaihn's' lifetime pension made him instantly popular in the area. *Kelem kitem ani zalem kitem* (what did I do, and what is the result—my Machiavellian scheming came to nothing)!

6

OPERATION VIJAY*
(THE ACTUAL MILITARY OPS)

Invasion Begins

Prof. John Kenneth Galbraith, the US Ambassador to India, kept meeting Nehru from early December 1961, pressurizing him to abandon military action.

On 13 December 1961, the USA put pressure on both India and Portugal to avoid war and settle the Goa issue peacefully. India's D-day of 14 December was postponed by two days, to 16 December.

On 15 December, Prof. Galbraith met Nehru again and then briefed Finance Minister Morarji Desai on the USA's position. Desai was the chief opponent of using force in Goa. He expressed an

> ... inability to support violent means because of his strong personal belief in the validity and necessity of non-violence ... as the true means of solving the colonial problem.[†]

He counselled patience and steadfastly debated with Krishna Menon against using force in Goa—famously known as the 'Morarji vs Menon' debate. On the same day (15 December), Prof. Galbraith informed Washington:

---

[*] Called Operation Vijay-1 after Kargil 1999 was also named Operation Vijay, necessitating the use of numerals 1 and 2 to distinguish one from the other.

[†] Gaitonde, 2016, p. 164.

It is my feeling that I may have moved him [Nehru] a bit, that he was even looking for arguments [to put off the military action]. Would also note he was very sensitive to the reactions of the President [Kennedy]. It is still my feeling that the decision is to act on Goa or conceivably other enclaves [Daman and/or Diu] probably tomorrow but possibly we may have produced one more pause [postponement of India's D-day] for reflection and pressure from Krishna Menon …*

On 16 December, President Kennedy personally messaged Nehru. D-day was postponed again to midnight of 17/18 December.†

So optimistic were the Portuguese that last-minute USA diplomacy would succeed that, on Saturday 16 December, the governor-general and commander-in-chief of the armed forces in Goa attended the wedding reception of his Goan friend's daughter.

On 17 December, the USA ambassador met Nehru again and proposed that India postpone military action by six months, to give diplomacy one last chance. An alarmed Krishna Menon, who was present at that meeting, told Nehru and Prof. Galbraith that it was too late. He told them that the troops had already moved inside Goa and they could not be pulled back now. Moreover, he had no means of communication.

Years later, Krishna Menon, in a press interview, would admit that this was not true. At the time Menon told Nehru and Prof. Galbraith the lie (morning of 17 December), Indian troops were still at Goa's borders, bracing for the midnight hour, the H-hour (alliteration for 'hour'), the zero hour of invasion. Later that night (17 December), Krishna Menon would head to the borders of Goa to inspect the troops. Menon informed Nehru of the H-hour only after the operation had begun.

---

* Ramesh, Penguin Viking, 2019, p. 550.

† https://timesofindia.indiatimes.com/india/john-f-kennedy/article-show/26169547.cms

Nehru's friend Lord Louis Mountbatten, the former viceroy, blamed Nehru for letting Krishna Menon 'bounce him' into military action. Mountbatten held that Menon had put Nehru

> ... in a position where he would either have to sanction the march into Goa, or it would be known that it was Nehru who had stopped it. Later, Mountbatten elaborated this, saying that Menon did 'the most frightful thing' to Nehru by forcing him to bless the Goa operation, thereby destroying him: 'Not only his credibility, his prestige, his reputation, but he destroyed his faith in himself, for he felt that he had been betrayed'.[*]

At the stroke of midnight of 17/18 December, India's military might crossed the international borders with 'a mighty thunder of guns' (as described by India) and rolled into Goa, Daman and Diu in a three-pronged attack. According to the *Economic Weekly*, Operation Vijay rolled out the

> much-delayed according to some and, it is now known, postponed at least twice in the hope that diplomatic methods might yet succeed ...[†]

The *Times of India* (19 December) banner headline read: 'Our Troops Enter Goa, Diu and Daman at Last'.

There were sixteen foreign media men present in Goa at the time. The journalists had been invited by Portugal to witness the unprovoked border attacks and territorial violations by the Indian Army, Navy and Air Force. Their presence in Goa would, however, work against the Salazar regime as, once the invasion began, the journalists filed factual reports that exposed the crass fictional propaganda officially spread in the media in Portugal. Portuguese captain, João Aranha, describes it as:

---

[*] Gaitonde, 2016, pp. 175–76.

[†] *Economic Weekly*, Bombay, vol. XIII, nos 51 and 52, 23 December 1961.

... resulting in another tremendous defeat for Salazar's policy.[*]

India announced the action to the world later in the day on 18 December. Nehru said India reluctantly took military action

... because the Portuguese left us no alternative.[†]

Indian land forces stole a quick march in an almost bloodless conquest. There were some skirmishes in Daman and Diu. In Goa, brief combat was witnessed only in the naval action in Anjediva, in the Zuari-Mandovi estuary at Mormugao, and when an Indian army unit was briefly bogged down in Verna.

Let us take a peek at the action in Goa, service-wise.

The task of subduing the Portuguese and capturing Goa had been assigned to 17 Infantry Division under the command of the special task force commander, just-promoted Maj. Gen. K.P. Candeth.

17 Infantry Division being the main Task Force was given the shorter, better and easier route into Goa from Anmod in the east. Its objectives were to capture Panjim, Dabolim, Vasco da Gama (capture of Mormugao port was assigned to the Indian Navy) and Margao. Maj. Gen. Candeth had two brigades: 63 Infantry Brigade under Brig. K.S. Dhillon as the operational brigade and 48 Infantry Brigade under Brig. Gurbux Singh as the reserve brigade (the third brigade, 64 Infantry, was left behind at Kasauli).

The operational 50 Independent Parachute Brigade under Brig. Sagat Singh, in a diversionary role from Dodamarg in the north

---

[*] João Aranha, 2008, footnote no. 33, pp. 44–45.

[†] Keesing's Record of World Events, *Indian Occupation of Portuguese Territories in India: Invasion of Goa, Daman, and Diu—Incorporation in Indian Union*, vol. 8, March 1962, p. 8, accessed at: http://web.stanford.edu/group/tomzgroup/pmwiki/uploads/1074-1962-03-KS-a-RCW.pdf

(aimed at splitting the defenders who would otherwise stage a concerted resistance to 17 Infantry Division) was also placed at the command of Maj. Gen. Candeth.

A decoy/feint from the south (Karwar–Canacona–Margao) by a Company of the 4 Rajput Battalion was directly under HQ Southern Command.

Maj. Fonseca SO 2 (Signals) was tasked to extend/bridge the line of communication with two detachments of newly imported RS C41/R22 radio relay sets along with detachments of 1 Air Support Signal Unit under Capt. A.S. Kahlon in support of the advance of 17 Infantry Division on the Tinaighat–Anmod–Panjim axis. Similarly, Maj. Fonseca was to support the 50 Parachute Brigade along the Sawantwadi–Bicholim–Ponda axis with two radio relay sets under Capt. G.A. Newton.[*]

The 50 Parachute Brigade: A Subsidiary Role

Fifty Independent Parachute Brigade (hereafter, 50 Para) under Brig. Sagat Singh was tasked to mount a subsidiary thrust from Dodamarg in the north, to facilitate the work of the main Task Force by splitting the Portuguese defenders in Goa.

Nicknamed Pegasus Brigade, 50 Para was one of India's most elite airborne formations. (The word today means different things to different people—including telephone spyware!—but in Greek mythology, Pegasus was an immortal winged horse, reminiscent of the winged dagger on the badge of India's Special Forces.)

It was ironic that an elite formation was allotted a sideshow, but the brigade commander was not the kind of person who would allow his team to play second fiddle, knowing the potential of his men. Unfolding events would prove the point.

50 Para concentrated at Amboli road in Sawantwadi on 13 December and moved to the assembly area east of Dodamarg on

---

[*]   V.K. Singh, *History of the Corps of Signals*, vol. 3, Chapter 3.

16 December evening. Lt Gen. J.N. Chaudhuri confirmed that D-day would be midnight 17/18 December with the code word 'Bulldozer'. On 17 December, the order to enter Goa was issued under the code word 'Varaha' (wild boar). 50 Para was allowed to patrol across the border after last light on 17 December and enter in full strength at the H-hour.

50 Para consisted of three battalions of which one, 2 Sikh Light Infantry, was a regular infantry battalion, and the remaining two were better-trained parachute battalions.

The 50 Para Brigade entered Goa by two approaches from Dodamarg in the north: Sanquelim/Usgao/Ponda (the eastern approach allotted to 2 Para Maratha and 1 Para Punjab) and Assonora/Tivim/Betim (western approach allotted to 2 Sikh Light Infantry). Later, when Brig. Sagat Singh saw feeble opposition from the Portuguese defenders, he ordered 1 Para Punjab to change course and take the Bicholim/Pilgao/Amona/Banastari middle approach.

In effect, the brigade entered Goa from Dodamarg in the north and later split into three approaches/columns:

- 2 Sikh Light Infantry Battalion along the Assonora–Tivim–Betim route (western column),
- 2 Para Maratha Battalion along the Sanquelim–Usgao–Ponda route (eastern column), and
- 1 Para Punjab as the reserve battalion was to follow 2 Para Maratha but was later ordered along the Bicholim–Pilgao–Amona–Banastari–Panjim route (middle column).

All three approaches—eastern, western and middle—were longer and, running against the natural grain of the country (where rivers ran east to west), more difficult to negotiate than the route from Anmod in the east allotted to 17 Infantry Division.

2 Para Maratha was the main attack battalion of the 50 Para Brigade. The CO of 1 Para Punjab, the decorated Lt Col Sucha Singh,

… was a prickly character, short tempered and did not always get along with Sagat.[*]

1 Para Punjab, the only unit to advance on foot (the other two moved on wheels), was kept in reserve to take over the advance from 2 Para Maratha and capture Ponda. It was ordered to cross the border before the start time of D-day and tasked to secure Ibrampur, Dodamarg and Maulinguem to ensure the safe initial entry of the brigade into Goa.

Brig. Sagat Singh wrote in *Reminiscences of a Historic and Happy Association*[†] regarding a preliminary operation for intact capture of the Sanquelim bridge by a company of 2 Para Maratha:

> From a Portuguese map obtained through smugglers by 2 Para, we gathered information that they [the Portuguese in Goa] had constructed a 110-foot single span RCC bridge over the river flowing by the eastern boundary of the Sanquelim town. I felt strongly that if we could capture the bridge intact, it would speed up 2 Para's advance. We worked out a careful plan. A company of 2 Para led by Major Uthaya [C Company] set off on man–pack basis after last light on the night of December 15/16 [an obvious typo; should read as December 17/18; the 50 Para Brigade moved to the assembly area near Dodamarg only on 16 December 1961 evening; the attempt to capture was made at about 4.20 a.m. on 18 December 1961]. He [Major Uthaya] was guided by seasoned smugglers who knew their clandestine tracks across country. The tasks given to Major Uthaya were to capture the bridge intact; if not, to find out a crossing place across the river. The company got to their forming up place on the eastern end of the bridge. As they started crawling forward, trouble began in the form of incessant barking of dogs. Though the Portuguese map had not

---

[*] Randhir Sinh, *A Talent for War*, p. 56.

[†] Maj. Gen. Afsir Karim, *The Story of the India's Airborne Troops*, Lancer International, New Delhi, 1990, pp. 153–54.

shown it, some hutments of the labourers who had worked on the bridge construction had settled at the eastern end. Men of 2 Para crawled carefully forward a little at a time but the dogs would not give up.

The Portuguese guards became alert and suspicious. As our men were preparing to charge, the Portuguese blew up the demolition charges and scurried towards Usgaon. Major Uthaya was able to locate and mark a crossing place at which all vehicles, tanks and guns got through without difficulty. I can never forget the scene of Major Uthaya meeting me at the Sanquelim end of the bridge with tears rolling down his eyes and in choked voice telling me, 'Sorry. I have failed you'—meaning that he had not got the bridge intact. Actually, the mission was a great success. The crossing place enabled us to maintain the momentum of our advance in motor transport. What Major Uthaya did not realize at the time was that he had prevented the Portuguese from firing all the demolition charges affixed to the long single span. They could only fire the charges in the demolition chambers at either end of the single 110-foot span. In the aftermath, the span was lifted by marine jacks and with additions to the abutments on either side, the bridge was re-commissioned economically and in a short time. I have narrated this in some detail not only to commend the performance of the 2 Para Company but to say that in war, howsoever you might plan in detail, there would be imponderables (like barking of dogs at night) to contend with.

Advance of 50 Parachute Brigade

The diversionary thrust from the north assigned to 50 Para was perpendicular to the east-west flow of Goa's rivers. The route was longer and the riverine obstacles more difficult to cross. Due to this difficult terrain, the Portuguese expected the attack to come from the east, and not the north (i.e., from Anmod, the easier route that was allotted to the main Task Force, 17 Infantry Division). 50 Para was pressed from the north to divide the defenders and facilitate the work of the main Task Force.

When the Portuguese heard of an airborne brigade (50 Para) being deployed, they began to worry about air security, expecting the brigade to be airdropped, only to learn from All India Radio a little past midnight 17/18 December that Indian troops had also entered Goa from the north by land, not from the air.

At a brainstorming at army HQ in Delhi on 29 November, it was decided to airdrop the 2 Para Maratha Battalion of 50 Para to capture vital bridges before the enemy could destroy them. Brig. Sagat Singh was happy that a unit of his brigade would have an airborne role. He suggested that the battalion be dropped by night near Ponda, so that river obstacles at Sanquelim, Bicholim, Usgao and Khandepar could be bypassed. 2 Para Maratha was shifted to Begumpet, Hyderabad for exercises. The idea was later dropped, however, and all three battalions of 50 Para moved in overland.

As seen, 50 Para entered Goa from Dodamarg in the north and later split into three approaches. The shortest of the three approaches was the western one allotted to 2 Sikh Light Infantry, under the command of Lt Col Thomas Cherian.

Despite starting on time, 2 Sikh LI was delayed two hours with obstacles inside the border and crossed the start point only at 9 a.m. on 18 December. On the way, bridges at Assonora and Tivim as well as culverts were blown up, and trees felled across the road, to slow its advance. But with a good Pioneer Section, the lead armoured column of the unit ('A' squadron of 7 Cavalry's Stuart armoured vehicles and 'B' Squadron of 8 Cavalry's AMX tanks under Maj. Shivdev Singh Sidhu) rapidly crossed minefields, roadblocks and river obstacles to make stunningly swift progress. It reached Tivim at 10.15 a.m. and, after a diversion via Colvale on account of a broken bridge, occupied Mapusa by 3.30 p.m. the same day. The lead armoured element reached the Betim riverfront (northern bank of the Mandovi River, across Panjim) by 5 p.m.—just as the last of the retreating Portuguese troops from Bardez crossed the Mandovi into Panjim. The entire unit (2 Sikh LI) reached Betim by about 6 p.m.

Artillery of 2 Sikh LI was stationed at the Betim hilltop, while the armour was lined along the northern bank of the Mandovi, their cannons trained at Panjim. IAF fighter jets zoomed menacingly over Panjim.

Artillery fired two warning shells. One landed in front of the river-facing Hospital Escolar, the hospital attached to the Escola Médica-Cirúrgica de Goa (Asia's first medical college in allopathic medicine, later the Goa Medical College and now headquarters of the International Film Festival of India), damaging a wall. The second shell landed near the road leading to Altinho.

According to Portuguese cavalry (armour) officer João Aranha, however, four shells were fired: the other two landed near police HQ and in the backyard of his quarters.[*]

Senior officers of the small garrison defending Panjim (Agrupamento D. João de Castro) were in a hopeless situation without human or material means to resist the Indian troops, artillery, armour or the air force. Archbishop D. José Vieira Alvernaz was able to convince the CO to lay down arms and declare a ceasefire, saving Panjim and its inhabitants. The Portuguese hoisted a white flag atop a riverfront tree on the southern bank of Mandovi River.

Past dusk, closer to 8 p.m., a Goan priest, Msgr Gregório Magno de Souza Antão, carried a ceasefire letter from Maj. Acácio Nunes Tenreiro, military commander of Panjim, in a rowboat across the Mandovi. The letter read:

> The military Commander of Panjim declares that he wishes to open talks with the Commander of the Indian Forces of the Indian Union to finalise surrender, so that peace could take effect immediately. This is to avoid massacre of the population and damage to the city. Signed, The Commander, AcácioTenreiro, Major.[†]

Msgr Antão gave the letter to Maj. S.S. Sidhu of 7 Cavalry at Betim, who took the letter to Lt Col Thomas Cherian, CO 2 Sikh LI, on the Betim hilltop. The CO could not get through to the

---

[*] João Aranha, 2008, p. 111.
[†] Ramani, 2008, p. 161, and Khera, 1974, p. 70.

brigade HQ or Brig. Sagat Singh. The priest was verbally assured that there would be no firing until ten the next morning.

The Portuguese crumble had begun.

In Lisbon, the censored Portuguese press would be fed with fictitious and fantastic stories. Newspapers would report imaginary scenes of 'heroic resistance' put up by Portuguese troops in Goa, of hand-to-hand combat in many places including Panjim and Vasco da Gama, even of Indian troops being taken POW by Portuguese forces! Salazar's shocked nation was blatantly fed fairytales. (There were, however, a few cases of heroism in Daman and Diu.)

Newspapers were not provided with even a semblance of the ground reality: that the Portuguese forces in Goa were minuscule, not adequately trained or experienced and so pathetically equipped that even if there was any will to stage a token resistance to the invasion, there were no means to do so.

The Portuguese press instead reported fantasies of fierce battles fought in the streets and fields of Goa, resulting in 1500 dead. The lies continued even on 21 December—two days after Portugal moved the UNSC and the Portuguese forces had surrendered unconditionally without a fight in Goa.

The Portuguese author-journalist Maria Manuel Stocker wrote in the preface to *Xeque-Mate a Goa: O Principio do Fim do Império Português*:

> The [Salazarian] regime deceived its own sympathizers. An entire people were led to believe a horrible fiction ...[*]

The international media persons present in Goa, however, filed factual reports. The demoralized defenders were gripped with fear and uncertainty. Throughout the day, 18 December, Emissora de Goa, the local radio station, nervously broadcast martial music but not the news of the stunning advance of Indian troops into Goa.

---

[*] Maria Manuel Stocker, *Xeque-Mate a Goa: O Principio do Fim do Império Português* (Checkmate Goa: The Beginning of the End of the Portuguese Empire), Temas e Debates, 2005, pp. 9–10.

Students who had reported to schools early that morning amidst clatter from IAF bombings at Dabolim and Bambolim were ordered to forthwith return home by their equally nervous teachers.

2 Sikh LI at Betim: So Near, Yet So Far

Panjim, the capital of a once glorious Estado da Índia, capitulated on the evening of 18 December, but 2 Sikh LI had no orders to cross the river and enter the city to accept surrender and disarm the Portuguese soldiers. That task was assigned to 63 Infantry Brigade of 17 Infantry Division, the main Task Force. Maj. Gen. Candeth, who was in Molem, could not be contacted. Brig. Sagat Singh was also incommunicado. 2 Sikh LI, though just a shout away, had to harbour for the night at Betim across the capital city—agonizingly so near, yet so far, with just a fordable river in between.

The plan was for 2 Sikh LI, loaned to the 50 Para Brigade, to change command from HQ 17 Infantry Division to the direct command of HQ Southern Command with issue of the code words 'Sugar Loaf'. The loaf turned unsavoury before the nickname could be issued. It would be a tragic night.

While Maj. Sidhu was away taking the ceasefire letter of the Portuguese garrison in Panjim to his commanding officer, and trying to contact HQ 50 Para Brigade and Brig. Sagat Singh for permission to enter Panjim and accept the surrender, his troops captured two men who claimed to be demobilized local soldiers from a village (Reis Magos) that lay on the route his squadron would take the next morning. This was at about 9.45 p.m.

To check the antecedents of the two men, Maj. Sidhu decided to reconnoitre up to Reis Magos. Leaving in a Dodge 15 cwt truck with five officers, three other ranks and the two prisoners at 10.30 p.m., he released them after they were identified by residents. But another local told Maj. Sidhu that fifty to sixty political prisoners held at Aguada Jail would be killed that night by the five or six Portuguese soldiers guarding them.

In a spirit of sheer humanitarianism, Maj. Sidhu rushed without preparation but with the informer to set free the prisoners. It happened that the jail, with 120 prisoners, was held by a platoon of Companhia de Caçadores No. 8 (C.Cac. 8 or Company of Hunters No. 8) headed by Second Lt Casimiro José Pereira Pinto with eight soldiers and twenty-eight Portuguese military prisoners, armed with rifles, LMGs, an MMG, 2-inch mortars and grenade launchers—and no written orders from Panjim to surrender. (Captain of Ports, Comandante Abel de Oliveira, had earlier sent a river launch to fetch the platoon of C.Cac. 8 but Second Lt Pereira Pinto asked for a written order to leave the fort.)

Around 11.30 p.m., Second Lt Pereira Pinto was going to his residence within the fort when he saw the headlights of the Dodge. He came to the gate. The visitors outside the gate said they were Portuguese-Goans from the police post at Betim. However, they were unable to tell him the password. According to Portuguese records, Second Lt Pereira Pinto then heard the sound of the loading of arms. He ordered his troops to open fire. From within the Aguada gate, the Portuguese opened fire with rifles, light machine guns, a medium machine gun, 2-inch mortar and grenade launchers.

It was a reverse situation from that in the rest of Goa. Here were thirty-seven well-armed Portuguese soldiers versus nine Indian soldiers inadequately armed for the occasion. The Dodge 15 cwt truck, which contained explosives, was hit by a grenade and detonated, and Maj. Sidhu and the equally young Capt. Vinod K. Seghal and one other rank lost their lives.

Two officers and one other rank, wounded but not seriously, limped to the camp at 3.30 a.m. A troop of AMX tanks, a troop of Stuarts and two rifle platoons reached Aguada at 5.30 a.m. After an exchange of machine gun fire, the Portuguese garrison hoisted the white flag but did not come out. After a warning, they emerged from the gate and surrendered at 6.40 a.m. (Second Lt Pereira Pinto was later decorated with a Medalha de Cruz da Guerra de 2ª Classe, a war medal, in Portugal. The fate of the local informer was not known.)

Unbeknownst to 2 Sikh LI, seeing their spectacularly swift
advance (and the slow progress of 63 Infantry Brigade), Tactical HQ
Southern Command partly modified the plan and gave the capture of
Panjim to 50 Para at around 10 p.m. on 18 December. Orders were
conveyed over the radio relay link, but since Brig. Sagat Singh was
away visiting 2 Para Maratha at Ponda that night (he reportedly spent
the night in the temple area of Mardol—codenamed 'Coca Cola'—
and Mangueshi—codenamed 'Sabzi Mandi'), Lt Gen. Chaudhuri
personally spoke to the brigade major of 50 Para, who had to wait
for the return of Brig. Sagat Singh to issue orders authorizing 2 Sikh
LI to enter Panjim, as per the chain of command.

It was not the only occasion that Brig. Sagat Singh was out
of contact. Earlier the same day, Tactical HQ Southern Command
lost contact with him, perhaps because of the swift advance of his
brigade, and sent an IAF Harvard from Sambra–Belgaum to 'drop' a
message to the brigadier (about that hilarious 'airdrop' later).

50 Para had a Signals Company under Maj. R.R. Chatterjee
with normal communications equipment that was unreliable and an
added truck-mounted SCR 399 set that would be useless on Goa's
narrow roads. Brig. Sagat Singh got that enhanced with a section of
newly inducted UK-made C41/R22 radio relay sets of 1 Medium
Radio Relay Section under Capt. George A. Newton.

Maj. Gen. V.K. Singh provides an interesting account of how
this was done in his book, *Leadership in the Indian Army: Biographies
of Twelve Soldiers*. It relates that Maj. Gen. (later lieutenant general)
R.N. Batra, after his promotion from brigadier and appointment
as director signals and signal officer-in-chief in May 1961, visited
HQ 17 Infantry Division in Belgaum and 50 Para Brigade at the
concentration area in Sawantwadi a few days before the ops began.
Maj. Gen. Batra and Brig. Sagat Singh were good friends. Brig.
Sagat Singh

... had learned that 17 Division had been given some radio relay
sets for their rearward communications to Belgaum. He asked
Raj [Maj. Gen. Batra] to also give a radio relay detachment to his
brigade, as the existing arrangements were unreliable. Raj told

Sagat that the C41/R22 radio relay sets [imported from the UK] had been introduced in the army very recently, and had still to be blooded [made functional]. Only one section had been raised, which was directly under the control of Army HQ. Four sets had been supplied to 17 Infantry Division for trials while four were kept for training purpose at the Signal Training Centre at Jabalpur. These also comprised the GS reserve, and he could not give them to Sagat.

Sagat was not to be shaken off so easily. He asked Raj what sort of a friend he was, if he could not do this small favour. Raj thought for a moment, and then agreed to give the sets. But he told Sagat that he would have to arrange to pick them up from Jabalpur, and return them after the operation in one piece. Within minutes of assuring Raj that this would be done, Sagat got through to the Parachute Training Centre at Agra and got them to send an aircraft to Jabalpur the same day to pick up the sets. They reached Sagat just a day before he moved to the assembly area at Dodamarg. By a stroke of good luck, his signal officer, Major (later colonel) R.R. Chatterjee, found there was a permanent line route of the P&T Department running past Dodamarg. This was patched to the rear terminal of the radio relay link, and enabled the brigade exchange to get through to Belgaum ... The orders for his brigade to capture Panjim were conveyed to him on the radio relay link, because 17 Infantry Division's communications had broken down.[*]

After the ops, the P&T Department asked Maj. R.R. Chatterjee for an explanation as to how a civilian line was used without its permission!

Panjim Captured by 50 Para Brigade

The 1 Para Punjab Battalion of 50 Para Brigade was commanded by Lt Col (later brigadier) Sucha Singh, the gallantry decorated officer who was described by Maj. Gen. Randhir Sinh as

---

[*] V.K. Singh, 2005, 2012, p. 245.

a prickly character, short tempered and did not always get along with [the Brigade Commander] Sagat [Singh].*

1 Para Punjab was the only unit of 50 Para Brigade to advance on foot. It was a reserve battalion meant to take over the advance from 2 Para Maratha, the main attack battalion, in the capture of Ponda.

However, seeing the feeble opposition from Portuguese defenders, Brig. Sagat Singh ordered 1 Para Punjab to change course and head for Panjim instead, via the Bicholim–Pilgao–Amona–Banastari approach (middle column). Despite broken bridges, the column made surprisingly swift progress. It reached Pilgao by noon, bombarded Tonca by 2 p.m. and reached Banastari (codename: 'Baby Girl') by 5.45 p.m. the same day, 18 December. The bridge here had been blown up four hours before—under dramatic circumstances.

The bridge was readied for demolition by about 1 p.m., but realizing that the squadron E.Rec.2 retreating from Bicholim was yet to cross Banastari on its return to Panjim, Portuguese major, Francisco Morais, rushed Sergeant Carlos Almeida to delay the destruction until E.Rec.2 crossed. Personnel responsible for the demolition, already under enemy pressure at Tonca, were in no mood to pay heed to Sergeant Almeida's pleas and prepared to fire the demolition charges. That is when Sergeant Almeida drove to the middle of the bridge and told the personnel they could now blow up the bridge with him on it. E.Rec.2 crossed just before 1.30 p.m., when the bridge was destroyed.†

Shortly after 1 Para Punjab reached Banastari at about 5.30 p.m.,‡ a message was received from brigade HQ that the unit should stay put there and build a helipad for Army Commander Lt Gen. J.N. Chaudhuri, who decided to pay a visit in the thick of action

* Sinh, *A Talent for War*, p. 56.
† Ramani, *Operation Vijay*, pp. 204, 206 and 211–12.
‡ Khera, 1974, p. 66.

at 9.30 a.m. the next morning (19 December). As seen, later the same night at about 10 p.m., the army commander ordered 50 Para Brigade to advance on Panjim, instead of 17 Infantry Division as planned before.

No river craft were in sight. 1 Para Punjab decided to harbour at the eastern bank of Cumbarjua canal at Banastari for the night, just as 2 Sikh LI had done at the northern bank of the Mandovi at Betim. 1 Para Punjab was some 15 km away from Panjim while 2 Sikh LI was barely 0.5 km away. Early next morning, civilians arrived in cars and trucks on the opposite side to cheer the troops. Forward elements of 1 Para Punjab swam across. Two rafts were hastily constructed to carry the equipment of the two forward companies. One raft, with a rifle and a sten, sank. Using the motor transport, the advance element of 1 Para Punjab raced to Panjim.

Boats were meanwhile found in Banastari, and the main body of 1 Para Punjab crossed the canal and, taking either the rest of the civilian motorized transport on the other bank or marching via Old Goa (codename: 'Madhu Bala'), reached Panjim (codename: 'French Toast') by 8.30 a.m., 19 December. A contact party sent by 2 Para Maratha from Ponda reached Banastari at about 7.30 a.m. and met only the rear elements of 1 Para Punjab that stayed back preparing the helipad for the army commander's visit.

In Panjim, the unit took over the Governor's Palace/Secretariat, Treasury, High Court, Power House, Civil and Military hospitals and the government godown, among the important objectives.

1 Para Punjab also took the Portuguese soldiers and sailors POW. Most of the Portuguese soldiers in Panjim had assembled at the Altinho military camp and begun destroying their weapons to render them inoperative.

Men and officers of 1 Para Punjab removed their steel helmets and donned the maroon Para berets, as previously instructed by their proud commander, Brig. Sagat Singh. Then, at 9 a.m., Lt Col Sucha Singh, together with a major and a captain, went to the Altinho Mess for the surrender formality.

Portuguese officers and soldiers were found there in their undergarments, cowering in fright. When asked why, they explained that they had been told that Indian soldiers were so barbaric that they would kill any Portuguese they could identify by their uniform!

Portuguese POWs taken by 1 Para Punjab at Altinho military camp, Panjim, were later transferred to CO 13 Kumaon, Lt Col B.S. Chand (13 Kumaon was a unit of the reserve 48 Brigade of 17 Infantry Division). 1 Para's adjutant, Lt J.C.M. Rao, accompanied Lt Col Sucha Singh for the transfer ceremony.

A series of ironies played out here. 17 Infantry Division, the main Task Force that was to capture Panjim, did not do so. Brig. Sagat Singh's 50 Para that was on a subsidiary thrust did it. 2 Sikh LI battalion, loaned to the 50 Para Brigade, which was the first unit to reach Betim opposite Panjim, did not capture the city. 1 Para Punjab, a reserve battalion of the 50 Para Brigade moving on foot and ordered to change course, did it. And the man to first set his eyes on Panjim from across the river, Maj. S.S. Sidhu, armour in-charge of 2 Sikh LI, was, alas, dead.

In a display of the poor chain of command-and-control structure in the Portuguese Armed Forces (just as it had happened at Aguada Jail the previous night), some defenders still holed up at the Customs House in Panjim fired at Indian troops with rifles and two automatics despite the ceasefire declared by the military commander of Panjim the previous evening. The firing was neutralized by a platoon of the 'C' Company of 1 Para Punjab after the visit of the army commander to Panjim later that morning.

The army commander who had placed three bets that Brig. Sagat Singh would not meet his planned timings (and lost the bets and Rs 500 to Air Vice Marshal Erlic Pinto) was visiting Panjim that morning together with Chief of Staff Maj. Gen. Patrick O. Dunn and Air Vice Marshal Pinto. Brig. Sagat Singh left Ponda for Panjim by the ferry route with a platoon of 'C' Company of 2 Para Maratha, to meet the army commander.

2 Sikh LI, waiting at Betim, finally received orders from brigade HQ to cross the Mandovi on the morning of 19 December. Two advance rifle companies of the unit, using local ferries, entered Panjim and occupied the police HQ and the Customs House. Some accounts say that 2 Sikh LI won the race to Panjim. But then, if 2 Sikh LI entered Panjim at 7.35 a.m. and thereafter occupied the Customs House, how could there be Portuguese firing from the Customs House four hours later when the GOC-in-C was in Panjim? The Customs House firing was flamed out by men of 1 Para Punjab. Key buildings—the Secretariat, Treasury, High Court, hospitals, etc.—were occupied and Portuguese soldiers taken POW by 1 Para Punjab, clearly the unit that captured the city.

The previous day, 18 December, despite broken bridges at Sanquelim, Dicholim and Usgaó on the longest and most difficult of the three 50 Para Brigade's routes (the eastern route) allotted to the 2 Para Maratha, the main attack battalion of the 50 Para Brigade, its advance Alfa Company under Capt. K.S. Pannu reached Ponda at 1.45 p.m.

Capt. Pannu saw hooligans looting military barracks, which had been set ablaze by retreating Portuguese troops, and immediately posted a platoon at each of the three army barracks in Ponda. As more troops arrived, guards were posted at petrol pumps, the municipal office, post office, police station and taluka administrator's office. The bazaar area was patrolled and the unruly crowds finally dispersed.

Almost the entire of 2 Para Maratha and its CO, Lt Col U.K. Gupta reached Ponda by 2.30 p.m., 18 December. With his 2IC and some officers, the CO reconnoitred the area and found six mineral ore barges, each capable of carrying 500 men and two to three jeeps. He told the owners and crew to be prepared to move at short notice to Panjim during that night. As it transpired, there was no need for this, as 1 Para Punjab at Banastari and 2 Sikh LI at Betim were poised to take the 'French Toast', Panjim.

Lt Col Gupta found the culvert at Mardol exploded. Taking a detour, the CO and party went to the Banastari bridge, also demolished, and returned to Ponda by 8.30 p.m., by when the brigade commander had arrived from Khandepar.

Quickest Advance by the 50 Para Brigade

It was the quickest imaginable advance by all three units of the 50 Para Brigade. 2 Sikh LI reached Betim across Panjim, 1 Para Punjab reached Banastari some 15 km from Panjim, and 2 Para Maratha reached and occupied Ponda—all coming by the longer and more difficult routes from the north—the same afternoon/evening of 18 December. No one expected Brig. Sagat Singh to conduct such a super-fast operation, exceeding his brief.

The Portuguese government in Lisbon is said to have promptly placed a reward of US$ 10,000 (of the value of 1961) for the capture of Brig. Sagat Singh! The brigadier learnt of this himself when, mid-June 1962, the brigade was back at Agra, and one evening he was in mufti at the Clarks Shiraz Hotel. Some American tourists kept looking at him intently. Finally, one of them came over and asked if he was Brig. Sagat Singh. He said yes, and asked how the American recognized him. The tourist said he and the group had recently visited Lisbon, where posters with the brigadier's photograph were splashed across cafés all over town, announcing the reward. The brigadier had a hearty laugh and offered to be taken captive, but the Americans declined the bounty saying they were not going back to Lisbon.[*]

Brig. Sagat Singh was a Rathore Rajput from Bikaner. He joined the State Forces, then passed out of the Indian Military Academy in 1941 and saw action in Iraq during World War II. When promoted to brigadier in September 1961, he was, without precedent but thanks to Lt Gen. (later general and COAS) P.P. Kumaramangalam, adjutant general at army HQ, given charge of the 50 Independent Parachute Brigade at Agra.

---

[*] Singh, 2005, p. 307.

It was unprecedented because Brig. Sagat Singh was not a paratrooper. And at age forty, nobody jumps out of flying planes to earn wings and the maroon beret. But Brig. Sagat Singh was different. He did the tough probation, jumped twice a day and earned wings in record time. He was soon in Goa, where his performance was brilliant. The only blemishes, in this author's opinion, were his absence on the night of 18/19 December 1961, when HQ Southern Command changed plans and tasked his 50 Para Brigade to capture Panjim, and later, the avoidable assembling of Portuguese POWs before a firing squad, following an attempted escape by three POWs in Ponda. Describing him as 'India's finest combat leader', Maj. Gen. V.K. Singh said:

> Sagat Singh was one of India's most brilliant and audacious military leaders ... His standing among Indian military leaders is the same as that of Patton in the US Army, and of Rommel in the Wehrmacht.[*]
>
> As commander at various levels of his unmatched career—from Lieutenant Colonel to Lieutenant General, from commanding a battalion to commanding a Corps—Lt Gen Sagat Singh had never failed. Not content with the victory of an operation, he often went achieving far beyond his given battle objectives (Dacca in 1971 is a spectacular case in point). His exploits during the Goa operations are now part of the Indian Army's folklore, and are often used as examples for students of military science.[†]

Army Commander Heli-Lands in Goa

Lt Gen. J.N. Chaudhuri, GOC-in-C Southern Command, accompanied by Maj. Gen. Patrick O. Dunn, chief of staff, and Air Vice Marshal Erlic W. Pinto, AOC-in-C of the then unified Air Operations Command of the Indian Air Force, landed by a helicopter at Banastari at 9.00 a.m. on 19 December 1961. On being told that

---

[*] Ibid., p. 295.
[†] Ibid., p. 299.

the forward elements and the main body of 1 Para Punjab Battalion of 50 Parachute Brigade had already captured Panjim, he decided to visit Panjim. (However, P.N. Khera says in his book *Operation Vijay* that the army commander was accompanied by Air Vice Marshal Pinto and Shri B.N. Mullik of the Intelligence Bureau[*]—not Chief of Staff Maj. Gen. Patrick O. Dunn. It is evident that Khera has mixed up details of the army commander's second visit to Goa the next day. Air Vice Marshal Pinto and IB's Mullik accompanied the army commander on the second visit on 20 December.)

The previous evening's message of the army commander's visit to Banastari was followed by another at about 10 p.m., in which the army commander ordered 50 Para Brigade to capture Panjim. Accordingly, the advance elements in civilian motorized transport followed by the main body of 1 Para Punjab left Banastari for Panjim early that morning, leaving behind the rear elements of the battalion to build a helipad for the visiting party. HQ 50 Para Brigade made necessary arrangements to receive and escort the army commander, chief of staff and AOC-in-C of the IAF.

Lt Gen. Chaudhuri, when proceeding to Panjim, sent a wireless message to the chief of army staff breaking the news of the fall of Goa. He stopped at Ribandar to visit the hospital. The army commander then triumphantly drove to the Secretariat in Panjim, where he was mobbed by the joyous civilian population. They insisted he hoist the Indian National Flag on the Secretariat building. He gladly obliged the milling crowd.

The Signals Officer of 50 Para Brigade, Maj. R.R. Chatterjee, followed the army commander's motorcade in a jeep with a radio set, accompanied by the army commander's helicopter pilot, Sqn Ldr William Joseph Liddel. The roads were choked with cheering crowds and Maj. Chatterjee's jeep got separated from the army commander's motorcade. It was misdirected to a wrong direction.

---

[*] Khera, *Operation Vijay*, p. 85.

Maj. Chatterjee and Sqn Ldr Liddel found themselves at the Agasaim river front, miles away from Panjim, on an uncleared axis.

Military historian Major General V.K. Singh describes that, at the ferry point, the misdirected Indian military party found some sour-faced Portuguese officers and men and also noticed a number of armoured cars in an adjacent grove with their guns pointing menacingly in their direction. They did a quick about-turn and got away as fast as possible. According to Liddel, Chatterjee's Jeep moved faster than his aircraft.

At this point, the Portuguese military Quartel Geral (QG, meaning HQ) was still temporarily camped at Agasaim, although it was meant to be across the Zuari River at Cortalim (on its way to the last redoubt, the peninsula of Mormugao) by the previous day, 18 December. Major Francisco Morais, together with his officers and men, came to Cortalim to report to the QG after completing their last task of destroying the Zuari Bridge at Borim, which they did precisely at 1 p.m. on 18 December. Finding that the QG was still at Agasaim, Maj. Morais, together with Capt. Couto Leite, crossed the river to contact the QG at the Agasaim river front.[*]

Lt Gen. Chaudhuri then drove to Altinho in Panjim. He visited the Broadcasting House, met the Goan Secretary-General Abel Colaço in the latter's house and then went to the Portuguese officers' mess to accept surrender from the local military commander, Maj. Acácio Nunes Tenreiro.

Returning to downtown Panjim, the army commander said he wanted to visit the Mandovi Hotel. Small-arms fire still emanating from the Panjim customs house made him decide to go back to Belgaum.

Maj. Gen. Randhir Sinh wrote:

[CO 1 Para Punjab Lt Col] Sucha Singh mentions that in his typical flamboyant style, he (Lt Gen. Chaudhuri) desired to have

---

[*] Ramani, *Operation Vijay*, p. 212.

a drink at the Mandovi Hotel. However, while going there, some
Portuguese troops in the nearby Customs House opened fire. He
ordered 1 Para Punjab to clear them off, forgot about his drink
and proceeded ...*

On the way back to Banastari where he had landed, Lt Gen.
Chaudhuri stopped for a while at Velha Goa to visit the church
of St Francis Xavier. He took off for Belgaum in the helicopter at
around 1.30 p.m.

After the Army Commander took off, Maj. Gen. V.K. Singh tells
us, Maj. Chatterjee's Jeep got stuck till late in the evening between
two ferries, as the rear elements of 1 Para Punjab were moving up in
the opposite direction. Maj. Chatterjee and his driver had not eaten
anything that day and were agreeably surprised when the cheerful
proprietress of a taverna, housed in a dilapidated mud hut in a
small village—probably Banastari or Bhom or Kundai—brought
out chilled Becks beer out of a kerosene-powered refrigerator and
charged only one rupee for a bottle.

GOC-in-C Lt Gen. J.N. Chaudhuri would fly again to Goa
the next day, to call on the Portuguese governor-general, who
surrendered later that night.

Advance of the Main Task Force

17 Infantry Division, the main Task Force under just-promoted
Maj. Gen. Candeth, was allotted the easier route that was shorter,
followed the grain of the country running east-to-west in the
same direction as Goa's rivers, and largely had good, metalled
roads. Its operational brigade, 63 Infantry Brigade, was under
Brig. K.S. Dhillon (and the reserve brigade, 48 Infantry Brigade,
was under Brig. Gurbux Singh) and according to freedom fighter
Dr Suresh Kanekar:

---

* Sinh, *A Talent for War*, p. 65.

Brig. K.S. Dhillon's adjutant was Captain Pinto, a Goan, who naturally knew the language of the natives.*

63 Infantry Brigade was composed of three battalions: 3 Sikh under Lt Col John Diljit Bobb; 2 Bihar under Lt Col Kuldip Singh Chadha; and 4 Sikh Light Infantry under Lt Col Raghbir Bahadur Nanda. (Sikh and Sikh LI are different infantry regiments.)

The Sikh Light Infantry Regiment had the unique honour of contributing three battalions for the Goa ops: 1 Sikh LI under Lt Col Munshi Singh Brar with the reserve 48 Infantry Brigade of 17 Infantry Division; 2 Sikh LI under Lt Col Thomas Cherian with the operational 50 Para Brigade; and 4 Sikh LI under Lt Col Raghbir Bahadur Nanda with the operational 63 Infantry Brigade of 17 Infantry Division.[11]

The advance element of 3 Sikh reached Molem 7.30 a.m. and Colem at 9.30 a.m. on 18 December. The rest of the battalion reached Colem by 11 a.m. Learning that the Portuguese were fast withdrawing towards Ponda, the advance element pushed on as quickly as it could so that the enemy did not get time to regroup and resist at Ponda. At the Shigao mines, they

... found a number of vehicles belonging to a mining company (EMCO Mining Co.). The owners were very helpful and placed the vehicles at the disposal of the Indian troops.†

Using the mining vehicles, the advance element of 3 Sikh reached Darbandora at 5 p.m., to find the bridge blown. The rest of the 3 Sikh Battalion reached Darbandora at 10 p.m. They harboured there for the night. Ponda, it may be recalled, had already been occupied by 2 Para Maratha of the 50 Para Brigade earlier that afternoon.

---

* Suresh Kanekar, 2011, p. 146. This author, however, has not been able to trace the army captain Pinto.

† Ramani, 2008, p. 165, and Khera, 1974, p. 77.

The remainder of 63 Brigade—2 Bihar and 4 Sikh LI—marched from Anmod in two columns towards Ponda. They too were impeded by blown bridges and bad communications.

Due to broken bridges at Daukond and Darbandora, artillery and armour were ordered to change course and head south. They arrived at Sanvordem and harboured for the night. The sub-units crossed the Zuari River at Sanvordem the following morning to proceed to Vasco da Gama via Quepem, where the bridge had been blown the previous day, and Margao. There were two Goan-origin officers on this changed route, Maj. Luis Fonseca of Badem, Salvador do Mundo, who led AMX tanks of 8 Cavalry, and Capt. Paul Fernandes of Sarzora, who led the Black Cats motorized column.

(An aside: On 18 December, Maj. Luis Fonseca, of the 1 Armoured Division, was headed for Vasco da Gama. Starting from the ghats just past midnight, he had taken the diversion via Sanvordem–Quepem–Margao on account of demolished bridges, but knew it was a cakewalk. So, he parked the tanks and crew at Verna church grounds for the night and went to the Gama house of his aunt nearby ... he pined for her Goan cuisine! Crossing the river at a fordable point at Quepem—the bridge had been blown—Capt. Paul Fernandes was greeted in Hindi by a throng assembled at the town square. He replied in chaste Konkani. Not expecting a Goan, the crowd almost fainted—before the cheering began.)

From the broken bridge at Darbandora, the mounted B Company of 2 Bihar in four trucks refuelled by a mining company* took an alternative route to Ponda, called the Miners Road, and reached Khandepar at 4.15 p.m. (Portuguese records say this happened at 2 p.m.) to find another broken bridge. The company group waded · across to the far bank, where they camped for the night. The foot column of 2 Bihar arrived at Khandepar at 10 p.m. The river level had risen with the high tide and since wading through it was out of question, they pitched camp for the night at the near bank. The

---

* Khera, 1974, p. 79 footnote.

rear battalion troops of the 4 Sikh LI, after marching 43 km from the border with their heavy loads, reached Khandepar at about 1 a.m. on 19 December and also camped by the near bank.

Almost all of the operational 63 Brigade of the Main Task Force—3 Sikh, 2 Bihar and 4 Sikh LI battalions—rested by the Khandepar River, either at Darbandora or at Khandepar, on the night of 18/19 December 1961. (Artillery and armour was at the Zuari riverbank in Sanvordem.)

Troops by the near bank at Khandepar—4 Sikh LI and the foot column of 2 Bihar—crossed the Khandepar River at 6 a.m. of 19 December, wading through chest-high waters. From being a rear battalion, 4 Sikh LI would eventually become the vanguard of the brigade.

4 Sikh LI went via Ponda and arrived at Borim (code name: 'Dall Moth') at 8.30 a.m., to find another broken bridge—destroyed at 1 p.m. the previous day. Using ore transportation barges provided by Firma Chowgule (the mining house of the Chowgules), 4 Sikh LI crossed the river by 9.30 a.m. and, using motorized transport provided by the Chowgules and other private parties, reached Margao by noon (which by then was already secured by 'B' Company of 4 Rajput, named '20 Infantry Brigade').

4 Sikh LI had to halt in Margao for almost one-and-a-half hours for 2 Bihar to pass through as ordered.

2 Bihar, following 4 Sikh LI from Khandepar, crossed the river at Borim in the Chowgules barges at around 10.30 a.m., arrived in Margao early afternoon, passed through 4 Sikh LI and headed for Vasco da Gama. It met some resistance at Verna and some 5 km beyond Cortalim at 4 p.m., was ordered to halt, where it remained for a few days.

The main body of 4 Sikh LI started from Margao at 1.30 p.m. At Verna, by about 2.45 p.m., it was ordered to pass through 2 Bihar which was involved in a skirmish with Portuguese troops and head for Dabolim (code name: 'Rat Din') and Vasco da Gama (code name:

'Prem Pujari'). 4 Sikh LI reached the outskirts of Dabolim at 3.30 p.m. where its CO, Lt Col R.B. Nanda, was met by the Portuguese chief of staff Lt Col Marques de Andrade, in the company of either Archbishop Alvernaz or his emissary Msgr Gregório Magno de Souza Antão, with Capt. (Dr) Garcia da Silva as interpreter who conveyed the governor-general's decision to surrender.

Meanwhile, a tiny force of 4 Sikh LI led by Maj. Earl William ('Bill') Carvalho, later as a lieutenant colonel decorated with a M-in-D in the 1965 Indo–Pak War, with Capt. R.S.K. Bali, Capt. (later brigadier) R.K. Mehta, CO of the unit's 'B' Company, and a few men had raced in two vehicles towards Vasco da Gama. They were the first to reach Alpalqueiros Hill where the Portuguese governor and C-in-C, Maj. Gen. Vassalo e Silva, had camped. This tiny but bold group of officers and men was destined to storm the HQ of the last redoubt of the Portuguese forces in Goa. This event, of the highest significance, is best narrated by Brig. Ravi K. Mehta (veteran) himself:[*]

> ... in our race to Vasco da Gama just Maj. Bill Carvalho, Capt. R.S.K. Bali and I [Captain R.K. Mehta] with just a few boys from my Company (B Coy) and a couple of vehicles landed at the gates [of Alpalqueiros Camp].
>
> Bill decided, irrespective of the ground reality of our main column being far behind, to boldly move into the camp. We drove into the camp and the sentries did not stop us and on enquiry as to where their governor and general were, directed us to their officers club/mess.
>
> We entered the mess around early afternoon and again on enquiry headed to the table at which the governor and army chief were sitting. Apparently, the message had gone to them that the Indian Army had surrounded them in great strength and [there was] no possibility of resistance. Bill marched up to the table and saluted the governor who stood up and returned the salute. Bill stated that we had come to take over the base

---

[*] Interview with the author.

and the Portuguese soldiers (hundreds of them) be ordered to lay down their arms and remain confined to the barracks and to remain inside the camp perimeter and the governor to move to his residence and a guard of our soldiers would be posted.

The governor acknowledged and accepted the terms, and orders were issued by the army general to their troops. By late afternoon/evening most of my Company had arrived and the rest of the battalion was also catching up and we set up our positions around the camp.

'Prem Pujari' (Vasco da Gama, HQ of the Portuguese last redoubt) was now in the hands of the Indian Army. 4 Sikh LI Battalion CO, Lt Col Nanda, arrived later, had a meeting with the Portuguese brass and accepted the surrender of the governor/C-in-C and of the Goa garrison—a pertinent fact that was eclipsed by the stunning advance of 50 Para Brigade the previous day. Lt Col Nanda decided on a Formal Surrender Ceremony that was held later that night with the commander of 63 Brigade present.

Lt Col Nanda also took custody of the sword of the Portuguese governor-general/C-in-C. The sword is displayed at the museum of the Sikh LI Regimental Centre.

Sixty years later, however, mystery continues to shroud the whereabouts of the supreme symbol of Portuguese power in the East— the Portuguese governor's *bastão*. This ceremonial staff, or sceptre, was handed over by each outgoing governor to the incoming one at the Church of Bom Jesus in Old Goa. The holder of that staff or sceptre represented ultimate temporal power in Goa, once the nerve centre of all Portuguese possessions from East Africa to the Far East.

Governor-general Vassalo e Silva last held the staff. It was not sent by the ship *Índia* on 12 December 1961 or on the last flights out of Goa midnight of 18–19 December 1961, nor were there any records of the staff being destroyed before Indian soldiers marched in. Rumours were rife that a few days prior to 19 December 1961, Governor Vassalo e Silva handed over the staff to a dear Goan friend, a wealthy mine owner.

Meanwhile, a platoon of 4 Sikh LI captured some forty Portuguese troops still holding out at Baina, Vasco da Gama.

3 Sikh at Darbandora turned towards Sanvordem–Quepem and headed for Margao. Its mounted column reached Margao by last light and the marching column reached Dabolim by 10 p.m., both on 19 December. It was a topsy-turvy situation where the advance battalion arrived last and the rear unit (4 Sikh LI) led the advance of the brigade to its finale!

63 Brigade finally completed its task at 9.15 p.m. on 19 December when Brig. Dhillon formally accepted surrender from the Portuguese governor, a serving Major General, a rank higher than Brig. Dhillon's. (The army commander and the chief of army staff later paid personal visits to the Portuguese major general.)

No photograph exists of the formal surrender ceremony. Lt Col Nanda did arrange for a local photographer, but Dr Suresh Kanekar tells us that the signal to the photographer to click never came.

Lt Col Nanda unfortunately died in action on the China front ten months later when commanding the same battalion.

Bad Communications

If Brig. Sagat Singh was twice out of contact on 18 December, the main Task Force HQ 17 Infantry Division was also dogged by bad communications. Maj. Gen. Candeth was in Molem by 10 p.m. on 18 December night. He was out of touch with both Tactical HQ in Belgaum and his own operational 63 Brigade HQ.

Not aware that the army commander had changed plans and ordered the 50 Para Brigade to capture Panjim, Maj. Gen. Candeth ordered the 50 Para Brigade to hold on at Ponda and tasked the reserve 48 Infantry Brigade under Brig. Gurbux Singh to advance via Ponda and Old Goa and secure Panjim. The divisional commander was evidently unaware that Banastari and Betim near Panjim had already been occupied by 50 Para Brigade the previous evening— but without orders to enter the capital city.

Trudging behind a bridging fleet of ageing vehicles that frequently broke down on the narrow and steep Anmod ghat road, 48 Infantry Brigade reached Molem at 10 a.m., 19 December. By this time, the advance and main parts of 1 Para Punjab at Banastari were already in Panjim and the vanguard of 2 Sikh LI would shortly be there from across the river at Betim. Maj. Gen. Candeth would learn of this only later—by telephone, and later in the morning during a meeting with Brig. Sagat Singh, who informed the Task Force commander of the change in orders about the capture of Panjim in view of two units of 50 Para being in the vicinity of Panjim on the evening of 18 December itself.

Brig. Gurbux Singh was a singularly unlucky officer. He missed capturing Panjim in December 1961. And he would be soundly defeated by the Chinese at Bomdila ten months later; paying the price for political blunders of the time.

Later that night, the GOC was not aware that the 63 Infantry Brigade had taken Vasco da Gama and that Brig. Dhillon had accepted surrender from the Portuguese governor and C-in-C.

There was a breakdown in communication between HQ 63 Infantry Brigade and the main divisional headquarters, HQ 17 Infantry Division. The capture of the last Portuguese redoubt in Vasco da Gama was not known to Maj. Gen. Candeth until 11 p.m. on 19 December 1961.[*] Maj. Gen. V.K. Singh put the issue in perspective thus:

A major problem faced by the unit [Signals] was a shortage of secondary batteries. Against a deficiency of 700 secondary batteries of 125/175 AHC (ampere hour capacity), the unit was able to get only 102 new batteries. These had to be put through the 'initial charge' before they could be used. All available avenues such as the Police, Posts and Telegraphs Department and the local market at Belgaum were explored to get these batteries charged

---

[*] Khera, 1974, p. 88.

quickly. There was also an acute shortage of portable batteries used by Signals as well as other units. Against an overall shortage of over 2,000 portable batteries, only about 200 were released. These were delivered on 24 December 1961, after the operation was over.[*]

With limited mobility, the truck-mounted SCR 399 communication sets with the 17 Infantry Division and with the swiftly moving 50 Para Brigade also led to 'calamitous results'.

There were lighter moments too.

In a deceptive move from Karwar (Canacona–Balli–Margao), B Company of 4 Rajput was supplemented with Special Reserve Police personnel—and called an eighteen times bigger '20 Infantry Brigade'—to mislead the enemy.[†] The outrageous 'brigade' was under the command of Capt. D.P. Nayar, who must have enjoyed acting four ranks higher as a brigadier!

Save a brief encounter with an LMG detachment, Esquadrão de Reconhecimento No. 4 (E.Rec.4) at Ardhafond near Canacona town, the feint was the first to reach Margao, the third objective of the main Task Force after Panjim and Vasco da Gama. B Coy of 4 Rajput arrived just in time prior to noon on 19 December in Margao—where looting of cash and burning of government records was merrily in progress. The bold 'brigade' did a splendid job of taking charge of the Treasury, bank and other public buildings and restoring order.

The 1 Maratha Light Infantry (called the Jangi Paltan or the 'fighting unit') was deployed to capture Daman. A few days later, the chief of general staff, Army HQ, Lt Gen. B.M. Kaul, one of Krishna Menon's men behind Operation Vijay, paid a visit to Daman.

Lt Gen. Vijay Oberoi, later the vice chief of army staff, now a veteran, was then a newly commissioned second lieutenant with 1 MLI. He tells the story inimitably:

---

[*]   *History of the Corps of Signals*, vol. 3, Chapter 3.

[†]   Six companies form a battalion, the army's basic fighting unit, and three battalions form a brigade.

When leaving, Lt Gen. Kaul stopped near his jeep to shake everyone's hand. That's when a stray dog suddenly rushed across and for no reason bit the General on the leg and scooted. After his departure, the officers got together to delve into the probable reason why the dog chose the general. I put forth my two-anna worth suggestions … firstly, that it could be the sixth sense of dogs about disliking a person with bad vibes …

I was tasked to keep an eye on the dog … and send a daily signal to the General's secretariat about the [health of the] dog.

For the next few days, Second Lieutenant Oberoi drafted and routinely sent a short, three-worded, monotonous report, 'Dog behaving normally'. One day, he decided to break the monotony, change the repetitive signal, and make it slightly longer. It read, 'Dog normal. How is the General?' All hell broke loose when the unit's adjutant saw the office copy of that report. A quick reply was received. It said, 'No more reports required.'*

2 Para Maratha (erstwhile 3 Maratha Light Infantry before its conversion to a Parachute battalion), the main attack unit of 50 Para Brigade, had some young officers like Maj. 'Minnie' Mohite (his younger brother Capt. Shahji Mohite led the advance of 1 MLI in Daman) and Lt 'Jumbo' Badha. They had studied under Jesuits at St Paul's, Belgaum. When marching across Old Goa, the young officers took permission of their CO and went to quickly greet and hug their ex-Paulite Jesuit priest-teachers now at the Bom Jesus/Casa Professa. When Maj. Gen. Candeth, a Malayali Hindu, was military governor—from 20 December 1961 (the day after the Portuguese surrender) until 17 June 1962, when a civilian lieutenant governor (T. Shivshankar) took over—he made sure to attend Sunday Mass at the Bom Jesus Basilica to assuage Goan Catholics.

(There are no religious differences in the armed forces. A Hindu soldier could well worship in a masjid, a Muslim in a gurdwara, a Sikh in a temple, a Christian in a masjid, gurdwara, temple or in

---

* https://www.indianpolitics.co.in/when-a-dog-bit-a-general-and-the-2-lt-the-bullet/

the battalion chapel, where any jawan of any religious persuasion could join in worship. A pujari could well hold for a maulvi, a maulvi for a granthi, a granthi for a Catholic priest and a Catholic priest—called the military chaplain—could well Sunday sermonize soldiers of all faiths on moral science. It is unlike the bigoted civil society. The Indian soldier knows that all paths of faith lead to the same destination.)

The Navy Bashes In

The Indian Navy was tasked with blockading Goa, taking out the sole defending destroyer at Mormugao, taking over the port, and capturing Anjediva. The island became an all-Navy job because the Army said it had no resources to spare (a stance since questioned).

The Navy deployed sixteen warships and one oil tanker (Task Force 332) for the purpose. As already seen, there was false intelligence of the presence in Goa of four surface warships, three S class submarines and possible Pakistan and NATO intervention.

The INS *Vikrant* and her carrier group of five warships was deployed to resist any attempt of external intervention. Patrolling 80 km seaward, the group blockaded Goa by gaining control of all seaward approaches. Carrier borne Alizé anti-submarine aircraft reconnoitred the seas and Sea Hawk fighter aircraft stood by to strike any Portuguese warship slipping out of Goa and reaching within gun range of Indian territory, especially Bombay.

Minesweepers sanitized entry to Mormugao harbour (and would continue sanitizing Panjim harbour to the end of the hostilities). The support vessel, INS *Dharini*, carrying the Naval officer in-charge Goa Ops, Capt. H.A. Agate, as well as the oil tanker of the fleet, INS *Shakti*, stood by.

The Navy's assault squadron of three frigates—INS *Betwa,* INS *Cauveri* and INS *Beas*—positioned 13 km off the Goa coast, then bashed in to neutralize any coastal battery opening fire, blockade the port to ensure that no Portuguese ships entered or exited (non-Portuguese merchant vessels were allowed free egress) and finally took on the lone Portuguese destroyer, NRP *Afonso de Albuquerque*, from the noon of 18 December (which we shall see in another section).

Cruiser INS *Mysore*, the command ship for the surface action at Mormugao and Anjediva under Capt. (later rear admiral) Douglas St John Cameron, and frigate INS *Trishul*, under Capt. (later vice admiral) K.L. Kulkarni, were tasked to capture Anjediva Island.

Anjediva was a historic isle that provided refreshing water to discoverer Vasco da Gama in 1498 and shelter and water to conqueror Afonso de Albuquerque in 1510. It was celebrated as an 'isle of love' by poet Luis Vaz de Camões in *Os Lusíadas*. Now was the turn of the two Indian warships to record some history on the island (today part of the Indian Navy's INS *Kadamba*, the largest integrated naval base in Asia, the brainchild of Chief of Naval Staff Admiral Oscar Stanley Dawson in the early 1980s).

The island was defended by some thirty-six Portuguese troops, at least one of them Goan.

While INS *Mysore*, positioned northeast of Anjediva, would provide cover fire, INS *Trishul*, positioned close to Binge Bay near Karwar towards the southeast, would land three assault parties on the island. Some 75–80 officers and sailors from the gunnery school at the naval station, INS *Venduruthy* at Cochin, were hurriedly trained for this novel duty. They were rushed through basic land-fighting training, like army-style firing, crawling with heavy loads of weapons and ammunition in hilly terrain resembling Anjediva.

Keeping a watch for opposition from the island with her 4.7-inch Bofors gun, INS *Trishul* would lower the boats. After a burst on the beaches with close-range weapons (40-mm Bofors guns), the landing parties would be sent, one after the other, in a motorboat with a towing whaler and an LMG mounted on the bow. If the situation was favourable, INS *Mysore* would provide a motor cutter and a whaler to expedite the landings.

The operation began at 7 a.m. on 18 December. The first assault party, *Rustum,* led by Lt (later rear admiral) Arun Auditto, later a submarine specialist, landed successfully at 7.15 a.m. It proceeded to the island's beach without any resistance.

As the second assault party—led by Lt (later commander) Noel Kelman, a senior commissioned naval gunner—approached the island by 7.45 a.m., he saw a white flag being hoisted up near Lima beach. The Portuguese later said that political prisoners detained at the fort hoisted the flag. There were no political prisoners on the island. White flags went up from different points on the island and could be seen from the Indian warships. The white flags confirmed the initial suspicion that the defenders wanted to surrender, as they had not resisted the first landing. The second landing party relaxed guard and continued towards the island.

The Portuguese Bateria de Artilharia 2 (B.Art.2) suddenly opened machine gun fire. Lt Kelman pressed ahead towards the beach, zigzagging his boat to avoid the gunfire. By the time the bullet-riddled boat beached, three of his men were killed and Lt Kelman was wounded in both legs.

When the firing on the second landing party began, Chief Petty Officer Gunnery Instructor Ali Mohammed, the most experienced member in land-fighting from the first landing party already on the island, threw a hand grenade and was the first to jump over and lead his men into action, drawing off much of the fire opened on the second boat. The INS *Trishul* opened up with her 40-mm Bofors gun and silenced the enemy machine gun.

Radio-telephony also failed. The main wireless set of the landing parties had been damaged and the walkie-talkies were out of range of the warships. Such a breakdown of communications could have led to disastrous results.

Cdr (later captain) A.F. Collaco, a Goan who knew a smattering of the Portuguese language (he later interrogated the POWs), a specialist in naval communications, was the fleet operations officer of the Indian fleet aboard the INS *Mysore*. He volunteered to lead a team ashore to re-establish communications and aid the landing parties. The problem was he had never fired a gun before, not even his service revolver. The surface action commander and skipper of the INS *Mysore*, Capt. Douglas St John Cameron, very reluctantly allowed him to go.

. That difficult decision of Capt. Cameron was to change the course of the naval assault.

Cdr. Collaco got a team with two wireless operators with backpack radios and two signals sailors with portable 'Aldis' signalling lamps and some sailors. An IAF squadron leader—liaison officer on board the INS *Mysore*—and a cameraman joined them. Upon landing safely, Cdr. Collaco quickly re-established communications between the landing parties and the ships, and, taking Lt Kelman's combat sailors, went in aid of the first landing party. When he and team advanced to capture a wireless transmitter, they were fired upon from the church, resulting in the death of one sailor.

That was it.

The assault parties were ordered to descend to the beaches. The two Indian warships then pounded the Portuguese positions with high explosive shells as well as 40-mm Bofors guns, taking care to avoid the two churches. In the words of Cdr. Collaco,

> ... trees being uprooted by *Trishul's* firing, scenic beauty mixed with death and devastation. It was all over soon ...[*]

Seven defenders were killed, four wounded. According to a report quoted by author Shrikant Ramani, Portuguese fatalities included Damuno Vassu Canencar (Damu Vassu Kanekar, a Goan).[†] Casualties on the Indian side were seven killed, two officers and twenty-two sailors wounded. Twenty-one defenders surrendered at about 4.30 p.m.

Of the four remaining defenders, two were smoked out the next day, one was stung by sea urchins to death when trying to escape by swimming to the shore, while Private Manuel Caetano, a white Portuguese, managed to swim to the mainland. He was

---

[*] Indian Navy's official account of the ops, *Sun Sets on Portugal's Asian Empire: Liberation of Goa, Daman and Diu.*

[†] Ramani, 2008, p. 342.

fed, sheltered and advised to turn himself in by a Karwar fisherman family. Caetano surrendered to Karwar police on 22 December 1961. In all, twenty-four were taken POW. The Indian tricolour went up the flag mast at Anjediva at 2.25 p.m., 19 December, after the Indian Naval Forces were held at bay for some thirty hours.[12]

When the INS *Mysore* returned to Mormugao, Capt. Agate gave Cdr. Collaco the keys of a captured jeep, telling him to gallivant around in his home state. So, along with Surg. Cdr. Frederick Nazareth, a fellow Goan also aboard the INS *Mysore,* Cdr. Collaco went visiting relatives at an aristocratic house in Margao.

'Are the Indians coming to burn us all?' the relatives asked.

Cdr. Collaco replied:

> The only thing burning will be the two tongues of these Indians after eating your sorpotel [actually sarapatel, a highly spicy local pork preparation] and drinking your Johnnie Walker.
>
> At least our relatives were reassured but it took quite a bit of Scotch to complete the job. They had much more reassurance and much less Scotch. They could hardly believe that they had become as much Indian as we were. They still felt they were Portuguese subjects.

Cdr Collaco wrote the above the Indian Navy's 1961 account—written long after his retirement, when he had relocated to Canada.

Despite the injuries and heavy bleeding in both legs, Lt Kelman continued to assist in the operations throughout the day. It was only at end of ops—after the National Flag was hoisted at Anjediva—that he sought medical attention.

Lt Noel Kelman won the Indian Navy's first Kirti Chakra, India's second highest peace-time gallantry award, then called the Ashoka Chakra Class II. He was also the first Indian naval officer to win a gallantry award in post-Independence India.

Lt Arun Auditto, shot in the shoulder, was decorated with a peace-time award (Nao Sena Medal). Chief Petty Officer, Gunnery Instructor Ali Mohammed was awarded the Ashoka Chakra Class

III (Shaurya Chakra) for his gallantry. Others were also decorated, but none were given War Gallantry awards because, like Hyderabad, India dubbed this a 'police action'.

Cdr. Noel Kelman, who was decorated in World War II for his role in sinking a Japanese submarine, was later the commanding officer of Goa Naval Area and lived in Goa after retirement, still coping with the consequences of the 1961 injury in his legs, until he passed away at ninety-two on 23 August 2019 at Porvorim. The Navy built memorials at Anjediva and INS *Gomantak* at Vasco da Gama in memory of the fallen heroes.

The Navy's decision to capture Anjediva on its own has been questioned. Air Vice Marshal Arjun Subramaniam (veteran) writes,

> A small amphibious force comprising trained army units of even a platoon or company strength may have done the job in a more professional manner. In a scathing critique of the operation, Maj. Gen. D.K. Palit, then a brigadier and director of military operations, recounts how he had identified a platoon of Gorkhas from the 4th Battalion of the 9th Gorkha Rifles and had them positioned in Bombay. To his surprise the GOC-in-C, Lieutenant General Chaudhuri had no intentions of sharing any glory with the Indian Navy and decided that if the army had to assault Anjadiv, it would do so on its own despite having no expertise. Bravely, the navy attempted it, but succeeded against amateurish opposition only after suffering heavy casualties ...[*]

Indian Air Force Silences Radio Goa, Bombards Dabolim

At 7 a.m., 18 December, six Hawker Hunter fighter aircraft of the IAF's 17 Squadron led by Squadron Leader Jayvant Singh from the Poona airbase and the Sambra, Belgaum, airfield mounted a

---

[*] Arjun Subramaniam, *India's Wars,* 2016, p. 193.

rocket and gun-cannon attack on the radio centre at Bambolim and destroyed it in ten minutes.

In one fell swoop, Goa was totally isolated from the outside world. Goans would never again hear the familiar 7 a.m. welcome line of Radio Goa's *Alvorada Musicala*, the opening programme: '*Aqui é Portugal, fala Emissora de Goa*' (Here is Portugal, you are tuned to Radio Goa).

Simultaneously, twelve Canberra bombers of 35 Squadron, led by Wing Commander N.B. Menon from the Poona airbase, escorted by four Hawker Hunters of 37 Squadron also from Poona, dropped sixty-three bombs, each of 1000 pounds, to disable the Dabolim runway.

As if 63,000 pounds of explosive did not suffice, a second wave of eight Canberras of 16 Squadron, led by Wing Commander Surinder Singh from the Poona airbase, escorted by four Hawker Hunters of 17 Squadron from Sambra, Belgaum, dropped another 48,000 pounds of bombs at about 7.40 a.m.

Within thirty minutes, Flt Lt Vivian Christopher Goodwin was scrambled up to fly over Dabolim and photograph the bombing results. Damage to the runway was not satisfactory. Hence yet another bombing raid—Green 4—with Flt Lt Goodwin was undertaken from Poona with four unescorted Canberras (hence the name, Green 4, without the cover of fighter jets).

Green 4 dropped another 24,000 pounds of bombs at about 11.40 a.m., causing some damage to the runway. The Portuguese described it as the 'most violent' bombardment of the airport.

The bombing of a civilian aerodrome was later debated. Intelligence reports, however, said the Força Aérea Portuguesa (Portuguese Air Force) had transonic jet fighters like US-made F-86 Sabres, a section of France-made Fouga Magister, some interceptor F-104 Starfighters and transport aircraft modified to carry bombs at Dabolim. With the onset of the invasion, such aircraft would best be left grounded by immobilizing the runway. (As it transpired, there was not a single defence aircraft at Dabolim; it was false intelligence yet again.)

The bombing, however, was largely ineffective. The quantum of 1,35,000 pounds of explosive that were rained down on Dabolim should have disabled many airfields its size. But most bombs were World War II duds, dropped from a height of six kilometres (20,000 feet, when the enemy's obsolete 4 cms AA guns, even if serviceable and had sufficient ammunition, would be ineffective at half that height). Many bombs veered off target. Some unexploded ones were found—decades later—some distance away in the wooded hill slopes of Chicalim. There were reports of unexploded bombs being found at Sada plateau in Vasco da Gama, some three miles away. That was possible because an airstrip had been constructed at Sada headland in 1930 (a quarter of a century before Dabolim) to receive the first flight from Portugal—and IAF bomber pilots may have relied more on visual indicators than navigational ones and mistaken Sada for Dabolim.

Prof. Valentino Viegas, then a Goan youngster at Betim, now in Portugal, says in *18 de Dezembro de 1961—Uma Data Histórica*, published in the *Diario de Noticias*, that he heard the deafening roar of the Hawker Hunters flying low over Betim towards Panjim just before 7 a.m. on 18 December 1961. One neighbour said Panjim was bombed. Another said the explosions came from further afield. A curious Valentino hopped onto a ferryboat to Panjim to find out.

People walked briskly. Outside a café opposite Police HQ was a young *mestiço* (Luso-Indian) soldier, a known loudmouth, rifle in hand. Asked what he was doing, the soldier said he had been ordered to remain there. When Valentino pressed for the reason, the braggart replied, 'Recognizing my accurate marksmanship, I've been posted here to take on the enemy transonics zooming overhead.'

At the Adilshah Palace (governor's office), Valentino saw the charade of troops crouched in combat position, their ancient Mausers pointing towards the river—as if waiting for a non-existent enemy to appear from the Mandovi amphibiously or from underwater and launch an assault at the palace.

That was the tragi-comic reaction of Portuguese defenders—who, without the requisite manpower, material and training, could hardly have been expected to do any better.

During the second bombing mission (7.40 a.m.), Flt Lt Trevor Joseph Fernandes of Siolim–Goa, who had earlier been a part of the disabling of the radio centre at Bambolim, flew a Hunter to provide cover for the Canberra bombers. He noticed the tail of a Lockheed Martin Super Constellation sticking out of a hangar at Dabolim. He radioed 2 Tactical Air Centre in Poona for permission to immobilize the aircraft.

Permission was declined ostensibly on grounds of possible civilian casualties. The real reason may have been to capture the civilian aircraft intact as a war trophy.

The Super Constellation, a civilian aircraft belonging to TAP, the Portuguese airline, was actually one of only three aircraft then present at Dabolim. The others were a Douglas DC-4 Skymaster of the local airline, TAIP and a TAIP Viking undergoing repairs in a hangar, not visible to Flt Lt Fernandes from the sky.

The TAP Super Constellation had landed earlier the previous night with a load of sausages—and by those sausages hangs a queer story.

The Portuguese Air Force sought to transport ten tonnes of Instalaza anti-tank grenades in two of its DC6 transports to Goa. The DCs were denied landing at the American Wheelus Air Base in Libya. They returned to Portugal and chartered a civilian plane from TAP (the Super Constellation) to which the cargo was switched—now mixed with bags of sausages—but Pakistan refused to let them transport weapons through Karachi. The ordnance was offloaded and the remaining cargo was allowed to proceed to Goa.

When the TAP Super Constellation eventually landed at Dabolim, anxious troops rushed to open the boxes, to be greeted by a strange sight: bags of sausages instead of boxes of grenades!

The flight also brought a group of female paratroopers to help in the evacuation of Portuguese civilians. An officer wryly quipped,

'Lisbon must have sent them [the sausages, one figures] to celebrate *The Soldier's Christmas.'*

Had the grenades arrived as well, and had the Panjim garrison launched them on the 7 Light Cavalry's Stuarts and AMX tanks at the open river front at Betim the next evening, one shudders to think of the consequences for Panjim. The 2 Sikh LI's artillery and armour had enough fire power to flatten the town.

Daring Escape by the Civvies

The IAF's bombing of Dabolim had succeeded in creating only a few craters in the runway. Facing an uncertain future, Portuguese officials in Goa anxiously sought to send their wives and children to safety, after the evacuation by commercial flights and by the overloaded ship *Índia* on 12 December.

There were two operational civilian aircraft at Dabolim—the TAP Super Constellation that had ferried the sausages and female paratroopers just the previous night, and TAIP's DC-4 Skymaster. As darkness fell, some of the runway's craters were quickly patched up.

Governor-general/C-in-C Maj. Gen. Vassalo e Silva permitted the TAP Super Constellation and the TAIP DC-4 Skymaster to take off from Dabolim, despite commencement of hostilities and Goa being surrounded from land, sea and air.

The two aircraft were readied with the wives and children of Portuguese officials and important documents of state. All dispensable stuff onboard—including extra seats—was offloaded to reduce aircraft weight.

With its lights switched off and throttles at the minimum to avoid visual and sound detection, the two aircraft had their tryst with destiny—first making a daringly short but a highly risky take-off over just 700 metres of the bombed runway in complete darkness and using only a part of the engine power around that midnight (18/19 December 1961), and then dodging enemy radars all the way to the point of destination.

The first to take off was the TAP's Super Constellation piloted by Capt. Manuel Correia Reis and his navigation and engineer cockpit crew. The Super Constellation's loud engines drew shots-in-the-dark from Indian warships arrayed offshore in the general direction of Dabolim.

In quick succession, TAIP's DC-4 Skymaster—piloted by Maj. Austen Goodman Solano de Almeida, a Portuguese Air Force pilot from the Lages Air Force Base in Azores, Portugal, on deputation with the local airline as its director of operations—took off in complete darkness and least sound.[*] Honouring his British mother (which explains his Christian names), Maj. Solano de Almeida had served the Royal Air Force during World War II.[†]

The two aircraft were headed for Karachi, the nearest friendly airport, at a distance of about 1300 km by the normal aerial route. But times were not normal, and instead of flying northwards along the coast, the two aircraft sped out west, seaward.

Before they got out of Indian airspace, they were spotted by IAF radars. The two aircraft split in different directions as a diversionary tactic. An IAF Vampire NF54 Night Fighter was scrambled from Poona to intercept the Skymaster, but could not make contact.

Both the civilian aircraft flew a circuitous and longer route at a very low altitude ('almost at tree-top level') to avoid radar detection—what is called as *razzo moto* flying, particularly dangerous for propeller-driven aircraft of the time, due to turbulence, cross winds and over consumption of fuel—all the way to Karachi.

Upon arrival, the crew received a standing ovation for having undertaken such a daring mission.

Maj. Solano de Almeida, later a lieutenant colonel, was married to a girl living in Goa, Celeste Vidigal. Of their three sons, two

---

[*] Portuguese Army (Exército) and Air Force (Força Aérea) ranks are common land military ranks; only their navy (Marinha) has traditional naval ranks.

[†] Email interview with Antonio Palhinha Machado, a neighbour of (now deceased) Maj. Almeida in Lisbon.

became distinguished TAP pilots, as also did their only grandson.[*] Maj. Solano de Almeida demitted commission with the Portuguese Air Force and took to commercial flying with the TAP. He flew Boeing 737s with Air Malta in the 1980s.

Air ops went smoothly over Goa, save two aberrations, both involving ground forces of the 50 Para Brigade.

As mentioned earlier, on the afternoon of 18 December, Tactical HQ Southern Command lost contact with Brig. Sagat Singh perhaps due to the unexpectedly swift advance of his 50 Para Brigade. Tactical HQ sent an IAF Harvard of 122 Squadron from Sambra, Belgaum, to literally 'drop' a message to the brigadier. The aircraft did not have the IAF markings painted on the underside. Unable to identify the aircraft as friend or foe, troops of 2 Sikh LI fired with small arms at the Harvard, puncturing two holes in the aircraft's belly.

In the second case, IAF repaid the compliment when four Vampires were scrambled to attack Portuguese armoured recce vehicles. Instead, in the words of military historian Maj. Gen. V.K. Singh, the four aircraft 'put in a set piece rocket attack' on artillery vehicles of 50 Para Brigade's 17 Para Field Regiment near Piliem— fortunately, with no casualties. Capt. George A. Newton rushed to his radio relay set, opened communications with Belgaum, and frantically radioed: 'Request the IAF to cease and desist'.

Later, All India Radio (AIR) sought the Army's help to salvage the equipment of Emissora de Goa, the Portuguese broadcasting station. On directions of the Military Governor, Capt. Newton was made available to AIR. From 25 to 29 December, he and the AIR engineers rigged up a 5-kilowatt transmitter at Bambolim.

Around the time, two powerful Phillips radio transmitters bought by Goa's Cosme Matias Menezes group (CMM), deployed at the Bambolim radio centre, bombed by the IAF, were being ferried by the Indian Armed Forces. Both transmitters were lost in the Mandovi River due to a mishap. CMM sued the Government

---

[*] Ibid.

of India, won the case, and was paid the cost of the transmitters with interest.*

Foreign correspondents in Goa had a tough time getting their despatches transmitted since the Portuguese transmitter at Bambolim was destroyed and the telegraph line to Belgaum cut off. A staff officer from brigade HQ was detailed to collect the despatches and send them to Tactical Headquarters Southern Command by returning helicopters. Despatches were then cabled from Belgaum.

Two More Acts of Portuguese Resistance (Other Than at Anjediva)

A few minutes past 8 a.m. of 18 December, or about one hour after the bombing of the radio centre at Bambolim and the bombing of the airport at Dabolim, the Portuguese governor-general/C-in-C left the capital city and headed for the last redoubt of Mormugao.

(Of the many fabricated stories floating around at the time, one story said that he went to Mormugao because he wanted to flee from Goa by air. If that was so, he would have easily travelled aboard either of the two civilian aircraft that, as seen, escaped from Dabolim—with his permission—later that night. Another fantastic story was that Air Vice Marshal Erlic Pinto came snooping into Goa some days before the ops. Only the thoroughly unlettered could produce such stories. Air Vice Marshal Pinto was India's AOC-in-C Operational Command, Indian Air Force, responsible for the direction of air ops throughout India—and the most likely next air chief, but for an unfortunate helicopter accident in J&K on 22 November 1963 that killed him together with four top Indian Army officers. Air Vice Marshal Pinto was way too big in the military's hierarchy to be a common snooper!)

The governor-general/C-in-C issued no fresh orders now that the assault had begun. This meant that the defence plan, Plano

---

* Teotónio R. de Souza, *Goa in Retrospect* in *Portuguese Literary and Cultural Studies,* University of Massachusetts, Dartmouth, 2010, p. 158.

Sentinela, would remain in force: that is, delay the enemy at the borders with conventional or guerrilla tactics, fall back to the riverfronts when no longer possible to halt the enemy advance and explode the bridges, hold back the enemy on the other bank of the river for as long as possible, and when that too was difficult, gradually fall back to the last redoubt, Mormugao, and defend it at any cost, until UN intervention arrived.

By 10.30 a.m., 18 December, Capt. (later general) Carlos de Azeredo, appointed as the coordinating officer of the security forces in Goa only days before, took command of around 500 troops retreating from other positions, to form the second line of defence—from St Jacinto Island to Issorcim, across the isthmus of the Mormugao peninsula. He had trenches dug rapidly, fortified with coconut trunks to fend off enemy artillery, and for weapons, an equally ridiculous duo of Lewis light machine guns and ancient rifles. Recall that Capt. Azeredo believed the Plano Sentinela was 'totally unrealistic and unachievable'.

Yet, one could say foolhardily, Portuguese defenders staged three acts of resistance in Goa. The first as seen was at the Anjediva Island, where they held Indian Naval Forces at bay for some thirty hours, with a comparatively high loss of lives. There were two other notable acts of resistance in Goa proper.

One was a skirmish at Verna staged by Portuguese troops retreating from Margao to the last redoubt at Mormugao. The other was the resistance put up by the lone naval destroyer in Goa against three Indian frigates at Mormugao.

Oddly, both incidents heralding the Portuguese exit evoked the history of their entry into Goa 451 years before—and the name of the man who had conquered Goa in 1510. Let us consider the Verna skirmish of 19 December first.

2 Bihar Battalion of the 63 Infantry Brigade was pressing from Margao towards Vasco da Gama. When it reached Verna at around 2 p.m., it was told of the presence of more than 450 Portuguese soldiers of the Agrupamento Afonso de Albuquerque, an undersized battalion, retreating from the military camp at

Rawanfond, Aquem Baixo, near Margao. They were in a fallback to the last redoubt at Mormugao and had halted at Verna.

C Company of 2 Bihar, under Capt. N.K. Bhandari, was ordered on the left flank to cut off the road behind the enemy position. B Company under Maj. M.M. Bose charged from the right flank. The Portuguese opened up with small arms fire. The brief but fierce encounter accounted for the largest number of casualties on both sides in Goa. On the Portuguese side, twenty-seven officers, twenty-three sergeants and 398 soldiers surrendered (448 in all; the rest perished), and fourteen armoured cars, twenty-one jeeps and a large quantity of arms and equipment were seized.

'There were about 450 prisoners [Portuguese POWs at Verna],' recalls freedom fighter Dr Suresh Kanekar, who, together with Purushottam Kakodkar and Ronald Coutinho of Margao, was proceeding to Vasco da Gama in Coutinho's car. Kanekar says he . . .

> . . . naturally thought of the number matching closely the years of
> Portuguese colonial rule imposed on Goa.*

As the encounter progressed, 4 Sikh LI reached Verna and as seen before, was ordered to pass through 2 Bihar and race to Dabolim and Vasco da Gama. A tiny force of the unit in two vehicles led by Maj. Bill Carvalho reached Alpalqueiros Hill in Vasco da Gama early afternoon, confined the Portuguese governor-general/C-in-C to his house, and got scores of soldiers present there to lay down arms and remain within the barracks. The CO of 4 Sikh LI, Lt Col R.B. Nanda arrived later in the evening, accepted surrender of the governor and of the Portuguese garrison and organized a formal surrender ceremony later that night (19 December). 2 Bihar was ordered to halt some 5 km beyond Cortalim.

And a controversial act of non-resistance: Second Lieutenant Manuel José Marques da Silva had arrived in Goa by the evacuee ship *Índia* two weeks before to take over command of the NRP

---

* Suresh Kanekar, 2011, pp. 146–47.

Sírius and her eleven-member crew. As seen, the Portuguese patrol vessel was armed with a lone 20-mm Oerlikon gun.

Of this author's two mentors in journalism, B.G. Koshy edited Bombay's the *Current Weekly* (while D.M. Silveira of Goltim–Divar, now no more, edited the *Onlooker*). Koshy later joined the corporate world and was long with Oerlikon in Zurich, Switzerland. He recalls the 20-mm Oerlikon gun—an ubiquitous weapon fitted to patrol boats, warships and aircraft of all the major militaries in the world—was sold to Portugal ('at excellent prices') by Dr Emile Buhrle, chairman of Oerlikon. Oerlikon's 20-mm gun was a bestseller in the 1930s.[*]

When the naval battle between the Portuguese destroyer and the three Indian frigates began at Mormugao on 18 December, 2/Lt Marques da Silva saw the rapid and superior enemy firepower that only destroyer NRP *Afonso de Albuquerque,* armed with four 120-mm cannons, could respond to. His patrol boat was like a lame chicken before rampaging elephants.

2/Lt Marques da Silva decided to scuttle the vessel. He claimed to follow the rule book—avoid capture and destroy equipment before it falls into enemy hands. He evacuated the crew and tried to sink the vessel by opening the bottom hatches. Finding them rusty, he said he smashed the boat against the rocks at Dona Paula.

Portuguese records, however, said that the patrol boat was abandoned with its engines running and implied that 2/Lt Marques da Silva had concocted the story in order to run away from battle.

Boarding the MV *Olga Minakoulis*, a Greek freighter, at Mormugao, with his crew—believed dead in Portugal—2/Lt Marques da Silva escaped to Pakistan. Arriving in Karachi on 25 December, he and the crew took a flight and arrived in Lisbon 30 December 1961.

The PIDE took them into custody upon arrival. 2/Lt Marques da Silva was accused of treachery and expelled from the armed

---

[*] Author's telephonic interview with B.G. Koshy.

forces. Portuguese authorities held that 2/Lt Marques da Silva had been a coward and had sunk the vessel prematurely.

2/Lt Marques da Silva wrote his version in a book titled *NRP Sírius.*[*]

The Other Act of Portuguese Resistance

This was the valiant, even if purposeless, resistance by the NRP *Afonso de Albuquerque,* a medium-sized (2434 tonne) Portuguese destroyer (an Aviso de 1ª Classe or Escoltador Oceânico, which means destroyer) that Portugal—for reasons not clear—called a frigate, but the Lisbon media called a Cruzador or a cruiser. Indian intelligence seemed to rely on the Portuguese media description.

A cruiser is larger than a destroyer, and a destroyer is bigger and more powerful than a frigate. The Indian Navy took no chances. It pressed three frigates to take on what was thought to be a cruiser (and two other frigates and three S-class submarines wrongly believed to be at Mormugao). *Afonso de Albuquerque* was, in the words of Commodore Gilbert Menezes, VSM, from Raia, Goa, 'a junk destroyer'.[†]

The Portuguese destroyer was built in the UK in 1934. After World War II, she was revamped and rebranded as F470, although always accounted for in Portuguese Navy registers as a destroyer. Developing 21 knots, she had an operating radius of 8000 nautical miles. Besides two depth-charge throwers and two mine-laying rails, she was armed with six Vickers-Armstrong multiple Pom-Pom guns (quick firing anti-aircraft guns nicknamed after the sound they produced when firing) two of 80-mm and four of 40-mm calibre, and four 120-mm Vickers-Armstrong cannons, two fore and two aft, each capable of firing about one round a minute, or in the aggregate, five times a minute effectively. The guns were manually controlled.

---

[*]   *Visão História-Queda Índia Portuguesa*, vol. 14, 2011, p. 29.

[†]   Author's interview with Cmde Gilbert Menezes (veteran).

Albuquerque was under the command of fifty-seven-year-old Capt. (later commodore) António da Cunha Aragão Teixeira, who was looking forward to his transfer orders to Portugal, expected in January 1962. *Albuquerque* was anchored at Mormugao. The warship could hold a complement of 229 sailors. At the time of action on 18 December 1961, she had 185 sailors, all ranks.

The three Indian frigates tasked to engage the *Albuquerque* were INS *Betwa* (under Cdr R.K.S. Gandhi, head of the assault squadron), INS *Cauvery* (under Lt Cdr S.V. Mahadevan) and INS *Beas* (under Cdr. T.J. Kunnenkeril). *Betwa* and *Beas,* both diesel-propelled Type 41 Leopard class frigates built in Newcastle, UK, in 1958/59, made speeds of 24 knots and, armed with twin semi-auto 4.5" (115-mm) Mark 6 turrets, could fire 16 rounds per minute each, with the latest British radar-controlled precision fire. The older *Cauvery* was slower, but the three Indian frigates could fire a total of forty rounds per minute, against five of the *Albuquerque*, or eight times faster.

Albuquerque was battle ready at 6.55 a.m. on 18 December 1961. Although the radio centre at Bambolim was put out of action by the IAF by 7.10 a.m., communications were kept open with Lisbon from this destroyer until about 10.30 a.m.

The Indian Task Force of the three frigates entered Goan waters by 9 a.m. From around 11 a.m., the IAF began bombing the Mormugao harbour. Despite a shortage of personnel to man them, *Albuquerque* trained her pom-poms toward the IAF aircraft zooming overhead, without effect.

Leader of the assault squadron, Cdr. Gandhi, received orders to take on the Portuguese destroyer just before noon. Within seconds, signalling to the *Beas* and *Cauvery* to follow, he sped towards Mormugao at 23 knots, with the *Beas* sliding in astern of the *Betwa*.

The *Betwa* fired a warning shot at around 12.15 p.m. from about 7 km and signalled to the *Albuquerque* by light, 'Please surrender or I open fire'. *Albuquerque* replied, 'Wait'. Cdr. Gandhi waited precisely three minutes and then ordered, 'Open fire!'

As each of the three Indian frigates took turns firing, they continuously radioed in Morse calling upon the *Albuquerque* to surrender—direct orders from New Delhi were to capture the warship intact.

Besides facing far more rapid and superior (radar-controlled) firepower and being outnumbered, the Portuguese warship was in a confined position, restricting her manoeuvrability. Yet, instead of surrendering, the defending warship lifted anchor and headed out to return the fire.

Skipper of the destroyer, Capt. Aragão, told the naval radio station at Alges, Portugal, 'We are being attacked. We are answering.'

Albuquerque then returned and slid behind a Panama flag ore carrier, *Ranger*, docked in Mormugao. Indian naval fire hit the *Ranger* and 'great quantities of ore started gushing out', according to a Portuguese version.

The exchange of fire—at a distance of about 5 km—continued for some ten minutes. Portuguese sources claimed that the *Albuquerque* knocked off two Indian frigates that were quickly replaced by reserve frigates from the carrier group. Capt. Aragão himself thought, mistakenly again, that he had hit the *Betwa* (F139) twice; he was going by the thick clouds of dark smoke produced by the diesel of Type 41 frigates when suddenly revved up to high speeds.[13]

Portuguese sources said the Indian frigates then used anti-personnel shrapnel bombs at about 12.25 p.m.

Lt Cdr John Eric Gomes, who was on the *Cauvery*, rubbishes this, maintaining that no Indian frigate was hit and none replaced.[*] He said the *Cauvery* used only conventional ordnance (it was a 4-inch conventional shell fired by the *Cauvery* that finally did the *Albuquerque* in).

However, in the Indian Navy's official account of the ops, Cdr. Gandhi states that 25 per cent of *Betwa's* armament comprised of HE/VT (high explosive, variable time) shells filled with shrapnel and fitted with fuses that go off when only a few feet away from the target. His second broadside was a direct hit on the *Albuquerque's*

---

[*] Interview with the author.

anti-aircraft gun director, which fell on the main director. Shrapnel killed and wounded several crew members of the *Albuquerque,* including Capt. Aragão. The warship's radio officer and four others were killed, and twelve sailors were wounded.

Capt. Aragão was wounded in the chest (a three-inch long piece of shrapnel was later surgically extracted from his chest, just short of his heart). London's *Daily Telegraph* described him as 'the only hero of this whole tragic episode'.

Command was handed over to the No. 2, Capt. José Maria Caldas Frazão Pinto da Cruz. Around 12.35 p.m., the crew immobilized and wrecked the engines and boilers of the destroyer.

A little past 1 p.m., the *Albuquerque* took a direct hit, swerved 180 degrees, and beached upright in 10 feet of water at the shore opposite Mormugao harbour. The *coup de grâce* was delivered by the *Cauvery,* with a 4-inch salvo.

Hoisting a large white flag, which curled around the mast (and was probably not seen by Indian naval personnel), the crew set the vessel on fire and disembarked by about 1.10 p.m., swimming a distance of about 150 metres to the shore. Several of the 180 Portuguese sailors said they came under Indian naval fire when swimming ashore. Portuguese colonel, Carlos A. Morais, in his book *A Queda da Índia Portuguesa,* wrote that Indian warships continued to fire at the area where the crew took shelter.

Cdr. Gandhi said that the moment he saw the *Albuquerque* had beached, he ordered cease fire and furthermore,

> ... ordered the other two ships to withdraw and we made the necessary signals to Naval Headquarters to say that *Albuquerque* had been destroyed and was now lying sunk in Goa harbour ... We had received a fair amount of duff [faulty] intelligence from Naval Headquarters.*

---

* Indian Navy's official account of the ops, *Sun Sets on Portugal's Asian Empire: Liberation of Goa, Daman and Diu.*

That night (18 December), *Betwa* was ordered to Tiracol, where intelligence reported the presence of a Portuguese frigate. When the *Betwa* got there, she saw a well-illuminated merchant ship loading iron ore at Redi port. *Betwa* fired a star shell to illuminate the area. Police in the village phoned Bombay to say that another Portuguese frigate was firing on them!

The *Albuquerque* crew was evacuated by Portuguese ground forces led by *Comandante* Abel de Oliveira to the Naval Club in Caranzalem. 1/Lt Mendes Rebelo evacuated the wounded in a vehicle and finally shifted Capt. Aragão to the Hospital Escolar (teaching hospital) attached to the Escola Médica-Cirúrgica de Goa at Panjim by 5 p.m. on 18 December.

There were many unsung heroes at the Hospital Escolar, all were Goan: doctors and nurses tirelessly attending to casualties streaming in. They were led by Dr João Manuel Pacheco de Figueiredo, professor of medicine and director of the medical school and hospital (later the first dean of Goa Medical College), and Dr Renato Fernandes, professor of surgery, from Siolim. Dr Pacheco de Figueiredo's son, Dr John, a medical student at the time, recalls telling his father: 'You should have been a general', to which his senior replied:

In a sense, I am; my enemies are disease and death.*

There were lighter moments in the lull before the storm …

Four young officers of the *Albuquerque* had purchased a fifth-hand cream coloured Fiat 1100. On their off days, they visited temples, churches and beaches and toured the hinterland of Goa in the car. Around three weeks before 18 December, they took a narrow road that ended at a surprisingly beautiful palace. They probably strayed into the domain of the Lamgao *Dessaiado*† of Rao

---

* Interview with the author.

† A large, state-granted estate free of levy for services rendered to the state, such as border defence of a sector with one's standing private army.

Desai, traditional feudatory lords of a large area in what is today the Bicholim taluka. The palace is located about a kilometre from the Bicholim municipality, now a part of the Bicholim municipal area.[*]

The lone guard at the palace was armed with a Kropatschek. The foursome carried a machine gun, grenades and personal handguns when venturing into uncharted territory.

Just then, a Rolls Royce drove in, halted, and from it emerged a man, who asked in chaste Portuguese, 'Who are you gentlemen?'

The officers identified themselves, and then the man said, 'I am the king of Bicholim.'

He insisted on playing host to the visitors—overnight, *à la* Omar Khayyam, with wine, women and song—at a palace the likes of which none of the four had seen before. They invited the 'king' aboard the *Albuquerque* and treated him to a lavish lunch about a fortnight before the hostilities. While departing, the 'king' insisted the four should visit his palace again. It was a 'dinner suspended by history'.[†]

As happens, enemy heroism, too, was recognized. The Task Force leader, Cdr. Rusi Gandhi, and Cdr. Tommy Kunnenkeril, skipper of the *Beas* (a 'very modest and likeable Malayali' in the words of Cmde. Gilbert Menezes[‡]), visited Capt. Aragão in hospital. Cdr. Gandhi presented him with chocolates, flowers and brandy.

The Portuguese destroyer was refloated, renamed *Sarasvati*, and towed to the Naval Dockyard in Bombay on 4 May 1962. *Sarasvati* was sold as scrap for Rs 7.71 lakh on 5 June 1965. Some retrieved parts are displayed at the Naval Museum in Mumbai. The sword of the commanding officer of *Albuquerque* is at the National Defence Academy at Khadakvasla in Pune.

The queer historical significance of the two acts of Portuguese resistance in Goa:

---

[*] Author's interview with journalist residing at Bicholim, Anant Salkar, now deceased.

[†] *Visão História,* vol. 14, 2011, p. 81.

[‡] Interview with the author.

- Verna was the village that staged stiff resistance to Bijapuri rule in the early sixteenth century. Mhal Pai, a *sardesai* (chief headman) with *sardeshmukhi* (tax collecting) rights over twenty-eight *mahals* (administrative units of the time, more or less comparable to contemporary talukas or tehsils), equalling some 500 to 800 villages, constantly fought and chased Arab Muslim Navaiyats, aka Rumis, out of Goa. Navaiyats vented their spleen on the largely Hindu natives every time Vijayanagar thwarted their sea trade of Arabian horses. Wealthy Navaiyats enjoyed the patronage of Mallik Yusuf Gurgi, the Turkish governor of Bijapur in Goa. Mhal Pai captured and held some Navaiyats. Gurgi forcibly released them and intensified persecution of natives. According to the Konkanakhyana, a historical poem written in 1721, when frustration crept in, Mhal Pai—with the help of Vijaynagar's friend of the Portuguese, naval captain Thimayya in Honavar—invited the Portuguese to liberate Goa from Bijapuri Muslims in 1510. A *betala sanyasi* (a nude mendicant/yogi) had prophesied that a foreign people from a distant land would free Goa from the Muslims. Mhal Pai knew it had to be the *topikar* (Portuguese) who were then stationed in Cochin (now Kochi). Mhal Pai lived in Verna—the village where, 451 years later, 450-plus Portuguese troops of the *Agrupamento Afonso de Albuquerque* retreating from Margao to the last redoubt at Mormugao, as seen before, offered the bloodiest resistance in Goa.
- The Portuguese army formation that resisted the invading forces at Verna as well as the Portuguese destroyer that resisted the three frigates of the Indian Navy at Mormugao were named after the same man who, at Mhal Pai's invitation, liberated Goa from the stranglehold of Bijapuri Muslims in 1510 but did not, as may have been expected, take a fee and return to Cochin. He stayed back and laid the foundations for Portugal's littoral empire in Asia. His name was Afonso de Albuquerque. The incapacitated destroyer

named after him had kept her four cannons ablaze until three became inoperative and she ran out of ordnance. She had fired 350–400 rounds (cannons and pom-poms) during the engagement. Her capitulation marked the end of Portuguese India. Symbolically, the Portuguese had arrived at Kapped (Kappakadavu/Kappukad) some 12 km north of Calicut (Kozhikode) in India 463 years before (on 20 May 1498) with cannons blazing from their sail ships—much the same way as they did when they were forced to depart.

A list (probably incomplete) of Goan-origin commissioned officers from the army, navy and air force who participated in Operation Vijay for India to free their homeland from foreign occupation, appears in the endnotes.[14]

India's defence minister Krishna Menon, a native of Calicut, declared on 19 December 1961:

> The unfinished part of the Indian revolution was completed this morning when the Indian Defence Services took over Goa, Daman and Diu and hoisted the Indian flag on our soil … We waited for years, we argued and gave opportunities for a settlement, but were then forced to adopt means which were not of our choice.*

---

* Khera, 1974, p. 135.

7

PORTUGUESE SURRENDER
AND POW REPATRIATION

The Curtain Falls

The Portuguese were the first Europeans to enter India and the last to exit. They were in Cochin when Goans led by Mhala Pai, together with Vijayanagar's naval captain at Honavar, Thimayya, a friend of the Portuguese, met the Portuguese governor in India.

Afonso de Albuquerque was refitting his ships for an important mission at Ormuz (Hormuz) in the Persian Gulf. Ormuz was a strategic point of control on the sea route between Asia and Europe. Thimayya and Mhal Pai somehow convinced Albuquerque that the time was opportune to liberate Goa from the oppressive rule of Bijapur. On his second attempt on 25 November 1510, Albuquerque succeeded in driving the Bijapuris out of Goa.

Knowing that Albuquerque was chiefly interested in Oriental spices, Mhal Pai—arguably the most powerful Goan at the time (as mentioned earlier, he lorded over some 500–800 villages)—perhaps expected Albuquerque to take a fee for the job and return to Cochin, leaving Goa to be ruled by him. Thimayya may have also had his own plans and ambitions. However, Albuquerque recognized Goa's strategic importance on the west coast of India and decided to stay for good. He had grand designs of creating a *mare nostrum* (our sea) for Portugal, with centrally located Goa as headquarters. Projecting himself as a liberator and not a conqueror, he was good to the natives and assured them that his quarrel was with the Muslims and not with Hindus. He did not interfere with the local religion or customs, save banning sati.

The rot set in after he was deposed through court intrigue in Lisbon and his resultant death in Goa in December 1515. The 'liberation', eventually, turned out to be a mere replacement of the Bijapuri by the Portuguese. Goans, however, continued to worship him as a demigod. It is said that when they faced oppression after his death, Goans prayed at Albuquerque's tomb.[*]

Albuquerque was Portugal's greatest strategist in Asia. The foundations he laid enabled Portugal to rule the waves for about a century from Asia to Europe with a few strategically located forts along the sea route—and hold Goa for four-and-a-half centuries.

The Portuguese did many things, both good and bad, during that time. For the world, they opened the Age of Discovery and the first signs of a world economy. For India, they started a plant gene bank at the southernmost tip of Mumbai, took India's mango to the world and brought to India tropical fruits and vegetables—even tobacco! Without them, we would have continued flavouring our food with black pepper. No pav-bhaji and what have you ... the Portuguese brought chillies, potatoes and the skills of baking bread and fermenting wine to India—and much more.

Goa was already a *sunaparanta* (golden Goa) from long before. The Portuguese influence added a different dimension, without which Goa would be indistinguishable from the other coastal areas of south Maharashtra or north Karnataka. The Konkan region on the western seaboard of India from south Gujarat to the tip of Kerala is dotted with beautiful beaches. But tourists flock to Goa. Not just because it is God's Own Country[†] or for her beaches alone. Goa's ambience is different. It is a delightful fusion of the East and the West, if you will.

The Portuguese shaped *Goa Dourada* (golden Goa) in their own mould. They gave it a sound system of record-keeping and a

---

[*] Robert de Souza, *Goa and the Continent of Circe*, Wilco Publishing House, Bombay, 1973, p. 109.

[†] According to the Suta Samhita (part of Vedic literature), Aparanta or Goa was the land that 'destroys all sins'.

uniform civil code. With compulsory music at the *Escolas Paroquiais* (parish schools), they added Western harmonic notes to the melodic Indian classical notes—producing a legion of Goan music conductors for the Indian film industry, particularly Bollywood, in the mid-20th century ... names like Roque Gonsalves, Sebastian Fernandes, Sebastian D'Souza, Chic Chocolate, Frank Fernand, Chris Perry and Anthony Gonsalves immediately spring to mind. (The Hindi film hit 'My Name is Anthony Gonsalves', enacted by Amitabh Bachchan in the 1977 Manmohan Desai film *Amar, Akbar, Anthony*, was actually a tribute to the Goan maestro from Majorda, Anthony Gonsalves, who taught the violin to Bollywood giants, Pyarelal and R.D. Burman.) Even the architecture of the relocated (and later, reconstructed) major Hindu temples in the New Conquests have a distinctively Portuguese appearance. Within India, it is only in Goa that one will find Hindu temple gates with a discernible Muslim influence (pre-Portuguese Bahamani) and domes that clearly bear Christian architectural overtones. Goa is a harmonious fusion, indeed, of the Oriental and the Occidental.

But there was also the bad, chief among which was the forced conversion to Christianity and western culture in a land that was a far older civilization than any in Europe. In 1521, John III became king of Portugal and the maxim, *Cujus regio illius religio*, meaning 'religion of the king is religion of the people', gained currency. Proselytization began in Goa. Most, if not all, converted to Christianity were native Hindus. Sir William Hunter writes:

> The native Christians who form more than half of the population
> are the descendants of the Hindus converted to Christianity after
> the subjugation of the country by the Portuguese and they can
> even now declare the caste to which they originally belonged.*

(The Danes, the Dutch, the British and the French who followed them into India did not overtly interfere with the religion of the

---

* William Hunter, *Imperial Gazetteer of India*.

land; the British quietly plundered the land, enriched themselves, impoverished India and when the going got tough, quit; the Portuguese enriched neither themselves nor the Goans, and refused to quit—unfortunately, they had to be shoved out with the use of force.)

Their second biggest blunder was that they converted only some, not all, to their faith (they ought to have converted none, but if they truly believed that the principle of *cujus regio* was valid, they ought to have converted all). By converting only some, the Portuguese wedged a chasm between Goans, virtually creating two Goas out of one.

Catholic priest Fr Cosme da Costa—the 'miracle baby', whose birth in medically impossible circumstances eventually led to the canonization of the 17th–18th century Goan priest, now St Joseph Vaz, in his book, *A Missiological Conflict Between Padroado and Propaganda in the East*, stated that the Portuguese even tried, but failed, to impose their culture on St Thomas Christians of Kerala— far older Christians than themselves.[*] He also touches this subject in his book *Apostolic Christianity in Goa and in the West Coast of India*.[†]

Among their lesser sins: unable to pronounce local words replete with consonants, they changed the names of places and people (including of Hindu natives) with a merry interspersal of vowels. 'A' in the native language changed to 'O' for converts. *Udak* (water) became *udok*, *sarvespar* (god) became *sorvespor*, *dev barem karum* (thank you) became *dev borem korum*. Vithal Sadashiv Shenvi Sukhtankar became Vittola Sadassiva Sinai Sunctancar and Digambar Pundalik Pai Kamat became Digambora Pundolica Poy Camotim. (Goan Catholic emigrants to British India on their own shed their Luso names and adopted or tweaked to Anglo-sounding ones. João Leão Fernandes became John Leon Fernandez and Irvino Estrocio became Irwin Extross. All double-barrelled 'de Costa', 'de Souza' became D'Costa and D'Souza.)[15]

---

[*] Pilar Publications, 1997.

[†] Rev. Cosme Jose Costa, Xaverian Publication Society, Pilar, 2009.

The early period of Portuguese rule was traumatic for the native. He was persecuted in various ways to change his faith or lose his property and leave Portuguese-held territory. The Goan Hindu was discriminated against, including under the law of segregation in the later period until Portugal turned into a republic in 1910. Five months after the republic was established, the *Lei da Separação da Igreja do Estado* (Law of Separation between Church and State) was promulgated. The Catholic religion ceased to be the state religion of Portugal and her colonies.

The proverbial last straw came with Salazar's Colonial Act (Law No. 18570) of 8 July 1930, which reduced Goans—both Hindu and Catholic—to subjects, abrogated their civil liberties, replaced Goans with whites in public posts and led to increased discrimination of the major segment of Goa's populace.

More than half of Goa's working population emigrated, the bulk of it to Indian cities—although this emigration was more for economic reasons than political and had begun more than a century before the Colonial Act of 1930.

As stated before, most of the Indian military officers of Goan origin hailed from these émigrés—Goans in Goa could only join the Portuguese forces and, irrespective of merit, could not rise above a middle rank. Senior ranks were a preserve of the white-skinned. A person of the calibre of Gen. S.F. Rodrigues, India's 'Thinking General' and chief of the Indian Army, or for that matter the 'Original Thinking General' Lt Gen. Eric Vas, like fellow army commanders Lt Gen. Stanley Menezes and Lt Gen. Walter Pinto, sixteen other generals, thirty-nine one-star generals (called brigadiers in India) and fifty-nine full colonels of Goan origin in the far bigger and superior Indian Army—not to mention the high ranks to which Goans rose in India's navy and the air force—may not have risen beyond tenente coronel or lieutenant colonel in the Portuguese Army.

Furthermore, Goans—prominently Goan Catholics—wanted the Portuguese out of Goa, from the planned armed insurrection masterminded by the first native Bishop Mateus Castro Mahale in the mid-1600s and the better-known Pinto Revolt of 1787, that also aimed to militarily evict them from Goa (more on these revolts below), to what finally culminated in India's armed action in 1961.

India planned to finish Operation Vijay in three days. Portuguese defenders, on the other hand, were ordered to fend off the invaders for three days at the borders, another ten days within Goa on the riverbanks and more at the last redoubt—time enough for a UN-called ceasefire and enemy pullback.

In the face of the impending Indian attack, aware that defending so long against an overwhelming, better-trained and better-equipped enemy was impossible, Salazar told his governor to hold out for at least eight days. Maj. Gen. Manuel António Vassalo e Silva replied that it would be

> ... possible to resist for eight days only if the Presidente do Conselho [Salazar] expects a miracle.*

The Indian 50 Para Brigade and 17 Infantry Division ended the 451 years of Portuguese rule in thirty-six hours flat.

50 Para Brigade's artillery officer, the Goa-origin Maj. (later colonel) Peter Mendonca's elite 17 Parachute Field Regiment, had an officer, then a major, by the name of Prakash Rao Jesus. The birth of Jesus Christ is generally observed on 25 December, Christmas Day. During the build-up, Maj. Jesus posted Vassalo e Silva a Christmas card. Scribbled on the card was a message, 'See you on my birthday—Jesus!' to which he added a postscript, 'I have Peter with me'. Peter alluded literally to Col Peter Mendonca and figuratively to St Peter, an Apostle of Jesus Christ, keeper of the 'pearly gates' of heaven. The card was intercepted by military intelligence. The two young officers were reprimanded. But later the director general of Military Intelligence invited them home for evening drinks, evidently appreciating their humour. The Christmas

---

* Carlos Alexandre de Morais, *A Queda da Índia Portuguesa*, 1995, p. 118.

card is framed in the office of the DGMI. Col Prakash Rao Jesus
from Warangal, Andhra Pradesh, now in Telangana, went on to
become a 1965 war hero who picked USA-made Pakistani Patton
tanks 'like cherries' at the tank battle in Kasur–Khemkaran village
of Asal Uttar (literally, real answer). Pak soldiers yelled into their
radio sets,

> Their artillery is playing hell into us, their man in command is
> called Jesus Christ!*

All Indian troops in Operation Vijay received the General Service
Medal 1947 with the Goa 1961 bar. As mentioned earlier, no
military gallantry awards were given for this 'police action' (similar
to Hyderabad). Officers and other ranks who displayed remarkable
gallantry were given civilian bravery awards.

Operation Vijay cost twenty-two lives on the Indian side
and seventeen lives on the Portuguese side as per Government
of India figures as reported in *Asian Recorder*.† According to Maj.
K.C. Praval, the figures were twenty-two on the Indian side
and thirty lives on the Portuguese side.‡ Air Vice Marshal Arjun
Subramaniam says,

> The Portuguese lost thirty men, had another fifty-seven wounded
> and, more humiliatingly, had over 3,000 taken prisoners.§

Col Morais in *A Queda da Índia Portuguesa* stated that twenty-five lives
were lost on the Portuguese side—fifteen in Goa (including Anjediva),

---

* Interview with Brig. Michael Mendonca (V), son of late Col Peter
  Mendonca, and story at: https://www.thequint.com/news/India/bat-
  tle-of-asal-uttar-indo-pak-war-65-how-jesus-fought-for-india
† Journal/Magazine, Delhi, 1962, p. 4383.
‡ *Indian Army after Independence*, Lancer, 2009, p. 214.
§ Subramaniam, *India's Wars*, 2016, pp. 191–92.

seven in Daman, three in Diu.[*] He did not count the nine policemen who died at Maulinguem and Dodamarog, as P.N. Khera did.[†]

Compared to the unthinkable number of casualties that were bound to occur if better-trained and better-armed defenders had put up a fight, this was a virtually bloodless walkover for India.

Heavily outnumbered and wholly outgunned by superior troops, Maj. Gen. Vassalo e Silva described Operation Vijay as a fight between the Indian elephant and the Portuguese mosquito.

There was little choice for the Portuguese but to remove the rail tracks from the border to Collem and block the rail tunnels in the Western Ghats, and explode some bridges and culverts to delay the Indian advance, viz. at Sanquelim, Bicholim, Darbandora, Usgao, Khandepar, Assonora, Chapora, Tivim, Banastari, Borim, Sanvordem, Quepem and Ardhafond. (Maj. Gen. Vassalo e Silva told a press conference on 13 February 1962 that 'more than thirty bridges' were blown up.)

Interestingly, trucks and explosives to blow the bridges came courtesy Goan mine owners. The very next morning, the same mine owners assisted Indian forces with barges to cross the same rivers whose bridges they had just helped the Portuguese to explode.

When the demolition of bridges failed to deter the Indian advance, the only option for the Portuguese was to surrender.

But surrender was contrary to the orders received from Lisbon. Had those orders been followed, both attackers and defenders, and with them Goa itself, would have been reduced to a pile of ashes. Let us take a closer look at that crucial aspect.

Scorched Earth: Destroy Goa!

Portugal's dictator, Dr António de Oliveira Salazar, was told years before that it was impossible to defend Goa militarily. By 12

---

[*] 1995, p. 17.

[†] P.N. Khera, 1974, provides a detailed list of casualties during the operations, Appendix XXII, p. 238.

December 1961, it was clear to him that he was grossly overwhelmed by a combination of Indian land, sea and air forces. The author of the Indian Navy's official account of the 1961 operations said that the suicidal way the Portuguese went about preparing to meet the challenge was 'as if they were firm believers in euthanasia'.

Initially, Salazar ordered resistance until all ammunition and provisions were exhausted.

> [It was] a ridiculous expectation given the asymmetry of forces and the ragtag army at his disposal for the defence of Goa.[*]

Air Vice Marshal Arjun Subramaniam was referring to Salazar's governor-general in Goa, but the quote is equally applicable to Salazar himself, the man calling the shots.

Salazar changed the order in a radio message on 14 December 1961 and instead ordered his governor-general in Goa to not surrender. Salazar told his governor-general,

> It is horrible to think that this may mean total sacrifice … I do not foresee the possibility of truce or of Portuguese prisoners … because I feel that our soldiers and sailors can be either victorious or dead …[†]

In other words, Salazar wanted a hopeless fight to the last man and the last round. The devious intent behind this drastic measure was to scandalize the world with 'pacifist' India's brutal massacre of a tiny Portuguese force in Goa. Salazar was willing to have each and every of his 3300 ill-trained and ill-equipped defenders dead in order to create a worldwide political backlash against India.

It may be recalled that Governor-General Vassalo e Silva detained the passenger ship *Índia*—sent to Goa to specifically shift the liquid assets like foreign currency reserves and gold and other

---

[*] *India's Wars*, 2016, p. 188.
[†] Carlos A. Morais, *A Queda da Índia Portuguesa,* 1995, p. 117.

securities pawned by locals with the Banco Nacional Ultramarino—
so as to enable Portuguese civilians, especially women and children,
to embark on the vessel and reach the safety of their home in
Portugal. The governor's act of kindness was not regarded kindly by
Lisbon. Meaning that, together with the defenders, the dictator did
not mind innocent citizens of his own country also perishing.

Even that, Salazar decided, was not enough. He was not a man
of half measures.

Three days later, he rounded the Portuguese response. In
an ominous secret radio message on 17 December 1961, Salazar
further ordered the complete destruction of all traces of Portuguese
civilization in Goa—major towns, centuries-old heritage buildings
and ancient churches—so that nothing fell into the hands of India.
In other words, a scorched-earth policy, just as he had done in São
João Batista de Ajudá, Dahomey/Benin, Africa, five months before.

Freedom fighter and Goa's first elected Legislative Assembly
speaker from 1963, Pandurang P. Shirodkar quoted Salazar as
having said,

Não deixe pedra sobre pedra (Don't leave stone on stone, destroy
everything).[*]

There shall be neither victors nor vanquished, only heroes and
martyrs, said Salazar. In other words, all would die, the attackers
and the defenders, including the hapless innocents unwittingly
caught in the crossfire. Only Goa's ashes would remain. (The
Geneva Conventions would ban the Scorched Earth policy only
later in 1977.)

This fellow is mad, Governor-General Maj. Gen. Vassalo e Silva
remarked upon reading the orders.

Vassalo e Silva was a military officer true to traditions. In
January 1959, at São Pedro on the way to the ceremonial bestowal
of the symbolic bastão (sceptre) in the Bom Jesus Basilica, Old Goa,

---

[*] Pandurang P. Shirodkar, *My Life in Exile*, 2012, p. 252.

a dog suddenly charged out and went under the wheels of the two-cylinder BMW motorcycle of his lead outrider, flinging him 10 metres away. The governor stopped the motorcade and got out to inquire about the fallen outrider, João Aranha, a young motorcycle stuntman, who rose immediately, and declared he was ready to proceed. However, Vassalo e Silva insisted that Aranha be taken forthwith to the Ribandar hospital, where he spent fifteen days under the care of Dr Belarmino Lobo, a Goan whose father had worked long years in Daman. The governor had someone regularly visit the hospital and report Aranha's progress to him.[*]

Vassalo e Silva was a brigadier-general when he was appointed Goa's governor-general on 4 December 1958. He was promoted to major general in 1960.

Just as the first governor, Afonso de Albuquerque, had done in 1510, the last governor Vassalo e Silva had fallen in love with Goa. Not once during his three years in Goa did Vassalo e Silva visit Portugal—something that was not regarded kindly by the regime in Lisbon. He displayed a manifest sense of caring towards Goa. As a military engineer, he crafted and implemented projects designed to improve the lives of the local populace.

Vassalo e Silva conceived Goa's most vital bridge linking north and south Goa across the Zuari at Cortalim–Agasaim. Execution of the steel bridge may have commenced in 1961 but for a dispute with the contractor, says former chief engineer Goa PWD, Anil Parulekar from Gogol, Margao, who saw the tender papers in Portuguese. (It took the Indian administration almost a quarter of a century to build an RCC bridge with a 670-metre span and 16-metre average navigational clearance using newly developed technology.)

The last Portuguese governor-general, then sixty-one, travelled in civvies in a jeep and mixed with people freely, to the consternation

---

[*] Aranha, who was a cavalry captain, served at the *Polícia do Estado da Índia* and describes the motorcade incident at pp. 81–82 of his book, *Enquanto Se Esperam As Naus Do Reino*.

of his security detail. According to freedom fighter Dr Suresh Kanekar, he was

> ... possibly the all-time most popular governor-general of Goa.*

It must have been the most painful decision in the life of Maj. Gen. Vassalo e Silva—to obey Lisbon's orders and destroy his men and Goa (Lisbon had sent him cyanide) or defy the orders and save his men and Goa—a Hobson's choice, between the devil and the deep blue sea.

As a loyal soldier, he chose to obey orders.

Following the Lisbon despatch of 17 December, the governor ordered the mining of the huge petrol storage bunkers at Mormugao, major towns, centuries-old heritage civil buildings and ancient churches, to ready them all for demolition. (On 14 December, the Ministry for Overseas Affairs ordered the relics of St Francis Xavier to be transferred to Lisbon, but there was neither the time nor the means to implement the order.)

Mormugao was a mid-latitude location. Petrol bunkers exploding there would perhaps suffice to destroy north, central and south Goa.

Explosives were duly placed. The governor's order to detonate was awaited.

Word of the impending destruction spread like wildfire. It is said (one cannot confirm the veracity) that India intercepted Lisbon's ominous radio message of 17 December and forthwith decided to ignore Washington's entreaties and launched Operation Vijay that very night.

In any case, leaflets in Konkani, Marathi, Portuguese and English dropped by IAF aircraft on the morning of 18 December, read in part:

> *The Portuguese will do everything to leave Goa in ruin[s] and the Goan people in misery. They do not care what happens to Goa, now. For they*

---

* Suresh Kanekar, 2011, p. 115.

*must and will depart. They have nothing to lose by sowing destruction
in this land. Their Portugal is at a safe distance. They will try to destroy
our bridges, our railways, our temples and churches, our schools and public
buildings, and the fine and God-given harbour ... Goans cannot and
must not allow this to happen at any cost. Be calm and brave. Rejoice in
your freedom and help to safeguard it.***

On 1 January 1962, the *Statesman* reported that Papal Nuncio, Msgr
James Knox, addressing 5000 people at St Francis Church, thanked
God for saving Goa from 'one of the world's worst destructions
planned by the Portuguese'. He also thanked Indian soldiers for
avoiding bloodshed in Goa and saving Goa from Portuguese
tyranny. The congregation included 100 Indian soldiers.

When the windowpanes rattled from 7 a.m. on 18 December
(with the IAF bombings), Goans deserted their towns and villages
and fled to the hills and forests. A fourteen-year-old, polio-crippled
boy in Banastari was carried in a *pantlo* (bamboo basket used for
coconuts and paddy) by his father as a head load, rushing for the
hills. The people neither knew nor cared whether it was the curtain
raiser of Salazar's scorched-earth policy or the Indian invasion, or
both. They just fled.

The Surrender

Goan journalist Mario Cabral e Sa says that, around noon, 18
December, the archbishop-patriarch of Goa, D. José Vieira
Alvernaz, and the secretario-general (chief secretary), Justice Abel
Colaço of Margao, met Maj. Gen. Vassalo e Silva in Chicalim at his
provisional camp, on his slow march to the last redoubt.[†]

Col Carlos Alexandre Morais in *A Queda da Índia Portuguesa* says
that the archbishop, together with the police chief, Capt. Joaquim
Pinto Brás, arrived at the camp around 3.30 p.m. on 18 December

---

* Khera, 1974, p. 132.
† Mario Cabral e Sa, *Gomantak Times*, 7 November 2005.

1961. According to Adv. Fernando Jorge Colaço, the archbishop of
Goa, through

> ... an emissary, a priest, Monsignor Gregório Magno Antão and
> the Secretary-General Dr Abel Regalado de Álvares Colaço,
> risking his high post and career for the love of Goa, contacted an
> Indian commander with the Governor-General at Chicalim ...[*]

French professor Sandrine Bègue says that it was a certain 'Fr. Santos'
who accompanied the archbishop to meet the governor-general.[†]

Whoever the two persons were, they did their utmost to persuade
the by now 'very shaken' governor-general to not destroy Goa,
to surrender and prevent a fatal confrontation with the advancing
army. In doing so, they told him, the governor-general would not
lose his honour but, on the contrary, would avoid senseless bloodshed
and destruction.

Col Carlos Morais says the governor did not agree with this
proposal of surrender. Vassalo e Silva's ultimate response to their
entreaties was

> ... A General in campaign uses the resources he has at his
> command and when he doesn't have them, he awaits. *I await* ...[‡]

What he may have meant was that he awaited Lisbon's final
orders to destroy Goa, together with themselves and the
invading forces.

According to Cabral e Sa, after they left, forty-three-year-old
Maj. Antonio Areias Peixoto, backed by a handful of like-minded
young leftist officers, went to the governor-general, stood to
attention, saluted and told him in slow, measured words:

---

[*] Fernando Jorge Colaço, 2017, p. 94.

[†] Europress, 2007.

[‡] Mario Cabral e Sa, *Gomantak Times*, 7 November 2005.

Waiting for what, my General? The radio station has been
bombed, and there is no question of you contacting Lisbon or of
Lisbon contacting you. You now are the final authority. These
people [Goans] are at no fault because we can't defend them. Let
us leave happy memories behind us.[*]

The governor-general listened pensively and, almost immediately,
ordered the fuses of the powerful bombs placed in the huge petrol
bunkers at Mormugao port remain unplugged, like all else that
had been mined elsewhere, contrary to his earlier orders. Vassalo
e Silva said,

I cannot destroy the evidence of our greatness in the Orient ...
Destruction of Goa is a useless sacrifice *(sacrifício inútil).*

Goa was saved.

Very few Goans had heard of Maj. Antonio Areias Peixoto. The
'miracle' he had wrought was credited to St Francis Xavier. It had
happened twice before.

In 1683 and in 1726, the Marathas were at the point of ousting
the Portuguese from Goa but turned away at the last moment, to
rush to their northern borders that were just as suddenly attacked by
huge Mughal forces. Miracles they were in a way and were attributed
to the intercession of the saint. Such was the resultant faith that the
transfer of the highest temporal power in Goa took place before a
statue of St Francis Xavier at the Bom Jesus Basilica in Old Goa.

Jesuit history tells us that a Genoese woman, Francisca de
Sopranis, who later became a nun taking the name of Maria Francisca
Xaveria, gifted 3000 crusados in 1670, from which an Italian-styled
statue of St Francis Xavier was sculpted. The statue, in pure silver,
was bejewelled with a crown of gold. The outgoing governor placed
his credentials at the foot and the bastão (sceptre) in the right hand

---

[*]   Ibid.

of the statue. The incoming governor, in all solemnity, then picked the credentials and bastão from there.

Just like Maj. Peixoto in 1961, no Goan had heard of Juliana Dias da Costa (*Juliana Fiddawie*), the powerful Indo-Portuguese woman in the Mughal court who crowned incoming Mughal emperors. It was she who got the Mughal emperors of the time to intervene and save the Portuguese in Goa from the Marathas in 1683 and 1726.

The following day, 19 December, from around 11 a.m., Maj. Gen. Vassalo e Silva was briefed by his field commanders who managed to reach Chicalim, one by one. At 12.15 p.m., he told his forces:

> ... situation does not allow me to proceed with the fight without great sacrifice of lives ... I have decided to contact the enemy ... I order all my forces to cease fire.

The decision was conveyed to all commanders by 12.45 p.m.

A Letter of Ceasefire was signed by the governor-general at 2 p.m. on 19 December. The letter, typed on the letterhead of the Independent Territorial Command of Portuguese India, read:

> To the C-in-C of the Indian Armed Forces,
>
> According to the annexed communication I sent to you, and with the powers given to me by the Commanding letter of Portuguese Central Government, I request you to cease fire between our forces from this moment.[*]

Vassalo e Silva then shifted from Chicalim to HQ Agrupamento Vasco da Gama at Alpalqueiros Hill, Vasco da Gama, the last redoubt (presently housing INS *Gomantak*) at 2.45 p.m.

He would shortly be met by Maj. Earl William Carvalho, Capt. R.S.K. Bali, Capt. R.K. Mehta and a few men of B Company of 4 Sikh Light Infantry who had raced in two vehicles to Vasco da Gama.

---

[*] Khera, 1974, p. 198.

The tiny but daring Indian Army group confined the governor-general to his house and the disarmed Portuguese troops present at the camp—multiple times the number of the Indian group—to their barracks. By around 3.45 p.m., the remaining troops of B Company of 4 Sikh LI reached Alpalqueiros Hill and took up their positions around the camp.

The ceasefire letter was carried to the Indian forces by the Portuguese chief of staff Lt Col Marques de Andrade, in the company of either Archbishop Alvernaz or his emissary Msgr Gregório Magno de Souza Antão, with Capt. (Dr) Garcia da Silva as interpreter. They handed over the letter to Lt Col R.B. Nanda, who they met near Dabolim (possibly in Chicalim).

Later the same evening, Lt Col Nanda reached Vasco da Gama and placed Maj. Gen. Vassalo e Silva in POW custody. Brig. K.S. Dhillon reached the town early that night and formally accepted surrender of the Portuguese forces in Goa.

Let's now turn to a rare—perhaps the only—first-hand eyewitness account of that surrender ceremony, recorded by a Goan freedom fighter whose major handicap (not a virtue for someone involved in covert activities in a police state like Goa) was that he could not tell a lie.

A Goan Freedom Fighter Recalls

Just past noon on 19 December, freedom fighters Purushottam Kakodkar and Dr Suresh Kanekar called at the house of their nationalist colleague Ronald Coutinho in Borda, Margao. Coutinho's hospitable wife—the cousin of India's future army chief Gen. S.F. Rodrigues—served them a quick lunch.

The three set off in Coutinho's car for Vasco da Gama to see what was happening there. Trudging behind a slow-moving convoy of Indian Army trucks, it took them about eight hours; they finally got there by about 8 p.m. They would be the only freedom fighters—among the handful of Goans—to witness the formal surrender ceremony of Portuguese forces in India.

Dr Kanekar wrote about the ceremony in his 2011 book, *Goa's Liberation and Thereafter: Chronicles of a Fragmented Life*. In his words:

When we reached Vasco, it was about 8 p.m. Lt. Col [Raghbir Bahadur] Nanda had reached Vasco ahead of us and was holding Vassalo e Silva in custody. When we learned about the arrest of the Portuguese governor-general, Purushottam [Kakodkar] told Brigadier Dhillon that he and I [Dr Suresh Kanekar] had known Vassalo e Silva personally and requested permission for us to talk with him. Dhillon denied permission, but he said we could, if we wanted, attend the formal surrender ceremony that was going to take place in a short while. So we decided to wait ...

We went back to where the surrender was to take place right out in the open. Dhillon was sitting in a jeep, while Nanda arranged to have the few cars including ours that were there placed in a semi-circle, with the headlights converging at where the governor-general would be surrendering to Dhillon. At about 8:45 p.m. Vassalo e Silva was brought to the spot along with his adjutant or chief of staff, probably named Andrade [Chief of Staff Lt Col Marques de Andrade], and made to wait while adjustments were being made to the cars and the lighting ...

All this while I was watching Vassalo e Silva very closely and I found his demeanour very dignified under the trying circumstances. He had allegedly (the allegation being of dubious veracity) fled from Panaji to the south with the intent of flying out from the Dabolim airport, but could not manage to do so because the airport had been rendered inoperative with pinpoint bombing of the airstrip by the Indian air force.

[Those allegations doing the rounds in Goa at the time were completely unfounded. One, Vassalo e Silva shifted to the south in accordance with the defence plan, Plano Sentinela, which fixed Mormugao as the last redoubt. As commander-in-chief, he had to be there, not in Panjim. Two, the Dabolim airport bombing with World War II vintage duds was unsatisfactory, necessitating a third bombing raid, Green 4, despite which two civilian aircraft took off midnight of 18/19 December 1961.

Three, and most pertinently, even if Vassalo e Silva wished to escape leaving behind his wife and children in Goa, he could have easily done so in one of those two aircraft that he himself had permitted to take off.]

There was occasionally the hint of a wry smile on his otherwise impassive face, probably at the irony of the situation. He had to stand there with his companion for about half an hour, in between Indian soldiers who had been lined up on both sides.

When Brigadier Dhillon was told that the arrangements were completed, he came out of his jeep and stood facing the governor-general. Addressing the Brigadier, Nanda announced that the governor-general of Goa, Daman and Diu was surrendering to him. At Nanda's order, Vassalo e Silva stepped forward, saluted Dhillon (Dhillon did not salute back, which surprised me especially as Vassalo e Silva was an army general, but then I have no expertise in military etiquette), and handed over the instrument of surrender to Dhillon, after which Dhillon went back to sit in his vehicle and Vassalo e Silva returned with his adjutant to the place of his confinement. Neither Dhillon nor Vassalo e Silva had uttered a single word during the brief ceremony.

... The ceremony had taken place at 9:15 p.m. on Tuesday, December 19, 1961, with very few people in attendance. I had looked at my watch at the conclusion of the ceremony.[*]

Although Brig. Dhillon accepted surrender (at 9.15 p.m.) from a major general, a rank his senior, India's official account of the operations states that the formal surrender took place at Alpalqueiros Hill in Vasco da Gama at 8.30 p.m. on 19 December, and that Maj. Gen. K.P. Candeth accepted the unconditional surrender.

The time recorded on the instrument of surrender—8.30 p.m.—was probably the time when the governor-general signed it. The instrument of surrender carried the signature of Brig. Dhillon and not of Maj. Gen. K.P. Candeth. The two attesting witnesses

---

[*] Kanekar, 2011, pp. 147–49.

were Lt Col R.B. Nanda (admittedly present in person) and Lt Col K.S. Chadha, CO 2 Bihar (whose unit, part of the same 63 Infantry Brigade, was ordered to halt some 5 km beyond Cortalim for some days and could have well been present).

Maj. Gen. K.P. Candeth could not have accepted the surrender for the simple reason that he was nowhere near Vasco da Gama when the formal ceremony took place. In fact, at the time of the surrender ceremony, Maj.Gen. Candeth was not even aware that Vasco da Gama was captured. He learnt of the capture and surrender at 11 p.m. that day; the information was relayed to him on the telephone.

No photograph exists of the formal surrender ceremony. Dr Suresh Kanekar tells us that

> [CO 4 Sikh LI, Lt Col RB] Nanda had found a photographer to take the picture of the ceremony, but the photographer did not have a flash for his camera. Nanda instructed the photographer that he was to take the photograph at the signal that Nanda would give him.*

However, something went wrong at the last moment, no signal was given and no photograph exists of the surrender ceremony.

Army Commander and COAS Visit Vassalo e Silva

Lt Gen. J.N. Chaudhuri, together with AOC-in-C Air Vice Marshal E.W. Pinto and B.N. Mullik of the Intelligence Bureau, took a helicopter from Belgaum to Goa the following day, 20 December. Lt Gen. Chaudhuri visited Maj. Gen. Vassalo e Silva at Vasco da Gama at 2 p.m.

Gen. Carlos de Azeredo, then a captain, was with Maj. Gen. Vassalo e Silva and was the official interpreter. In his book, *Trabalhos e dias de um soldado do império* (Work and days of a soldier of the empire), he says,

---

*   Kanekar, 2011, p. 147.

General Chaudhuri entered the cell alone and cordially greeted Vassalo. Vassalo wanted to stand up to compliment [salute] the Indian, but the latter rested his hand on his shoulder and did not let him. He [Lt Gen. Chaudhuri] pulled up a chair and sat down. He had words of praise for the Portuguese forces.

Col Carlos A. de Morais says that Lt Gen. Chaudhuri congratulated Maj. Gen. Vassalo e Silva for the combats in Mapusa, Bicholim, Diu and Daman.

Despite the scarce means the Portuguese [forces] had reacted well against the action by the Indian troops.

The GOC-in-C said that he had ordered POWs from Diu to be evacuated to Goa. Lt Gen. Chaudhuri

... ended the meeting saying that if he [Maj. Gen. Vassalo e Silva] wanted anything he could request the Indian camp commander [Maj. Bill Carvalho of 4 Sikh LI].[*]

Lt Gen. Chaudhuri assured Vassalo e Silva that his wife, Fernanda Pereira Monteiro e Silva, was well and safe and that the Government of India would soon be sending her to Lisbon.

Lt Gen. Chaudhuri then drove to Panjim in an army jeep, accompanied by Air Vice Marshal Erlic Pinto and B.N. Mullik. On the way, the trio encountered two white men happily motoring along, oblivious towhat was happening around. The two were stopped and quizzed. They told the Indian military officers that they were German and not Portuguese—and seemed quite unperturbed in the hands of the Indian jawans.

Hearing that, Air Vice Marshal Pinto pulled out two bullets from his personal weapon and, showing them to the two Germans, said, 'These bullets are illiterate. Can they recognize your nationality?'

---

[*] Morais, *A Queda da* Índia *Portuguesa*, 1995, p. 151.

Lt Gen. Chaudhuri chuckled and he then told the Germans politely that they would be better off at home and to remain indoors until the situation in Goa grew less volatile. The Germans made an about turn and vanished. P.N. Khera, on page 85 of his book *Operation Vijay*, mentions this incident as occurring during the army commander's visit to Goa the previous day.

Lt Gen. Chaudhuri and his companions then visited hospitals in Panjim and assured the wounded POWs that no harm would come to them. He ordered due medical attention and supplies be given to them. The party then returned to Dabolim and helicoptered back to Belgaum.

Later, the chief of army staff, Gen. Pran Nath Thapar, visited the governor-general at the POW camp in Vasco da Gama. The meeting was warm and cordial—and led to a more comfortable living for the Portuguese C-in-C, now a POW.

Vassalo e Silva was soon shifted to a better house in the woods within the Alpha POW Camp in Ponda (he remained at Alpalqueiros, Vasco da Gama, for less than ten days). Indian major, Cezar P.F. Lobo, a pilot with the Air Observation Post of the Artillery Regiment, a Goan from Aldona fluent in the Portuguese language, was tasked to take charge and look after the VIP POW.

On 20 December 1961, Maj. Gen. Candeth was appointed military governor, with R.C.V.P. Noronha, ICS, as chief civic administrator and G.K. Handoo, IPS, as special advisor. Brig. Donald Viegas of Curtorim, then a colonel at Army HQ, was sent to Goa on 21 December to assist the military governor. Lt Col Paul Baylon Fernandes of Sarzora and Lt Cdr John Eric Gomes of Margao (both part of Operation Vijay) were retained to assist in the takeover of the Goa administration. Maj. Gerson R.A. de Souza of Moira served as aide to the military governor. N.R. Nagoo, IPS, was appointed the first inspector general of police of Goa (there was no DGP system then).

R.C.V.P. Noronha, or Ronald Carlton Vivian Piedade Noronha or 'Ron' or 'RP' to his friends, was born in 1916 in Hyderabad of Goan parents, educated at Loyola College, Madras and at the London School of Economics; topped the ICS exam, was twice chief secretary of Madhya Pradesh, 1963–68 and 1972–74 when he retired, and was honoured with the Padma Bhushan the following year. The Madhya Pradesh Academy for state civil service officers was later named after him. Two villages—one in Bhopalpatnam *tehsil* of the erstwhile Bastar district (now in Bijapur district of Chhattisgarh) where he opted to serve as district collector, called Noronhapalli, and another near Bhopal, where he lived in a small, simple house post-retirement called Noronha Sankal—were named after him. He wrote an autobiography titled *A Tale Told by an Idiot*, before passing away in 1982.

Handoo, responsible for the 'faulty intelligence' that resulted in avoidable loss to the nation, was Nehru's trouble-shooter in Goa. As special advisor placed between the military governor and the chief civic administrator, Handoo became the author of misgovernance in Goa.

An immediate fallout of 'His White Majesty' (a title given to him by a Calcutta journalist who visited Goa in January 1962, while Portuguese POWs called him *Eminência Parda* or 'Grey Eminence') Handoo's overbearing attitude was based on his assumption that many Goans in service of Government of India, who were deputed to serve in Goa, wanted to go back and sought repatriation to their parent department in India. Some Goa-based officers opted to join the Union government service, for instance, Eng. Vitorino Pinto who went from the Goa PWD to CPWD.

Fernanda Monteiro e Silva, wife of the erstwhile governor-general, was treated rather shabbily and physically evicted from the official residence at Cabo, Dona Paula. She roamed the streets of Panjim as if lost. Former chief secretary, Abel Colaço, rescued her and sheltered her at his own official residence in Panjim. He was summoned to the Secretariat and threatened with sedition by Handoo, who then said, 'I can have you shot.'

This incident rocked the Lok Sabha. Nehru said that Colaço's act was chivalrous, the gesture of a gentleman towards a woman in distress. Fernanda Monteiro e Silva was flown out of Dabolim to Bombay by IAF's Fg Offr Srinivasan on 29 December 1961, en route to Lisbon. Her husband's return would follow only five months later. Portuguese non-combatants in Goa were also taken to Bombay by 29 December and repatriated to Portugal.

POW Portuguese Military Officers Recall ...

Portuguese troops, 3306 in number (including policemen), were taken prisoner of war in the three enclaves of Goa, Daman and Diu. Krishna Menon's lie of 7 December 1961, of 'heavy reinforcements' reaching Goa, lay bare. But history is written by the victor, not the vanquished. As the ancient Greek tragedian–dramatist Aeschylus had said long ago, 'In war, truth is the first casualty.'

Including non-combatants, 4668 were taken prisoner—3412 in Goa, 853 in Daman (shifted to Vasco da Gama aboard the INS *Delhi* on 31 January 1962) and 403 in Diu (shifted to Goa by the INS *Delhi* mid-January and lodged at the Ponda POW camp on 29 January 1962). Many of the non-combatants were released and repatriated.

The POWs were alive because the Indian forces did not kill them, records Portuguese cavalry (armour) Capt. João Aranha, himself a POW.[*] When retreating from Mapusa to Panjim on 18 December 1961, he and his party were spotted by IAF Hunters that flew low over them but did not open fire. The same had happened all over Goa: Portuguese soldiers were allowed to retreat but not fired upon.

POWs were initially held in five camps: Aquem Baixo (under 2 Bihar), Ponda (under 2 Para Maratha), Vasco (under 4 Sikh LI), Panjim (under 13 Kumaon) and Panjim MDS/Aguada (under 152 Field Amb-T). The five camps were later consolidated into three:

---

[*] João Aranha, 2008, p. 146.

Ponda, Vasco and Aguada. On 16 January 1962, POWs from Aquem-Baixo, numbering 459, were shifted to the Ponda camp. There were 1716 POWs in Ponda now; the rest were in Vasco (1631) and Aguada (eighty-five). This total number of 3432 POWs included 294 white policemen, forty-two white civilians, eighty-four Goan personnel and three Portuguese journalists held by mistake.

The three POW camps were brought under the 50 Para Brigade and troops of the 63 Infantry Brigade were withdrawn. The commander of the camps was Brig. Sagat Singh, who based himself at the Ponda camp. Maj. Gen. Vassalo e Silva was held in a separate house in the Ponda camp.

The Ponda POW camp was named Alpha Detenue Camp. POWs called it a 'mass graveyard'. There was an attempted escape by three POWs on 19 March 1962. The plan was simple: armed with pipes that they would use to breathe under mounds of refuse, they would escape in a garbage truck. The Portuguese accomplice POW in charge of garbage disposal developed cold feet at the eleventh hour (it was 6.30 p.m.). Brig. Sagat Singh assembled all the POWs, surrounded them with machine guns on all sides and a firing squad in front. Then, in English, he asked if any of them desired to exact revenge on the POW who turned informer. Their answer surprised the brigadier. 'Yes,' they shouted in unison. An ugly showdown was averted by the intervention of the Portuguese military chaplain, Fr Joaquim Ferreira da Silva.

There were conflicting reports of the treatment meted out to the POWs. Some (but not all) Portuguese narratives alleged that the POWs were ill-treated. The Government of India documented stray cases of abuse, for instance at the Alpalqueiros Camp in Vasco da Gama following an attempted escape (details below), where erring Indian troops were punished.

Rev. James Knox, the Apostolic Nuncio in New Delhi, was allowed to visit the POWs in January 1962. He reported that they were being treated well and the wounded were receiving medical attention.

> Prisoners of war were treated very humanely and had covered
> accommodation while many Indian soldiers remained in the
> open ... A helicopter was specially sent to Daman airfield on the
> 19th to evacuate the Portuguese Governor of Daman who had
> been wounded ...[*]

There were also first-hand published accounts by POW officers that praised the treatment they received.

Maj. (later colonel) Minnie Mohite of 2 Para Maratha was officer-in-charge of the Alpha Detenue Camp at Ponda. POW officers praised his conduct. Also praised was the conduct of Maj. Bill Carvalho of 4 Sikh Light Infantry who was the first officer-in-charge of the Alpalqueiros Camp in Vasco da Gama.

Gen. Carlos de Azeredo, then a captain, in his book has words of praise for the Indian troops in charge of the POW camp at Alpalqueiros, Vasco da Gama.[†]

This is despite the fact that Gen. Azeredo was held responsible for the attempted escape of twelve POWs from the Vasco da Gama camp on 16 January 1962. Gen. Azeredo was beaten black and blue by Indian troops, who were later punished. The dozen escapees were duped by the captain of a Greek ocean liner at Mormugao port, who took their money and then refused to let them embark. When they frantically turned to an Italian captain, he said he needed time to think about it and called them the next day—only to hand them over to Indian Army officials.[‡]

Maj. Gen. Francisco Cabral Couto was twenty-six and fresh from the military academy when he arrived in Goa on 27 March 1961. He commanded 47 Caçadores (Hunters) Battalion at the Afonso de Albuquerque military camp at Aquem Baixo-Navelim

---

[*] Khera, 1974, p. 140.

[†] *Trabalhos e dias de um soldado do império* (Work and days of a soldier of the empire).

[‡] POW António Correia de Lima details this incident in his book, *O Fim dos Séculos*.

near Margao. In his book *O Fim do Estado Português da Índia* (The
End of the Portuguese State of India), Maj. Gen. Couto says the
worst humiliation was when his captors forced his men

> ... to break their weapons and arrange them in mounds.*

At the Aquem-Baixo-Navelim camp he once commanded, 463
POWs slept back-to-back on a plain cement floor towards the rear
of the camp. They were ordered

> ... to dig trenches to serve as open-air latrines and had to make do
> with a jar of water supplied by tanks of the Margao municipality.

He admits the water shortage had been caused by the Portuguese
themselves; they had destroyed bridges and supply lines. He
remembers Christmas 1961 was celebrated with some dry biscuits,
which meant much in the given situation.

Among the Indian soldiers guarding them, he recognized three
he had seen around in Margao in recent months: one as a train TC,
another as a worker at Margao's Longuinhos restaurant and the third
as a beggar sitting under a banyan tree. They were Indian military
spies. He admired the discipline of the Indian Army.

Like Gen. Carlos de Azeredo, who describes the sorry state
of Portuguese fighting equipment, Maj. Gen. Couto describes the
complete lack of resources for any meaningful defence. His unit
HQ had a non-functioning generator set, and they depended on
kerosene lamps at night. He and his men were later shifted to the
Ponda POW camp.

Three Portuguese media persons—Urbano Carrasco (of *Diário
Popular*), José Neves da Costa and cameraman José Serras Fernandes
(both of *Rádio e Televisão de Portugal* or RTP)—were held POW
initially at Altinho and later at Ponda, in all for sixty days (they

---

* Tribuna da História, 2006.

departed from Goa by air on 17 February 1962 for Bombay, en route Lisbon). They too had words of praise for the Indian Army officers.

POW Repatriation and After

Carrasco, upon his return to Portugal, did a series of feel-good articles (*Diário de prisioneiro* or 'Diary of a Prisoner' in the daily newspaper *Diário Popular*), meant to reassure the families of POWs back home. This led to unintended results: the POWs felt the reports delayed their repatriation. Salazar was incensed to learn that the POWs in Goa were being treated as per the Geneva Convention. Furious that his orders to follow a scorched-earth policy and 'fight to the last man' had been disobeyed, Salazar practically abandoned the Portuguese POWs. He did not want the 'traitors' back any time soon. He wanted them to suffer (for 'not having died for Salazar'). As noted by Portuguese cavalry officer João Aranha, Salazar wanted them to 'accept' the 'holocaust' in exchange for a sung 'glory' expressed in his politically ill-thought-out and militarily ill-written orders (to the Goa governor-general).*

The Portuguese dictator derailed repatriation talks with a stubborn stance.

On 12 January 1962, he detained and later expelled 2274 Indians from Mozambique (the figure is usually mentioned as 1200, but as 12,000 by South African, US and British newspapers, and about 3500 by Indian newspapers). Also detained were fewer numbers in Angola and 51 in Macau—even 5 Indian passengers in transit at Lisbon airport!

This no doubt annoyed India, but the government continued to pursue early repatriation of the POWs from Goa.

The negotiations dragged on because Salazar insisted that the POWs be repatriated from Mormugao port in a Portuguese vessel, while India insisted it would be by air from Bombay. Salazar then

---

* Aranha, 2008, p. 109.

said the repatriation should be in Portuguese aircraft, and India insisted on aircraft from a neutral country.

An exasperated Prime Minister Nehru threatened to allow the POWs to fly out on their own. On 24 March 1962, the Government of India officially informed the POWs in writing that they were free to return to Portugal or go to any country of their choice at their own cost.[*]

Things changed immediately. Salazar's 'secret agent or James Bond', Jorge Jardim, an influential man living in Mozambique since 1952, negotiated the repatriation.[†] According to Portuguese media person Fernanda ('Nene') Paraiso, Jardim took the help of K.B. Kakoobhai, a rich trader in Beira and Lourenço Marques (now Maputo) and his brother Kumar Hemendra in Nairobi, to establish contact with Morarji Desai and V.C. Trivedi, joint secretary in the Ministry of External Affairs. Hemendra also wrote to Nehru on 25 March 1962.[‡]

The repatriation was finally agreed upon on 13 April 1962. POWs would be flown via an 'air bridge' from Dabolim to Karachi in chartered F-BGSN aircraft of UAT (*Union Aéromaritime de Transport*, which merged in 1963 into a new *Union de Transports Aériens* or UTA), a French company.

The repatriation began on 4 May 1962 in the presence of the Apostolic Nuncio and Leal Ferreira, secretary of the Brazilian Embassy in New Delhi. (The Apostolic Nuncio was present at India's request; Brazil looked after Portugal's interests in India.) All Portuguese POWs were in Karachi by 5 May 1962.

---

[*] Ibid., p. 147.

[†] Portrayed as Salazar's James Bond by author José Freire Antunes in one of his books, see: https://sites.google.com/site/pequenashistorietas/person-alidades/jorge-jardim. Jorge Jardim evidently was a shady man. General Kaulza de Arriaga, Mozambique's military chief, later said in an interview that Jorge Jardim appropriated Kakoobhai's house. Pedro Vieira, author of this essay, says that Jardim took Kakoobhai's belongings too.

[‡] Email interview of Fernanda Paraiso with author.

The POWs had suffered five months detention 'thanks to the stupid stubbornness of Lisbon' observed Gen. Carlos de Azeredo in his book.* He also had words of anger for the way his compatriots back in Portugal received them and judged them very unfairly in a military court.

The POWs sailed from Karachi for Lisbon in three ships: *Vera Cruz* (departed Karachi 8 May 1962 and arrived in Lisbon on 22 May 1962), *Pátria* (12 May, 26 May 1962) and *Moçambique* (15 May, 30 May 1962).

A worse fate awaited them in Portugal.

Upon arrival, like a gang of ordinary criminals, they were all taken into custody at gunpoint by the military police and whisked away without being permitted to greet their families who had gathered to receive them—some from nights before.

They were publicly discredited as cowards, traitors and malefactors of high treason and were court-martialled for defying the express orders of the supreme commander to not surrender. During the court-martial, they had no right of defence. The verdict was out on 22 March 1963.

A dozen officers—Maj. Gen. Vassalo e Silva, his military commander, the chief of staff, one naval captain, six majors, a sub lieutenant and a sergeant—were stripped of their rank, expelled from the armed forces and barred from holding any public office for life. Five were compulsorily retired and nine sentenced to half a year's suspension from military service. No appeal lay.

A military chaplain, Fr António da Silva Mendes, who had fixed a truce flag at Daman hospital, was also punished.

Being an engineer, Vassalo e Silva began working for his father-in-law's construction company.

The penalized were rehabilitated only after Portugal's 25 April 1974 Carnation Revolution overthrew Salazar's successor, Marcelo Caetano.[16]

---

* *Trabalhos e dias de um soldado do império* (Work and Days of a Soldier of the Empire).

The rehabilitation was formalized by enactment of Law No. 727/74 of 19 December 1974 (note the date—19 December 'was not an unexpected coincidence; Portuguese lawmakers could teach lessons to their Damascus Caliphate's peers'!*).

The order of rehabilitation was signed by the President of the Republic, retired Gen. Costa Gomes (who, as Portugal's undersecretary of war in 1960, had told Salazar that even the entire army of Portugal would not be able to resist an invasion of Goa by India for more than five hours).

Maj. Gen. Vassalo e Silva regained his rank—with an even more popular sobriquet, Vacila e Salva (literally, 'vacillate and save').

Goans Celebrate, Sulk, Worry

In 1961, Goans, especially those at the short end of the colonial regime's stick, celebrated, some by going on a looting spree against perceived local enemies. Goans—mostly Catholic—living in Delhi, Bombay, Calcutta and Bangalore, also celebrated 19 December 1961.

Mine owners, importers and traders—facing the grim prospect of India's 'socialist' economic policies and the dreaded 'licence raj', 'permit raj', 'quota raj' and 'inspector raj'—silently grieved the loss, together with a small section of the elite, both Hindu and Catholic. The majority was muted, by and large relieved that an oppressive regime was dismantled but uncertain of the future.

For the family of famed freedom fighter Pandurang P. Shirodkar, there was no celebration. His wife, with two children still in college, lived in Dahisar, Bombay. They spent 19 December 1961 in penury. Shirodkar was jailed in Angola. He was released, but ordered not to leave Angola. He gave tuitions and worked at a Portuguese-language newspaper to make a living.

When revolt against the Portuguese broke out in Angola in February 1961, Shirodkar was again put into solitary confinement. Remittances and letters stopped. Reuters reported that Goan

---

* Email interview of Antonio Palhinha Machado, Lisbon, with the author.

prisoners in Angola were shot dead by the Portuguese, and that Goans in Nairobi met in condolence. The son kept the news from his mother but informed his paternal and maternal grandfathers in Goa.

On 19 December 1961, the son had only five rupees. He purchased the national flag for three-and-half rupees and hoisted it outside their block.* While India celebrated, Shirodkar's family ate *cunji* (or rice gruel) sweetened with borrowed jaggery.†

It turned out that Shirodkar was not among those killed. He returned the following year and was the first elected speaker of the Goa Legislative Assembly.

On Christmas Day, 1961, Air Marshal Mally Wollen, then a squadron leader heading 23 Squadron (Gnats), descended with Flying Officer Ramachandran at the controls of a T-11 Vampire at the Diu airfield, where children had gathered around a Christmas tree. The canopy opened and there emerged Santa Claus (Air Marshal Wollen). Santa told the kids that Rudolf (the reindeer) was not well that day, so he had to take a plane.

Fun, food and football—not necessarily in that order—are national passions in Portugal (so fun-loving that the French say: '*Les Portugais sonttoujours gaies*' or 'The Portuguese are always cheerful'). The traditional three Fs are, of course, Fátima (the Catholic shrine of Our Lady that draws pilgrims from the world over), Football (the national sport) and Fado (the melancholic even mournful ballad form of song).

In an uncharitable version, *fado* is anagrammatically spelt as *foda*. Illustration of its usage: circa 1929, the Portuguese governor of Goa, Gen. Pedro Francisco Massano de Amorim, suffered from an ailment and visited Tata Memorial Hospital in Bombay by train (there were no flights at the time). In the governor's retinue was a Goan interpreter of Portuguese-English-French, Vittola Sadassiva Sinai Sunctancar (Vithal Sadashiv Shenvi Sukhtankar). At every halt, the station master called on the governor, to the annoyance

---

* Interview of Dr P.P. Shirodkar, now deceased, with the author.
† Shirodkar, *My Life in Exile*, p. 242.

of the suffering man. At one station, he could take it no more and instructed Sukhtankar to tell the intruding station master, 'vá e foda' (F.O.). Sukhtankar promptly translated, 'I am well. Nothing needed. Thank you!'

To the cheerful Portuguese people, the loss of Goa was a spiritual bereavement. Like a funeral oration, Salazar told his Parliament on 3 January 1962 (not verbatim):

> What Goa means to Portugal cannot be measured by the smallness of its territory but by the greatness of the history of which it forms part, and the nobility of the mission that took the Portuguese there in the first place.[*]

Salazar himself was the chief architect of that disgraceful loss. By the end of World War II, the world view of colonialism underwent a drastic change. The world no longer viewed the domination of a people by a foreign power as something tolerable that could continue. One by one, colonial regimes that subjugated people in Asia and Africa were dismantled—either peacefully or by the use of force— and the anachronism called a colony was consigned to the annals of history. Recognizing the writing on the wall, some West European colonial masters vacated on their own. Those who hesitated were pushed out—for instance, the French from Indo-China and Algeria, the Dutch from Indonesia and the Portuguese themselves from the tiny area called São João Batista de Ajudá in Benin.

The world had changed. Salazar had not. He continued to follow 'absurd politics'[†] and ignored the counsel of his own ministers and officials, of Portugal's opposition leaders, of the respected geographer Prof. Orlando Ribeiro of Lisbon University,[‡] of prominent Goans who pleaded with him and, finally, of Portugal's undersecretary of

---

[*]   *Diario de Lisbòa,* 3 January 1962, second edition, http://casacomum. org/cc/visualizador?pasta=06544.082.17627

[†]   Aranha, 2008, p. 146.

[‡]   See *Relatórioao Governo* of 1956, referred to later.

war, Gen. Francisco Costa Gomes, who had pointed out, towards the end of 1960, that the situation in Goa was militarily untenable.

Salazar's obstinacy was clearly demonstrated yet again when he rejected the advice of others when contrary to his own opinion. The Goa situation unmistakably bore his insidious signature. His men in Goa had to be—and finally were—physically evicted.

For all his failings, Salazar was scrupulously honest, a man of impeccable personal integrity. Whatever one may accuse him of—an aversion to democratic processes, a misogynistic aversion to women except in housekeeping, kitchen and bed, an aversion to counsel other than his own ideas—the one thing none could accuse him of was personal corruption. His integrity was legendary.

Freedom fighter Prabhakar Sinari (later an IPS officer) once remarked to comrade-in-arms Dr Manu Fernandes that India needed a leader like Salazar. When Salazar passed, freedom fighter Adv. Gopal Apa Kamat (the second speaker of the Goa Legislative Assembly, 1967–72) publicly eulogized Salazar's virtue in a newspaper article.

Goans, meanwhile, were uniquely placed in India: they were *de jure* dual nationals!

Portugal refused to recognize India's annexation of Goa and continued to view all those born in Goa prior to 19 December 1961 (and their successive two generations) as Portuguese nationals. After the normalization of relations between India and Portugal on 31 December 1974, Portugal issued decree No. 308-A/75 on 24 June 1975 recognizing Goans as Portuguese nationals. The decree was normalized under the Portuguese nationality law (No. 37/81) and its amended Organic Law 2/2006 of 17 April 2006 that continued to recognize Goans as Portuguese nationals. The law enables Goans to obtain a Portuguese passport.[*]

India, pre- and post-Independence, conferred full Indian citizenship (including voting rights) to Goans settled in her territory.

---

[*] https://timesofindia.indiatimes.com/city/goa/portuguese-nationality-is-fundamental-right-by-law/articleshow/28808047.cms

India liberated Goa from the colonial yoke on 19 December 1961
and annexed the liberated territories to the Republic of India by
the Constitution (Twelfth Amendment) Act on 27 March 1962.
The following day, without asking the Goans to renounce their
Portuguese nationality, India granted them Indian citizenship,
vide Goa, Daman and Diu (Citizenship) Order promulgated on
28 March 1962.

Goans are the only Indians who are simultaneously Portuguese
as well as Indian citizens. Indian law does not permit dual nationality,
but the strange case of dual nationality granted to Goans by India
and Portugal is yet to undergo judicial scrutiny.

8

THE AFTERMATH

In the Wake of the Invasion

On 18 December 1961, the UN Security Council met twice in New York, at 3 p.m. and again at 8.45 p.m., over the issue of the invasion of Goa. Besides the permanent members—USA, USSR, Britain, France and Nationalist China—other members present and voting at the Security Council table that day were Sri Lanka, Chile, Liberia, Turkey, Ecuador and the UAE (chair).

India and Portugal were allowed to attend ... but without the right to vote.

Portugal complained to the UNSC that India had committed a fully premeditated and unprovoked aggression, violating Articles 2(3) and 2(4) of the UN Charter.

France agreed, adding that it was not only shocked but astonished as well that India, a country which always prided itself on its policy of non-violence, had stooped to this action.

Clearly, two issues were at play here: colonialism and invasion. For the US and most western countries, the twin issues were conundrums that could not be reconciled. Their stated policy was against colonialism; hence, they ought to have supported India; but they also professed to be against invasion; hence, a condemnation of India was to be expected. However, they ended up supporting Portugal and condemning India.

One doesn't need to look very far for the reason for their paradoxical behaviour. On the morning of 18 December, Portugal's foreign minister summoned the US ambassador in Lisbon and issued a blunt warning that a hostile US stance

at the UNSC meet would invite grave consequences. The
US had strategic naval and air bases in the Azores archipelago
of Portugal deep in the Atlantic. The US state department's
national interests veered their focus on aggression by India
and away from colonialism in Goa. At the UNSC meet,
the US envoy, Adlai Stevenson, began with ridicule:

> Few nations have done more to uphold the [UN] principles or
> to support its peace-making efforts all over the world, and none
> have espoused non-violence more vehemently [than India].[*]

That very year (1961), Stevenson said, Nehru had addressed the
UN on peaceful settlement of disputes and also said:

> [Nehru] who many look up to as an apostle of non-violence ...
> India's Minister of Defence, so well known in these halls for his
> advice on matters of peace and his tireless enjoinders to everyone
> else to seek the way of compromise, was on the borders of Goa
> inspecting his troops at the zero hour of invasion.[†]

Stevenson quoted the Indian delegate at the UN when the
Dutch used force in Indonesia in 1947. India's delegate had told
the UN then:

> Can any country be allowed to indulge in aggression of this type
> and refuse arbitration? ...If any power can act as it chooses in
> such matters then there is no purpose left for the United Nations.
> It will have no prestige or authority and [is] bound to fade away
> ... [Stevenson then added] When acts of violence take place
> between nations in this dangerous world, no matter where they
> occur or for what cause, there is reason for alarm. The news from
> Goa tells us of such acts of violence. It is alarming news and, in

---

[*] Record of UN proceedings.
[†] Ibid.

our judgment, the Security Council has urgent duty to act in the interests of international peace and security.[*]

India's permanent delegate, C.S. Jha, told the UNSC:

> It must be realized that this is a colonial question. It is a question of getting rid of the last vestiges of colonialism in India. That is a matter of faith with us. Whatever anyone else may think, [UN] Charter or no Charter, [UN Security] Council or no Council, that is our basic faith which we cannot afford to give up at any cost.[†]

Commenting on the UNSC debate, political analyst Margaret W. Fisher wrote in 'Goa in Wider Perspective',

> Somewhat paradoxically, the representative of the country which had achieved independence through a violent revolution [the USA] took the stand that whatever the circumstances, there was no excuse for the use of force, whereas the representative of the country which had achieved independence after a uniquely non-violent freedom movement [India] took the stand that if force was required to achieve independence from colonialism, the right to use it could not be questioned.[‡]

USA, China, Britain, France, Chile, Turkey and Ecuador (seven members out of eleven) condemned India's aggression. The remaining four—USSR, UAE, Liberia and Sri Lanka—sided with India.

Resolution S/5033 moved by the US and Britain deploring the use of force and, among other things, calling upon India to withdraw its forces to positions before 17 December 1961, was vetoed by USSR—exercising its UNSC permanent member's veto for the ninety-ninth time.[§]

---

[*] Ibid.

[†] Ibid.

[‡] Margaret W. Fisher, 'Goa in Wider Perspective', *Asian Survey*, 1962.

[§] *UN Review 14*, January 1962.

It was ironic. India had always opposed the UNSC veto.

A counter-resolution in support of India was rejected by a predictable majority of four votes (three for, seven against). The USSR, Liberia and Sri Lanka voted for it, while the UAE was in the chair.[*]

Following these deliberations at the UNSC, the UN General Assembly adopted Resolution 1699 (XVI) the following day, 19 December, condemning Portugal for failing to comply with its obligations as an administering power, without naming Goa.

Ultimately, even if several nations disagreed with India's use of force, few regretted the outcome. The world in the mid-twentieth century was clearly against colonialism. Most nations felt that colonialism was such an evil that even the use of force to eliminate it could be condoned.

Only South Africa, Spain and Brazil stood by Portugal. South Africa's white Dutch minority faced similar political problems, Spain was a neighbour and Brazil, which shared a long heritage with Portugal, maintained that the Indian armed action was not an enforcement of the principle of self-determination for the local population. Brazil said that it was a glaring case of annexation, a mere replacement of Portuguese rule by domination of the Indian Union.

Not many applauded India either. Only the Afro-Asian world supported India and the USSR stood rock solid with India.

Goa: Liberated or Conquered?

On 19 December 1961, India announced to the world that Goa had been 'liberated' from Portugal.

On 9 August 1965, the Supreme Court of India held that Goa was 'acquired by conquest in [an] act of war'. In other words, it had been conquered.

The verdict, by a full bench of the Supreme Court headed by the chief justice of India, was delivered in a unanimous judgement in Writ Petition No. 120 of 1965, Pema Chibar alias Preamabhai Chhibabai Tangal vs Union of India (AIR 1966 SC 472).

---

[*]   Ibid.

The case arose because Goa's post-1961 dispensation cancelled twenty-three licences issued by the Portuguese to Preamabhai, an alleged smuggler from Daman, to import 1 million pounds sterling worth of merchandise.

Caught in a difficult situation vis-à-vis Article 358 of the Constitution of India, the then solicitor general of India, S.V. Gupte, submitted before the court that Goa was acquired by conquest and that, as a successor sovereign, the Union of India was not bound to honour commitments of the vanquished sovereign.

The verdict of 9 August 1965 was given by Chief Justice P.B. Gajendra Gadkar together with Justice K.N. Wanchoo, Justice M. Hidayatullah, Justice J.C. Shah and Justice S.M. Sikri.

There were other verdicts of the Supreme Court of India in this context which in effect said the same thing: that Goa was conquered in an act of war.

In the celebrated case of Rev. Msgr Sebastião Francisco Xavier dos Remedios Monteiro v/s the State of Goa (1969 (3) SCC 419 and AIR 1970 SC 329), the verdict of 26 March 1969 given by Chief Justice M. Hidayatullah (later vice president of India) together with Justice S.M. Sikri, Justice R.S.Bachawat, Justice G.K. Mitter and Justice K.S. Hegde upheld that Goa was 'seized by force of arms' and annexed through conquest and subjugation.

Msgr Sebastião Francisco ('Padre Chico') Monteiro was a popular Goan priest from Candolim. He felt the invasion was immoral, retained his Portuguese passport and refused to register himself at the Foreigners Branch of Goa Police, as required under the law. The Government of Goa issued orders for his deportation to Portugal. He lost at the trial level, lost in appeal before the District Court, lost in 2nd Appeal before the Judicial Commissioner's Court (this was before the Judicial Commissioner's Court in Goa was replaced by a permanent Bench of the Bombay High Court) and lost in the final Appeal before the Supreme Court of India. Padre Chico was to be deported to Portugal. However, in a quid pro quo, Salazar agreed to release Adv. Telo Mascarenhas, a Goan freedom fighter from Majorda, held in political detention in Portugal.

All the Supreme Court judgements mentioned above were based on pleadings of the Union of India.

Politically, Goa was liberated. Legally, Goa was conquered.

Nehru's Volte-Face

Nehru had assured western powers, USA and UK in particular, that he would not use force against the Portuguese in Goa but would sort out the question using peaceful means. He made a complete 180-degree turn on that solemn assurance. It was not his only volte-face with regard to Goa. There was another that still rankles some Goans. It was the unceremonial annexation of Goa, without taking the natives into confidence. Nehru had asserted in Sitapur on 21 August 1955,

> ... to take Goa by force would be easy ... [but] ... would be contrary to the policy of the Government as well as to the dignity of India. We have assured Goans that it is for them to establish their own future.

Again, he solemnly declared in Bombay on 4 June 1956:

> If the people of Goa ... wish to retain their separate identity, I am not going to bring them by processes of compulsion or coercion into the Indian Union.

He not only used force but, within three months, annexed Goa into the Republic of India without consulting the native population.

The unilateral Constitution (Twelfth Amendment) Act annexing the liberated territories to the Republic of India on 27 March 1962 was a complete reversal of Nehru's steadfast pronouncements right from 1954—and was certainly not in line with the principles of self-determination. Self-determination was enshrined in the UN Charter of 20 June 1945 and in its General Assembly Resolutions No. 637 (VIII) of 16 December 1952 on self-determination and No. 1514 (XV) of 14 December 1960 on decolonization. India was a party to the Charter and both the Resolutions.

A plebiscite ('Opinion Poll') was held five years later, 16 January 1967—the first such held in India (the only other to date was held in Sikkim in 1975). It asked whether Goans want to continue as a centrally administered Union Territory or be merged with Maharashtra. There were no other choices.

The opinion-poll verdict went against merger with Maharashtra, 55:45. India declared the controversy of Goa's integration as closed forever. The principle of self-determination was conveniently swept under the carpet.

Outright annexation following conquest, without ascertaining the wishes of the local people as enshrined in the principle of self-determination, seems to be the chief grouse of some Goans—not the act of integration per se.

The inimitable Shankar Bhandari was a wise and witty man from Cumbarjua in Tiswadi. He was the author of that unique observation, *Goenkar rattche torrad, sokallche honrrad* (Sozzled at night, Goans are honourable by day). Bhandari, a fierce defender of the Goan identity, was not at all in favour of the continuance of the Portuguese in Goa. When India unilaterally annexed Goa, Bhandari penned the famous poem, *Ganarajya* (Republic), of which the telling line was, *Ganachem Ailam Raj / Khuincho Gana Konn Zanna?* (Gana's rule has arrived; who knows from where Gana comes?) Bhandari worked as a programme officer at the Panjim broadcasting station of All India Radio. When Goa was sought to be merged into Maharashtra and an opinion poll was held to decide the issue, Bhandari sloganeered, *Amkam naka puran poli, amkam zai Goenchi xit kodi* (We don't want Maharashtra's popular puran poli, we want Goan fish curry rice).

The first free elections by universal adult franchise in Goa's history—to the thirty-member Goa Legislative Assembly—were held about two years after liberation of the territory from colonial rule, on 9 December 1963. Nehru had visited Goa in May that year, had met Goans and had addressed some public meetings, including at Panjim and Margao—Goa's foremost towns then (and now). Unprecedented crowds thronged to hear the Indian leader. Nehru's ubiquitous Congress Party, which until then had seldom lost an election anywhere in India, contested Goa's first elections. The party had, after all, liberated Goa. It evidently expected to harvest rich returns.

Not a single Congress candidate won in Goa. Two-thirds of the party's candidates fared so badly and polled so few votes that they forfeited their security deposits.

Goa ke log ajeeb hain, Nehru is reported to have remarked upon hearing the election results. It was admirable that one of India's best-educated prime ministers and the great statesman that he was, could make such an accurate assessment sitting in faraway Delhi. It took a lesser mortal like this author, who was born and bred in Goa, half a lifetime to realize the correctness of that singular trait of Goan quirkiness!

What India Said

A majority of Indians celebrated the eviction of the last colonial power from the soil of the subcontinent. Defence minister Krishna Menon became an overnight hero for the masses. The opposition parties had the winds stolen from their sails. The Congress party would be returned to power in the February 1962 general elections. But not all Indian political leaders were happy with the means employed to achieve the end. Like their counterparts in the west, they raged at Krishna Menon. Prime Minister Nehru was not so much target of their outrage.

The Gandhian 'elder statesman' who was governor-general of India 1948–1950, Chakravarti Rajagopalachari ('Rajaji'), wrote in his journal, *Swarajya*, that, after the action in Goa, India

> ... totally lost the moral power to raise her voice against militarism ...

and could no longer claim to be on a mission for promoting peace. He repeated this during a press interview.[*] While Portugal's

---

[*] *Swarajya*, 27 December 1961, and *Times of India*, 27 December 1961.

occupation of Goa was a violation of Indian nationalism, it was not a greater offence than Red China's occupation of Indian territory. The 'great adventure' of seizing Goa may be the turning point in India's values of non-violence, he said.

> What message does India now carry in a world on the brink of moral collapse? Our nationalism has, I fear, led us into impatience at the wrong moment.[*]

Rajaji's Swatantra Party was the only Indian political party that had *ab initio* been against armed intervention in Goa, arguing that when there was tension with China on the northern borders, it would be foolish to divert troops to Goa. Fellow partyman, the irrepressible Minoo Masani (a former socialist), said the Goa operations were a calculated prelude to the 'khaki elections' due in February 1962. Rajaji's thoughts were echoed by the national daily *The Hindu*:

> It would be presenting a deceptive picture to suggest that everyone is supremely happy over the Goa developments without any reservations. Many in high places did hold a different view on the desirability of using force ... India might have endangered the high esteem in which she has been held all over the world.[†]

The same daily had editorially commented a few weeks before, on 29 November 1961, that the Portuguese had survived in India because of

> ... British tolerance and Indian endurance.

Within the Congress Party, Finance Minister Morarji Desai steadfastly opposed the use of force by India in Goa. Following the killing of satyagrahis at the Goa borders on 15 August 1955, when protestors marched to the secretariat in Bombay demanding action

---

[*] Ibid.

[†] *The Hindu*, 20 December 1961.

against the Portuguese in Goa, Morarji, then the chief minister Bombay State, had the protestors lathi-charged and tear-gassed. His views on Goa were reflected in the 'Morarji vs Menon' debate. After Operation Vijay, Morarji wrote that

> Krishna Menon forced the military action in December 1961 to bolster his electoral prospects two months later.[*]

Pandit Nehru's own sister, Vijaya Lakshmi Pandit, would tell Paul Gore-Booth, the British high commissioner to India, that Krishna Menon had pushed the prime minister to give his approval to Operation Vijay.[†] Rajkumari Amrit Kaur, then a cabinet minister, wrote in a letter:

> I have personally been very sad about Goa. It was really the enormous and continuous pressure from his own and all the other political parties of India, in particular that of the Jan Sangh and the Communists, that finally drove our Prime Minister to accede to their demands. I feel the triumph has not been worth the price we have had to pay for it. For some time, at any rate, India's voice will not count as much as it has done in the past in the world councils for peace.[‡]

Wrote the *Gandhi Marg*:

> From now on India must be content to remain in the common ranks of the nations which protest, maybe sincerely, that they stand for peace and at the same time resort to military action when it suits them.[§]

---

[*] Ramesh, Penguin Viking, 2019, p. 547.

[†] Ibid., p. 546.

[‡] Ramachandra Guha, 'Recalling the Liberation of Goa', *The Hindu*, 2 September 2007.

[§] *Gandhi Marg*, vol. 6, no.1, January 1962, p. 3.

Dom Moraes, the Goan-origin poet and son of editor–author Frank Moraes, in an article titled 'I Am an Indian, and on This Day, I Cannot but Feel Ashamed ...', wrote:

> Who knows what the Goan people want? I think this must be the first occasion, seen through the rain of Indian propaganda pamphlets fluttering down on Goa, where the 'liberation' of a country was achieved from outside rather than inside ... I am horrified, ashamed and appalled by the action of the Indian Government.[*]

Bombay High Court advocate, B.K. Bohman-Behram, in his book *Goa and Ourselves*, said that,

> ... the writer [he] discovered that the Goans had no desire to exchange the sovereignty of Lisbon for that of New Delhi ... The writer was told by Goans who knew their Goa that a referendum at the time would have yielded at least a ninety-five per cent poll in favour of the Portuguese and against a merger with the [Indian] Union ... In the result, one finds that a true Goan feels a bond of kinship with distant Portugal which he does not with his great Neighbour on our side of the frontier ... The voice of Goa seems unequivocal: Goans, Portuguese Nationals, do not want the integration of their country into the Union of India.[†]

Fellow Parsi, Astad Dinshaw Gorwala, a former ICS officer, attacked the government for fabricating incidents on the Goan borders to build a case for invasion. He said Nehru should have just taken Goa, offered no apologies and let the matter rest there.[‡]

---

[*] Nishtha Desai, *Liberation vs Armed Aggression*, Directorate of Art & Culture, Government of Goa, 2011, p. 109 and footnote no. 125.

[†] B.K. Bohman-Behram, *Goa and Ourselves*, New Book Company, Bombay, 1955, pp. i, iii, 58.

[‡] Astad Dinshaw Gorwala, *Janata Weekly*, vol. 16, 31 December 1961, Bombay, pp. 15–16.

On 2 September 2007, historian Ramachandra Guha, in his Sunday column in the daily newspaper *The Hindu*, wrote a thought-provoking piece titled 'Recalling the Liberation of Goa'. He observed:

> ... the charge that Indians were being hypocritical and sanctimonious falls away in the light of the behaviour, in later decades, of the world's superpowers. Who, in the face of the Soviet invasion of Afghanistan in 1979 or the American invasion of Iraq in 2003, could consider India's action in Goa to be illegitimate?

The takeover of Goa by the armed forces did not have the global results that were expected of it: it did not lead to an increase of India's influence in the Afro-Asian world, it did not bring down the Salazar regime in Portugal and it did not help the freedom struggles in Portugal's African colonies of Angola and Mozambique (both these countries, together with other colonies in Africa, became free in 1975 only after Portugal's Carnation Revolution overthrew the fascist regime on 25 April 1974).

What the World Said

After India had taken Goa, Krishna Menon hurried to New York to offer his explanations to the UN. Hardly had the Portuguese surrendered in Goa when Menon was in New York. The US State Department said:

> Menon came to flaunt India's action in Goa.[*]

Author Emil Lengyel wrote in his book on Krishna Menon:

> A phalanx of pressmen confronted him, wanting to know how he could reconcile Gandhi's spirit with the employment of jet

---

[*] Ramesh, Penguin Viking, 2009, p. 550.

bombers. The occupation of Goa, he told them, was not an act of aggression.

'What do you call it, then?' a reporter ventured to ask.

'I will not put up with such rudeness,' Krishna Menon exploded. 'Who are you to treat me like this?'

The bewildered reporter tried to explain that his question was purely factual, and that no harm had been meant.

'Apologize into the microphone,' Krishna Menon demanded, and the reporter apologized. Millions of TV viewers were privileged to witness this edifying encounter.[*]

The military action in Goa evoked worldwide indignation and few countries stood by India. Countries otherwise opposed to colonialism did not support the means used by India. Friendly countries that were trying to cultivate India and draw her to its side, like the United States of America, turned severe critics of the military action.

Quizzically, when Prime Minister Nehru met President John F. Kennedy during an official visit to Washington on 7 November 1961, observers

> ... wondered whether the President gave Nehru some kind of assurance that the United States would take no action if Goa were invaded. Salazar himself was convinced of this, and that 'Nehru only put the military machine into action after having received the green light from the United States'.[†]

President Kennedy was favourably disposed towards India, unlike the preceding Republican administration. When the US Senate Foreign Relations Committee attempted to cut the 1962 foreign aid appropriation to India by 25 per cent in displeasure over India's military action in Goa, President Kennedy objected.

However, as widely (and famously) quoted, President Kennedy is said to have told the Indian ambassador to the USA, B.K. Nehru:

---

[*] Lengyel, *Krishna Menon*, 1962, p. 207.

[†] Gaitonde, 2016, p. 167.

You spend the last fifteen years preaching morality to us, and then you go ahead and act the way any normal country would behave ... people are saying, the preacher has been caught coming out of the brothel.[*]

Red China supported the people's struggle against 'imperialist colonialism', but the Hong Kong newspaper *Ta Kung Pao* dubbed the attack on Goa as

... a desperate attempt by Mr. Nehru to regain his sagging prestige among the Afro-Asian nations ...

... and ridiculed Nehru for choosing to take on

the world's tiniest imperialist country.[†]

(It may be recalled that China favoured accepting Portugal's offer to take over Mormugao seaport and Dabolim airport, but Premier Chou En-lai had felt there was a lot of time to make a move; he did not think Nehru would attack Goa and ruin his pristine image as a pacifist.)

An American writer commented:

For a good deal of the world ...and particularly for the United States, still mesmerized by the memory of Mahatma Gandhi's credo of non-violence, the invasion of Goa by India was shocking news. It was as if Little Lord Fauntleroy had suddenly turned out to be a juvenile delinquent.[‡]

---

[*] *Times of India,* Mumbai edition of 23 November 2013, https://timesof-india.indiatimes.com/india/john-f-kennedy/articleshow/26169547.cms

[†] *International Reactions to Indian Attack on Goa,* Keesing's Record of World Events, vol. 8, March 1962, https://web.stanford.edu/group/tomzgroup/pmwiki/uploads/1074-1962-03-KS-b-RCW.pdf

[‡] Lengyel, *Krishna Menon,* 1962, p. 205; the phrase 'Little Lord Fauntleroy' implies a person with a pompous air of moral superiority.

American historian Arthur Schlesinger said that,

> The contrast between Nehru's incessant sanctimony on the subject of non-aggression and his brisk exercise of *Machtpolitik* was too comic not to cause comment. It was a little like catching the preacher in the hen-house; and it suggested that Harrow and Cambridge, in instilling the British virtues, had not neglected hypocrisy.[*] [Nehru had studied at Harrow School and Cambridge University in the UK.]

The German political news magazine *Der Spiegel* observed:

> Behind the violent occupation of Goa by India stands the economic interest as Goa's export of iron ore will yearly add 250 million DM [Deutsche Marks] into the Indian Treasury to build up its money reserves from only 982 Million Rupees or 825 million DM.[†]

The UK's *Daily Telegraph* reported:

> Goa earns more than 10 Million pounds a year at present from her mining operations by exporting mostly to Japan and West Germany. This incidentally is a good reason for grabbing the colony so far as hard-currency hungry India is concerned.[‡]

The *Miami Herald* reported of an American who spent a week in Goa negotiating the sale of three transport planes and who said, when back in America:

> Iron is so plentiful in Goa that they use it for building farm fences. Goa abounds in rich iron and manganese mines. While

---

[*] Arthur Schlesinger, *A Thousand Days*, p. 527; Gaitonde, *The Liberation of Goa*, pp. 182–83, and Ramachandra Guha, Goanet, available at https://www.mail-archive.com/goanet@lists.goanet.org/msg16687.html

[†] 10 January 1962.

[‡] 5 December 1961.

the Goanese may be poor compared with US standards, they are certainly not, compared with the peoples of the Middle and Far East. India's steel mills had reached their capacity and needed more iron ore.[*]

The British daily newspaper *News Chronicle* said:

India's armed invasion of Goa will be viewed with shocked surprise by the nations of the free world. Mr. Nehru, who had become the embodiment of pacifism, with the policy favouring peaceful negotiations before the International Court of Justice, has shed his role of peacemaker, and now, against a roar of Indian aircraft and the thunder of their bombs, says India felt she had 'no alternative' but to move into Goa.[†]

The *New York World-Telegram*, on 18 December 1961, said:

He [Mr Nehru] ranged from critical to indignant when Britain, France and Israel invaded Egypt; when Russia crushed the Hungarian revolt, and when the United States backed the rebel invasion of Fidel Castro's Cuba … The Prime Minister in this invasion of Goa ignored President Kennedy's plea to avoid the use of force … He has now adopted the philosophy that might makes right … Portugal has no more right to Goa than Britain has to India or France to Indochina. All three took territory because they had power to and held the natives under thumb. That was imperialism. Mr. Nehru has been a life-long foe of it. But action against Goa also is imperialism, although he may call it 'liberation'.[‡]

Only the *New York Times* in the western print media put the issue in perspective when it said:

---

[*] 19 December 1961.

[†] 20 December 1961.

[‡] Bonnie Lubega, http://goa-invasion-1961.blogspot.com/2013/04/goa-african-writers-perspective.html

It is true that Portugal's claim that Goa is a Portuguese province is unconvincing. Goa is a colony, no matter what legal fiction has been contrived in Lisbon ...[*]

However, the newspaper added that, despite Goa's being under a stubborn dictator in Lisbon,

... if the Goans agreed, it [Goa] should have been amicably transferred to India years ago, as were the small French enclaves that remained on Indian soil after India became independent ...It is nevertheless inexcusable that India—a self-styled champion of peace—should now resort to military invasion of Goa.

The newspaper also tagged on, rather blithely, that Portugal would have eventually relinquished Goa. The following day, the same newspaper supported India's claim to Goa but did not approve of the method used.

In an article titled 'India, the Aggressor', 19 December 1961, it said,

With his invasion of Goa Prime Minister Nehru has done irreparable damage to India's good name and to the principles of international morality.[†]

On 22 December 1961, *Los Angeles Tidings* said,

Overnight, Pandit Nehru had become Bandit Nehru.

A British newspaper ran the headline,

Nehru, Sanctimonious Bully.

---

[*] 'India Moves into Goa', *New York Times*, 18 December 1961.
[†] Desai, 2011, pp. 59 and 83.

Life International condemned India's military action. Its 12 February 1962 edition said in an article,

> Symbolic Pose by Goa's Governor: The world's initial outrage at pacifist India's resort to military violence for conquest has subsided into resigned disdain. And in Goa ... Governor K.P. Candeth ... as the very model of a modern Major General, betrayed no sign that he is finding Goans less than happy about their 'liberation'.

Krishna Menon told Henry Kissinger, visiting India as a consultant to the US National Security Council, on 8 January 1962:

> ... the American objection to the Indian action was a vestige of Western imperialism ... The attack on Goa was simply a continuation of India's struggle for independence ...[*]

On 13 January 1962, Krishna Menon told the UK high commissioner in India, Paul Gore-Booth:

> ... there had been two postponements [of the D-day of invasion] and a really worthwhile offer from the Portuguese could have prevented the use of force ...[†]

Role of Goan Catholics: Wrong Perceptions, Wrong Conclusions

Indian and western perceptions of Goa differed, often being at diametric opposites. At times, neither reflected the ground reality. Goan Catholics congregating at the Bom Jesus Basilica in the wake of Operation Vijay is a case in point. Indian media said people converged there to give thanks at being united with India. Western media said they were there to pray for protection from Indians. Neither was true. The reason they congregated was to thank the

---

[*] Ramesh, Penguin Viking, 2019, p. 558.

[†] Ibid., p. 560.

Almighty for saving them, and maybe even the basilica where they were, from destruction!

No opinion, Indian or western, was more erroneous than the one on the role of Goan Catholics. This was compounded by what appeared to be a deliberate local political agenda unleashed in the wake of 1961.

The entire Goan Catholic community was painted as pro-Portuguese, un-Indian and anti-national. A wedge was sought to be driven to distance the 60 per cent majority Goan Hindu from the Goan Catholic. In the mid-1970s, a chief minister of Goa openly called Goan Catholics 'anti-nationals, fit to be deported to Portugal'.

To further taunt the community—a minority already depleted from 38 per cent of the population in 1961 to around 30 per cent by the mid-1970s (it is estimated at 20 per cent today)—the Goa government withdrew the ferry-crossing priority of then Goan Archbishop Raul Gonsalves (during the colonial era, all Goa bishops were European). Wrongly labelling a local community for a real or imagined grouse of Portuguese miscegenation in one's own ancestry, or for the misdoings of the medieval-period Inquisition (which primarily victimized, between natives, Goan Catholics), was neither factually correct nor legitimate.

Another widely held and erroneous impression is that the various local approaches to resolving the situation in Goa were divided by caste and creed—when, in reality, each approach (e.g., integration with India, autonomy, status quo) had adherents from a mix of castes and creeds; no approach was exclusive to any particular caste or any particular creed.

One must, however, bear in mind that, at the time, unlike today, the majority of Goans were illiterate; only the upper strata from both the major religious communities were literate, into the professions and took part in politics.

Let us look further into these two misconceptions, starting with Goan Catholic patriotism or the lack of it. Let us arrive at the actuality on the basis of facts and figures, not false and untenable beliefs.

9

FALLACIES

Goan Catholics: Un-Indian?

Most Western critics laboured under two misconceptions: that the bulk of Goa was Catholic and that Goan Catholics were pro-Portuguese (the latter impression, as seen, was/is shared by some Goans too!).

Westerners saw a fundamental incompatibility between the cultures of Goa and India. A British writer argued that Goans were as much Mediterranean Europeans as descendants of various European nationalities were Americans. The argument was ridiculous both in construct and factual foundation. Goans were not Caucasian, like the Europeans settled in America, they did not migrate to the Mediterranean region as did Europeans to America, and the majority of Goa's population was totally alien to the Mediterranean region culture even after 451 years of Portugal's domination. Comparing Europeans settled in America to Goans who remained in their homeland was like comparing a pear to an apple—there was just no basis for comparison. The British journal *Catholic Herald* said:

> Wherever he goes in India, a Goan remains a Goan, and tends to form a self contained Goan community. He certainly does not see himself as an Indian. Five hundred years of religious, social, and racial and cultural interpretations have sharply differentiated him from other peoples of the Indian subcontinent.

The journal—obviously alluding to Goan Catholics—forgot that any community, especially a tiny one like the Goan, domiciled outside its native land 'tends to form a self-contained community' anywhere in the world, not just Goan Catholics in India. Goans had their own gymkhanas and clubs wherever they settled in the world (especially in British East Africa).

A Casa de Goa was established by Goans in Lisbon in 1988. Going by the *Catholic Herald*'s logic, Goans in Portugal did not see themselves as Portuguese. What are we talking about? That Goans were neither Indian nor Portuguese? (Technically and legally, as seen, they were, and are, both Indian and Portuguese!) And, just to remind the reader: far more Goan Catholics went to India rather than to Portugal. The argument of religion, Christianity in this case, was clearly facetious.

Salazar too used Christianity in Goa as an argument to support continued Portuguese rule. In a speech on 25 November 1947, Salazar said:

> ... if geographically Goa is India, socially and in religion and culture Goa is Europe.[*]

Salazar and most westerners forgot that Christians were a 38 per cent minority in Goa, the bulk of which was against foreign rule anyway. They also forgot the more important fact that Christianity arrived in India less than two decades from Christ's crucifixion—long before Portugal (yet to be born as a nation) and the west became Christian—and that there already were, as of 1961, 8 million Christians in India, equal to the entire population of Portugal. (Indian Christians are 24 million today.)

India's intervention with the Vatican led to Salazar losing control over some archdioceses in India beyond Goa and Daman vide a renegotiated pact of 18 July 1950 between India and the Vatican. The Vatican disregarded Salazar's expectation of having

---

[*] Franco Nogueira, *Salazar*, Livraria Castro e Silva, Lisbon, 1985, vol. 4, p. 87.

the Portuguese Archbishop of Goa, D. José da Costa Nunes, as the first cardinal from India, and instead raised the archbishop of Bombay, Valerian Gracias—a Goan from Dramapur in Salcete—as the historic first cardinal from India in 1953. The Portuguese alleged that Valerian Cardinal Gracias curried favour with Nehru to secure the appointment. What mattered was that this diplomatic defeat was the first major sign of loss of influence of the Salazar regime (Estado Novo) on the international stage.[*]

As for distinctness, Goa was distinct right from its earliest recorded history, more than sixteen centuries before the Portuguese arrived. While European-origin Indo-Aryans settled in north India, peninsular south India (south of the Vindhyas) was inhabited by Dravidians and tribals. Goa was a tribal habitat, until it became the first—and for long, the only—place south of the Vindhyas inhabited by Indo-Aryans who migrated from north India. Goa was always different. Nowhere in mainstream India is there a deity called Shantadurga (a peaceful Durga)—amongst the principal deities of Goa—the very antithesis of Ma Durga. Nowhere in India is a demon called Narkasura symbolically burned on the eve of Diwali as in Goa. Ravana may be burned on the eve of Dussehra in the rest of India. Goa was different in a variety of ways since ancient times. Author Robert de Souza writes that these pre-Portuguese

> ... characteristics of the individuality of Goa [were] by virtue of political and territorial separation from the neighbouring lands during the several [successive] Hindu and Muslim kingdoms.[†]
>
> [He further adds] While ethnically or genetically the Goan race remained just as pure as the Indian race elsewhere [an admixture of several races], culturally and politically it yielded to several pressures from within and from without the territory.

---

[*] Estado Novo, literally 'a new state', was the direct fallout of Salazar assuming dictatorial powers, which lasted from 1932 to 1968 until his death and thereafter under his successor Marcelo Caetano, until the latter was deposed in a military coup in 1974.

[†] Robert de Souza, *Goa and the Continent of Circe*, 1973, p. 37.

But to suggest that after 451 years of Portuguese subjugation, Goans—or at least Goan Catholics—became un-Indian or alien to India is to stretch the argument to the absurd.

Doubtless, the long Portuguese rule added to Goa's already distinct culture. T.B. Cunha in 1944 called it 'denationalisation of Goans' (denationalization of *all* Goans, both Catholic and Hindu, as Dr Nishtha Desai skilfully spotlights in her analytical essay on the subject).[*] If not for this distinctness, Goa would be no different from the neighbouring coastal areas of Maharashtra and Karnataka—and would not be the tourist draw it is today.

The American crusader for civil rights and racial equality, Homer Alexander Jack, who was in Goa in August 1955 (and witnessed the killing of unarmed Indian satyagrahis), put the issue in another perspective:[†]

> There are cultural differences among the various sections of the Indian Union—Assam and Punjab to name only two. Surely Assam is no less different from 'India' than Goa.

India, indeed, is a composite of diverse cultures. It is probably the most diverse nation in the world—culturally, racially, ethnically, climatically, linguistically, economically and religiously.[‡]

More than 19,500 languages are spoken in India. The French Ambassador to the UN described India as

> ... the spiritual mother of all mankind.[§]

The Vedic way of life, called 'Hinduism' only in the modern era, is considered to be the world's oldest religion.

---

[*] https://www.persee.fr/doc/luso_1257-0273_2000_num_7_1_1390

[†] His impressions were published as 'Callous mentality of Portuguese' by the Information Service of India.

[‡] A video by Knowledge Junction.

[§] Year 2015 UN debate on the Yoga Resolution introduced by India and co-sponsored by a historic 177 out of 193 member nations.

The Goan-origin, Switzerland-based retired chemical engineer Bernardo Elvino de Sousa (a Prabhu descendant from Aldona, Goa), who uses DNA sequencing to trace ancestries, notes,

> If ever there was a melting pot, then it was certainly India. The diversity of the country's population is unique with regard to its cultural and genetic diversity[*]

and

> In short, all Indians are a mixture and there is no such thing as a pure Indian race [a mixture of ancestral north Indian and ancestral south Indian that started circa 4000 BC, occurred in multiple waves and went on for two millennia until the caste system crystallized][†]

and, more tellingly:

> Goa is thus not any different [genetically] from the rest of the Indian sub-continent.[‡]

Robert de Souza writes:

> [Goa's] genetic ethnology is not different from that of India of which geographically she is a territory ...[§]

and that

> ... no native of Hindustan can claim to be a pure [European Indo] Aryan more than a native of Pakistan can claim to be a pure Arab

---

[*] Bernardo Elvino de Sousa, *The Last Prabhu*, 2020, p. 95.

[†] Ibid., pp. 98 and 99.

[‡] Ibid., p. 127.

[§] Robert de Souza, *Goa and the Continent of Circe*, 1973, p. 37.

or Ottoman [meaning that all in the sub-continent are admixtures of different races, cultures, ethnicities and anthropologies].*

T.B. Cunha famously said:

Any attempt to prove that Goa is an integral part of India looks as ridiculous as trying to break open an unlocked door.†

The natural Goan affinity was clearly tilted heavily towards India to the exclusion of any other country.

Portugal's converting only a part of the Goan populace permanently divided the community. There was the Hindu Goa (60 per cent of the population) and the Catholic Goa (38 per cent) in 1961. The previously one but now two communities mercifully were like twin rails of a railway track: parallel and complementing one another.

Many Goans—Hindu and Catholic—and non-Goans, including foreigners, did not fail to notice, and often wrote about, this uncommon harmony between the two major communities of Goa. Goan pop star Remo Fernandes in his autobiography writes about his childhood in Panjim. For neighbours, he had a Sardesai family, Goan Hindu, whose eldest son was a very respected professor at the Liceu.‡ His two sisters, Kumud and Suman, much older to Remo, loved teasing Remo, calling him Kiristão (Christian in Konkani).

'*Chee*,' they would say in mock disdain, 'you're a Kiristão and you eat meat!'

'Chee,' Remo would reply in the same vein, 'you're a Konknò and your God is an elephant!'§ Friendly ribbing about differences

---

* Ibid., pp. 192 and 193.
† T.B. Cunha, in one of his monograms.
‡ He was Professor Naraina Naique Pratap Rau Sardessai according to his son, Adv. Nitin Sardessai, designated senior counsel, Bombay High Court, in an interview with the author.
§ Remo Fernandes, 2021, p. 41.

was quite representative of how different communities got along in Goa then.

Goan Hindus and Catholics co-existed in perfect camaraderie. There were differences in names, customs, cuisines and the like, but no malice was involved, no offence meant and none taken. Scratch the surface of the religious divide and the Goan, be it Hindu or Catholic, knows that he is a kindred brother of the other, within his own social grouping.

Differences between Goan Hindus and Catholics were acknowledged, but seldom with rancour. Konkani adages embody that:

> ... *padri-chi ghantt zali, botta-achem xentt gelem* (the Catholic priest's call to prayer does not affect the Hindu priest), or *padri-chem okod botta-k poddlem?* (was medicine for the Catholic priest administered to the Hindu priest?).

Nirad Chaudhuri, who shredded Goan Christians to bits in his book *The Continent of Circe*, acknowledged that,

> ... between them [Goan Christians] and the Hindus of Goa there did not exist that antithesis and antipathy which was present in the Eurasian [Anglo-Indian]-Hindu relationship in India.[*]

His refuter, Robert de Souza, wrote,

> There is no antagonism in their ways of life and social intercourse [between Goan Hindus and Catholics]. Whereas, there are some basic differences in the ethnographic and religious practices of all of them as compared with those of the Hindus of the rest of India.[†]

---

[*] As quoted by Robert de Souza who refuted Nirad Chaudhuri's charges in his book *Goa and the Continent of Circe*, Wilco Publishing House, Bombay, 1973, p. 9.

[†] Ibid., p. 38.

At least until Portugal became a republic in 1910, the foreign colonizer did not treat the Goan Hindu and the Goan Catholic at par. The Lei da Separação (segregation law, much like apartheid in South Africa or hotel/club boards in British India that said, 'Dogs and Indians Not Allowed') that discriminated against Hindus was repealed in 1911. This led to a general renaissance of the Goan Hindu community that then established schools, associations and other religious and social fora. Vernacular newspapers also began publication. The first Hindu political forum, Pragatik Sangh, was established in 1920.

Goan Catholics were given more favourable treatment, even if this permeated only to a small elite, and not to the general Goan Catholic community. The imposition of the Acto Colonial (Law No. 18570 of 8 July 1930) nullified all that. All Goans—Hindu and Christian, elite or otherwise—were made colonial subjects of Portugal ('objects of possession' as advocate Antonio Bruto da Costa put it), bereft of civil liberties.

The Goan Catholic, generally, remained Indian in blood and bone.

When the Portuguese began converting Goans to Christianity (the majority of residents of the Old Conquest talukas of Tiswadi, Bardez and Salcete were converted by the early 17th century), there was a legal equality between the converts and the Portuguese, points out Ângela Barreto Xavier, a Portugal-based historian with roots in Margao, Goa. This meant upsetting the imperial equation. Hence, the colonial order was reconfigured, resulting in greater differentiation. Converts fought for better positions and power.

> Eventually, their power acquisition strategies reduced the distance that separated them from the *casados* [casados were descendants of 16th-century marriages between Portuguese men and Goan women].*

---

* Ângela Barreto Xavier, 'Purity of Blood and Caste' in *Race and Blood in the Iberian World*, p. 126.

The convert—the Goan Catholic—was neither equal to the Portuguese nor totally alienated from his native Indian culture. Natives generally held the whites in awe, even if the whites were far less civilized than themselves. The story is told that during the tenure of an early corrupt Portuguese governor, Diogo Lopes de Sequeira (1518–22), his agent, Martim Correa, was on a looting spree on the Coromandel coast in 1521. Correa met an old man, too old to work, who was among those taken captive by his soldiers. The man offered £3 for his liberty. Having no friend, he asked that he be allowed to fetch the money himself. Correa, more in jest than earnest, gave the man his liberty after making him swear on his Brahmin sacred thread that he would return with the money. A few days later, to the amazement of the Portuguese, the old Brahmin returned with half the money and eight fowls in lieu of the balance—all that he could scrape together. Correa was so moved that he refused to take anything and gave the old man a certificate (the chit of the modern Anglo-Indian).*

During the same voyage of loot, Correa came upon a large country house with courtyards and gardens, and many poor people sitting around. The philanthropic Mohammedan owner, who spent part of his wealth giving alms, treated the Portuguese with hospitality. When a friendly understanding had been arrived at, Correa had the curiosity and the naivety to ask him why he gave alms and what satisfaction he derived from it.† Almsgiving was wholly alien to Correa. Goa is known to have had a public charity at Govapuri, the capital city, as far back as the 10th and 11th centuries of the Current Era. India has had charitable institutions even before that—from the Gupta Period in the fifth century AD—hospitals for poor patients, orphans, widows and cripples, and guest houses for travellers.

---

* R.S. Whiteway, *The Rise of Portuguese Power in India 1497–1550*, Asian Educational Services, third reprint, New Delhi, 2007 (first published, 1899), pp. 28–29.

† Ibid., p. 29.

Not all Goans felt culturally inferior to the Portuguese, though. Goan converts like the first native bishop, Mateus de Castro Mahale of Divar (circa 1594 to 1679), said the Portuguese were mixed-blood, hence lower than Goans. In his *Espelho de Brâmanes*, Bishop Castro Mahale described the Portuguese as a 'vile people, not humans, worse than goats'. He described the casados (offspring of White men married to natives) as

... sons and daughters of low-caste Indian women and downgraded Portuguese men [and] sons of Goan market women, Malabars, Bengalis and blacks ... very inferior ...*

Reputed to be a descendant of King Gaspar, one of the three Magi who went to Bethlehem on the birth of Jesus Christ, Bishop Castro Mahale said the Goan elite were superior to the 'Old Christian' nobility of Portugal.

Goan Catholics were moulded into the Portuguese culture—so that the converts would not intermingle with their Hindu brethren and relapse into old customs, traditions and faith. They were made to eat beef and pork (taboo to the native Hindu) and even change the way they cooked rice (made to add salt before straining the rice). The Goan Catholic was thus made 'untouchable' to the Goan Hindu.

Educated Goans, both Hindu and Christian, were accustomed to the Portuguese way of life. It is not that they disliked Portugal or her people (Salazar's iron-fisted rule under the Colonial Act of 1930 was a different story). But for not being averse to Portuguese culture, could Goan Catholics be labelled as 'un-Indian'? Author Robert de Souza observes:

Secondly, this homogenious society [the Goan Hindu, Catholic and Muslim] did not become alienated from the original (crude) society, but evolved from it into a refined modern society, by

---

* Ângela Barreto Xavier in *Race and Blood in the Iberian World*, pp. 135–36.

the force and operation both of internal [native] and external [colonial Portuguese] circumstances.[*]

Despite being forced into changing his faith, name, language and script, and his sartorial, culinary, musical and other tastes to resemble those of the European, the Goan Catholic did not entirely lose his ancient Indian roots. Even after two centuries (or say six generations) of a new faith, the Goan Catholic still went to Hindu temples to propitiate his old gods or seek divine remedy. The Autos da Fé (cases) tried by the Goa Inquisition in the last decade of the eighteenth century are particularly revealing. The collection of verdicts was painstakingly transcribed in a 630-page volume by Antonio Joaquim Moreira in the year 1863, which is available in PDF format at the National Library of Lisbon. For instance, on 20 November 1795, José Joaquim Faleiro, born in Margao and residing at Benaulim—a widower—was accused of idolatry and returning from a 'Pagode' (Hindu temple) with some sheets touched to the idol.[†] He was acquitted for old age and poor health.

The Goan Catholic adhered to India's caste system, especially in matters of marriage. Justice A.B. Bragança Pereira wrote in his book, *Etnografia da India Portuguesa*[‡] in 1940:

> In each village, the Hindu temples were substituted by churches
> ... The [lay] religious confraternities ... instituted in the churches,
> were cast in the social structure in the moulds of the devasthans
> (Hindu religious associations)... Both the devasthans as well as
> the village communities were based on the caste system which

---

[*] *Goa and the Continent of Circe*, 1973, p. 34.

[†] Moreira, cod-866_0000_capa-capa_124-C-R0150.pdf, Lisbon: Biblio-theca Nacional de Lisboa, 1863, p. 575.

[‡] As quoted in *Goa and the Continent of Circe*, 1973, p. 90. *Etnografia* was originally published in the Portuguese language in two volumes in 1940. Volume 2 thereof was translated into English by Padmashri Maria Aurora Couto and republished as *Ethnography of Goa, Daman and Diu*, New Delhi: Penguin Viking, 2008.

even today persists among the Christians in their domestic and matrimonial relations ...

Recall the statement of Sir William Hunter in the *Imperial Gazetteer of India* that Goan Christians

> ... can even now declare the caste to which they originally belonged.

Dr Leo J. de Souza (now departed) of Parra, Goa, was born in Tanganyika (now Tanzania) in 1926 and educated in India (St Joseph's High School, Arpora, Goa, St. Xavier's College and Grant Medical College, both in Bombay) and in Edinburgh, where he got his FRCS. He was later associate professor of orthopaedic surgery at the University of Minnesota and was awarded the Lifetime Achievement Award for his commitment to resident education. He wrote in his book:

> Goan Catholics, despite colonial Portuguese influence, retained the Hindu caste system of their ancestors [in matters of marriage]. This practice made for peace of mind. No rules were broken, no customs transgressed, all deities appeased, and all relatives kept content.[*]

Nurse turned artist-author Clarice Vaz of Saligao, Goa, points out in her latest book that Christianity in Goa was rooted in Indian culture:

> It has been noted by some historians that a different brand of Christianity was practiced by Goans ... Pope Gregory XV gave special dispensation in 1623 that Brahmins converted to Catholicism might continue to wear their sacred thread provided it was blessed by a [Catholic] priest and use their caste marks.[†]

---

[*] Leo J. De Souza, *No Place for Me: A Memoir of an Indian Doctor in East Africa,* Beaver's Pond Press, Minnesota (USA), 2021, p. 38.

[†] Clarice Vaz, *Romalina: Goodbye Africa, Adeus Portugal, Namaste Goa,* self-published, Goa, 2022, p. 253.

Another ancient ritual blessed by the Catholic Church in Goa was the Addav, where the temple priest prayed for a bountiful harvest. The tradition continues to this day—only the Hindu priest has been replaced by a Catholic one. Similarly, the Maadi—a pre-novena Catholic ritual held at a Nagina tree (*Sterculia foetida, Linn.*), unseen anywhere in the Catholic world—is reminiscent of pre-Portuguese times. The Nagina was planted in place of the pipal (*ficus religiosa*) that stood in front of the erstwhile Hindu temple. There are many such instances: all indicate that Goan Christianity was steeped in Indian traditions.

The Goan Catholic not only adhered to India's caste system but also diligently observed so many other traditional Indian systems, beliefs, customs, even superstitions!

As in the days of yore, he relied on the *mahar* to exorcise the evil eye. *Sottve rati* (the sixth night after a child's birth when Hindu goddess Satty writes the child's destiny on its forehead) still formed part of his aphorism, song, paean and proverb. A few days before a Goan Catholic marriage, the poor were fed in a ceremony called *bhikaranchem jevonn*, in memory of the dead of the family. On her wedding eve, the Goan Catholic bride still followed *haldi* or *ros*, a ritual bath in turmeric, rice flour and coconut milk. (Many of these customs, ironically, were banned by the colonizer in the sixteenth century to persecute natives resisting conversion, but survived surreptitiously among the converted!) A regular application of cow dung slurry to the floor still maintained the coolness and salubrity of his house. Before the advent of domestic plumbing, the Goan Catholic took his daily 'bucket bath'—unlike the public baths in Europe. And, like a good Indian, he still cleaned his butt with water—not toilet paper!

Goan Catholics: Pro-Portuguese?

I was born in India, cradle of poetry, philosophy and history, today its tomb ... I belong to that race which wrote the Mahabharata and invented Chess—two conceptions that bear in them the eternal and the infinite. India is imprisoned. I pray for India, liberty and light.

Aravind Adiga wrote in his column:

> Given that these sentences were written in 1861, it would be
> natural enough to assume that their author was a Bengali Hindu,
> writing either in Calcutta or in London. In fact, it was a young
> Goan Catholic in Lisbon who composed these stirring phrases
> ... Not only have most Indians not heard about [Francisco
> Luis] Gomes, but many would find it jarring to think of a Goan
> Catholic who wrote in Portuguese as a nationalist.[*]

Dr Prakashchandra P. Shirodkar, Goa's former director of archives,
wrote in his preface to the Goa Gazetteers book, *Who's Who of
Freedom Fighters, Vol. 1* (1986), that Gomes was:

> ... one of first Indians to demand freedom for India from
> alien hands.

Francisco Luis Gomes propounded the idea of freedom long before
the Indian National Congress was founded in India on 28 December
1885. The idea of freedom from foreign rule was carried forward
by Goan Catholics like Luis de Menezes Braganza in the early
20th century. T.B. Cunha launched the Goa National Congress in
1928 to fight for freedom from alien rule. Inaugurating the year-
long sixtieth anniversary of Goa's liberation on 19 December 2020,
India's then president, Ramnath Kovind, recalled the contribution of
these pioneer Goan Catholic stalwarts to the Goa freedom struggle.

Throughout history, Goan Catholics—often including Catholic
priests—propounded the idea of freedom from Portugal's rule.

The history of Goan revolts against the Portuguese power is
almost as old as colonial rule. Salcete came under the definitive
possession of the Portuguese in 1543. Within seventeen years, in
1560, tribal residents of Salcete's frontier village, Cola/Khola (now

---

[*] 'The Lusitanian in Hind', *Outlook*, 30 September 2021.

in Canacona taluka), where the 'Agaçaim Pass' tax was collected, revolted over the steep increase in local taxes. It resulted in the residents fleeing and their village confiscated.

This was followed by the revolt in Assolna–Ambelim–Velim in 1575, also over the exorbitant taxes. Villagers killed the Salcete tax collector Estevão Rodrigues and his sepoys before fleeing. The three villages were confiscated (and finally ended up with the Jesuits).

Trouble that had been brewing in Cuncolim and Veroda over taxes and religious persecution finally came to a head in 1583, when five Jesuits and fifteen others were killed. In reprisal, fifteen village chieftains were killed at Assolna fort and six or eight chieftains and mob leaders were eliminated through private killers in Bijapuri lands. The villages, both in Salcete, were confiscated (and were later constituted into a *condado* or the estate of a Portuguese Count).

> Revolts [against the Portuguese power] became a regular feature of Goan history, so much so that they occurred at the average rate of one in every ten years. Almost all classes of society, from peasants and soldiers to priests and noblemen, were involved in these revolts at one time or another.*

The first Indian bishop in the Latin rite appointed directly by the Vatican (*Propaganda Fide*), Bishop Mateus Castro Mahale, was the first Goan to think of ousting the Portuguese from Goa with the use of force—his banner of revolt went much beyond unreasonably high taxes and religious persecution. He had not been allowed to join the Franciscan priestly order because he was not white. With the help of some Carmelites, he went to Rome, studied, was ordained priest and a few years later—exhibiting a manifest intelligence of a high order—was consecrated as bishop.

When Portugal was on the ascendant, discovering new lands in Africa and Asia in the sixteenth century, the Vatican entered into

---

* Khera, 1974, p. 29.

a treaty (popularly known as the *padroado* or patronage), tasking the king of Portugal to Christianize the eastern territories held by Portugal, with his monetary patronage, in return for power to the Lisbon crown to control all Vatican functions in such territories— like sending missionaries, appointing clergy and bishops, building and maintaining churches, etc. When the decline of Portuguese power began from the 17th century, the Vatican created a department called the *Propaganda Fide* (propagation of the faith), which resumed control of religious matters previously exercised by Portugal in the territories lost to other powers like the Dutch, the British and the French.

Bishop Castro Mahale was appointed bishop by the *Propaganda Fide* in 1635 for territories in the domain of the Mughals, Bijapur and Golconda. He soon endeared himself to the Delhi emperors and the Deccani sultans, but the Portuguese civil and religious administration in Goa stoutly refused to recognize his authority and tried various means to undermine him. (While Bishop Castro Mahale remained bishop from 1637 to 1677, Goa, incidentally, was without a bishop during the period of 1652 to 1675.)

Bishop Castro Mahale conspired with the Dutch and Adil Shah to oust the Portuguese from Goa. He was the first to sow the idea of an independent Goa. His revolt was such that the viceroy in Goa complained to the king in Lisbon. But nothing could be done as Bishop Mahale was beyond Portuguese jurisdiction. He was in places like Mangalore, Bicholim (where he built his modest cathedral), Banda and Vengurla (although largely at Bicholim, then under Bijapur; Bicholim directly overlooked his native island of Divar). Dr P.D. Gaitonde says in his book *The Liberation of Goa*:

> The people of Goa proclaimed him [Bishop Castro Mahale] Governor on 2 January 1654 and his government lasted almost two years.[*]

---

[*] Gaitonde, *The Liberation of Goa*, 2016, p. 3.

With the help of the Adil Shahis of Bijapur, Bishop Castro Mahale surreptitiously raised an armed force to liberate Goa from the Portuguese. But before the plans could roll out and fructify, information was leaked to the Portuguese in Goa. They raised a case of sedition against him, with a warrant for his capture. He fled from Vengurla to Rome, where he eventually died in 1679. In its Preliminary Objection of April 1957 in the 'Rights of Passage' case before The Hague, the Government of India stated that Bishop Castro Mahale's armed attempt had occurred in 1654.*

The second native bishop was Custódio de Pinho (1638–97) of Bamborda, Verna. Like Bishop Castro Mahale, Pinho too was appointed by the *Propaganda Fide* as bishop (1669 to 1683) for non-Portuguese territories.

When very young, Pinho cut unripe jackfruits at home and, fearful of parental retribution, ran away from home weeping. On foot, he eventually reached Cortalim, where a priest from the capital city (Old Goa) who was due to return to Lisbon sheltered him, and finally, via Lisbon, to priestly studies in Rome. Out of shame he changed his original Curtorim surname of Costa to Pinho.†

Bishop Pinho succeeded Bishop Castro Mahale. He retained his cathedral in Bijapuri Bicholim, which was later conquered by the Marathas. In 1683, Sambhaji invited him to the Maratha court and discussed plans for an all-out attack on Goa to chase the Portuguese away.

At the point of victory, Sambhaji was informed of a huge Mughal force at his northern borders (as seen, sent at the behest of Juliana Dias da Costa, the influential Indo-Portuguese woman in the Mughal court) and turned back. Fearing that Sambhaji may hold him responsible for the unexpected turn of events, Bishop Pinho fled to Goa and, at the request of the Vatican, was not harmed by the Portuguese until he died at the Benaulim parochial house in 1697.

---

* https://www.icj-cij.org/public/files/case-related/32/9113.pdf, p. 99.
† The family was from Curtorim but lived in Bamborda, Verna.

Following these revolts, from 1746, came seventeen Rane rebellions over feudal/manorial rights.

An organized revolt, however, that aimed at militarily ousting the Portuguese and establishing a sovereign republic in Goa, was the Pinto Revolt of 1787. It was led by two Goan Catholic priests, Fr Caetano Francisco da Couto and Fr José António Gonçalves. The two Goan priests had gone to Portugal to complain about the ecclesiastical policy being heavily tilted against Goan native clergy. Finding no sympathetic ears, they had a series of meetings at the home of Fr Caetano Vitorino de Faria, the Colvale (Goa) born father of the world renowned Father of Hypnotism, Fr José Custodio de Faria, better known as *Abbé Faria* (Abade de Faria in Portuguese). It was here that the idea of the rebellion to oust the Portuguese from Goa was born. Back in Goa, the priestly duo met at the palatial Pinto mansion in Candolim to fine-tune details of the military plan, from where the planned revolt got its name. The Pinto plan was discovered by the betrayal of a Goan conspirator and foiled in the nick of time. Goan military conspirators were brutally killed, their heads piked and put on display in their respective villages. Priests were arrested, humiliated and exiled to Portugal. Before he could be arrested in Portugal, Fr José Custodio de Faria fled to France, where he would develop the theory and practice of hypnotism, participate in the French Revolution and be immortalized by Alexandre Dumas in *The Count of Monte Cristo*. His life-size bronze statue next to the old Secretariat in Panjim was sculpted by the famed Goan sculptor, Ramchandra Pandurang Kamat. (The only other serious attempts to oust the Portuguese until then had come from the Marathas in 1683 and 1726, and by their successor Peshwas in 1739.)

Fr Pedro António Ribeiro (1769–1824) was a descendant of Mangarna Shenoy, a native of Cortalim, reputed to have the most intelligent of all Saraswats settled in Goa. Mangarna Shenoy resettled in Pilerne and became the first convert to Christianity of the Franciscans in Bardez. Fr Ribeiro was an anti-monarchist. In 1822, he led an armed insurrection against the colonial power from the fort at Colvale. Defeated, he fled to Malvan, returning to Pilerne just months before he passed.

In 1835, Dr Bernardo Peres da Silva of Neura was the only Goan ever appointed as prefect (effectively governor) of Goa. Portuguese officials feared he planned to oust them from Goa. Barely seventeen days in office, he was overthrown in a military coup that saw the massacre of Goan troops at Fort Gaspar Dias in Panjim, at the Dona Paula fort and the garrison under Mariano Rocha of Aldona at the Tiracol fort.

In 1852, Msgr Estevão Jeremias Mascarenhas (1802–57), a Goan priest from Bastora who was elected as member of the Côrtes (Portugal's national parliament), gave a clarion call for Goa's freedom. He told the Lisbon Parliament on 24 May 1853:

> Independence, Gentlemen! … Its love is a right inherent to the gift of liberty … and the power to live by oneself, without necessity of tutelage, when it is not required; unworthy would be the people who having the necessary strength and intelligence to live independently would not desire it, would not employ all the means to achieve it … Nay, gentlemen, Portuguese India … none should wonder if she desired to be [independent], just as nobody wonders if a son owes his father his being … This is the natural course of the world, common to individuals and to colonies … [as] experience has shown as regards to England with America, to Portugal with Brasil. I, Mr. President, confess with all frankness … I would desire from my heart her Independence …*

In 1861–62, it was Dr Francisco Luis Gomes of Colmorod, Margao, also a Goan member of the Côrtes, who, as seen at the outset, called for freedom—a call that reverberated throughout western Europe. When his fiery speeches in the Lisbon Parliament agitated Luís Vicente de Affonseca, member from the Portuguese archipelago of Madeira, Gomes quietened Affonseca, telling Parliament,

---

* Souza, 1973, pp. 114 and 115.

... In India there are no banquets of human flesh; on the contrary, there are sects whose hands are innocent of all blood; who abstain from meat diet; who show compassion even towards animals ...*

Nineteenth-century Fr António Francisco Xavier Álvares of Dignem, Verna (born 1836), who openly demanded liberty and independence for Goa, was imprisoned by civil authorities and excommunicated by the Lisbon-controlled Catholic Church in Goa. Fr Álvares joined Malabar's Malankara Orthodox Syrian Church in 1887 and became Alvares Mar Julius, Metropolitan (bishop) of Brahmawar near Mangalore in 1889.

Returning to Goa in 1894, Bishop Álvares launched the *O Brado Indiano* (The Indian Cry), and wrote in 1895,

Vipers of my country, bite and poison the descendants of those conquerors who have put us to shame! Down with European banditry!

He was arrested, paraded half-naked on the streets of Panjim and slapped with sedition. The Portuguese judge laughed and then set him free. He was arrested a second time for wearing the robes of a Syrian bishop! He then led a rebellion of 298, mostly Goan Hindu soldiers, who were on transfer orders to Mozambique, at the Nanuz Fort in 1895. (The Syrian faithful settled in Goa observe a solemn annual procession from Ribandar to Panjim in his memory.)

Predicated by assumed superiority of the white ruler over the brown inferiority of the ruled, Goans were victims of crass discrimination by a despotic colonial rule that rode roughshod over them. Portugal signed a treaty with Britain on 26 December 1878 in Lisbon, which Goans viewed as the Portuguese selling them out to the British. Over and above their linking Mormugao port with the railway network of British India, the treaty bartered local currency

---

* Sharmila Pais e Martins, *The Encounter: With the Ballot in Colonial Goa 1821-1961*, Goa, 1556, 2021, p. 124.

and customs duties (standardized on British lines), gave them control over age-old local industries with exclusive rights of production and sale of salt, taxing country liquor (*feni*) and outlawing opium. For an annual 4 lakh rupees, the Portuguese handed to the British commercial control over Goa. (The tax on feni resulted in the first-ever workmen strike in Goa: by toddy tappers, in 1891.)

A quickly composed *mando* (Goan Catholic Konkani song in the western metre), mourned:

> *Chintileary kalliz fapsota* (The thought suffocates the heart)
> *Odruxtt kosolem* (What a misfortune)
> *Libranche axen Ingleza* (For the greed of pounds sterling
> the British)
> *Goiam entrado dilem* (Are allowed to enter Goa)

The mando is always followed by a quick-paced *dulpod*. A famous dulpod of the time cautioned the Portuguese not to take Goans for granted:

> *Undra mhojea mama,* (Big mouse, my uncle—
> alluding to the colonizer)
> *ani hanv sangtam tuka* (I caution you)
> *Tea mazorichea pilea lagim,* (With that small kitten—
> alluding to the colonized)
> *khell mandu naka.* (play not hide-and-seek)
> *Undir mama ailo,* (Mouse uncle came)
> *ani bazu pondak liplo* (and hid under the bed)
> *Ani mazorichea pilan taka,* (And the kitten—did not play but)
> *ek-a ghansan khailo* (ate the mouse in one bite)

After studying Goa, the respected Portuguese geographer, Prof. Orlando Ribeiro (1911–97) of Lisbon University wrote:

However, Goan Christians, in *mandós* or in *tiatr* (folk plays), surrender to the protection of St. Francis Xavier but do not have a word of sympathy or thanks to those who came here to defend the integrity of their territory, the quiet of their homes and the free exercise of their beliefs. Gratitude is not their forte. Give [them] a lot, but receive very little ...*

Without adequate educational facilities and jobs in a Goa left impoverished by the Portuguese, Goans—especially Goan Catholics from the Old Conquests—migrated in droves to the rest of India and the world beyond.

As a result of this mass emigration, Goan Catholics turned from a local majority population of 64 per cent in 1850 to a minority of 38 per cent in 1961.

The Goan in the diaspora is estimated to be far more populous than the Goan in Goa. With better education and job prospects, Goan emigrants fared much better than most Goans at home— as doctors, engineers, educationists, sportspersons ... even in that rather unusual avenue of human endeavour: 'Miss World' beauty pageants. It was Goan Catholic Reita Faria (now Powell), born of Goa-origin parents based in Bombay, who was crowned Miss World in London in 1966 and paved the way for Asian and Indian girls to claim the crown.

And to the most pertinent question: roughly nine out of ten Goan-origin commissioned officers in India's defence services were Catholics.[†] Did these hundreds of officers in the country's armed forces, who served India with a good degree of dedication and distinction in the military uniform in practically every department, every role and every war fought by India—1947/48 J&K Ops,

---

* *Relatório ao Governo* (Report to the Government), 1956, p. 132; can be viewed online at https://gloriainacselsis.wordpress.com/2008/04/13/goa-em-1956-relatorio-de-orlando-ribeiro/

[†] Valmiki Faleiro, *Patriotism in Action: Goans in India's Defence Services*, by this author, 2010, Goa, 1556.

1948 Operation Polo, nineteen out of twenty of them in the 1961
Operation Vijay that actually relieved Goa of its colonial yoke,
1962 Indo–China, 1965 Indo–Pak, 1971 Operation Cactus Lily
(Bangladesh), 1987/88 Operation Pawan (IPKF, Sri Lanka), 1999
Operation Vijay–2 (Kargil), UN peacekeeping missions and the
continuing anti-terrorism and counter-insurgency ops in J&K and
the Northeast—in inhospitable terrains from the icy heights of the
Himalayas (including Siachen, 'the world's highest battlefield') to
the searing deserts of Rajasthan—indicate that the Goan Catholic is
'un-Indian, unpatriotic and anti-national, fit to be deported to
Portugal'?

Let us pan to the present.

Advocate-Notary Fernando Jorge Colaço hailed from the
local elite. He studied and graduated from the University of
Lisbon in 1956. He worked some years as notary/civil registrar
and judge of criminal investigation in Portugal, with a promising
career there. He had spent the greater part of his life in Portugal.
Yet, he chose to return to Goa for good in December 1959.[*]
He was appointed legal adviser to the Law Department (1965),
OSD–Goa Law Commission (1968–71) and secretary to the Goa
Government Committee on Personal Laws.

Like him, several Goan Catholics studied and grew up in
Portugal during their formative years but returned to Goa and served
their motherland. Suffice to cite just one: Eduardo Faleiro,[†] five-
time elected member of Parliament (Lok Sabha), Union minister of
state in New Delhi's Ministry of External Affairs (later Ministry of
Finance) and then a member of the Rajya Sabha. Prior to all that,
he was an elected member of the Goa Legislative Assembly. He was
a student in Lisbon in 1961 and speaks Portuguese as fluently as any
ethnic Portuguese. He helped bring back Goan gold pawned with
Banco Nacional Ultramarino from Portugal in the 1990s.

---

[*] Colaço, 2017, pp. 70–71.

[†] No relation to the author, but the latter's college professor in mercantile
    law who continues to be a respected senior friend.

Antonio Piedade da Cruz from Velim was among the greatest Indian portrait painters and sculptors. He was the first Asian to be admitted into the Academy of Arts in Berlin. Da Cruz was commissioned to do portraits and sculptures of princes, rajas and maharajas (including of Louis Mountbatten in India), and of royalty and assorted VIPs of the West. He was counted among the leading European-style painters of his time. He was the first Indian artist to exhibit his paintings in several European capitals. When, at an exhibition of his work in Europe, he was hailed as a 'Portuguese from Goa', Cruz promptly refuted this and described himself as a 'pure Indian'.

Take the case of pharmacist Antonio Sequeira. To the manor born, he was from Raia, also a lawyer and from May 1946, editor of *A Voz da India*, a leading daily newspaper that was started to espouse autonomy for Goa. In the mid-1940s, despite censorship (first imposed in 1926 and again on 3 January 1934 after the rise of Salazar), he subtly exposed the ineptitude and injustice of the authoritarian Salazarian regime in Goa. Together with Purushottam Kakodkar and Prof. Dionisio Ribeiro, he met Ram Manohar Lohia at Assolna in 1946.* He helped freedom fighters escape. His rented house in Pajifond, Margao, was searched by the police. In February 1950, when Nehru told Parliament about Portuguese repression in Goa, the colonial regime directed local editors to condemn Nehru's statement; Sequeira refused. The daily was banned and a warrant of arrest was issued against him.

Disguised as a priest, Sequeira was driven across the border by Dr Nazazieno Fernandes and Prof. Albano Costa. He lost his investment in the newspaper, his pharma and wines factory, and his legal practice. He lived for some time in Belgaum and eventually moved to Mombasa. He returned to Goa in February 1962, soon after the Portuguese were militarily evicted. A farewell in Mombasa was graced by an Indian diplomat in that coastal East African city.

---

* Evagrio Jorge, *Goa's Awakening: Reminiscences of the 1946 Civil Disobedience Movement*, p. 10.

Sequeira did not use the diplomat's letter of recommendation to 'important Government officials in India', ignored G.K. Handoo's advice to go to New Delhi, spurned a top job offered by Goa's first chief minister, D.B. Bandodkar, and refused to register himself as a freedom fighter, maintaining that he had only done his duty to Goa.[*]

All the above persons are/were the so-called 'anti-national' Goan Catholics!

When the Father of Goan Nationalism passed away in 1958, a Dr T.B. Cunha Memorial Committee was formed under the chairmanship of the *Father of Scientific Indian History*, Prof. Damodar Dharmanand Kossambi (1907–66), the illustrious polymath son of Goa—mathematician, statistician, historian on ancient India and Marxism and a numismatic. Graduating in math, history and languages from Harvard University, Kossambi taught at Benares Hindu University then at Aligarh Muslim University and for fourteen years at Pune's Fergusson College, before joining the Tata Institute of Fundamental Research. (The composition of the T.B. Cunha Memorial Committee, which in itself tells a story, is provided in the Annexures.)

Orlando Ribeiro, the respected professor and head of department of geography at Lisbon University, was personally commissioned by Salazar to visit Goa, study its people (their predilections vis-à-vis the Portuguese) and submit a report to the Lisbon government.[†] On a *Missão de Geografia da Índia* (Geographic Mission of Portuguese India), Prof. Ribeiro visited Goa with his assistant Raquel Soeiro de Brito in 1955. How imbued with Portuguese culture and 'pro-Portuguese' Goan Catholics were, was amply stated by Prof. Orlando Ribeiro in his 1956 *Relatório ao Governo* (report to the government). Prof. Ribeiro described Goa as the 'least Portuguese' of all of Portugal's colonies (in Africa and Asia).

---

[*] Fonseca, *The Journey of an Unsung Hero*, 2021.

[†] Correia, *Once Upon a Time in Goa,* 2022, p. 260.

I have visited all the Portuguese territories in Africa, starting from Mozambique, and have studied Guinea and the islands of Cape Verde; I have spent four months in Brazil and observed its deep recesses. I have thus acquired a good preparation to initiate my research. Goa appeared to me as the least Portuguese of all the Portuguese territories I had seen so far, even less than Guinea, which was pacified in 1912! ...The predominant relationship is of distance and suspicion, when it is not an outright or camouflaged antipathy. I have witnessed a near total ignorance of our language, the persistence of a society, not only strange and indifferent, but even hostile to our presence ...*

The Freedom Movement: Goan Catholic Quality and Leadership

Luis de Menezes Bragança called for Goa's autonomy in 1910. In 1918, he demanded freedom at a rally in Margao. In 1928, his Paris-returned engineer cousin, T.B. Cunha, the Father of Goan Nationalism, launched the Goa National Congress to foster nationalist fervour in Goa.

The well-known, Goan-origin, Portugal-based historical researcher, Dr Sandra Ataíde Lobo, in an authoritative essay, 'The Return to Indianness', writes that in the early 1920s, T.B. Cunha aired his anti-colonial views in the French press, especially in journals like *Clarté* and *L'Europe Nouvelle*.

T.B. Cunha's older brother, Francisco de Bragança Cunha, who studied in London and later at the Sorbonne in Paris, translated Rabindranath Tagore's nationalist views and was invited to teach at Shantiniketan. The eldest, Vicente de Bragança Cunha, was also an active nationalist.

---

* http://analisesocial.ics.ul.pt/documentos/1223992527N9sRA6mc-3Mk47CE2.pdf; or https://docplayer.com.br/18979224-Orlando-ribeiro-goa-em-1956-relatorio-ao-governo-lisboa-cncdp-1999.html, https://histheory.tripod.com/OR.html; or http://revisitargoa.blogspot.com/2016/01/relatorio-ao-governo-goa-1956-orlando.html

Political activism and a yearning for freedom in Goa amplified, ironically, in Europe. In Portugal, Goan students like Adeodato Barreto, Aires Gracias, António de Noronha, António Furtado, Benedito Fulgêncio de Brito, Cipriano da Cunha Gomes, Druston Rodrigues, Fernando da Costa, Joaquim Otto Xavier de Siqueira Coutinho, Lúcio de Miranda, Telo Mascarenhas (once a student and supporter of Salazar at the Coimbra University, decorated with a Padma Shri, who wrote an autobiography titled *When the Mango-Trees Blossomed*) and Zacarias Antão were vocal about freedom for Goa. The Portuguese press dubbed them communist. Dr Ataíde Lobo says that medical student Santana Rodrigues elucidated to Portuguese dailies *Imprensa da Manhã* and *Diário de Notícias* the ancient glories of the Indian civilization and the federalism that would be adopted once the British left. In 1926, his views were published in a book—*The Indian National Movement*.

Above all, these Goan Catholic nationalists decried that constitutional equality in the republic translated to practical inequality in Goa. They called for equal treatment of all Goans, especially Hindus and those in the *Novas Conquistas* (New Conquest talukas), in the citizenship equation.

It was Dr Julião de Menezes of Assolna who brought Ram Manohar Lohia to Goa and reignited Goa's freedom struggle in 1946.

Goa being a police state, various organizations for Goa's freedom sprung up in Bombay and Belgaum. Leadership and direction of the Bombay groups came largely from Goan Catholics.

It was the Goan Catholic political leadership in Bombay that prevailed upon Nehru to impose the economic blockade in 1953 with a view to creating a local rebellion.

Francisco Mascarenhas and Vaman Desai, with volunteers of their United Front of Goans, captured Dadra on 22 July 1954.

George Vaz of the Goan People's Party was an active participant in freeing Nagar Haveli by 2 August 1954.

The satyagraha staged at Tiracol, Banda and Polem on 15 August 1954 was organized by the Goan Catholic Peter Alvares, a prominent member of India's Praja Socialist Party. All the three groups of satyagrahis were led by Goan Catholics: Alfred Afonso, Mark Fernandes and Anthony D'Souza, respectively.

When, for the first time, Nehru met a cross-section of leadership of the Goa freedom movement in New Delhi in June 1957, seven of the eleven leaders were Goan Catholics.

Four out of the five Goan leaders deputed for the Casablanca Conference in April 1961 were Goan Catholics.

Two of the three Goans invited to the seminar on colonialism at the Constitution Club in New Delhi in October 1961 were Goan Catholics.

Meanwhile, a group of prominent allopathic doctors from Salcete, led by Dr Gambeta da Costa of Margao, decided to turn Gandhian just as the struggle for freedom for Goa heated up in the 1940s. Mostly Catholic—like Dr Constancio Roque Monteiro, a former taluka administrator and a very popular medical practitioner of Nagoa, Verna, Dr Barónio Monteiro of Loutulim and Dr Peregrino da Costa of Aquem Baixo—they turned the clock back 400 years when their converted ancestors were forcibly made to change their native form of dress to Western attire.

They changed to khadi kurta-pyjama, often topped by a Gandhi cap. Dr Barónio Monteiro, an allopathic doctor who opted for Ayurvedic cures and fought against some aspects of Portuguese culture including the wearing of western suits in Goa's hot and humid climate, championed the use of cotton gowns by medical doctors.

While hand-spun khadi and the kurta-pyjama were passable, the Gandhi *topi* was anathema for a Goan Catholic in Portuguese Goa. For refusing to remove his Gandhi topi in a Mapusa court, freedom fighter Frank Raphael Paul Andrades had his house in Parra seized and sold in auction by the colonial regime. Freedom fighter Vicente Agostinho Francisco da Cunha's Gandhi topi was snatched in public by Portuguese policemen, who wiped their shoes with it and returned it. Vicente Cunha took it back with a loud *Jai Hind!* Passed round for donations, a sum of 200 rupees was placed in the topi. (Cunha never left off wearing a linen suit, tie and shoes all his life; during the Portuguese era, this trademark attire was topped by a Gandhi topi.)

Grave was the disdain of the Portuguese towards this symbol of India's resurgence. Most of the topi-crowned Salcete doctors, Goan Catholic, were not registered freedom fighters.

The seed sowed by a chief minister of Goa in the mid-'70s continues to bear fruit. There is still criticism of the community, in blatant contradiction of fact. In 1987, a dozen freedom fighters 'vehemently condemned and protested against the calumny' that Goan Catholics did not welcome Goa's liberation (oHERALDo, 2 February 1987). They traced the history of Goan Catholic resistance to Portuguese colonial rule right from the seventeenth to the twentieth century—within Goa, in the rest of India and in the world at large. They recalled that the Goa freedom movement in Bombay, steered by the National Congress Goa, United Front of Goans, Goan People's Party, Azad Gomantak Dal, Goa Liberation Council and the Goan National Union, was 'over 90 per cent Goan Christian both in composition and direction'.[17]

The Goan Catholic community provided quality—leadership and direction—as well as numbers to the twentieth-century freedom struggle. While official records list 116 registered Goan Catholic freedom fighters, a far-from-complete list of Goan Catholic freedom fighters compiled by this author, lists 200-plus (registered or not, but genuine Goan Catholic nationalists). The list heads the Annexures.

Goan Catholics: Freedom Lovers No Less

Quite a few Goan Catholic freedom fighters met the criteria for registration but chose not to. Freedom fighter Adv. Cristovam Furtado of Chinchinim refused to accept a Central government *tamrapatra* on grounds that he had merely discharged a moral duty. A few Goan Hindu freedom fighters too did not register, including litterateurs/ poets B.B. ('Bakibab') Borkar and Dr Manohar Rai Sar Dessai. Dr Julião de Menezes, who brought Ram Manohar Lohia to Goa, returned the money sent to him by Nehru, saying that he did not fight for freedom of Goa from the Portuguese for monetary benefits.

The Goan Catholic participation in the freedom struggle was at least, if not more than, its proportionate share of the population (around 38 per cent in 1960).

G.K. Handoo, who played a major role in the run up to 1961, acknowledged the 'far greater contribution of Goan Catholics to the Goa freedom struggle than any other community', in his signed article 'Nehru and Goa'.* He would surely know.

India's first cardinal, Valerian Cardinal Gracias, Archbishop of Bombay—as seen, a Goan Catholic—addressing a Goan congregation on 24 December 1961 in the metropolis, welcomed the freedom to Goa, stating that this opened vast potential for Goa's economic development.†

The Western media's understanding of Goa's minority Catholic population, at times unfortunately shared by some locals, was clearly wide off the mark. Bombay's *Times of India* had reported seven years before (16 August 1954):

> The belief held in certain quarters that Goans themselves are not in the thick of the fight for the liberation of Goa was belied on Sunday when thousands of Goans, predominantly Christians and many members of the clergy attended mass rallies in Bombay to celebrate [India's] Independence Day and to hail the Satyagraha movement scheduled to begin in Goa that day.

It is also true that a tiny Goan minority, estimated at a single-digit percentage of between 5–9 per cent favoured the Portuguese. No one likes to be under foreign domination. It is evident that the votaries of this school of thought stood to benefit—economically, socially or in other ways—from Portuguese rule in Goa.

---

* 'Goan Catholics Are Not Anti-Nationals!', *oHERALDo*, 2 February 1987.
† *Free Press Journal*, 25 December 1961.

This group was led by Goan Hindu big-business (mine owners), importers and traders. At no point was this starker than during the India-imposed economic blockade of Goa.

Recall that Goan Hindu traders imported Indian goods via Aden, Singapore and South Africa to stymie the effects of India's economic blockade. Compliant mine owners actively collaborated with the colonial rulers by producing more to buoy the economy. Militant Goan freedom fighters targeted mines with attacks and blasts.

The elite mining barons, importers and businessmen had reason to be wary of India. In place of the laissez-faire ambience of doing business in Portuguese Goa, India's then socialist policies, state monopoly mining and channelized exports of mineral ore through the Metals and Minerals Trading Corporation Ltd (that would weed out the rampant malpractice of tax evasion through under-invoicing), the 'licence raj', 'permit raj', 'quota raj', 'inspector raj' and rather heavy taxes were less conducive to conduct business.

Dr P.D. Gaitonde told Nehru that the majority of Goans were in favour of Goa's merger with India.

> However, there were exceptions. These represented a tiny proportion of the Goan population, say about 200 families. They had for centuries enjoyed positions of privilege, and their voice, and only theirs, was heard all over the world. Lisbon had used them with skill and to great effect ... with the result that Delhi therefore had distorted views about Goa.[*]

The fact is that the pro-Portugal school of thought was the tiniest among all on Goa's future. Dr Gaitonde's statement also underscored that most Goans, Hindu and the 'pro-Portuguese' Catholic, favoured Goa's integration with India.

Two prominent Hindus in Goa favoured continued Portuguese rule. One was the Soundekar (aka Savaikar), Raja Savai Veer Sadashiv Rajendra Basavalinga Wodeyar, whose ancestors were granted refuge

---

[*] Gaitonde, 2016, p. 76.

by the Portuguese in exchange of the approximate talukas of Ponda, Quepem, Sanguem and Canacona when the raja was threatened by Haidar Ali. He continued to receive patronage and recognition as a king—his was the only car in Goa, other than that of the Portuguese governor-general, that carried a coat of arms instead of a registration number on the number plates. With liberation, the Soundekar lost a lot of land in the former domain (the four talukas). Portugal still sends a Christmas card to the Soundekar royals annually.

The other was Vasantrao Dempo, arguably the richest Goan mine owner of the time, who was a personal friend of the last governor-general and commander-in-chief of the armed forces in Goa, Maj. Gen. Vassalo e Silva—so thick a friend that the governor, in the face of India's invasion on 18 December 1961, attended the Saturday, 16 December wedding reception of Dempo's daughter. Dempo led the coterie of Goans who joined the governor-general at the Cabo palace every Thursday evening for high tea. (Oddly, down the centuries, Goan Hindus were trusted friends of Portuguese governors. One has not come across a Goan Catholic who was so friendly. Outside food was not allowed into the governor's residence, save from the nearby palatial house of Mhamai Kamat. Another Goan Hindu was a regular evening-tea guest of the governor. Instances are many.)

It is said that the majority of Goan Catholic elites favoured continuance of the Portuguese. That may be only partly true. Although many regarded their culture as distinct from the rest of India, and disliked India's marching into Goa, neither would they have liked the Acto Colonial repression to continue. This was true of Goan Hindu elites too.

Approaches to Goa's Future Not Based on Caste or Creed

Another popular misconception (prevailing in Goa even today) was that opinions on Goa's future were divided on the lines of religion and caste.

This is far from reality.

As seen, there were broadly four distinct schools of thought regarding Goa's future. Each group had adherents from both the Hindu and Catholic sections and from different castes and backgrounds. A delectable mix, if you will. It must be remembered, though, that barely 30 per cent Goans were educated at the time and generally only professionals and the highly educated participated in politics. Let us briefly take a closer look at each of these four groups.

1. The majority group was of those who stood for integration of Goa with India. Comprising both Hindus and Catholics—more or less in proportion to their population—this group's adherents hailed from different castes and social backgrounds. All the Goan organizations fighting for freedom either peacefully or by violent means, based in Bombay and Belgaum, belonged to this grouping.[18]
2. There were two groups that thought differently and were not in favour of integration with India. Neither were they in favour of Portuguese rule continuing in Goa. Both these groups demanded autonomy for Goa but with differing statuses. The first group sought autonomy under Portugal's sovereignty. One of its members, Purushottam Kakodkar, even went to Lisbon—where he had earlier been jailed for a decade—to pursue this objective in early 1961.[19]
3. The next group demanded total autonomy with Goa as a quasi-nation aligned to a Portuguese Commonwealth. It was neither pro-India nor pro-Portugal. This group was called The Group of Margao. Led by Adv. Antonio Bruto da Costa of Margao, its proponents were both Goan Catholic and Goan Hindu.[20]
4. The smallest group comprised Goans who wanted Portugal to continue to rule over Goa, in other words, for continuance of the status quo. Those who subscribed to this idea, as already seen, were estimated to be in a single-digit

percentage figure of Goa's population. They comprised
members of the business class and some elite, both Hindu
and Catholic.

Each of the four divergent schools of thought had a mix of Hindus and
Catholics, and no opinion was exclusive to any one religion. There
was a healthy disconnect between religion and political persuasion.[21]

Caste, it seems, was ironically at play to some extent among
the technically 'casteless' Goan Catholics: there were more *Chardó*
activists demanding integration with India than there were Brahmin,
who were more inclined towards autonomy or a quasi-nation.* But
it is beyond doubt that the vast majority of both Goan Hindus and
Catholics, across castes, converged on one common aspiration: that
Portugal's colonial hold of Goa must end.

Majority Goans Certainly Not Pro-Portuguese!

Several western commentators, both around 1961 and thereafter,
stated—incorrectly again—that Goans themselves were indifferent
to the question of freedom from foreign colonial rule. To suggest
that Goans—Hindu or Catholic—acquiesced in colonial bondage
was far from fact.

The vast majority from both of Goa's major religious
communities wanted an end to colonial rule. At least fifteen Goan
organizations, six of them militant, fought for Goa's freedom.

In 1961, barely 1.46 per cent Goans, Hindu and Catholic,
knew or conversed in the Portuguese language. While 686 studied
in Portuguese schools, 11,914 studied in English schools. Recall
the statement in the report of the respected Lisbon university

---

* Chardó was a new caste created by the Portuguese, who did not understand India's ancient varna system. Converted (to Christianity)
  Kshatriyas and Vaishyas were bundled together into a single caste called
  Chardó. So, while Goan Hindus have four castes, Goan Catholics have
  three (Brahmin, Chardó and Shudra).

geographer, Prof. Orlando Ribeiro, in 1956: that Goa was the 'least Portuguese' of all of Portugal's colonies in Africa and Asia. Prof. Ribeiro pointedly mentioned the general lack of knowledge of the Portuguese language. And of a people hostile to colonial rule in Goa.

It is also true, however, that some Goans abroad, practically all Catholic, vehemently protested India's action in Goa.

In the months following the Goa action, the Portuguese government drew up *Plano Gralha* (Operation Crow/propaganda) and another called *Plano Nemasté* (Operation Namaste), urging Goans, in Goa and in the diaspora, to resist and weaken Indian presence in Goa.

Two organizations, Movimento de Resistência de Goa (Goa Resistance Movement) and the Movimento Revolucionário da *Índia* Portuguesa (Revolutionary Movement of Portuguese India) were formed by some Goans—again, mostly Catholic—in Portugal, Pakistan, Persian Gulf, East Africa, France, UK, Brazil and USA to oppose Goa's takeover by India.

On 20 June 1964, some bombs went off in Goa and the organizations were implicated in the 'Goa Bomb Case', the second such case since 1947, after the 'Kashmir Conspiracy Case', where Sheikh Abdullah, Mirza Afzal Beg and twenty-two others were accused of conspiracy for an independent Kashmir. Nothing came out of either case. And for Portugal, nothing out *Plano Gralha* or *Plano Nemasté* either.

An organization named Goan Freedom Movement, established by expatriate Goans, professed to be equidistant from India and Portugal. It made repeated requests to the UNO to place Goa under UN Trusteeship and ascertain the wishes of the Goans through a plebiscite. It held conferences around 1963 in Paris, Nairobi, Kampala, Angola, Mozambique, Macao, Ceylon, Pakistan, India, the Arabian Gulf area, Ethiopia, Iraq, the UK, Germany and Brazil. (It may be recalled that Adv. Antonio Bruto da Costa and The Group of Margao had been making a similar demand for years, but Salazar turned a deaf ear. As seen, Salazar also did not favour a plebiscite in Goa. No one—within Goa or outside—protested at that time against the Portuguese dictator blocking a plebiscite in Goa.)

The Goan author-writer in Portugal, Orlando Costa, penned a play, *Sem Flores nem Coroas* (Without Flowers or Wreaths) ending with Goa, 19 December 1961. Highly critical of Salazar's rule, it was banned in Portugal during the Salazarian regime. The play was published only in book form in 2003.

Which brings us to a singular irony. How many, say just half a century ago, would even imagine that a colonial subject (the 'object of possession' of Portugal) would govern the erstwhile colonial master's own lair? The playwright's son is the present second consecutive term elected prime minister of Portugal. Before António da Costa, his distant relative, Alfredo Jorge Nobre da Costa, was prime minister of Portugal in August 1978. He was invited to form the government by Portugal's president, Gen. Ramalho Eanes, after the fall of the Mario Soares ministry on 27 July 1978. Both prime ministers of Portugal of Goan origin, António da Costa and Nobre da Costa, belong to the same Costa clan of Margao, whose 20th-century scion Adv. António Bruto da Costa demanded an end to colonialism and repression under the Colonial Act, and who wanted a quasi-nation status for Goa. Two more Goan-origin persons, both economists, were/are in Portugal's national government: Nelson de Souza, minister for planning, and João Leão, minister of state for finance.

Relations between India and Portugal would thaw only after authoritarian rule was overthrown in a military coup d'état in 1974 in Portugal. In a bilateral treaty signed in New Delhi on 31 December 1974, Portugal recognized India's sovereignty over Goa, Daman and Diu.

In June 1980, Goan industrialist VasantraoDempo invited Maj. Gen. Vassalo e Silva to Goa, which the former governor-general described as

... a land and a people I deeply admire and respect.[*]

---

[*] *New York Times,* 13 August 1985, p. 23.

The last Portuguese governor-general of Goa, who passed away in 1985 aged eighty-six, was held in such esteem that the welcome was graced by the likes of Vassudev Tamba, freedom fighter Froilano Machado, Eng.Eufemiano Dias, Dr Gurudas Desai, Mohan Nadkarni, Upendra Counto, Bernadinho Silva, Vishwanath Rao Valauliker, Eng. Borkar, Adv. Fernando Colaço, Shashikant Mandrekar, Ramesh Kamat, Arch. Ralino Souza, Govind Bharne, Prof. Dr Mascarenhas, Eng. Sebastião Pinto, Francis Menezes, Eng. Balkrishna Naik and Eng. Ramesh Mandrekar.

Small mercies that these gentlemen were not collectively labelled 'un-Indian, pro-Portuguese, and anti-national'!

10

SITUATION AT GROUND ZERO

Aftermath of Operation Vijay at Ground Zero

On 18 December 1961, the Indian armed forces air dropped printed leaflets from Liberator bomber aircraft all over Goa. The opening paragraph read:

> The defence forces that are now with you are for your protection ... They will take every step to ensure your safety and uphold your dignity and honour, whatever the cost.

The ground reality was a bit different from that solemn promise.

Ugly incidents of looting, rape and murder followed in the wake of the military takeover. Goa was a peaceful place where occurrences of rape and murder were like the proverbial blue moon. Some Goan-origin retired Indian army officers told this author that excesses could be put down to soldiery drawn largely from peasant backgrounds of Punjab, who had never before seen what they did in Goa: shops full of foreign goods, women dressed in skirts, households brimming with riches. Air Marshal S. Raghavendran, then a young squadron leader with 23 Squadron, wrote:

> Goa was a shoppers' delight as the shops were filled with imported goods at very cheap prices. Liquor and beer was cheap and there were roadside wine shops etc everywhere ... I bought my very first 'Transistor' and cine camera.[*]

---

[*] https://www.bharat-rakshak.com/IAF/history/1961goa/raghaven-dran/.

This was honesty. Unfortunately, there was not much in evidence. Shops were looted, and practically emptied.

However, it was not just the *jawan*. Officers, too, ransacked shops of imported merchandise and even stole the antiques and carved furniture from the governor's palace.

Moved by a shopkeeper's wails, one kindly Indian officer restored all the refrigerators and other bulky merchandise loaded in a three-tonne truck by another officer, recalled a long-retired Goan military officer.*

In February 1962, the editor of the *Illustrated Weekly of India*, A.S. Raman, wrote about his visit to a Panjim store.

> *Salesman*: We've got some very nice German ball-points for you, sir.
> *Raman*: Only ball-points! Your signboard lists bigger and more luxurious items. Where are all the transistors and tape-recorders, refrigerators and radiograms?
> *Salesman*: All gone, sir, thanks to the liberation.†

Wrote Emil Lengyel:

> When an American correspondent visited the territory half a year later, he reported: 'The Goan shopkeeper said with a grimace and a grumble that his shelves had been empty since the Indian army came in. Then he said thoughtfully that the political jails had been, too.'‡

Panjim resident and eye-witness Francisco Monteiro said Indian forces entered Panjim on the morning of 19 December 1961 and almost immediately began looting shops and canteens. Among the

---

* Interview with the author.

† A.S. Raman, *Illustrated Weekly of India*, edition LXXXIII.7 of 18 February 1962 (Special Issue on Goa), p. 39.

‡ Emil Lengyel, *Krishna Menon,* pp. 207–08.

many victims was the tall and slim Eloy Sequeira. Sequeira had a shop, Relógaria, and was the main dealer for Tissot watches. He employed a survivor from the German spy ships blasted by the British at Mormugao harbour during World War II. The shop was cleaned of its Swiss merchandise.

Such was the mistrust that a wealthy mine owner shifted to Margao and lived at the house of his firm's official for three days together with his pots of gold, literally.

Educationist, litterateur and nationalist, the Goan-origin Prof. Armando Menezes, (he was appointed India's Consul to Goa in 1947 after M.R.A. Baig, but Portugal refused to accept his credentials!*), observed in verse in his 1962 poem titled *Freedom*:[†]

> *Freedom is greed, is violence*
> *Lust, and the lordship of the fool*
> *... Freedom's image cannot keep*
> *Even a poet's loyalty*

A decade later, Lt Col (later a major general) Antonio Caetano D'Silva of Benaulim commanded the 59 Mountain Artillery Regiment during the 1971 war in East Pakistan. The unit adjutant, Lt Col Krishna Chander, recalled:

> The CO told his officers and men, 'If anyone picked up anything, I give you 24 hours to go and keep it back where you picked it from. We in Goa suffered in 1961.'[‡]

Even the judiciary was not spared. Without the slightest courtesy, the local judiciary—chief justice of the high court, justices, advocate

---

[*] Gaitonde, *The Liberation of Goa*, 2016, p. 49.

[†] Edward Joachim D'Lima, *Creative and Critical Writings of Armando Menezes*, Goa University, Goa, 2003, p. 94; or *Armando Menezes and his Writings (1902–1983)*, Institute Menezes Braganza, Panjim, 2007, p. 58.

[‡] Interview with Maj. Gen. D'Silva's son, Arun D'Silva, in Bengaluru.

general, registrar of the high court, subordinate judges, land registrars
and taluka ex-officio notaries who also belonged to the judicial
cadre in those days, twenty-five in number, all Goan, all Catholic,
save Mahadev Lawande and Dilip Kaissare—were targeted with
an ultimatum of a single day to either sign an oath of allegiance
or be summarily dismissed from their posts. The Fourth Geneva
Convention of 1949, 'Protection of Civilian Persons in Time of
War', was clearly ignored!

(In 1961, it was not just the judiciary that was headed by Goans.
Civil administration was led by a Goan chief secretary, the directors
of Public Administration, Customs, Treasury, Posts and Telegraphs,
Government Printing Press, Goa Medical College, etc., were all
Goans. All had to sign the oath of allegiance to India or quit.)

Another Goan judge, doing his job in the Military Tribunal,
which meant dispensing harsh prison sentences including exile on
nationalists, was not handled as per the law: he was allowed to be
dragged out of his official residence in his underclothes, thrashed
soundly and paraded on the streets of Panjim by a mob of locals,
within the sight of armed Indian soldiers.

Lt Col Paul Fernandes of Sarzora, who led a motorized column
into Goa, told this author about an Indian captain's inebriated
misconduct at the 1961–62 New Year's dance at Clube Harmonia
in Margao. The incident was a culture shock of sorts to the local
people. It was not the done thing in Goa. If one had had one too
many, the norm was to retire to one's home and avoid misbehaving
in public. The incident of the young, uniformed military officer's
indecorum in public within a few days of marching into Goa did
not augur well for the otherwise celebratory liberation of Goa. Lt
Col Fernandes, who was a guest of honour on the occasion, had
to send his rambunctious subordinate home with a flea in his ear.
The war diary of the 50 Para Brigade, which captured Panjim,
read in parts:

The hardest part of Operation VIJAY for the Parachute Brigade
was the occupation and administration of PANJIM on 19, 20 and

21 Dec 61 ... On the 19th, streets of PANJIM were full with people intoxicated with joy, freedom and doubtful pleasantness of being intoxicated with liquor ... the main concern was to prevent looting, restore law and order ...[*]

There were shocks of another kind. Remo Fernandes felt deprived of the music, films and comic books he was used to during the Portuguese days. As a child of eight he would sob with frustration at the taste of Indian butter and missed his usual Blue Peter butter.[†]

Remo remembers a neighbour booking an Indian Fiat and receiving it after years of waiting. The man had opted for sky-blue colour but received a black car instead. When driving home from the dealer, the steering wheel came loose in the man's hands! For the Goans, accustomed as they were to being pampered by the salesmen of Mercedes Benz, Vauxhall, Opel, Simca, Datsun and the Volkswagen, such slapdash treatment was unprecedented.

First Taste of Freedom

Among the first measures on Maj. Gen. K.P. Candeth taking over as military governor on 20 December was an order declaring both Indian and Portuguese currencies as legal tender (the exchange rate being six escudos to the rupee), a ban on export of gold, jewellery and currency, the closing of Banco Nacional Ultramarino pending decision by the Reserve Bank of India, dissolution of the União Nacional (Salazar's single-party outfit) and the teaching of Portuguese as a subject in schools was made optional (it had been compulsory hitherto).

Maj. Gen. Candeth also assured Goans that no violence would be tolerated and that the lives and property of all would be respected. (Directive No. 12 (g) issued by his HQ 17 Infantry Division on

---

[*] Khera, 1974, p. 190.
[†] Remo Fernandes, 2021, pp. 102–03.

16 December 1961 told the troops to take firm action to prevent rioting and to give protection to sections of public whose life and property could be in danger.)

Yet, the first taste of freedom was not sweet for many. Far from it, it was traumatic.

Freedom fighter Dr Suresh Kanekar speaks of the gang rape of a Christian girl in a stationary railway goods-train wagon by armed Indian troops in Margao.* Leo Lawrence speaks of two young Hindu ladies being kidnapped from their home in Alto de Porvorim; enraged villagers rushed to their rescue and horse-whipped the Indian soldiers at the risk of their own lives.†

There were plain, cold-blooded murders. Germano D'Souza of Cobravaddo, Calangute was a primary-school teacher, who, suited and booted, as was customary at the time, pedalled to school on his bicycle. On 19 December, he was on his way to work on the main Calangute–Candolim road, when he was waylaid by a sub-unit of Indian troops. D'Souza did not understand Hindi. Nobody knew what actually occurred. What was known was that his bullet-riddled body lay motionless by the roadside a full twenty-four hours before it was finally retrieved and given a decent burial.

The list of atrocities—symbolized by the mindless tossing of a hand grenade into a Bogmalo bedroom that killed a fourteen-year-old girl on 16 January 1962 at 1 a.m.—is far too long to be recounted here.

Perhaps the jawan, influenced by higher-level politics of regional lobbies, squeezing out Anglo-Indians who were reaching the top echelons of the defence forces (causing the Anglo-Indians to mass emigrate), may have laboured under the delusion that Goan Catholics were Anglo-Indian!

---

* Suresh Kanekar, *Goa's Liberation and Thereafter: Chronicles of a Fragmented Life*, 2011, p. 156.

† Lawrence, *Nehru Seizes Goa,* 1963, p. 207, https://babel.hathitrust.org/cgi/pt?id=mdp.39015016919634&view=1up&seq=227&skin=2021

Directive No. 12 (h) issued by HQ 17 Infantry Division on 16 December 1961 had cautioned troops to maintain 'exemplary discipline' and that 'cases of looting and maltreatment by troops will be dealt with firmly'.* There was no evidence of any of such cases having been 'dealt with' at all—firmly or otherwise. Writes Leo Lawrence:

> In the villages, Indian troops made it a point to pay nightly visits, in groups, on the Catholic Churches, ostensibly for the purpose of looking for concealed white Portuguese soldiers, and then to threaten the priests with reprisals in case they refused to accede to their demands and hand over all the cash and valuables belonging to the congregation. For this reason, during the Christmas that followed the conquest, few parish priests dared to hold the time-honoured midnight services in Goan churches.†

There were several instances of churches and shrines being desecrated. Christian religious statues and other sacred objects were later found discarded in the most unseemly places—like gutters, dustbins and open garbage dumps, shorn of their gold and silver trimmings.

An image of Christ holding an olive branch was lifted from Panjim's Mary Immaculate Church and found in a gutter at Altinho–Panjim—with the Indian tricolour in the hand, and the slogan *Jai Hind* scribbled across it.

Soldiers, who had perhaps never seen lace in their villages, ripped the delicate and exquisite lace trimmings from the church altar cloths to take it home.

Significantly, there was no such occurrence of abuse reported from any of Goa's Hindu temples.

Goan mothers changed 'bogey man' to 'Sikh man' to frighten kids into obedience. (In earlier times, it was 'Albuquerque' and his long beard!)

---

* Khera, 1974, p. 194.
† Lawrence, *Nehru Seizes Goa*, pp. 210.

In a 'Special Order of the Day' of 16–17 December 1961, read out to all troops before they entered Goa, Army Chief General P.N. Thapar had said (quoted in part):

> Secondly, the people of GOA are Indians ...
>
> Thirdly, you will now enter GOA NOT as conquerors of a foreign land ...
>
> Sixthly, in GOA you are in India and with your compatriots. Your duty is as at home GO DEFEND and PROTECT the people. Let no one suffer violence.
>
> Eighthly ... you will take special care to respect sanctity of places of worship and see that no damage is done to them.*

Unfortunately, all of these mandates were ignored.

The Goan Catholic community was ruthlessly targeted by locals—in plain sight of Indian soldiers—labouring beneath the warped reasoning that the Goan community was responsible for acts of the 16th-century Inquisition! At the Cortalim ferryboat crossing, the Portuguese Archbishop-Patriarch of Goa, who had played a key role to ensure that Goa was not destroyed, was almost manhandled by some locals.

The official account of the operations of the Sikh Light Infantry Regiment, three of whose battalions participated, said:

> On night 18/19 December 1961, locals wrecked their vengeance by looting Portuguese houses and threatening Goans who they felt were pro-Portuguese.

The tragicomic scene went to bizarre lengths. Marauding mobs of 'Goan nationalists' (not Catholics) rampaged the streets of Panjim breaking anything and everything that appeared 'Portuguese' to them. At a quaint little bridge near the then Escola Médico-Cirúrgica de Goa (Goa Medical College), they destroyed a beautiful statuette

---

*   Khera, 1974, Appendix VII, p. 186.

of Minerva, the Roman Goddess of knowledge, counterpart of Goddess Saraswati, thinking it was a Portuguese queen. (Owing to a long tradition, the Portuguese invariably placed a statue of Minerva near an academic institution.)

In like manner, the statue of Manuel Antonio de Souza of Mapusa, a great Goan nineteenth-century pioneer in Mozambique, was demolished by local 'nationalists' under the ignorant impression that it was some Portuguese hero!

But Paul Grimes, special correspondent of the *New York Times* who was in Goa during this period, said in a despatch,

> Well-equipped Indian forces moved forth with precision. Even many of their enemies credited them with extreme care in safeguarding civilian population, preserving historical and religious landmarks and treating Portuguese prisoners.[*]

Shoe on the Other Foot, Ten Months Later ...

What followed the month-or-two-long orgy of violence, loot, rape and murder was even more surprising. Maj. Gen. Candeth had two top-level civil service officers to assist him: R.C.V.P. Noronha, ICS, as chief civic administrator, and G.K. Handoo, IPS, as special advisor. It is generally accepted that Handoo was the author of misgovernance in Goa. Handoo's overbearing attitude was detested by local government officials. The unceremonious eviction of the last Portuguese governor's wife from the official residence and the shabby treatment meted out to Goan judicial officers were cited as examples.

Dr Remy Dias, associate professor of history, Government College of Arts, Science and Commerce, Quepem, Goa, and deputy director, Higher Education, Government of Goa, wrote,

> Goans in general did not approve of the cavalier and insensitive manner in which the new administration handled the transition.

---

[*] Ibid., p. 140.

Surely, it would have not caused much economic harm if the 'unnecessary' colonial departments were allowed to continue functioning for some time. By forcing the transition thoughtlessly, by refusing to give local people time to adjust, the new administration caused much bitterness.[*]

Even euphoric freedom fighters criticized the transition. Dr Suresh Kanekar wrote a letter to *The Times of India*, early in 1962, critical of Handoo.[†]

A respected former schoolteacher from Margao, this author's neighbour, named his post-1961 pup 'Handoo'. (Interestingly, freedom fighter Dr Suresh Kanekar, who spent some years at Aguada Jail, tells us that Portuguese jail guards had a dog named 'Nehru' and another named 'Salazar'.)[‡]

Handoo was aware he was unpopular with Goans, particularly Goan Catholics. One day, Handoo asked a Goan Catholic who had gone to meet him at the Panjim Secretariat, 'Do you see the two horns [the devil is popularly portrayed with two horns] on my head that you people think I have?'

Despite all the ugly acts and criminal offences that occurred during the month or two following 19 December 1961, not a single arrestor prosecution was made, or trial held—not even a single court martial carried out. Maj. Gen. Candeth is said to have sent back a unit, marching on foot as punishment. Lt Gen. H.S. Panag wrote in his book:

The only sour note was that some units indulged in looting and were forced to march on foot on the way back.[§]

---

[*] Remy Dias, 'Trials and Turbulences of Goa's Post-colonial Transition to Democracy, 1961–63', *Radix International Journal of Research in Social Science*, ISSN 2320-1738, vol. 2, issue 6, June 2014, p. 26.

[†] Suresh Kanekar, 'Goa's Liberation and Thereafter: Chronicles of a Fragmented Life', *Times of India*, 2011, pp. 157–58.

[‡] Ibid., p. 73.

[§] H.S. Panag, *The Indian Army: Reminiscences, Reforms and Romance*, Westland Publications, Chennai, 2020.

Pertinently, 803 Goans, mostly Catholics, left India immediately in the wake of liberation. By the end of January 1962, the Brazilian Embassy in New Delhi looking after Portugal's interests in India had issued 5000 Portuguese passports to Goans in Goa, with a few thousand more applications under process. Many Goan Hindus (besides those from Gujarat) settled in Portugal, some rising to high offices, including as Supreme Court justices.

Goan emigration, both Catholic and Hindu, continued to rise in later years for other reasons. Today, the Goan is said to be a minority in Goa. The 16th-century Spanish Jesuit, St Francis Xavier, is credited to have said, *Gôa ninguém levará, ela por si acabará* (Nobody will conquer Goa, she will end by herself). Looks like the words are turning prophetic.

India's Use of Force Emboldens China?

The armed forces' victory in Goa had serious repercussions elsewhere. Air Vice Marshal Arjun Subramaniam wrote:

> In a scathing critique of the manner in which the GOC-in-C of Southern Command, Chaudhuri, and other senior commanders overplayed the preparation for the operation, thereby diverting attention from the more serious China border situation ...

Maj. Gen. D.K. Palit recounts:

> Yet, in its consequences, Operation Vijay eventually took on greater significance: the easy conquest was taken too seriously in many quarters. The euphoria of success inflated a passing interlude of secondary military consequence into a famous victory.

Brian Cloughley, an Australian colonel who spent two years as the deputy head of the UN Military Observer Group (UNMOG) in India and Pakistan, made these observations on India's reaction to its Goa victory:

Unfortunately for the army and Indian prestige, the invasion of the tiny Portuguese enclave of Goa had been greeted with euphoric approval by an Indian public which considered it to be a great feat in arms, which it patently was not.

As seen, Operation Vijay was a cakewalk, not a great military victory. It was meant to demonstrate to the Indian voter that the Congress Party was capable of handling foreign intrusions and bolster the defence minister's prospects at the ensuing February 1962 general elections. Never mind that Pakistan was holding large areas of Kashmir (POK) and China, after encroaching on a substantial sliver of Indian land in Aksai Chin, kept urging India to resolve the Indo–China boundary 'dispute'.

In the final analysis, Operation Vijay was a reasonably well-planned and well-executed military operation against a significantly weaker adversary after almost thirteen years of peaceful existence. Though the Indian armed forces gained valuable battle experience, little did they realize that barely a year later they would be pitted against an enemy who would prove to be of a different mettle in a completely different environment.[*]

The easy military victory in Goa over an undersized, underarmed and demoralized enemy appeared to have lulled India into smug complacence.

Goa may well have given Krishna Menon and Kaul [Lt General B.M. Kaul who was in command of the China front in the northeast in 1962] a swollen head and a false sense of India's military prowess.[†]

---

[*] Arjun Subramaniam, 2016, pp. 193–94.
[†] Ramesh, Penguin Viking, 2019, p. 551.

Maj. Gen. D.K. Palit later wrote,

> Rather than being alarmed by the military inadequacies displayed
> by the Operation ...the powers that be preened themselves as
> though they had struck a stunning blow at a major enemy; that in
> turn led to a false confidence in our military dynamics.[*]

This false sense of confidence is acknowledged by other Indian
military authors. It was to lead to a sense of complacency in the
ruling establishment, which in turn led to the ignominy ten months
later with the Chinese aggression. Maj. Gen. Randhir Sinh said in
his book *A Talent for War*:

> Goa was in many ways a cake walk and should not be considered
> a major feat of arms. Nevertheless, even under such easy
> circumstances the main thrust line got bogged down, enabling the
> secondary thrust of the Para Brigade to go beyond the objectives
> set for it ...
>
>   Unfortunately, everyone seems to have been more than
> willing to bask in the swift victory over a demoralised Portuguese
> soldiery achieved by the Para Brigade. The heady feeling blinkered
> the vision of the politician and bureaucrat and affected senior
> officers too. A certain amount of overweening arrogance appears
> to have crept into our attitude. That balloon was well and truly
> pricked by the disaster of 1962 [with China, ten months later].[†]

At the world level, *Time* magazine had, in an article titled, 'India:
End of an Image', dubbed Jawaharlal Nehru

> ...a hypocrite who preached peace abroad but used force at home.[‡]

---

[*] D.K. Palit, 2004, p. 113.

[†] Randhir Sinh, *A Talent for War*, 2013, p. 67.

[‡] 'India: End of an Image', *Time*, 29 December 1961.

The following week, when the same magazine asked what if India were to be obliged to leave Goa, Nehru thundered,

> The whole world will be ablaze if such a thing comes to pass.[*]

He may have forgotten his words in the Lok Sabha on 17 September 1955, in the wake of the bloodied satyagraha earlier in August that year:

> There is nothing I can argue with any person who thinks that the methods employed in regard to Goa must be other than peaceful, because we rule out non-peaceful methods completely … One cannot have it both ways. One either adopts military methods or keeps to peaceful methods. To mix them up is to fall between two policies, and to nowhere … If we suddenly reverse our policy, the world will get an opportunity to say that we are deceitful … Once we accept the position that we can use the army for the solution to our problems, we cannot deny the same right to other countries.

China evidently took Nehru's words seriously. The change of stance from non-violence to use of force in Goa, many believe, emboldened China to attack India ten months later. If Portugal had refused to negotiate Goa with India, India had refused to negotiate the common border with China.

Nehru had been ill since late 1961 [from a little after the Goa invasion in December 1961] but his health took a sharp turn for the worse in November–December 1962 [after the China invasion in October 1962].[†] (Nehru suffered a paralytic stroke on 8 January 1964 and passed away on 27 May 1964.)

There was another nexus between the Goa invasion and the China invasion. The mutual aversion between the mastermind of

---

[*] *Time*, 5 January 1962, p. 16.

[†] Ramesh, Penguin Viking, 2019, p. 610.

the Goa action, Krishna Menon, and the US Ambassador to India, Prof. John Kenneth Galbraith, had sharply increased after the Goa invasion. When China invaded and India requested the USA for urgent military supplies, Prof. Galbraith got the US to agree on one condition: that Krishna Menon be dropped from the union cabinet. One of Menon's many *suo moto* letters of resignation was forwarded by Nehru to the president, Dr Sarvapalli Radhakrishnan, who was only too happy to drop the other Krishna.

The hunter in Goa ten months before was now the quarry. Menon sowed the wind in December 1961. He reaped the whirlwind in October 1962.

EPILOGUE

Goa has been free of Portuguese colonial rule sixty-two years now. Goans, or at least Goan politicos, quickly learnt the ropes of our brand of democracy from national counterparts. Most would have heard of India's *Aya Ram Gaya Ram* variety of politicians, the worthies who inspired the Anti-Defection Act, 1985. Few would know that Goa, India's smallest state, had eight chief ministers between the years 1990 and 1994 and thirteen in the last decade of the twentieth century. Between 1990 and 2005, Goa had eighteen governments in fifteen years—including three interspersed tenures of president's rule. Goa taught the rest of India how to circumvent the law against floor-crossing. From a mortal fear of the law during the harsh colonial regime, the Goan had now graduated to fiddling with it.

Goa produced the maximum 'case law' (verdicts of the high courts and of the Supreme Court of India) under the Anti-Defection Act. Where a split of one-third of the elected legislative strength of a party could not be attained, Goan MLAs resigned from their seats, contested the ensuing by-polls on the ticket of the party they wanted to cross to and were promptly re-elected.

The Anti-defection law was amended by Parliament in 2004, making its dodging more difficult. It did not matter to Goa, which continued to show the way. In 2019, thirteen (out of seventeen) Congress MLAs merged into the ruling BJP. More recently in September 2022, eight (out of eleven) Congress MLAs who had taken a pre-election oath in a temple, church and masjid to not defect, merged into the ruling BJP. One defecting MLA told the media that the almighty had endorsed the step in a temple *prasad*. Just prior to the end of the term of the seventh Goa Legislative

Assembly and fresh polls in February 2022, seventeen (out of forty) MLAs resigned from their seats—to be in a position to defect and contest from the ticket of another political party.

If India's smallest state led the way in political defections, its root—political corruption—would not lag far behind. In its 'India Corruption Study – 2008', Transparency International India placed Goa's level of corruption at an eminent 'alarming' (of its four descending categories: Alarming, Very High, High and Moderate). While Goan politicians continue playing the game, Goans continue leaving Goa for greener pastures of the honest kind. Emigration, ironically, has been made easy by passports of the former colonial power, Portugal.

Nature abhors vacuum. The place left vacant by the Goan emigrant has been taken by people from all over the country, literally from Kashmir to Kerala (even neighbouring Nepal). A journo-humourist wondered if he had his geography wrong: all this time he thought Goa was within India. Writing in *The Times of India* (20 November 2021), he said:

... But it was the other way round; India was in Goa, or so it appeared during my recent visit there.

The Goan is reduced to a minority in his own land. Goa may, a few decades into the future, remain only in name.

Liberation also ushered in a world of good, particularly on the parameters of education, health and welfare legislation. Practically every village has a government primary school; towns witnessed a proliferation of secondary, higher secondary, college and even technical/ professional education. Goa saw an unprecedented rise in rural and urban health centres, upgraded hospital facilities and a doctor-to-patient ratio improving from one doctor for 1500 inhabitants in 1961 to about one doctor for 800 inhabitants today. Villages no longer lack asphalt roads, electricity and piped water, whatever be their quality. Goa is today counted among the leading states of India (and not just in the matter of political defections!). Slice it any way you will, Goa has come a long way since colonial rule ended.

ACKNOWLEDGEMENTS

If you are holding a copy of this book published by a world's prominent publishing house, it is thanks to two women: my fellow writer-author friend Selma Carvalho (Nuvem/London) and Deepthi Talwar, editor at Penguin Random House, India.

I write with the object of resuscitating and sharing by now largely forgotten information about Goa, my native region (no, not for money! I have been blessed enough). In simpler words, it translates to 'A writer writes to be read'. In the normal course of things, I should have gone to a local publisher, but with a worldwide publisher, the exposure to this humble work would be exponentially larger.

My sincere thanks to Selma and Deepthi, to Rachna Pratap of Penguin's legal team, to the copy-edit and line-edit teams and to all at Penguin Random House, India, and people in the production process who made this book possible. Contrary to my initial apprehensions of having to work with a large multinational, it was truly a breeze working with them. They made things seem so effortless, easy and quick!

In particular, it would not be easy to thank Ms Deepthi Talwar enough. Evidently gifted with a fine intellect and excellent professional competence, she not only quickly grasped in a jiffy the intricacies of the subject with international ramifications and complexities, but deftly edited the manuscript to greatly improve the flow and quality of the narrative. I am thankful to her patience too: for having put up with my frequent requests for changes, with a smile instead of a frown!

In a special way, my sincere gratitude to the estate of Lieutenant General Eric Vas (V), Lieutenant General Stanislaus Menezes (V),

Major General D.K. Palit (V) and to my respected senior friend Prabhakar D. Bhide, chair of Rajhauns Sankalpana Pvt. Ltd that republished Dr Pundalik D. Gaitonde's 1987 book, *The Liberation of Goa*, in 2016. I have also quoted from the book by Dr Gaitonde's widow Edila (now also no more), *As Maçãs Azuis*, and its English version, *In Search of Tomorrow*, published by Rajhauns Vitaran.

I stand obliged to Lieutenant General Walter Pinto (V, now departed), Lieutenant General Vijay Oberoi (V), Major General Ian Cardozo (V), Major General V.K. Singh (V), Major General Randhir Sinh (V), Major General P.K. Mallick (chairman Corps of Signals History Cell)—all military historians and commentators—and Major General Anil Raikar (V), Air Vice Marshal Arjun Subramaniam (V, military historian), Brigadier Ravi K. Mehta (V, Sikh LI), Colonel Harjeet Singh (V, Sikh LI, military historian), Lieutenant Colonel Pravinkumar Shirodkar (V), civilian authors Dr Suresh Kanekar, Adv. Fernando Jorge Colaco, Dr Prakashchandra Shirodkar (now departed), Dr Sushila Fonseca, Dr Nishtha Desai, Gabriel de Figueiredo, Bernardo Elvino de Souza, Martin Menino Fernandes and all the other authors whose work helped me and who graciously allowed me to freely quote from their published work, use photographs and other copyrighted material, and all the authors whose names feature in the text and in the select bibliography.

Major General Anil Raikar (V, Sikh Light Infantry Regiment) and Major General Dinesh Merchant (Pai Raikar, V, Madras Regiment, who grew up in Altinho, Panjim, with fond memories in the dying years of the colonial regime), both of Goan origin, reviewed a part of the manuscript and offered me valuable comments and suggestions, for which I am grateful. Lieutenant Colonel Vishwas Bhandare (veteran paratrooper) and my respected senior neighbour, Dr Francisco Colaco, gifted me copies of their books that were of much help. About forty years ago, (the now late) Mr Norton Pires of Velim (ex-Kenya) thrust in my hands a 1973-published book, *Goa and the Continent of Circe* by Robert de Souza, saying, 'Keep it, Valmiki, it may come in handy someday.' It did, Mr Pires, in the final stages of finalizing this book. Thank you!

Especial thanks are due to Arun K. Batra (New Delhi/Noida) son of a defence officer—his father, Brigadier S.K. Batra, was chief signals officer, Southern Command—who is actually a chartered accountant (he was financial controller at Nestlé India and spent some years at HQ in Vevey, Switzerland) but more, is a well-read and erudite person who took the pains of running through an early draft of this book with a fine-tooth comb and made valuable improvements and corrections. And to one of my two gurus in journalism, B.G. Koshy (Bangalore, now Bengaluru) for his constant support and guidance—and, of course, for kindly consenting to write the Foreword to this book. BGK, as he is known to friends, spent some post-1961 years in Goa and was among my lecturers of the English language at college before he moved into full-time journalism and then into the corporate world, most of it with Oerlikon in Switzerland.

Last but not least, to my knowledgeable friends Antonio Palhinha Machado (in Portugal), Prof. Valentino Viegas and Pedro Mascarenhas (both Goans in Portugal), Dr John de Figueiredo (a Goan medico in the US), Rafael Viegas (in Curtorim, Goa), cousin, academic, writer-author Eugenio Viassa Monteiro (Nagoa/Portugal/New Delhi/Bombay), another cousin Dr Sandra Ataíde Lobo (Siolim/Panjim/Portugal) and Bengaluru-based author Alan Machado Prabhu for providing me information and some excellent source material, teacher-historian-writer Tensing Rodrigues (Carmona/Santa Cruz, Goa) who added diacritical marks to Portuguese words/names from the orthography of that language and Augusto Pinto (Moira, Goa), lecturer-writer-translator-reviewer who made time to read an early draft of the manuscript and offered me his valuable suggestions.

Being human, I might be forgetting names. To all those I have, my sincere apologies for the entirely unintended omission and a big thank you!

ANNEXURES

Goan Catholic Freedom Fighters

†Denotes those who either did not seek registration or are not registered freedom fighters (but are genuine nationalists who fought for a Goa free from the colonial yoke). The reader may note that this list is far from complete.

Full details of the authors' works mentioned below are in the Bibliography.

Sources

Fernandes, Martin Menino, *Goa, Daman & Diu Catholic Freedom Fighters*, Goa: Goeam Tujea Mogakhatir (Gurunath Kelekar), 2011.

Fonseca, Sushila S., *Antonio Sequeira: His Quest for Goa's Freedom—Dictatorship & Freedom of the Press in Goa in the Forties*, Goa: Dr Sushila S. Fonseca, M.D., D.P.B., 2021. [ISBN: 978-81-910150-2-7]

Goa Gazetteer, *Who's Who of Freedom Fighters—Goa, Daman & Diu (volume One and volume Two)* edited by P.P. Shirodkar (Jr), Goa: Goa Gazetteer Department, Government of the Union Territory of Goa, Daman and Diu, 1986 (volume 1) and 1990 (volume 2).

Goa Gazetteer, *Trial of the Four*, edited by P.P. Shirodkar (Jr.), Goa: Goa Gazetteer Department, Government of Goa, 1999.

Kanekar, Suresh, *Goa's Liberation and Thereafter: Chronicles of a Fragmented Life*, Goa: Goa, 1556, 2011. [ISBN: 978-93-80739-30-4]

Shirodkar, Dr P.P. (Jr.), *Goa's Struggle For Freedom*, Goa: self-published by Mrs Sulabha P. Shirodkar, Alto Porvorim, Goa, 1988 (revised edition 1999). [ISBN: 81-202-0195-7]

Shirodkar, P.P. (Sr), translated into English by Lt Col Dr Pravinkumar P. Shirodkar, *My Life in Exile*, Goa: Pradnya-Darshan Prakashan, 2012.

oHERALDo daily newspaper, edition of 2 February 1987, which carried the Newspaper Statement issued by some Goan Catholic Freedom Fighters.

1. Albano Souza: was a nationalist leader based in Bombay.
2. Militant Albert L.R. Fernandes: Cuncolim, Azad Gomantak Dal (hereafter, AGD), arrested and tortured on 25 August 1954 for offering satyagraha in Ponda, sentenced to five years' rigorous imprisonment plus one year simple imprisonment. *Goa Gazetteer* vol. 1 listing at pp. 98–99; Fernandes (2011) at p. 64.
3. Alex Fernandes: *Goa Gazetteer* vol. 1 reference under George Louis Pereira at p. 119. Fernandes (2011) at p. 84.
4. Alfred Afonso: Galgibaga–Canacona, worked in Bombay Telephones, quit, led the batch of fourteen satyagrahis who occupied Tiracol fort, was released in September 1959. Goa Gazetteer vol. 1 listing at pp. 3–4 and references under Kamat Gopal Apa at p. 153, under Karpe Ramkrisna Arjun at p. 171, under Kerkar Janardan Krishna at p. 179, under Mayenkar Pandurang Sokdo at p. 218, under Parsekar Sriram and Parsekar Vasu Ramakant at p. 265, under Priolkar Prafull V. at p. 286, under Sardesai Shankar Pandurang Naik Prataprao at p. 304, Fernandes (2011) at p. 16, Kanekar (2011) at p. 71.
5. Journalist Alfred Braganza: *Goa Gazetteer* vol. 1 reference under Shinkre Janardan Jagannath (later the first general

secretary of MGP from 1962 and elected Lok Sabha MP from 1967) at p. 322.

6. Prof. Aloysius Soares[†]: Ucassaim, Bombay-based professor of English at the University of Bombay and prolific writer, wrote about freedom for Goa, founded The Goa Liberation Council and was its president in June 1954. He was among the leaders who provided direction to organizations that fought for Goa's freedom by peaceful means. *Goa Gazetteer* vol. 1 reference under Mascarenhas Emilio Francisco Lamberto *alias* Mascarenhas Lambert at p. 215, Fernandes (2011) at p. 17.

7. Salcete municipal president Alvaro da Costa: Margao–Colva, was editor of *Diário de Goa* and former president of Salcete municipality, arrested on political charges in the mid-1950s.

8. Alvaro Antonio Precioso Pereira: Divar, completed a pharmacy course and joined medical studies but gave up; joined the freedom movement. In the words of Mario Cabral Sa, 'He travelled all over Goa, distributing pamphlets highlighting Goa's humbling submission to the dictatorial regime of Dr António de Oliveira Salazar [until he was] denounced to the Margao police by a civil administration official.' Pereira was fond of referring to his Aguada Jail travails as 'my university years'. He went into business post 1961 (farm products). Goa Gazetteer vol. 1 listing at pp. 276–77 and references, among others, under Gude Vishwanath Jaiwant at p. 123, under Joshi Pandurang Narayan at p. 142, under Kanekar (Dr) Suresh Viaswambar at p. 161, under Panvelkar Anant (Abu) Vitthal Naik at p. 262, under Raiturkar Ravindranath Yeshwant Pai at p. 291, under Virginkar Mohandas Narayan at p. 374, Fernandes (2011) at p. 110, Kanekar (2011) at pp. 51, 86–88, 108–109, 112, 138.

9. Municipal president and militant Alvaro Pinto Furtado: Chinchinim, advocate and former president of Salcete

municipality, specialized in despatching bomb parcels, was arrested and imprisoned from 1956, dismissed from government service. *Goa Gazetteer* vol. 1 reference under Saldanha Jose Ladislau at p. 299. Listing at *Goa Gazetteer* vol. 2 at p. 30, Fernandes (2011) at p. 83.

10. Alvinho (Alwin) Belarmino Coelho: Saligao, led satyagrahis to Tiracol on 16 September 1954, arrested and released after four years, worked as panchayat secretary after 1961. *Goa Gazetteer* vol. 1 listing at pp. 51–52, reference under Lanjekar Krupavant Shambhu at p. 195, under Rane Murlidhar Vishwanath at p. 295. Fernandes (2011) at p. 44.

11. Trade-union leader Anastacio Almeida: Velim, graduate in arts and journalism, worked for Bank of Baroda in Bombay, resigned after the 15 August 1954 satyagraha and returned to Goa, arrested the following month and released September 1958, turned to trade unionism after 1961. *Goa Gazetteer* vol. 1 listing at pp. 6–7 and reference under Narvenkar Shashikant Dutta at p. 249. Fernandes (2011) at p. 19, Kanekar (2011) at first photo after p. 90 and pp. 108 and 138.

12. Former MLA/minister Anthony ('Tony') John D'Souza: born in Bombay 1920, joined a seminary but gave up, went to Kashi to study the Vedas but gave up, finally joined Lloyd's Bank, resigned in 1952 and plunged into the Goa freedom struggle, led the 15 August 1954 satyagrahis from Polem and was awarded the highest sentence of twenty-eight years' rigorous imprisonment, joined the MGP after the opinion poll and was cabinet minister but resigned in 1970. *Goa Gazetteer* vol. 1 listing at pp. 336–37, references under Narvenkar Shashikant Dutta at p. 249, Pai Srirang Vishnu at p. 254, Priolkar Prafull V. at p. 286, Sardesai Shankar Pandurang Naik Prataprao at p. 304, Thali Dinkar Govind at p. 352, Virginkar Gopal ('Sadanand') Narayan (businessman from Margao who escorted Dr Ram

Manohar Lohia and Dr Juliao Menezes from a lodge at Francisco Luis Gomes Road to what would be known as Lohia Maidan on 18 June 1946—although most accounts say it was Laxmidas Borkar who escorted the two leaders) at p. 374, Fernandes (2011) at p. 135, Kanekar (2011) at pp. 26 and 28.

13. Militant Anthony Leo Sequeira: Chinchinim, AGD, armed action on Supangudi and Cotigao police stations, guided Indian troops entering via Majali on 18 December 1961. *Goa Gazetteer* vol.1 listing at p. 312, Fernandes (2011) at p. 130.

14. Antonio Braganza†: *Goa Gazetteer* vol.1 reference under Manjrekar Vasant Ganpat at p. 212.

15. Judge Antonio Blasio de Souza: Velsao/Margao, newspaper statement, 1987.

16. Antonio Conceicao Fernandes: Cuncolim, was with the National Congress Goa (hereafter, NCG) between 1954 and 1960 when he joined the Indian National Congress, arrested in 1954 for offering satyagraha at Ponda and sentenced to five years' simple imprisonment. *Goa Gazetteer* vol. 1 listing at p. 99, Fernandes (2011) at p. 65.

17. Adv./Judge Antonio Furtado: Chinchinim but born in Carmona, was a student activist with a law degree from Lisbon. He was the brother of Dr Jose Maria Furtado (No. 132 in this list). Due to his nationalist activities he was threatened with deportation to Portuguese Africa and he went into self-exile in Belgaum from where, in 1954, he was called upon by the Bombay Government to work as administrator of Dadra and Nagar Haveli six years after 1954. He was additional judicial commissioner of Goa post 1961. *Goa Gazetteer* vol. 1 listing at pp. 102–103 and reference under Rana Babubhai Laxmanbhai at p. 292; Fernandes (2011) at p. 73.

18. Militant Antonio Jose E. dá Gama S. de Costa Frias: was born in Inhabane–Mozambique in 1930, did first-

year medicine in Goa but joined the NCG in 1950 and later the AGD-Rancour Patriotica group (hereafter, RP), gathered important intelligence on bridges and airport while working for Panjim Municipal Council, arrested in 1956, tortured and imprisoned for more than three years, tried but acquitted, rearrested in 1960, retired from Panjim Municipal Council post 1961. Listing at *Goa Gazetteer* vol. 2 pp. 29–30, Fernandes (2011) at p. 82.

19. Antonio Piedade Antao†: *Goa Gazetteer* vol. 2 reference under Budholkar Vasant Rama at p. 12.

20. Member of Parliament (nominated 1962) Dr António Colaço: Margao, was doctor of Hospicio Hospital and brother of the bishop of Cabo Verde, D. Jose Colaço. He was under PIDE watch and was questioned by police in the 1950s. Following liberation, he was nominated to the Lok Sabha in 1962 as one of the two representatives from Goa.

21. Militant Antonio Rosario Menino Egidio Gregorio Lume Jose Vaz: Orlim, was with the Goa Liberation Army (hereafter, GLA) from 1956 and worked under Peter Alvares, was arrested in Margao, Fernandes (2011) at p. 152.

22. Antonio Silva: Goa Velha, was an associate of the president of NCG, Pandurang P. Shirodkar, and helped the latter in raising funds for the organization. Goa Gazetteer, *Trial of the Four*, p. 24.

23. Militant Antonio Rosario Policarpo/Polycarpo ('Polly') Teodosio da Silva: Chinchinim, always daring, joined the RP in 1954, sent bomb-parcels to TMT (military tribunal) Judge Jose Joaquim Militao de Quadros, administrator Jose Fortunato de Miranda, mine owner Damodar Mangalji and Viscount Kaka Deshprabhu. *Goa Gazetteer* vol. 1 listing at p. 332 and references under Almeida Rodolfo J. at p. 8, Bhise Raghuvir Dattu p. 27, Desai Dattaram Uttam at p. 63, Halarnkar Gajanan Govind p. 125, Kolvenkar Dattaram Ganesh at p. 187, Manjrekar Vasant Ganpat at

p. 212. *Goa Gazetteer* vol. 2 reference under Kharangate Shripad Narahari at p. 56, Fernandes (2011) at p. 131.

24. Pharmacist Antonio Sequeira[†]: Raia was the fearless editor of *A Voz da India*, a daily newspaper. In the mid-1940s, despite censorship (imposed on 3 January 1934), he subtly exposed the authoritarian Salazarist regime in Goa. When a warrant of arrest was issued against him, he escaped to Belgaum disguised as a priest, and thence to Mombasa. He refused to register as a freedom fighter, maintaining that he had only done his duty to Goa (Fonseca, *The Journey of an Unsung Hero*, 2021).

25. Antonio Viegas[†]: associate of Luis Antonio ('Jose Luis') de Costa, was among the seventy-five members of the NCG arrested on 18 June 1954 to frustrate the proposed satyagraha demonstration. *Goa Gazetteer* vol. 1 references under Costa Luis Antonio de at p. 52, under Desai Narendra Govind Hegde at p. 72, Souza Jacinto de at p. 338, Fernandes (2011) at pp. 47, 132, 140, Kanekar (2011) at pp. 92, 95–96, 100, 135.

26. Adv. Ariosto Tovar Dias: Chinchinim/Margao, joined the NCG when doing BA, LLB, BEd., participated in secret meetings from 1946 onwards, helped freedom fighters financially, was dismissed as additional public prosecutor, arrested in June 1956 and a second time later. Listing at *Goa Gazetteer* vol. 2 p. 27 and reference at *Goa Gazetteer* vol. 1 under Kalangutkar Vasudev Rama at p. 151, Fernandes (2011) at p. 63. Shirodkar, *My Life in Exile*, 2012, pp. 35 and 37.

27. University professor Armando Menezes[†]: Divar, was among the leading intellectuals of the time to lead the freedom movement. He was appointed India's consul-general to Portuguese Goa, but the colonial administration refused to accept his credentials. His brother Nicolau Menezes, a teacher, was also a freedom fighter.

28. Salcete municipal president Adv. Armando Teodoro Valente Santana Pereira: Chinchinim, completed 7th-year Lyceum and obtained a degree in law but was refused licence to practise law on account of nationalist activities. Was with AGD, arrested five times and his house was raided ten times. Post 1961 he was appointed president of Quepem municipality, administrator of Comunidades-South and president of Salcete Municipality. *Goa Gazetteer* vol. 1 listing at pp. 277–78 and references under Desai Gajanan Vitthal Prabhu at p. 64, Jaques Arsenio at p. 136 and Sanzguiri (Dr) Kashinath Ladu at p. 301, Fernandes (2011) at p. 111. Newspaper statement, 1987.

29. Journalist Arsenio Jacques: Majorda, hailed from one of the biggest land-owning families in the village. *Goa Gazetteer* vol. 1 listing at p. 136 and reference under Mense Krishna Parasharam at p. 222, Fernandes (2011) at p. 87.

30. Militant Artur Fernandes: Sarzora–Chinchinim, joined the NCG in 1952 and participated in organizing satyagrahis in 1955. Later joined the GLA where he worked underground. Post 1961 he worked as chief archivist at Margao Municipal Council. *Goa Gazetteer* vol. 1 listing at p. 99 and reference under Nagvenkar Jaiwant Vitthal at p. 229, Fernandes (2011) at p. 66.

31. Militant Augusto (Augustus) Alvares: born in Bombay, science graduate, co-founded the GLA as one of its six commanders on 30 September 1955, dynamited barges and mines. *Goa Gazetteer* vol. 1 listing at p. 9 and references, among others, under Kakodkar Manohar Jaiwant at p. 148, Kerkar Pandurang Dulba at p. 181, Madkaikar Khushali Rama at p. 204, Rane Jaisingrao Venkatrao at p. 294, Sardesai Pandurangrao Dadasaheb Rane at p. 304, Tupkar Manu ('Hemraj') Mohanlal at p. 356, Fernandes (2011) at p. 24.

32. Augusto Monteiro: Loutulim, referenced at Shirodkar, *My Life in Exile*, 2012, pp. 236–37.

33. Balduino Arnaldo Fernandes: Colva, was a seaman during World War II, worked thereafter in the Royal Indian Dockyard, joined the NCG in 1954 and entered from Majali–Polem in the 15 August 1954 satyagraha, arrested at Mashem, was sentenced to five years' imprisonment. *Goa Gazetteer* vol. 1 listing at p. 99, Fernandes (2011) at p. 67.

34. Adv. Baptist Rebello[†]: Deussua, was a freedom fighter when in Bombay, was expelled from the Deussua Club in the metropolis for his nationalistic activities.

35. Barbosa Barreto[†]: referenced at Shirodkar, *My Life in Exile*, 2012, pp. 236–37.

36. Dr (PhD) Beatris de Menezes Braganza: Chandor, daughter of Luis de Menzes Braganza, was a scientist at the Haffkine Institute (where, among other things, she developed an antidote for cobra poison), at the Tata Memorial Hospital (where she was director, research, and made significant contributions to cancer therapy) and further research in Paris, Copenhagen and London. She was research director of the Tata Institute for Cancer Research and, in 1974, was the first dean of the institute. A founder member of the Goa Youth League, she was active in the freedom movement and led protest marches in Bombay, met Pandit Nehru with Adv. Joachim Dias in 1946, carried the Goa message abroad during her many visits attending conferences, Fernandes (2011) at p. 34.

37. Benjamin Fernandes[†]: *Goa Gazetteer* vol. 1 reference under Desai SripadGoona at p. 79.

38. Editor Berta de Menezes Braganza: Chandor, sister of Beatris at no. 36 above, she was married to Adv. Antonio Furtado (at no. 17 above), escaped to Belgaum when her husband was threatened with deportation to Portuguese Africa, took up the editorship of the fortnightly *Free Goa* from her husband in 1958 until it ceased publication in 1962, attended conferences in Cairo and Moscow where

she highlighted the Goa situation, toured India to mobilize opinion in favour of military action. *Goa Gazetteer* vol. 1 references under Harmalkar Namdev Shankar at p. 128 and Jambawalikar (Dr) Pandurang Gaeca at p. 135, Fernandes (2011) at p. 36.

39. Journalist Bonifacio Eusebio Inacio Dias: Cavelossim, younger brother of Thomas Dias at no. 200 below, was a legal clerk in Bombay when he left and returned to Goa to plunge in the freedom struggle. His old grandmother was interrogated and severely beaten for not divulging his whereabouts. Finally arrested, he was released from prison only on 19 December 1961. He edited the *A Vanguarda* in Mapusa. *Goa Gazetteer* vol. 1 listing at pp. 93–94, Fernandes (2011) at p. 56.

40. Dr Caesar Monteiro†: reference in Shirodkar, *My Life in Exile*, 2012, pp. 236–37.

41. Caetano (Cajetan) Braganza†: Majorda, worked at Dabolim airport/TAIP as a ground crew marshaller (person who helps a pilot to taxi an aircraft with two table tennis bats in hand signals). He was arrested and beaten up so badly that it left him with a permanent hearing problem. Imprisoned at Aguada, he was buried neck-deep as punishment. He made friends with Felicio Cardoso at Aguada and was his close associate.

42. Caetano Manuel de Souza: Cortalim, offered satyagraha in 1955. Was an important member of the NCG. *Goa Gazetteer* vol. 1 listing at p. 337, Fernandes (2011) at p. 137. *Goa Gazetteer, Trial of the Four*, Appendix V (letter of 27 August 1947 of Dr Vinayak Sinai Mayenkar to Guilherme de Souza Ticlo asking the latter to meet Caetano Souza at Saligao and bring him to the working committee meeting of NCG) at p. 254 and at Appendix VI (NCG working committee meeting on 6 September 1947) at p. 255.

43. Journalist Caetano (Cajetan) Ludger Teodor Lobo: Aldona, publisher *Goa Tribune*, attended national and

international conferences on freedom, including the three-day Casablanca Conference of Portugal-subjugated countries in Asia and Africa in April 1961 together with George Vaz, Aquino de Bragança, Dr Pundalik Gaitonde and Adv. João Cabral. *Goa Gazetteer* vol. 1 listing at p. 199 and references, among others, under Afonso Francisco Correia p. 4, under Mascarenhas Emilio Francisco Lamberto alias Mascarenhas Lambert at p. 215, Fernandes (2011) at pp. 17 and 91. Newspaper statement, 1987.

44. Martyr Camilo Pereira: Bandora–Ponda, GLA, raided mines, shot dead by police together with Suresh A. Kerkar at Curti on 17 February 1957 while they were in the process of blowing up a pipeline supplying water to the Portuguese garrison at Ponda. *Goa Gazetteer* vol. 1 listing at p. 278 and references under Chari Naguesh Babu at p. 43, Dhawlikar Gurudas Krishna at p. 92, Kerkar Janardhan Mangesh at p. 180, Padwalkar Vitthal Krishna at p. 251, Sapte Vinayak Dharma at p. 302 and Shirodkar Raghunath Pundalik at p. 329, Fernandes (2011) at p. 113.

45. Journalist Carlos da Cruz[†]: Chandor, was active in Bombay in the early 1940s, was the subject of much diplomatic correspondence between the Portuguese in Goa and the British in Bombay. Was under the watch of Bombay police, summoned and warned several times about his nationalistic writings. He moved to Dadra and Nagar Haveli from 1954 (*oHERALDo*, edition of 25 August 2010).

46. Teacher Celina Olga Moniz: born Mombassa 1926, joined satyagraha movement in Goa, was jailed but later asked for pardon at the Military Tribunal in Panjim, migrated back to Africa in 1957, was a schoolteacher, then settled in London. *Goa Gazetteer* vol. 1 listing at p. 224 and references, among others, under Pai Srirang Vishnu at p. 254, Fernandes (2011) at p. 109, Kanekar (2011) at p. 54.

47. Militant Chagas de Cunha: Chinchinim, participated in underground nationalist activities of AGD, arrested in Colem, released for young age on condition that he should not leave Goa. He escaped and was part of the action in freeing Dadra & Nagar Haveli. *Goa Gazetteer* vol. 1 listing at p. 53, Fernandes (2011) at p. 50.

48. Militant Christopher Silva Lobo: Velim, joined the AGD after 2nd year Portuguese Lyceum, was arrested in Margao, detained and later shifted to Panjim jail. *Goa Gazetteer* vol. 1 listing at p. 199, Fernandes (2011) at p. 92.

49. Dr Clementino J.N.L. Jorge: Carmona, medical doctor, his house was raided and a copy of the Constitution of India and other 'incriminating' documents seized. Tried and sentenced to rigorous imprisonment and fine. *Goa Gazetteer* vol. 1 listing at p. 137, Fernandes (2011) at p. 88.

50. Cristovam (Kaka) Furtado: *Goa Gazetteer* vol. 1 reference under Desai Vaman Narayan at p. 81, Kanekar (2011) at first photo after p. 90.

51. Adv. Cristovam Furtado: Chinchinim, rebelled against Portuguese authority in Mozambique, deported to Goa, formed the CRC Club in Chinchinim that was dissolved by the Portuguese in 1946, demanded the release of Dr Jose Maria Furtado (at no. 132 below) and was promptly put behind bars, president of NCG-Bombay branch in 1950, founder general secretary of United Front of Goans (hereafter UFG), Bombay in 1952, vice-president of UGP in 1962, spurned the Tamrapatra on grounds that he only did his moral duty. *Goa Gazetteer* vol. 1 listing at p. 103 and referred, among others, under Kakodkar Chandrakant Bapu at p. 147, Fernandes (2011) at p. 75.

52. Militant Cristovam Gabriel Paulo das Angustias Furtado: Chinchinim (not be confused with the other famed civil and criminal advocate of Goa by the same name and from the same village at no. 51), AGD, participated in the

liberation of Nagar Haveli in 1954. In Goa, he carried out subversive activities, was arrested in 1955 and sentenced to six years' rigorous imprisonment. His car was seized and sold in public auction. *Goa Gazetteer* vol. 1 listing at pp. 103–104, references under Fernandes Roque Santana at p. 101 and Kenkre Rajnikant (Rajaram) at p. 178, Fernandes (2011) at p. 77.

53. Militant Cruz Viegas†: RP, *Goa Gazetteer* vol. 2 reference under Viegas Eusebio Martires at p. 124, Fernandes (2011) at p. 155.

54. Prof. Dionisio Ribeiro†: Margao–Raia, referenced by journo-freedom fighter Evagrio Jorge in his book *Goa's Awakening* at p. 10.

55. Domingos Aguiar: Cuncolim, joined the freedom struggle with Dr Ram Manohar Lohia's meet at Margao on 18 June 1946, fled to Bombay to avoid arrest. *Goa Gazetteer* vol. 1 listing at p. 6, Fernandes (2011) at p. 18.

56. Dr Eclito de Souza: Assolna, was vice president of East African Goan League, constantly wrote to the western media about Goa, was part of the delegation sent by Government of India to make a factual report on the aftermath of 19 December 1961. Listing at *Goa Gazetteer* vol. 2 pp. 113–14, Fernandes (2011) at p. 145.

57. Dr Eduardo Furtado: co-organized together with Dr Jose Maria Furtado (at no. 132 below) a *Prabhatferi* in Chinchinim in 1947. *Goa Gazetteer* vol. 1 reference under AGD activist Kolvenkar Dattaram Ganesh at p. 187.

58. Edward Soares†: Aldona, educationist and founder of St Thomas Boys School (1923, when he was just twenty-five years of age), brother of the English grammar author Anthony Soares. His statue occupies a prominent place in the village.

59. Elphinstone Dias†: *Goa Gazetteer* vol. 1 references under Lobo Jose Piedade at p. 200 and under Palekar Gangadhar Govind at p. 256.

60. Militant Emiterio Sebastiao Paes: Assolna, was dismissed from government service, participated in the liberation movement of Dadra and Nagar Haveli, was publicity officer of UFG from 1951 to 1961 in Bombay. *Goa Gazetteer* vol. 1 listing at p. 251 and references under Almeida Felix at p. 7 and George Louis Pereira at p. 119, Fernandes (2011) at p. 20.

61. Ex-MLA Enio Pimenta: Curtorim, graduate in arts and teacher by profession, offered satyagraha in Margao on 21 June 1946 with Purushottam Kakodkar, wrote for national mastheads on Goa's freedom struggle, escaped to Bombay to evade arrest, joined NCG Bombay branch, assisted Dr Telo Mascarenhas in editing English section of *Resurge Goa*. *Goa Gazetteer* vol. 1 listing at p. 280 and reference under Shinkre Janardan Jagannath (later the first general secretary of MGP from 1962 and elected MP, Lok Sabha, in 1967) at p. 322, Fernandes (2011) at p. 116. Newspaper statement, 1987.

62. Dr Eric D'Melo[†]: was secretary of NCG, Bombay Branch, in 1948, Fernandes (2011) at p. 30.

63. Militant Ernesto Costa Frias[†]: member of RP, *Goa Gazetteer* vol. 2 references under Sinari Dinkar Vitthal Porobo and under Sinari Purushottam ('Syam') Vitthal Porob (both brothers of Prabhakar V. Sinari, IPS, former RP leader) all at p. 110, Kanekar (2011) at pp. 66, 152.

64. Militant Eusebio Martires P. Viegas: Chinchinim, member of RP, mined the rail line between Chandor and Margao, rearrested for last time in June 1961 and released 19 December 1961. Listing in *Goa Gazetteer* vol. 2 pp. 124–25 and reference in *Goa Gazetteer* vol. 1 under Fernandes Artur at p. 99, Fernandes (2011) at p. 155.

65. Journo/Editor Evagrio Francisco Jorge: Carmona, as a twenty-one-year-old youth then with the Portuguese-language daily *oHERALDo,* met Dr Ram Manohar Lohia

and participated in his movement, wrote copiously on the Goa problem, including *Goa's Awakening: Reminiscences of the 1946 Civil Disobedience Movement*. Wrote about sixteen booklets and pamphlets between 1942 and 1961. Was tried and sentenced to imprisonment a number of times. Worked in All India Radio up to 1970 and then edited the Konkani daily *Uzvadd*. *Goa Gazetteer* vol. 1 listing at pp. 137–38 and referred, among others, under Kakodkar Purushottam at p. 149, Kudchadkar Shivaji Venkatesh at p. 191 and Sardesai Vaman Balkrishna Naique Prataprau at p. 305, Fernandes (2011) at p. 89. Shirodkar, *My Life in Exile*, 2012, pp. 15, 28 and 41.

66. Journalist F.M. Pinto[†]: Fernandes (2011) at p. 122.
67. Fabiao de Costa: Seraulim, was born in Zanzibar in 1928, arrested first time in June 1954, again in 1955 serving a longer prison sentence that included fifteen days' solitary confinement. *Goa Gazetteer* vol. 1 listing at p. 52 and references under Nagvenkar Jaiwant Vitthal at p. 229 and Nagvenkar Sadanand Purushottam at p. 230, Fernandes (2011) at p. 45, Kanekar (2011) at pp. 71–72 and 113. Newspaper statement, 1987.
68. Journo/Editor Felicio Cardoso (Felicio Xavier Esperdiao Caetano da Rosa Cardoso): Seraulim, wrote extensively about Goa in the Bombay media, participated in the freedom struggle in Goa, later started his own periodicals from Margao in Romi Konkani, high school teacher by profession. *Goa Gazetteer* vol. 1 listing at p. 38 and references, among others, under Verenkar Venkatesh Krishna (who rushed to shield Dr Ram Manohar when Portuguese police pointed a handgun at Lohia in Margao and was not allowed to attend his young daughter's funeral for refusing to abjure from nationalistic activities) at p. 372, Fernandes (2011) at p. 40, Kanekar (2011) at pp. 38 and 153–54.

69. Felix Almeida: Velim–Margao, born in Calcutta, mobilized opinion for Goa there, rushed medicines for satyagrahis in August 1955 with the help of the Indian Medical Association and pharma companies. *Goa Gazetteer* vol. 1 listing at p. 7, Fernandes (2011) at p. 20.

70. Journo Felix Valois Rodrigues: Chicalim, was based in Karachi and participated in the Quit India Movement. Worked with MPs Joachim and Violet Alva, Adv. Joachim Dias, journalist F.M. Pinto and others for the sake of Goa's freedom. *Goa Gazetteer* vol. 1 listing at p. 296, Fernandes (2011) at p. 122.

71. Adv. Fernando Costa†: Fernandes (2011) at p. 148. Was active right ever since his student days in Portugal.

72. Fernando Gomes†: an associate of Felicio Cardoso, *Goa Gazetteer* vol. 1 reference at p. 38, Fernandes (2011) at p. 40.

73. Filipe Cardozo†: *Goa Gazetteer* vol. 1 reference under Kelkar Pandurang Anant at p. 175.

74. Journo Flaviano Piedade Francis Dias: Velim, returned to Goa after doing MA, plunged in underground work in Goa but had to escape to Bombay to avoid arrest. Post 1961, he was general secretary of Bombay Union of Journalists and organizing secretary of Maharashtra Union of Working Journalists for long years and after a lifetime of journalism in Bombay, returned as PTI correspondent in Goa where he was president of Goa Union of Journalists. *Goa Gazetteer* vol. 1 listing at p. 94 and reference under Naik Rohidas Harishchandra at p. 241, Fernandes (2011) at p. 58.

75. Priest Fr Furtado: Pilerne, *Goa Gazetteer* vol. 1 reference under Shinkre Janardan Jagannath (later the first general secretary of MGP from 1962 and elected MP, Lok Sabha, in 1967) at p. 322.

76. Priest Fr Pinto: Guirim, *Goa Gazetteer* vol. 1 reference under Shinkre Janardan Jagannath (later the first general

secretary of MGP from 1962 and elected MP, Lok Sabha, in 1967) at p. 322.

77. Militant Francis (Francisco) Mascarenhas: was president of the militant UFG in Bombay in 1951 with Vaman N. Desai as general secretary. Led a group of thirty-five UFG volunteers in the liberation of Dadra on 23 July 1954. *Goa Gazetteer* vol. 1 reference under Desai Vaman Narayan at p. 80.

78. Prof. Francisco Correia-Afonso: Benaulim, Chancellor's Gold Medallist at MA, ex Oxford, principal of several colleges, wrote and articulated extensively on the Goa situation. Was founder member of Goa Liberation Council. *Goa Gazetteer* vol. 1 listing at p. 4 and references, among others, under Sardesai Vaman Balkrishna Naique Prataprau at p. 305, Fernandes (2011) at p. 17.

79. Francisco Menezes: *Goa Gazetteer* vol. 1 reference under Chimulkar Govind P.P. at p. 45.

80. Dr Frank de Sequeira†: Panjim, businessman, brother of later day political leader Dr Jack de Sequeira of the United Goans Party. Was arrested in the mid-1950s.

81. Militant Frank Raphael Paul Andrades: Parra, born in Bombay 1918, post-graduated in arts, quit the Anglo-Iranian Oil Co. in Iran, supported the Naval Mutiny in Bombay, immersed in the Goa freedom struggle from 1946 in militant underground activity of Quit Goa Organisation (hereafter, QGO), when he refused to remove his Gandhi *topi* in a Mapusa Court, his house in Parra was seized and sold in auction by the colonial regime. *Goa Gazetteer* vol. 1 listing at pp. 12–13, references under Chandelkar Gopinath Sriniwas Prabhu at p. 41 and Shinkre Janardan Jagannath at p. 322, Fernandes (2011) at p. 29. *Goa Gazetteer, Trial of the Four*, p. 9.

82. Franklin Moraes†: Cuncolim, associate of Albert L.R. Fernandes (at no. 2 above) and Antonio Conceicao

Fernandes (at no. 16 above), was arrested in 1954 for offering satyagraha at Ponda and sentenced to five years' simple imprisonment. *Goa Gazetteer* vol. 1 reference under Fernandes Antonio Conceicao at p. 99, Fernandes (2011) at p. 65.

83. Former MLA/Speaker of the Goa Legislative Assembly Froilano Carmelino da Rocha Machado: Nagoa–Verna, hailed from a *Morgado* family with its own coat of arms. *Goa Gazetteer* vol. 1 listing at p. 203 and reference under Desai Narendra Govind Hegde at p. 72, Fernandes (2011) at p. 98. Newspaper statement, 1987.

84. Dy. S.P. (Goa Police) Fulgencio Moraes†: Veroda, was an underground activist with the AGD. Underwent arms and explosives training at Amboli Camp in 1956. *Goa Gazetteer* vol. 1 reference under Pednekar Bhagwant Damodar at p. 274, Fernandes (2011) at pp. 50 and147.

85. Dr Gambeta da Costa: Margao; hailing from a large land-owning family, he was a Gandhian who led a group of Salcete allopathic medical practitioners who were not only conversant with Gandhian philosophy but changed their western attire to khadi kurta-pyjama and even a Gandhi topi. The urn carrying Mahatma Gandhi's ashes was displayed for public homage at his Padre Miranda mansion in Margao before immersion in the sea at Colva beach. Dr Gambeta da Costa was registered as a bonafide Freedom Fighter under no. 1233, as per a certificate issued by Home Department of the Goa Government.

86. George Francisco Caetano Andrade: Ambajim–Margao, composed poems on nationalistic themes, arrested in June 1954, post-1961 worked as supervisor in a mining company. *Goa Gazetteer* vol. 1 listing at p. 12, references under Bhat Vaikunth Narsinva at p. 23, Desai Narendra Govind Hegde at p. 72 and Kerkar Chandrakant at p. 179, Fernandes (2011) at p. 28, Kanekar (2011) at pp. 38 and 119.

87. Militant George Louis Pereira†: St Estevam, after MA, he joined the Goa Action Committee (hereafter, GAC) in Bombay, was beaten by Portuguese police at a public meeting at Mapusa in 1946, was betrayed and arrested on the night he brought a hand bomb to be planted at Adil Shah palace and served a four-year sentence. Shifted back to Bombay and participated in meetings, processions and hartals, Fernandes (2011) at p. 84.

88. Trade Union Leader George Vaz: born in Bombay 1919, was first arrested in Sanquelim in 1946, he was art director of several films like *Lal Batti*, participated in the three-day Casablanca Conference in April 1961 together with Dr Pundalik Gaitonde and Cajetan Lobo. Was founder-member of the Goan People's Party (hereafter, GPP) in Bombay. *Goa Gazetteer* vol. 1 listing and references, among others, under Madkaikar Shamrao Narayan at p. 205, Mandrekar Jaiwant Mukund Shenvi at p. 209, Mense Krishna Parasharam at p. 222, Palekar Gangadhar Govind at p. 256, Palekar Narayan Vitthal at p. 257, Shetye Jairam Vaikunth at p. 318, Shinkre Janardan Jagannath (later the first general secretary of MGP from 1962 and elected MP, Lok Sabha, in 1967) at p. 322, Shirsat Sridhar Sadashiv at p. 331, Fernandes (2011) at p. 153. Shirodkar, *My Life in Exile*, 2012, p. 21. Newspaper statement, 1987. *Goa Gazetteer, Trial of the Four*, in Biographical Sketch of Nilkanth M. Karapurkar, p. 1 thereof (unnumbered page) and p. 22.

89. Trade Union Leader Adv. Gerald Xavier Pereira: based in Vasco da Gama, wrote several monograms, was the first trade unionist in free Goa, organizing the Mormugao Port and Dock Workers Union in 1962. *Goa Gazetteer* vol. 1 listing at p. 278 and reference under Lamberto Emilio Francisco Mascarenhas Lambert at p. 215, Fernandes (2011) at p. 114.

90. Glorio Rosario Furtado: Cusmane–Quepem, joined the NCG in 1947, wrote patriotic songs and articles, started a free English school in Quepem in 1949, arrested twice in the late 1950s. *Goa Gazetteer* vol. 1 listing at p. 104, Fernandes (2011) at p. 78.

91. Gosalino Coutinho[†]: *Goa Gazetteer* vol. 1 reference under Desai Devidas Ramkrishna Prabhu, p. 63.

92. Guilherme de Souza Ticlo: Assagao–Saligao, although born in Zanzibar 1911, was a teacher, he resigned and plunged into the freedom movement organizing the NCG, was its vice president and then general secretary. Arrested in 1947, he was deported to Angola. He was accused no.1 in the *Trial of the Four* who were tried together and exiled together, the three others being acc. no. 2, Adv. Pandurang P. Shirodkar (Sr) president NCG, acc. no. 3 Nilkanth Manguesh Karapurkar, executive member NCG and acc. no. 4 Dr Vinayak N. Sinai Mayenkar, treasurer NCG. (Also arrested were brothers Ramkrishna Farjand, owner and Mahadev Farjand, compositor, who printed material for NCG at Laxmi Printing Press, Mapusa.) *Goa Gazetteer* vol. 1 listing at pp. 353–54 and references, among others, under Karapurkar Nilkanth at pp. 165–66, Kunde Jaiwant Sinai at p. 193, Lawande Vishwanath Narayan at p. 197 (last line), Mayenkar (Dr) Vinayak Narayan at p. 219, Shirodkar Pandurang Purushottam at p. 327, Fernandes (2011) at p. 150. Shirodkar, *My Life in Exile*, 2012, pp. 25, 29, 45, 50, 114 and 143. *Goa Gazetteer, Trial of the Four*, in Biographical Sketch of Pandurang Purushottam Shirodkar, p. 2 thereof and at Biographical Sketch of Guilherme de Souza Ticlo (both unnumbered pages) and then practically throughout the book, *Trial of the Four*.

93. Adv. Gilman Fernandes: Cuncolim, was with the Bombay branch of AGD.

94. Guilman D'Souza[†]: *Goa Gazetteer* vol. 1 reference under Lawande Sriniwas Janardan at p. 196.

95. Dr H. C. Denis/Diniz[†]: co-founder and chairman of the Goa League in London. Secretary of the League was Adv. João Cabral (at no. 113 below).

96. Rev. Fr (Dr) Hubert OlympioMascarenhas: Porvorim, a versatile linguist including in Sanskrit, he was principal of several schools in Bombay, authored several books, especially on religions and religious philosophies. Brother of the famous engineer, William Xavier Mascarenhas who was the first Indian principal of the College of Engineering, Poona, member of the War Memorial Committee, designed the campus of the National Defence Academy at Khadakvasla, was later chief engineer of Maharashtra and the first chairman of Goa Planning Board. *Goa Gazetteer* vol. 1 listing at pp. 215–16 and references, among others, under prominent Hindu priest and Marathi litterateur Joshi Pandit Mahadev Shastri at p. 142, Fernandes (2011) at p. 101.

97. Ignatius de Souza: Aldona, imprisoned for six years and released in September 1958. *Goa Gazetteer* vol. 1 listing at p. 337, Fernandes (2011) at p. 138.

98. Militant Ilidio (Elidio) Francisco do Carmo Costa: Betim, he graduated in arts but joined the militant RP, participated in underground subversive activities, arrested and tortured. Listing at *Goa Gazetteer* vol. 1 at p. 52. References in *Goa Gazetteer* vol. 1 under Halarnkar Gajanan Govind at p. 125, in *Goa Gazetteer* vol. 2 under Antonio Jose Costa Frias at p. 29, Sinari Dinkar Vitthal Porobo and Sinari Purushottam ('Syam') Vitthal Porob (both brothers of Prabhakar V. Sinari, IPS, former RP leader) all at p. 110, Fernandes (2011) at p. 46. Newspaper Statement, *oHERALDo*, edition of 2 February 1987.

99. Inacinho Lobo: Chinchinim, was a medical compounder, participated in Quit India Movement in Bombay, was summoned to Margao police station on suspicion in 1951 but was detained and interrogated for several days. *Goa Gazetteer* vol. 2 listing at pp. 63–64, Fernandes (2011) at p. 97.

100. Inacinho Martinho Santana de Souza: Aldona, worked at BEST in Bombay before plunging into the Goa freedom movement. Was sentenced to three years' imprisonment. *Goa Gazetteer* vol. 1 listing at p. 338, Fernandes (2011) at p. 139.

101. Militant Inacinho Viegas[†]: RP activist who participated in subversive activities. *Goa Gazetteer* vol. 2 reference under Viegas Eusebio Martires P. at p. 125, Fernandes (2011) at p. 155.

102. Irene Heredia[†]: Divar, hailed from one of the leading Goan business families in Bombay, Fernandes (2011) at p. 92.

103. Adv. J. Carvalho: referenced in Shirodkar, *My Life in Exile*, 2012, pp. 35 and 37. Newspaper statement, 1987.

104. J. Mendes: *Goa Gazetteer* vol. 1 reference under CPI-affiliated trade union leader Palekar Narayan Vitthal at p. 257.

105. J.J. Pinto[†]: Fernandes (2011) at p. 138.

106. Journo J.M. Pinto (*The Times of India*)[†]: active in Bombay, *Goa Gazetteer* vol. 1 references under Afonso Francisco Correia at p. 4, Lobo Caetano/Cajetan Ludger Teodor at p. 199, Mascarenhas Emilio Francisco Lamberto alias Mascarenhas Lambert at p. 215, Fernandes (2011) at pp. 17, 92 and 100.

107. Jacinto de Souza: Majorda, escaped arrest in 1954 by fleeing to Belgaum. *Goa Gazetteer* vol. 1 listing at p. 338 and reference under Cardoso Felicio at p. 38, Fernandes (2011) at p. 140.

108. University Lecturer James (Jaime) Fernandes: Assonora, joined NCG in 1954. He was captured by Portuguese

Captain Santos Borges, arrested in March 1955 and was sentenced to ten years' rigorous imprisonment plus four years' simple imprisonment. *Goa Gazetteer* vol. 1 listing at pp. 99–100 and references under Chodankar Kashinath Rama at p. 48 and Pereira Januario Joaquim at p. 279, Fernandes (2011) at p. 68.

109. Januario Joaquim Pereira: born in Jodhpur in the Marwar district of Rajasthan in 1908, he graduated in arts and plunged into the Goa freedom struggle. He was tried and sentenced to nine years' rigorous imprisonment. *Goa Gazetteer* vol. 1 listing at p. 279, Fernandes (2011) at p. 115, Kanekar (2011) at p. 64.

110. Jeremias Lobo[†]: NCG activist, *Goa Gazetteer* vol. 1 reference under Thali Ramchandra Trivikram at p. 352.

111. Jeremias ('Jerry') Francis Pinto: Aldona, accountant by profession. Joined NCG and held secret meetings together with Mohan Nair, tried and sentenced to three years' rigorous imprisonment. *Goa Gazetteer* vol. 1 listing at p. 281, Fernandes (2011) at p. 117, Kanekar (2011) at p. 64.

112. J.N. Heredia[†]: Divar, belonged to one of the leading Goan business families in Bombay of the time who started a general insurance business (subsequently nationalized) and a steamer service between Bombay and Goa. Founded the Goan National Union (GNU) in Bombay. *Goa Gazetteer* vol. 1 reference under Mascarenhas Emilio Francisco Lamberto alias Mascarenhas Lambert at p. 215, Fernandes (2011) at p. 100.

113. Adv. /Goa's first Advocate General Joachim Dias: Cuncolim, participated in the Indian freedom movement when a student of BA, LLB, was arrested in Castlerock and fined in Belgaum, was founder president of Goan Youth League, Bombay (1943), met Mahatma Gandhi in Pune and Nehru in Delhi, and helped create awareness among the masses. *Goa Gazetteer* vol. 1 listing at pp. 94–95 and referred, among others, under Kakodkar Chandrakant Bapu at p. 146,

Kakodkar Divakar Balkrishna at p. 148 and writer-journalist Pandit Raghunath Vishnu at p. 261, Fernandes (2011) at p. 59. Shirodkar, *My Life in Exile*, 2012, p. 298.

114. Advocate João Francisco Caraciolo Cabral: Nagoa–Verna, co-founder of the Goan League in London, attended the Conference on Colonialism in Delhi, 20–23 October 1961, represented Angola, Mozambique and Guinea organizations and part of Committee of African Organisations (CAO) in London, addressed the House of Commons in London and spoke in Rabat, Sweden and Belgium. He returned to Goa post 1961 and started a business. He was father of Goa Cabinet Minister Nilesh Cabral and brother of José Cabral, who had a famous bicycle shop *(Jos Cabral)* in Margao. *Goa Gazetteer* vol. 1 listing at pp. 37–38, Fernandes (2011) at p. 38.

115. Joaozinho Furtado: Chinchinim. Details not known.

116. Joao Joaquim Lourdinho da Cunha: Cansaulim, arrested in Vasco da Gama and detained without trial, suffered imprisonment for four years. *Goa Gazetteer* vol. 1 listing at p. 54, Fernandes (2011) at p. 51.

117. Joaquim Araujo†: referred to in *Goa Gazetteer*, vol. 1 under Afonso Alfred at pp. 3–4 and under Mayenkar Pandurang Sukdo at p. 218, Fernandes (2011) at p. 128.

118. Ex-MLA Joaquim Luis Gonsalo Araujo: Santa Cruz–Kalapur, participated in Quit India Movement and joined the Goa Youth League (GYL) in Bombay. He returned to Goa, was arrested, and served three years in jail. He attended the Afro-Asian Conference in 1961 in New Delhi, was elected member of the first Goa Legislative Assembly in 1963. *Goa Gazetteer*, vol. 1 listing at p. 14, Fernandes (2011) at p. 31.

119. Joaquim Joao Carvalho†: referred to in *Goa Gazetteer* vol. 1 under Desai Sripad Goona, at p. 79.

120. Joaquim Xavier Pinto: Bodiem–Bardez, joined the NCG after matriculation in 1954 and participated in subversive

activities, arrested in 1955, sentenced to two-and-a-half years' imprisonment. *Goa Gazetteer* vol. 1 listing at p. 281, and reference under Souza Inacinho Martinho Santana de at p. 338, Fernandes (2011) at p. 118.

121. Dr (Homeopathy) John Carvalho†: Veroda–Cuncolim, participated in India's freedom struggle from 1929 and later that of Goa, writing articles in the Bombay and Calcutta press, arrested in 1951 but was acquitted. *Goa Gazetteer* vol. 1 listing at p. 39 and references under Bir Madhav Ramkrishna Pai at p. 30, Dubhashi Shivaji Raoji at p. 97 and Shirodkar Madhusudan Purushottam (brother of P.P. Shirodkar Sr) at p. 326, Fernandes (2011) at p. 42.

122. Dr (Ayurveda) John Costa Bir: Nagoa–Verna, was with the Sadakat Ashram in Santa Cruz, Bombay, when he joined the underground AGD and was active at the borders in Sawantwadi and Banda. *Goa Gazetteer* vol. 1 listing at p. 29, Fernandes (2011) at p. 33.

123. Militant John Gilbert Rebello: Revora–Bardez but born in Tanzania, co-founded the QGO, led a number of armed actions in Pernem and Bardez including an attack on Mapusa police station. *Goa Gazetteer* vol. 1 listing at p. 295, references, among others, under Andrade Frank Rafael Paul at p. 13, Bir (Dr) John Costa at p. 29, Cuncolienkar Pandurang Ramchandra Shenvi at p. 53, Gaundalkar Ravindra Vassudev at p. 116, Karpe Govind Shamba at p. 171, Keni Bala Vasu at p. 176, Khalap Chandrakant Ganpat at p. 183, Shetye Govind Vasudev at p. 317, Shinkre Janardan Jagannath at p. 322, Shinkre Vaikunth Jagannath Prabhu at p. 322 and Simepurushkar Tukaram Dhaku at p. 333, Fernandes (2011) at p. 121.

124. Ex-MLA John Mariano (J.M.) D'Souza: Siolim, co-founded the GNU in Bombay in 1954, wrote nationalist pamphlets, was held in Goa and was released by the Indian Army on 19 December 1961. He was founder-member of UGP and elected MLA of the first Goa Legislative Assembly in 1963.

Goa Gazetteer vol. 2 listing at p. 114 and reference in *Goa Gazetteer* vol. 1 under Lobo Porfirio Maria Gaspar Silva at p. 200, Fernandes (2011) at p. 146.

125. Jose Antonio do Rosario Alvares: Chinchinim, commanded the Portuguese garrison at Tiracol on 15 August 1954 when he ordered his men to abandon the fort and run away at the first sight of fifteen unarmed satyagrahis. He was dismissed from service and imprisoned for three-and-a-half years. *Goa Gazetteer* vol. 1 listing at pp. 9–10, Fernandes (2011) at p. 25.

126. Dr Jose Francisco Martins: Salvador do Mundo, offered Satyagraha in the freedom movement of India when still a student at Dharwar in 1942, joined the NCG and with his associates decided to organize Satyagraha campaign from 2 October 1954, arrested same year and sentenced to eight years' rigorous imprisonment. *Goa Gazetteer* vol. 1 listing at p. 214 and references, among others, under Dubashi (Dr) Ganba Naguexa Sinai at p. 97, under Kamat Gopal Apa at p. 153, under Madkaikar Shamrao Narayan at p. 205, under Priolkar Prafull V at page 286 and under Sardesai Shankar Pandurang Naik Prataprao at p. 304, Fernandes (2011) at p. 99, Kanekar (2011) at p. 26. Newspaper statement, 1987.

127. Adv. Jose Inacio ('Fanchu') de Loyola Jr: Orlim, was parliamentary secretary to Labour Minister of Portugal, co-founded *A Voz da India* with Vicente Joao Figueiredo (see under pharmacist Antonio Sequeira at no. 24 above), to champion autonomy for Goa, deported and imprisoned in Portugal. Met Pandit Nehru a couple of times but was not in favour of Goa's integration with India. *Goa Gazetteer* vol. 1 listing at pp. 202–203, Fernandes (2011) at p. 96. Shirodkar, *My Life in Exile*, 2012, pp. 16, 20 and 55.

128. Jose Jeremias Lobo: Oxel–Bardez, joined the freedom movement after 3rd year Lyceum and Secondary School in English, arrested in 1955 and sentenced to three years

jail, rearrested 1 February 1960 and released 19 December 1961. *Goa Gazetteer* vol. 1 listing at p. 199 and references under Harmalkar Ramnath Raghunath at p. 129, under Harmalkar Srikant Murari at p. 129 and under Naik Vaman Vasu at p. 245, Fernandes (2011) at p. 93.

129. Jose Joachim (Joaquim) Lume Pereira[†]: referred to in *Goa Gazetteer* vol. 1 under Shinkre Janardan Jagannath (later the first General Secretary of MGP from 1962 and elected Lok Sabha MP from 1967) at p. 322.

130. Jose Ladislau Saldanha: St Estevam, worked for freedom under various organizations after completing secondary school in English. He was arrested in Canacona and served the sentence of imprisonment at Aguada jail. *Goa Gazetteer* vol. 1 listing at p. 299, Fernandes (2011) at p. 128, Kanekar (2011) at p. 41.

131. Jose Lourdes Gomes: associate of Felicio Cardoso. *Goa Gazetteer* vol. 1 listing at p. 38 and reference under Souza Jacinto de at p. 338, Fernandes (2011) at pp. 40 and 140.

132. Militant Jose Manuel ('Manuelinho') Viegas[†]: associate of Mukund Pawar, Roque Santan Fernandes and A.R. Polly Silva (RP). References in *Goa Gazetteer* vol. 1 under Fernandes Roque Santan at p. 101, Kenkre Rajnikant (Rajaram) at p. 178 and Matha Prabhakar Narayan Sinai at p. 217, Fernandes (2011) at pp. 71, 132 and 148.

133. Dr Jose Maria Furtado[†]: brother of Advocate/Judge Dr Antonio Furtado (at no. 17 above) who was married to Berta de Menezes Braganza (at no. 38 above), was a popular medical practitioner in his native Chinchinim. He co-organized with Dr Eduardo Furtado (at no. 57 above) a *Prabhatferi* in Chinchinim in 1947. Was president of NCG in 1948. References in *Goa Gazetteer* vol. 1 under Kolvenkar Dattaram Ganesh (AGD activist, of post-parcel-bombs fame) at p. 187, Kurade Gopinath Krishna Naik at p. 194, Sanzguiri (Dr) Kashinath Ladu at p. 301. Shirodkar, *My Life in Exile*, 2012, pp. 35 and 36.

134. Jose Minguel Saldanha†: *Goa Gazetteer* vol. 1 reference under Desai Narendra Govind Hegde at p. 72.

135. Dr Jose Vicente Paulo Francisco Gomes: St Estevam, US-trained surgeon who headed the frontline medical team during the 15 August 1955 satyagraha on Goa's borders. Was dismissed from Health Services by the colonial government in 1955. Continued to support the cause of Goa when in the US and collected contributions to the 'Defence of India Fund' in New York during the Chinese aggression in 1962. *Goa Gazetteer* vol. 2 listing at p. 37, Fernandes (2011) at p. 86.

136. Adv./Judge Jose Paulo Santana Desiderio Lucas Teles: Ponda, did legal studies in Lisbon where he co-founded *National Hindu Party* in 1925, resigned as substitute judge and defended T.B. Cunha at the TMT (military tribunal), subsequently defended various other nationalists and was blacklisted by the colonial regime. Was appointed additional judicial commissioner of Goa after 1961. *Goa Gazetteer* vol. 1 listing at p. 349 and references under Madkaikar Shamrao Narayan at p. 205, under Nachinolkar (Dr) Raghunath Vishram Prabhu at p. 228 and under Shirodkar Pandurang Purushottam at p. 327, Fernandes (2011) at p. 148. Shirodkar, *My Life in Exile*, 2012, p. 298. *Goa Gazetteer, Trial of the Four*, in Biographical Sketch of Pandurang Purushottam Shirodkar, p. 1 thereof (unnumbered page) and p. 61.

137. Jose Piedade (J.P.) Lobo: Bombay-based, always khadi clad, met Netaji Subhas Chandra Bose and pleaded for the inclusion of Goa in India's freedom struggle. *Goa Gazetteer* vol. 1 listing at p. 200 and reference under Mayenkar Vitthal alias Ana Narayan at p. 220 and under Palekar Gangadhar Govind at p. 256, Fernandes (2011) at p. 94.

138. Teacher Joseph Godinho†: Aldona, inculcated a sense of nationalism among his students, *Goa Gazetteer* vol. 1 reference under Pereira Januario Joaquim at p. 279, Kanekar (2011) at p. 64.

139. Juliao Caridade ('JC') de Souza: Socorro–Bardez, was detained by Bombay Police for organizing 'Black Flag' demonstration against visiting Portuguese Goa governor-general, was later in government service in Bombay. *Goa Gazetteer* vol. 1 listing at p. 338, Fernandes (2011) at p. 141.

140. Juliao da Costa†: *Goa Gazetteer* vol. 1 reference under Souza Jacinto de at p. 338, Fernandes (2011) at p. 140.

141. Dr Juliao de Menezes: Assolna, did MD in Berlin (friend of Ram Manohar Lohia who studied at the same university), brought Lohia to Goa on 10 June 1946 and was thus responsible for rekindling the Goa freedom struggle with the public meeting at Margao on 18 June 1946. *Goa Gazetteer* vol. 1 listing at pp. 220–21 and references, among others, under Karmalkar Atmaram (Apa) Narsinha at p. 171, Madkaikar Narsinha at p. 204 and Manjrekar Vasant Ganpat at p. 212, Fernandes (2011) at p. 106. Shirodkar, *My Life in Exile*, 2012, pp. 4 and 28. *Goa Gazetteer, Trial of the Four*, p. 14.

142. L.A. Rodrigues†: *Goa Gazetteer* vol. 1 reference under Costa Luis Antonio de at p. 52.

143. Lopes (first name not known)†: *Goa Gazetteer* vol. 2 reference under Shankhwalkar Prabhakar Krishna Kamat at p. 104.

144. Journalist/editor/author Lambert Mascarenhas alias Emilio Francisco Lamberto Mascarenhas: Colva, served as information officer in the External Affairs Ministry, Government of India during late 1950s, vowed not to marry until Goa was free (a vow he kept), was joint editor of the *Navhind Times* (Goa), then started his own monthly *Goa Today* and passed away at the ripe old age of 100+. *Goa Gazetteer* vol. 1 listing at pp. 214–15 and reference under Desai Vaman Narayan at p. 81, Fernandes (2011) at p. 100. Newspaper statement, 1987.

145. Dr Laura Souza Rodrigues: Parra, wife of Prof. Lucio Rodrigues (at no. 149 below), gave up medical practice to plunge into the Goa freedom struggle. *Goa Gazetteer* vol.

1 listing at p. 296 and references under Gadekar Sadanand Mahadev at p. 106, Sanzguiri (Dr) Kashinath Ladu at p. 301, Sardesai Laxmanrao Sripad at p. 303 and Tamhankar Jagannath Arjun at p. 346, Fernandes (2011) at p. 123.

146. Militant Libano S. de Souza: born in Nairobi 1930, joined the QGO in 1954 and was active both in Bombay and Goa, where he was arrested at Altinho, Panjim. *Goa Gazetteer* vol. 1 listing at pp. 338–39 and reference under Chodankar Jayandrath Vitthal at p. 47. *Goa Gazetteer* vol. 2 reference under Prabhu Shyamsundar Atchyut at p. 92, Fernandes (2011) at p. 142.

147. Adv. Libia Lobo Sardesai: Porvorim, joined the GYL in 1947 but is known more for her underground radio station *Voice of Freedom* run together with Vaman B. Sardesai and Nicolau Menezes, broadcasting from Castle Rock and Belgaum since November 1955. Was very active on 18–19 December 1961, broadcasting from IAF aircraft flying overhead. She later married Vaman Sardesai. *Goa Gazetteer* vol. 1 listing at pp. 303–304, Fernandes (2011) at p. 129.

148. Ligorio Cota Carvalho[†]: Chandor–Margao, *Goa Gazetteer* vol. 1 reference under Rodolfo Almeida at p. 8, Fernandes (2011) at p. 22.

149. Lucio Miranda was a Lyceum teacher in Portugal, married to an Azorean from São Miguel. For the sake of Goa's freedom, he deserted his teaching job and Portugal, and moved to London to join the nationalist movement. (Edila Gaitonde, *As Maçãs Azuis,* p. 150.)

150. Dr Lucio Monteiro[†]: *Goa Gazetteer* vol. 1 reference under Palekar Gangadhar Govind at p. 256.

151. Prof. Lucio Rodrigues: Anjuna, taught in colleges in Dharwar, Bombay and, post-1961, at Dempe College, Panjim, edited *Goan Life* and authored *Soil and Soul* among other books in English on Konkani folk tales and folklore. *Goa Gazetteer* vol. 1 listing at p. 297 and references, among

others, under Sanzguiri (Dr) Kashinath Ladu at p. 301 and Sukhtankar Jagannath Sadashiv at p. 342. *Goa Gazetteer* vol. 2 reference under Borkar Vasant Pandurang at p. 11, Fernandes (2011) at p. 125.

152. Luis Cabral[†]: was part of the T.B. Cunha Memorial Committee chaired by Prof. D.D. Kosambi.

153. Luis Antonio ('Jose Luis') de Costa: Carmona, arrested in 1954. Was elected sarpanch of his village in 1975. *Goa Gazetteer* vol. 1 listing at p. 52, Fernandes (2011) at p. 47.

154. Adv. Luis (Louis) Gabriel Mendes: Velim, participated in Quit India Movement, his house in Velim was searched thrice by PIDE. He was appointed public prosecutor after liberation. *Goa Gazetteer* vol. 1 listing at p. 220 and references, among others, under Aguiar Domingos at p. 6 and Desai Gajanan Vitthal Prabhu, p. 64, Fernandes (2011) at p. 105.

155. Luis George[†]: Carmona (?), *Goa Gazetteer* vol. 1 reference under Keni Bala Vasu at p. 176.

156. Luis Gracias: Revora, joined the freedom movement in Bombay and after about four years shifted to Calcutta where he founded the branch of NCG. *Goa Gazetteer* vol. 1 listing at p. 123 and reference under Almeida Felix at p. 7, Fernandes (2011) at pp. 20 and 85.

157. Dr Luis Monteiro[†]: *Goa Gazetteer* vol. 1 reference under Lobo Jose Piedade at p. 200, Fernandes (2011) at p. 94.

158. Luis D'Souza[†]: based in Bombay, worked for the success of the 'Quit Goa' Resolution. *Goa Gazetteer* vol. 1 reference under Sukhtankar Jagannath Sadashiv at p. 341.

159. Eng. Luiz J. ('LJ') D'Souza[†]: served as member of the Dr T.B. Cunha Memorial Committee, *Goa Gazetteer* vol. 1 references under Lobo Jose Piedade at p. 200 and Silva Salvador Bermindo de ('SB') at p. 333, Fernandes (2011) at pp. 94 and 134.

160. Dr Luiza C. Pereira[†]: wife of Adv. Gerald Pereira (at no. 88 above), was a GPP sympathizer in Bombay, led the GVSS medical team to provide care during the 15 August 1955

satyagraha at Patradevi. *Goa Gazetteer* vol. 1 reference under Pereira Gerald Xavier at p. 278, Fernandes (2011) at p. 86.

161. M. Gonsalves[†]: *Goa Gazetteer* vol. 1 reference under Desai Manohar Vithoba at p. 69.

162. Militant Dr Manuel ('Manu') Estevam Fernandes: St Cruz/ Kalapur, member of GLA, he planted bombs at Margao Police Station and motor launch *Quintanilha* which exploded at Aldona in 1956, was arrested and imprisoned at Aguada three-and-a-half years. Prabhakar Sinari of RP often consulted him. *Goa Gazetteer* vol. 2 listing at pp. 28–29 and reference under Kantak (Dr) Ghanashyam Vinayak at p. 52, Fernandes (2011) at p. 80.

163. Maria Joaquina Calista Araujo: Siolim, arrested in 1947 and released in 1951, arrested again in 1956 and sentenced to fourteen years' rigorous imprisonment. *Goa Gazetteer*, vol. 1 listing at pp. 14–15, Fernandes (2011) at p. 32. Shirodkar, *My Life in Exile*, 2012, p. 23, Kanekar (2011) at photo caption.

164. Militant Mario Rodrigues: Cavelossim, worked for Indian Air Force but was influenced by the 1945 Naval Mutiny in Bombay, joined the AGD in 1947 and was its active member. *Goa Gazetteer* vol. 1 listing at pp. 297–98 and references under Mense Krishna Parasharam at p. 222 and Palekar Narayan Vitthal at p. 257, Fernandes (2011) at p. 126.

165. Trade Union Leader Mark Agostinho Fernandes: Calangute, born in Quetta–Baluchistan (now Pakistan) in 1926, was with Kuwait Oil Co. after Senior Cambridge but organized a Goan workers union there, came to Bombay 1946 and joined the GYL in 1951. Later joined the NCG and worked under the guidance of Peter Alvares, led twelve satyagrahis via Banda and Torxem–Pernem on 15 August 1954, arrested and sentenced to eight years' rigorous imprisonment. *Goa Gazetteer* vol. 1 listing at

p. 100, references, among others, under Hinde Chandrakant at p. 131, Karpe Govind Shamba at p. 171, Naik Uttam Dhakuji at p. 244, Narvenkar Shashikant Dutta at p. 249 and Fernandes (2011) at p. 69.

166. Journo Massilon de Almeida: Assolna, was a working journalist in Bombay, active throughout the liberation movement. *Goa Gazetteer* vol. 1 listing at p. 7, references, among others, under Karapurkar Vasant Mukund at p. 166, Palekar Gangadhar Govind at p. 256 and Sukhtankar Jagannath Sadashiv at p. 341, Fernandes (2011) at p. 21. Shirodkar, *My Life in Exile*, 2012, p. 6.

167. Mathew Rodrigues[†]: associate of Evagrio Jorge, L.A. de Costa, et al., *Goa Gazetteer* vol. 1 reference under Costa Luis Antonio de p. 52, Fernandes (2011) at p. 47.

168. Melba Dias Costa[†]: was active in Bombay. Wrote a scathing letter dated 23 April 1955 addressed to Paulo Bénard Guedes, the 'Governor General of Indian territories occupied militarily by the Portuguese', regards physical abuses by Portuguese police on unarmed satyagrahis including women.

169. Melicio Fernandes[†]: *Goa Gazetteer* vol. 1 reference under George Luis Pereira at p. 119, Fernandes (2011) at p. 84.

170. Dr Menino D'Souza[†]: *Goa Gazetteer* vol. 1 reference under Silva Salvador Bermindo ('SB') de at p. 333, Fernandes (2011) at p. 134.

171. Menino Fernandes: Colva, member of NCG, arrested at Pali–Usgao and sentenced to three-and-a-half years' rigorous imprisonment. *Goa Gazetteer* vol. 1 listing at pp. 100–101, Fernandes (2011) at p. 70.

172. Militant Mussolini Menezes: Tivim, after 3rd year Lyceum and matriculation in English, joined the NCG in 1947 but switched to AGD in 1954, his family in Goa faced much harassment from Portuguese police for his whereabouts. He remained outside Goa. *Goa Gazetteer* vol. 1 listing

at pp. 221–22 and reference under Lawande Sriniwas Janardan at p. 196. *Goa Gazetteer* vol. 2 references under Chaiwala Gopaldas Hiralal at p. 13 and Mistry (Mitna) Rambhai Govanbhai at p. 72, Fernandes (2011) at p. 108.

173. Teacher Nicolau Menezes[†]: Divar, also an educationist brother of Prof. Armando Menezes, assisted Vaman Sardesai and Libia Lobo (then unmarried) run the radio station *Voice of Freedom* from the forested areas around Goa. *Goa Gazetteer* vol. 1 references under George Luis Pereira at p. 119, Sardesai Libia Lobo at p. 304 and Sardesai Vaman Balkrishna Naique Prataprau at p. 305, Fernandes (2011) at pp. 84 and 129.

174. Adv. Norberto Carvalho or Antonio Norberto do Rosario Carvalho: Betalbatim, son of Erasmo Carvalho, participated in Quit India Movement in Pune where he studied, returned to Goa in 1947 to participate in the civil disobedience movement, arrested in 1954, wrote extensively on Portuguese barbarism in Goa, was rearrested in 1960. *Goa Gazetteer* vol. 1 listing at p. 38 and reference under Naik Yeshwant Vinayak at p. 246, Fernandes (2011) at p. 41.

175. Nuno Viegas[†]: an associate of Felico Cardoso, *Goa Gazetteer* vol. 1 reference under Cardoso Felicio at p. 38, Fernandes (2011) at p. 40.

176. Pascoal Rocha[†]: *Goa Gazetteer* vol. 1 reference under Souza Inacinho Martinho Santana de at p. 338, Fernandes (2011) at pp. 84 and 139.

177. Pedro Joao ('P.J.') Pinto: Aldona, passed Inter Science when he joined the NCG, was arrested in 1956 and sentenced to nine years' imprisonment. *Goa Gazetteer* vol. 1 listing at p. 282, Fernandes (2011) at p. 119.

178. Ex-MP Peter Alvares: Parra, quit a good job at the Bombay Port Trust to participate in the Quit India Movement, founded a number of trade unions in Bombay, was a leading member of Praja Socialist Party and was elected to the Bombay Presidency Legislative Assembly in 1949,

was president of the NCG in 1953, initiated the last phase of the Satyagraha Movement on 15 August 1954, and was later elected to the Lok Sabha from North Goa in 1963. *Goa Gazetteer* vol. 1 listing at p. 10 and references, among others, under Mascarenhas Emilio Francisco Lamberto alias Mascarenhas Lambert at p. 215 and Palekar Gangadhar Govind at p. 256, Fernandes (2011) at p. 26.

179. Militant Ponciano Pereira[†]: belonged to the militant RP, participated in subversive activities. *Goa Gazetteer* vol. 2 reference under Viegas Eusebio Martires at p. 125, Fernandes (2011) at p. 155.

180. Journo Porfirio Maria Gaspar Silva Lobo[†]: Assolna, after 3rd year Lyceum, did first-year arts and diploma in education and then joined NCG in Bombay, arrested in 1953 at Margao railway station and sentenced to one-and-a-half years in jail, later joined the *Diario de Goa*, Fernandes (2011) at p. 95.

181. Prisonio Tavares[†]: *Goa Gazetteer* vol. 1 references under Ambe Dinanath alias Dinkar Dattu Shenvi at p. 11 and Harmalkar Namdev Shankar at p. 128.

182. Dr Rogaciano Moraes[†]: Veroda, active in Bombay, was a founder member of the GLC formed by distinguished Goans based in Bombay. *Goa Gazetteer* vol. 1 reference under Afonso Francisco Correia at p. 4, Fernandes (2011) at p. 17.

183. Rafael Antonio de Souza: Assonora, joined NCG in Bombay in 1954, arrested on 19 March 1955 and after beatings and torture, was sentenced to two years' rigorous imprisonment. *Goa Gazetteer* vol. 1 listing at p. 339 and reference under Fernandes James at p. 100, Fernandes (2011) at p. 143.

184. Militant Rafael Tavares: Aldona, was based in Bombay when he joined the AGD with Fulgencio Moraes, underwent arms and explosives training at Amboli Camp in 1956, but died in a tragic accident in Bombay in 1957. *Goa Gazetteer* vol. 1 listing at p. 348, Fernandes (2011) at p. 147.

185. Teacher Raul Bose[†]: Canacona/Margao, a modest man, he was a schoolteacher by profession, Gandhian, always wore khadi clothes.

186. Teacher Rodolfo J. Almeida: Assolna, although he graduated in science and law and was qualified to practise law, chose the teaching profession, worked with Nath Pai during the 1955–56 Satyagraha while studying in Belgaum. *Goa Gazetteer* vol. 1 listing at pp. 7–8, Fernandes (2011) at p. 22.

187. Ronaldo Roque Carmo Coutinho: Borda–Margao, worked for Agencia Geral Limitada (a division of Salgaocar e Companhia) when he was accused of underground activities and imprisoned for 26 months from 1958 to 1960. Following his release, he continued to work in the same company. Together with Purushottam Kakodkar and Dr Suresh Kanekar, he was among the only three freedom fighters who witnessed first-hand the 'Surrender Ceremony' at Vasco da Gama on the night of 19 December 1961, Fernandes (2011) at p. 49, Kanekar (2011) at pp. 145–49 and p. 169.

188. Ex-MLA Roque Santan Fernandes: Sokolbhat–Velim, was an AGD activist. *Goa Gazetteer* vol. 1 listing at p. 101 and reference under Vaidya, Prabhakar Trivikram at p. 359, Fernandes (2011) at p. 71. Newspaper statement, 1987.

189. Roque Sequeira[†]: referenced in Shirodkar, *My Life in Exile*, 2012, p. 15.

190. Rosario Fernandes: Assolna, joined NCG in Bombay in 1951, was part of the satyagraha group that entered from Torxem–Pernem on 15 August 1954 under Mark Fernandes, was sentenced to seven years' imprisonment. *Goa Gazetteer* vol. 2 listing at p. 29, Fernandes (2011) at p. 81.

191. S.F. de Melo: Saligao, was joint treasurer with Vaman N. Desai of NCG in Bombay in 1948. *Goa Gazetteer* vol. 1 reference under Desai Vaman Narayan at p. 80. Sam de Melo is mentioned as active in Bombay and sent lists to

Goa to collect signatures of Goans who desired integration of Goa with India. Also referenced in *Goa Gazetteer, Trial of the Four*, p. 9.

192. S.M. Carvalho[†]: *Goa Gazetteer* vol. 1 reference under Gracias Luis at p. 123, Fernandes (2011) at p. 85.

193. S.M. Lemos[†]: Saligao, *Goa Gazetteer* vol. 1 reference under Gracias Luis at p. 123, Fernandes (2011) at p. 85.

194. Adv. Salvador Bermindo (SB) Silva: Cuchelim–Bardez, practised law in Bombay, met Mahatma Gandhi regarding Goa, was a special invitee to the AICC session in Nasik in 1949, escaped from Calangute to Belgaum, wrote plays for All India Radio to counter Portuguese propaganda. *Goa Gazetteer* vol. 1 listing at p. 332 and references under Borkar Laxmidas Krishna at p. 33, Santana Sebastaio (SS) Carvalho at p. 39, Jambawalikar (Dr) Pandurang Gaeca at p. 135 and Mascarenhas Emilio Francisco Lamberto alias Mascarenhas Lambert at p. 215. *Goa Gazetteer* vol. 2 reference under Borkar Vasant Pandurang at p. 11, Fernandes (2011) at p. 133. Dr Shirodkar, *Goa's Freedom Struggle*, 1999, p. 69.

195. Sampaul Cruzinho ('C.P.') de Costa: Carmona, arrested in 1954 and released with stern warning, rearrested prior to the 15 August 1955 satyagraha. Went into business with the firm, C.P. de Costa, in Margao, Fernandes (2011) at p. 48.

196. Editor Santana Sebastiao ('S.S.') Carvalho: Mapusa, participated in Quit India Movement and joined NCG in 1950, edited some periodicals in Bombay, arrested by Bombay Police for the 'black flag' demo protesting against the visiting Portuguese governor-general of Goa. *Goa Gazetteer* vol. 1 listing at p. 39 and reference under Golatkar Dinanath Sazu at p. 120, Fernandes (2011) at p. 43.

197. Ex-MLA/Minister Sebastiao ('Tony') Fernandes: Sanvordem, did BA, LLB from Karnataka University, joined AGD, participated in several armed actions, mined the Colem–Sonaulim rail tracks that led to the death of

thirteen white Portuguese soldiers on 13 August 1956 (six more would be killed later in December the same year), attacked a train carrying cash, attacked Pirla mines and dynamited Colem bridge. Elected in 1963 to the Goa Legislative Assembly and was the first law minister. *Goa Gazetteer* vol. 1 listing at pp. 101–102. Many references, Fernandes (2011) at p. 72.

198. Shashikala Hodarkar Almeida[†]: wife of Anastacio Almeida. *Goa Gazetteer* vol. 1 listing at p. 8, Fernandes (2011) at p. 32.

199. Militant Soccoro Costa[†]: Was an RP activist. Took part in laying land mines and other militant activities. *Goa Gazetteer* vol. 2 reference under Viegas Eusebio Martires P. at p. 125, Fernandes (2011) at p. 155.

200. Adv. Telo de Mascarenhas: Majorda, while studying law at Coimbra–Portugal, was a supporter of Salazar who taught economics at the same university. Mascarenhas started a periodical, *India Nova,* and serialized political articles under the title 'Death of the Idols', later worked as public prosecutor in Portugal before returning and plunging into the freedom struggle; worked for some time at All India Radio, New Delhi, was arrested, exiled and imprisoned in Portugal and was among the last Goan freedom fighters to be released in 1970; authored about two dozen books (prose and poetry). *Goa Gazetteer* vol. 1 listing at pp. 216–17 and references, among others, under Fernandes Antonio at pp. 102 and 103. *Goa Gazetteer* vol. 2 reference under Borkar Vasant Pandurang at p. 11, Fernandes (2011) at p. 103. Dr Shirodkar, *Goa's Freedom Struggle,*1999, p. 68.

201. Militant Thomas Aquino Jose Rosario Furtado: Deussua–Chinchinim, specialized in making cracker bombs to create fear, was sent to Bombay by his father to keep him away from nationalist activities but continued with them in Bombay. He was the first elected sarpanch of the Chinchinim–Deussua panchayat in 1962. *Goa Gazetteer* vol. 1 listing at p. 104, Fernandes (2011) at p. 79.

202. Thomas Dias: Cavelossim/Ambajim–Margao, older brother
     of journalist and freedom fighter Bonifacio Dias, arrested
     first time in 1951, then again in 1952 and again in 1954—
     and ten times thereafter until 1960. Days before the armed
     action by India, he was detained for interrogation and badly
     tortured (leading to permanent hearing defect) but escaped.
     Goa Gazetteer vol. 1 listing at p. 95–96. *Goa Gazetteer* vol. 2
     reference under Budholkar Vasant Rama at p. 12, Fernandes
     (2011) at p. 61.
203. Tony M. Rodrigues: Bicholim, joined the GYL in Bombay
     in 1945, moved on to other organizations, organized
     a mass rally at Cross Maidan–Bombay, participated in
     demonstrations and processions on and following the
     15 August 1955 satyagraha and helped the participants
     financially and otherwise. *Goa Gazetteer* vol. 1 listing at p.
     298, Fernandes (2011) at p. 127.
204. Eng. Tristao de Braganca Cunha: Cuelim–Cansaulim,
     educated in Pondicherry and Paris. Was a qualified engineer.
     He is recognized as the Father of Goan Nationalism. *Goa
     Gazetteer* vol. 1 listing at p. 54. Many references, Fernandes
     (2011) at p. 52. Shirodkar, *My Life in Exile,* 2012, pp. 2,
     5, 54, 298. *Goa Gazetteer, Trial of the Four,* in Biographical
     Sketch of Pandurang Purushottam Shirodkar, p. 1 thereof
     (unnumbered page).
205. Dr Ubaldo Mascarenhas[†]: presided over the NCG
     Conference in Bombay on 7–8 January 1950. He was a
     former mayor of Bombay. *Goa Gazetteer* vol. 1 reference
     under Sukhtankar Jagannath Sadashiv at p. 341.
206. Militant Urselino Almeida: Velim, was one of the leading
     lights of NCG, later co-founded the GLA on 30 September
     1955. *Goa Gazetteer* vol. 1 listing at pp. 8–9, references,
     among others, under Kerkar Janardan Krishna at p. 179,
     Kerkar Pandurang Dulba at p. 181, Prabhu Krishna Putu
     at p. 284, Rane Jaisingrao Venkatrao at p. 294, and Tupkar
     Manu ('Hemraj') Mohanlal at p. 356. *Goa Gazetteer* vol. 2

references under Kesarkar Vishnu Harishchandra at p. 55, Rao Narayan Bhikaji (N.B. Rao) at p. 94 and Sawal Mohan Bitu at p. 100, Fernandes (2011) at p. 23.

207. Vicente Agostinho Francisco da Cunha: Cansaulim, his Gandhi topi was snatched and Portuguese police wiped their shoes with it, he accepted it back with a shout of 'Jai Hind'. The topi fetched contributions that added up to Rs 200 when passed around the Goan public. *Goa Gazetteer* vol. 1 listing at p. 55, Fernandes (2011) at p. 55.

208. Xavier Pereira: Cavelossim, participated in Quit India Movement as a student and joined the GYL after matriculation, was part of the GAC, arrested in 1954 and served jail, was secretary of Bombay Branch of GPP. and was delegated to the 1961 Afro-Asian Conference in New Delhi. *Goa Gazetteer* vol. 2 listing at pp. 89–90, Fernandes (2011) at p. 120.

209. Militant Zotico Praxedes de Souza: Bodiem–Tivim, matriculated and joined the GYL, then was a part of the AGD since 1947, prepared volunteers for armed action and also worked secretly in Goa. Goa Gazetteer vol. 1 listing at p. 339 and references under Kandolkar Rajaram Laxman at p. 159 and under Lawande Sriniwas Janardan at p. 196, Fernandes (2011) at p. 144. He later joined the MGP and served on its executive committee, resigning with Vishwanath Lawande, Narayan Naik, Vithal Bablo Naik and M.S. Prabhu when Goa's first political split occurred in the MGP in 1970.

Officially, there were only 116 registered Goan Christian Freedom Fighters.

GOAN CATHOLIC FREEDOM
FIGHTERS' CLASSIFICATION

(SUMMARY)

Martyrs: 1. Camilo Pereira

Militants: 1. Albert L.R. Fernandes (AGD), 2. Anthony Leo Sequeira (AGD), 3. Antonio Jose E. da Gama S. de Costa Frias (RP), 4. Antonio Rosario Menino Egidio Gregorio Lume Jose Vaz (GLA), 5. Antonio Rosario Policarpo/Polycarpo ('Polly') Teodosio da Silva (RP), 6. Adv. Armando Teodoro Valente Santana Pereira (AGD), 7. Artur Fernandes (GLA), 8. Augusto (Augustus) Alvares (GLA), 9. Chagas de Cunha (AGD), 10. Christopher Silva Lobo (AGD), 11. Cristovam Gabriel Paulo das Angustias Furtado (AGD), 12. Cruz Viegas (RP), 13. Emiterio Paes (UFG), 14. Ernesto Costa Frias (RP), 15. Eusebio Martires P. Viegas (RP), 16. Francis (Francisco) Mascarenhas (UFG), 17. Frank Raphael Paul Andrades (QGO), 18. Fulgencio Moraes (AGD), 19. George Louis Pereira, 20. Ilidio (Elidio) Francisco do Carmo Costa (RP), 21. InacinhoViegas (RP), 22. John Gilbert Rebello (QGO), 23. Jose Manuel ('Manuelinho') Viegas (RP), 24. Libano S. de Souza (QGO), 25. Dr Manuel ('Manu') Estevam Fernandes (GLA), 26. Mario Rodrigues (AGD), 27. Mussolini Menezes (AGD), 28. Ponciano Pereira (RP), 29. Rafael Tavares (AGD), 30. Soccoro Costa (RP), 31. Thomas Aquino Jose Rosario Furtado, 32. Urselino Almeida (GLA) and 33. Zotico Praxedes de Souza (AGD).

Catholic Priests: 1. Fr Furtado (Pilerne), 2. Fr Pinto (Guirim) and 3. Fr (Dr) Hubert Olympio Mascarenhas (Bombay).

Medical Doctors: 1. Dr António Colaço (see Lok Sabha MPs), 2. Dr Caesar Monteiro, 3. Dr Clementino J.N.L. Jorge, 4. Dr Eclito de Souza, 5. Dr Eduardo Furtado, 6. Dr Eric D'Melo, 7. Dr Frank de Sequeira, 8. Dr Gambeta da Costa, 9. Dr H.C. Denis/Diniz, 10. Dr John Carvalho (Homeopathy), 11. Dr John Costa Bir (Ayurveda), 12. Dr Jose Francisco Martins, 13. Dr Jose Maria Furtado, 14. Dr Jose Vicente Paulo Francisco Gomes, 15. Dr Juliao de Menezes, 16. Dr Laura Souza Rodrigues, 17. Dr Lucio Monteiro, 18. Dr Luis Monteiro, 19. Dr Luiza C. Pereira, 20. Dr Manuel ('Manu') Estevam Fernandes (also Militant), 21. Dr Menino D'Souza, 22. Dr Rogaciano Moraes and 23. Dr Ubaldo Mascarenhas.

Pharmacists: 1. Alvaro Antonio Precioso Pereira and 2. Antonio Sequeira.

Scientist: 1. Dr Beatris de Menezes Braganza.

Engineers: 1. Eng. L.J. de Souza and 2. Eng. Tristao de Braganca Cunha.

University Lecturers/Professors: 1. Prof. Aloysius Soares, 2. Prof. Armando Menezes, 3. Prof. Dionisio Ribeiro, 4. Prof. Francisco Correia–Afonso, 5. Prof. James (Jaime) Fernandes and 6. Prof. Lucio Rodrigues.

Teachers: 1. Celina Olga Moniz, 2. Enio Pimenta (see MLAs), 3. Joseph Godinho, 4. Nicolau Menezes, 5. Raul Bose and 6. Rodolfo J. Almeida.

Additional Judicial Commissioners of Goa: 1. Adv. Antonio Furtado and 2. Adv. Jose Paulo Santana Desiderio Lucas Teles.

Civil and Criminal Judge: Antonio Blasio de Souza.

Advocates: 1. Adv. Ariosto Tovar Dias, 2. Adv. Baptist Rebello, 3. Adv. Cristovam Furtado, 4. Adv. Fernando Costa, 5. Adv. Gerald

Xavier Pereira (also trade unionist), 6. Adv. Gilman Fernandes, 7. Adv. J. Carvalho, 8. Adv./Goa's first Advocate General Joachim Dias, 9. Adv. João Francisco Caraciolo Cabral, 10. Adv. Jose Inacio ('Fanchu') de Loyola Jr., 11. Adv. Libia Lobo Sardesai, 12. Adv. Luis (Louis) Gabriel Mendes, 13. Adv. Norberto Carvalho, 14. Adv. Salvador Bermindo (SB) Silva and 15. Adv. Telo de Mascarenhas.

Editors: 1. Alvaro da Costa, 2. Berta de Menezes Braganza, 3. Evagrio Francisco Jorge, 4. Felicio Cardoso, 5. Lambert Mascarenhas and 6. Santana Sebastiao ('SS') Carvalho.

Journalists: 1. Alfred Braganza, 2. Arsenio Jacques, 3. Bonifacio Eusebio Inacio Dias, 4. Caetano (Cajetan) Ludger Teodor Lobo, 5. Carlos da Cruz, 6. F.M. Pinto, 7. Felix Valois Rodrigues, 8. Flaviano Piedade Francis Dias, 9. J.M. Pinto, 10. Massilon de Almeida and 11. Porfirio Maria Gaspar Silva Lobo.

Trade Unionists: 1. Anastacio Almeida, 2. George Vaz, 3. Adv. Gerald Xavier Pereira (also Advocate) and 4. Mark Agostinho Fernandes.

Lok Sabha MPs: 1. Dr António Colaço (also medical doctor)—nominated and 2. Peter Alvares—elected.

Goa Legislative Assembly Speaker: Froilano Carmelino da Rocha Machado.

Goa Ministers/MLAs: 1. Anthony ('Tony') John D'Souza, 2. Enio Pimenta (also Teacher), 3. Joaquim Luis Gonsalo Araujo, 4. John Mariano (J.M.) D'Souza, 5. Roque Santan Fernandes and 6. Sebastiao ('Tony') Fernandes.

Municipal Presidents: 1. Alvaro da Costa, 2. Alvaro Pinto Furtado and 3. Adv. Armando Teodoro Valente Santana Pereira (also militant/AGD)

Government Officials: 1. Alvinho (Alwin) Belarmino Coelho and 2. Dy SP Fulgencio Moraes (also militant).

GOA FREEDOM ORGANIZATIONS

1. AGD: Azad Gomantak Dal (Militant), 1947 (Vishwanath Lawande, Narayan Hari Naik, Dattatraya Deshpande)
2. GAC: Goa Action Committee, 1953 Bombay (T.B. Cunha, essentially to coordinate the efforts of National Congress (Goa), United Front of Goans and Goan People's Party)
3. GLA: Goa Liberation Army (Militant), 1955 Belgaum (Shivaji Desai, Urselino Almeida, Balkrishna Bhonsle, Augusto Alvares, Jaysingrao Rane and Madhavrao Rane)
4. GLC: Goa Liberation Council, 1954 Bombay (Prof. Aloysius Soares, Francisco Correia Afonso, L.J. de Souza, Prof. L.N. Velingkar, J.N. Heredia, J.M. Pinto and Nicolau Menezes)
5. GLF: Goa Liberation Front
6. GNC: Goan National Conference
7. GNU: Goan National Union, 1954 Bombay (J.M. D'Souza and J.N. Heredia)
8. GPC: Goan Political Convention/Goan League, London (H.C. Denis and João Cabral)
9. GPP: Goan People's Party (Militant), 1949 (George Vaz, Divakar Kakodkar, Berta de Menezes Bragança, joined by Aquino de Bragança in Mozambique)
10. GVSS: Goa Vimochan Sahayak Samiti, 1955 Pune (Jayantrao Tilak, Praja Socialist Party, Kisan Mazdoor Sabha, Hindu Mahasabha and Communist Party of India)
11. GYL: Goan Youth League, 1945 Bombay (T.B. Cunha)
12. NCG: National Congress (Goa), 1946 Londa (Dr Rama Hegde, Laxmanrao Sardesai, Balkrishna Borkar, Narayan Prabhu Bhembre, Venkatesh Vaidya and Vasant Kare)
13. QGO: Quit Goa Organisation (Militant), 1954 (Janardhan Shinkre)
14. RP: Rancour Patriotica (Militant, an offshoot of AGD, Prabhakar Sinari)
15. UFG: United Front of Goans (Militant), 1950 (Francisco de Mascarenhas, Vaman Desai, António Furtado)

GOAN-ORIGIN INDIAN ARMED FORCES OFFICERS IN OP VIJAY-1

1. Air Vice Mshl Erhlich Wilmot Pinto, 2. Brig. Donald Viegas, 3. Col Peter Mendonca, 4. Naval Captain Patrick Ivor Telles, 5. Naval Captain A.F. Collaco, 6. Gp Capt. Trevor Joseph Fernandes, 7. Lt Col Louis Fonseca, 8. Lt Col Vitalio de Paula Ribeiro Lobo, 9. Lt Col Paul Baylon Fernandes, 10. Surg. Cdr Joseph G. Rodrigues, 11. Surg. Cdr Frederick Nazareth, 12. Surg. Cdr Joel de Sa Cordeiro, 13. Wg Cdr Vishwanath B. Sawardekar, 14. Wg Cdr Mervyn Jude Pinto, 15. Wg Cdr Remegius ('Remy') V. Paul, 16. Maj. Gerson R.A. de Souza, 17. Maj. Ceasar P.F. Lobo, 18. Lt Cdr John Eric Gomes, 19. Captain Pinto (Kanekar, 2011, p. 146) and 20. Naval Lt Jose Figueiredo Melo.

(Future Gen. Sunith F. Rodrigues accompanied the troops into Goa but did not participate in the action.)

DR T.B. CUNHA MEMORIAL COMMITTEE

Prof. D.D. Kosambi	Hon. Chairman
Adv. Gerald Pereira	Hon. Secretary
Dr Beatriz de Menezes Braganza ...	Hon. Joint Treasurer
Antonio da Cruz	Hon. Joint Treasurer

Members: Prof. Armando Menezes, Dr Arthur E. D'Sa, Prof. A.N. Chikhalikar, A.P. D'Cruz, Dr Antonio Sequeira (Mombasa), B.P. Mhambrey, Evagrio Jorge (New Delhi), J. Cabral (London), Dr Jorge Andrade, J.M. Furtado (Nagar Haveli), J.S. Suktankar, Kant Desai (Nagar Haveli), L.J. D'Souza, Prof. Lucio Miranda (Essex, UK), Luis Cabral, M.D. Gaitonde, Dr M.U. Mascarenhas, Mussolini Menezes, Dr Oliver Britto (Saudi Arabia), Peter Alvares, Rosario da Gama Pinto (Nairobi, Pio's brother), S. Nadkarni, Victor Gonsalves, Vicente Cunha, V.N. Lawande (Belgaum), Verissimo Coutinho, Dr Waman Vinayak Laud, Prof. YG Naik and Zotico de Souza.

SELECT BIBLIOGRAPHY

Aranha, João (Captain), *Enquanto se esperam as naus do reino ...*, Lisbon: Espera do Caos Editores Lda., 2008.

Azeredo, Carlos de, *Trabalhos e Dias de Um Soldado do Império* (Work and Days of a Soldier of the Empire), Lisbon: Livraria Civilização Editora, 2004.

Bohman-Behram, B.K., *Goa and Ourselves*, Bombay: New Book Company, 1955.

Bruto da Costa, Mário, *Goa: A Terceira corrente (Discursos, artigos, cartas e defesas forenses de António A. Bruto da Costa)*, Goa: self published, 2013.

Cardozo, Major General Ian, *1971: Stories of Grit and Glory from the Indo-Pak War*, Gurugram: Penguin Random House India (Ebury Press), 2021.

Colaço, Fernando Jorge, *December 18–19, 1961: Before, During & After (Memoir of a 20th Century Voyager)*, Goa: jointly published by Goa, 1556–Saligao and Golden Heart Emporium-Margao, 2017.

Costa sfx, Cosme (Rev.), *A Missiological Conflict Between Padroado and Propaganda in the East*, Pilar Publications, 1997.

Costa sfx, Cosme (Rev.), *Apostolic Christianity in Goa and in the West Coast of India*, Pilar: Xaverian Publication Society, 2009.

Correia, Joaquim, *Once Upon a Time in Goa*, Goa, 1556 and GPR Associates, 2022.

Desai, Morarji, *The Story of My Life*, New Delhi: Macmillan (vols 1 and 2), 1974; S. Chand & Co., vol. 3, 1979.

Desai, Nishtha, *Liberation vs Armed Aggression: The Media Response to Goa's Liberation*, Goa: Directorate of Art & Culture, Government of Goa, 2011.

D'Lima, Edward Joachim, *Creative and Critical Writings of Armando Menezes*, Goa: Goa University, 2003.

D'Silva Themistocles, *Beyond the Beach: The Village of Arossim, Goa, in Historical Perspective*, Goa: Goa,1556, 2011.

Esteves, Sarto, *Politics and Political Leadership in Goa*, New Delhi: Sterling Publishers, 1986.

Fernandes, Martin Menino, *Goa, Daman & Diu Catholic Freedom Fighters*, Goa: Goeam Tujea Mogakhatir (Gurunath Kelekar), 2011.

Fernandes, Remo, *Remo: The Autobiography of Remo Fernandes*, Noida: HarperCollins, 2021.

Fonseca, Sushila S., *The Journey of an Unsung Hero: Antonio Sequeira, His Quest for Goa's Freedom—Dictatorship & Freedom of the Press in Goa in the Forties,* Goa: Dr Sushila S. Fonseca, M.D., D.P.B., 2021.

Forjaz, Jorge and Noronha, José Francisco de, *Luso-Descendentes da Índia Portuguesa,* vol. 3, Goa: Fundação Oriente, 2006.

Gaitonde, Edila, *As Maçãs Azuis: Portugal e Goa 1948–1961,* Dafundo (Portugal): Editorial Tágide, 2011.

Gaitonde, Edila, *In Search of Tomorrow,* Goa: Rajhauns Vitaran, 2010 (first published in 1987 by Allied Publishers).

Gaitonde, P.D., *The Liberation of Goa: A Participant's View of History,* Goa: Rajhauns Sankalpana, 2016 (first published in 1987 by C. Hurst & Co. Ltd., London).

Hangen, Welles, *After Nehru, Who?,* New York: Harcourt, Brace & World Inc., 1963.

Kanekar, Suresh, *Goa's Liberation and Thereafter: Chronicles of a Fragmented Life,* Goa: Goa, 1556, 2011.

Karim Afsir (Major General), *The Story of the India's Airborne Troops,* by New Delhi: Lancer International, 1990.

Khera, P.N. (Edited: S.N. Prasad), *Operation Vijay: The Liberation of Goa and Other Portuguese Colonies in India, (1961),* New Delhi: Historical Section, Ministry of Defence, Government of India, India Press–Nasik, 1974.

Jack, Homer Alexander, *Callous mentality of Portuguese: American reporter's impressions,* New Delhi: Information Service of India, 1955.

Jorge, Evagrio, *Goa's Awakening: Reminiscences of the 1946 Civil Desobedience [sic] Movement,* Goa: 18th kune (Goan Revolution Day) Silver Jubilee Celebrations, 1971 (originally published by the University of Michigan), 1971.

Lawrence, Leo, *Nehru Seizes Goa,* New York, Pageant Press (University of Michigan), 1963. Accessed at: https://babel.hathitrust.org/cgi/pt?id=mdp.39015016919634&view=1up&seq=7

Leasor, James, *Boarding Party,* Houghton Mifflin Harcourt, 1978.

Lengyel, Emil, *Krishna Menon,* New York: Walker and Company, 1962.

Lewis, Jon E., ed., *The Mammoth Book of War Correspondents,* London: Constable & Robinson Ltd, 2001.

Lopes, Filipa Alexandra Carvalho Sousa, *As Vozes da Oposição ao Estado Novo e a Questão de Goa (1950-1961),* Universidade do Porto (Faculdade de Letras), 2017.

Loyola–Nazareth, Yona, *Goa's Foremost Nationalist: José Inácio Cândido de Loyola: The Man and His Writings*, XCHR Studies Series No. 9, New Delhi: Concept Publishing, 2000.

Mankekar, D.R., *Goa Action,* Bombay: Popular Book Depot, 1962.

Mateus, Dalila Cabrita, *A PIDE/DGS na guerra colonial (1961-1974,* Lisbon: Terramar, 2004.

Menezes, Lieutenant General Stanley L., *Fidelity and Honour: The Indian Army from the Seventeenth to the Twenty-First Century*, New Delhi: Oxford University Press, 1999.

Moraes, Frank, *Jawaharlal Nehru: A Biography,* New York: The MacMillan Company, 1956.

Morais, Carlos Alexandre de (Col), *A Queda da Índia Portuguesa: Crónica da Invasão e do Cativeiro*, Lisbon: Editorial Estampa/University of Michigan, 2nd edition, 1995.

Moreira, Antonio Joaquim, cod-866_0000_capa-capa_124-C-R0150.pdf, Lisbon: Bibliotheca Nacional de Lisboa, 1863.

Nogueira, Franco, *Salazar* (vol. 4), Lisbon: Livraria Castro e Silva, 1985.

Pais e Martins, Sharmila, *The Encounter: With the Ballot in Colonial Goa 1821–1961*, Goa: Goa, 1556, 2021.

Palit, D.K., *War in High Himalaya: The Indian Army in Crisis*, 1962, New Delhi: Lancer International, 1991.

Palit, Major General D.K., VrC, *Musings & Memories, Vol–II*, New Delhi: Palit&Palit in association with Lancer Publishers & Distributors, 2004.

Palmer, Norman D., *The Indian Political System*, Boston: Houghton Mifflin Company, 1961.

Panag, H.S. (Lt General), *The Indian Army: Reminiscences, Reforms & Romance*, Chennai: Westland Publications, 2020.

Pearson, M.N., *The Portuguese in India,* Cambridgeshire, New York: Cambridge University Press, 1987.

Pinto, Lieutenant General W.A.G., *Bash on Regardless: A Record of a life in War and Peace*, Pune: Lt Gen. W.A.G. Pinto (printed at Repro India Ltd., Navi Mumbai), 2011.

Porch, Douglas, *The Portuguese Armed Forces and the Revolution*, Oxfordshire: Routledge, 1977.

Praval, Major K.C., *Indian Army after Independence*, New Delhi: Lancer Publishers & Distributors, 2009.

Ramagundam, Rahul, *The Life and Times of George Fernandes*, Gurugram: Penguin Random House, 2022.

Ramani, Shrikant Y., *Operation Vijay: The Ultimate Solution*, Goa: Broadway Book Centre, 2008.

Ramesh, Jairam, *A Chequered Brilliance: The Many Lives of V.K. Krishna Menon*, Gurgaon: Penguin Viking (Penguin Random House India), 2019.

Rao, R.P., *Portuguese Rule in India*, Bombay: Asia Publishing House, 1963.

Rotter, Andrew Jon, *Comrades at Odds: The United States and India, 1947–1964*, Cornell University Press, 2000.

Rubinoff, Arthur G., *India's Use of Force in Goa*, Bombay: Popular Prakashan, 1971.

Salazar (A. de O.), *The Case for Goa,* Lisbon: Secretariado Nacional da Informação, 1954.

Schlesinger Jr., Arthur M., *A Thousand Days: John F. Kennedy in the White House*, Mariner Books, reprint 2002.

Shirodkar, P.P. (Sr), translated into English by Lt Col Dr Pravinkumar P. Shirodkar, *My Life in Exile*, Goa: Pradnya-Darshan Prakashan, 2012.

Shirodkar, P.P. (Jr.), *Goa's Struggle for Freedom*, Goa: self-published by Sulabha P. Shirodkar, Ajanta Publications, Alto Porvorim, Goa, 1988 (revised edition 1999).

Shirodkar, P.P. (Jr), ed., *Who's Who of Freedom Fighters—Goa, Daman & Diu (volume one and volume two)*, Goa: Goa Gazetteer Department, Government of the Union Territory of Goa, Daman and Diu, 1986 (volume one) and 1990 (volume two).

Shirodkar, Dr P.P. (Jr), ed., *Trial of the Four*, Goa: Goa Gazetteer Department, Government of Goa, 1999.

Singh, Major General V.K., *Leadership in the Indian Army: Biographies of Twelve Soldiers*, New Delhi: Sage Publications India Pvt. Ltd, 2005 (Ninth Printing 2012).

Singh, Major General V.K. (former Chairman, History Cell of the Corps of Signals), *History of the Corps of Signals*, New Delhi: volume III (covering the period 1947–72), revised March 2013 (Chapter 3), manuscript.

Sinh, Major General Randhir, UYSM, AVSM, SM, *A Talent For War: The Military Biography of Lt Gen Sagat Singh*, New Delhi: Vij Books India Pvt. Ltd., 2013, Reprint 2014, Second Reprint 2015.

Sousa, Bernardo Elvino de, *The Last Prabhu: A Hunt for Roots—DNA, Ancient Documents and Migration in Goa*, first published by Goa,1556 in 2011, revised and self-published in 2020.

Sousa, Bernardo Elvino de, *The Denaming of Goans: Case Studies of Conversions in Medieval Goa*, Riehen, Switzerland, Pothi, 2022.

Souza, Leo J. De, *No Place for Me: A Memoir of an Indian Doctor in East Africa*, Minnesota (USA); Beaver's Pond Press, 2021.

Souza, Robert de, *Goa and the Continent of Circe*, Bombay: Wilco Publishing House, 1973.

Souza, Teotónio, *Portuguese Literary & Cultural Studies 17/18*, Dartmouth: University of Massachusetts, 2010.

Stocker, Maria Manuel, *Xeque-Mate a Goa: O Principio do Fim do Império Português,* Portugal: Temas e Debates, 2005.

Subramaniam, Arjun (Air Vice Marshal), *India's Wars: A Military History 1947–1971*, Noida: HarperCollins, 2016.

Trinidad, Jamie, *Self-Determination in Disputed Colonial Territories,* Cambridge University Press, 2018.

Thorat, S.P.P. (Lt Gen.), *From Reveille to Retreat*, New Delhi: Allied Publishers, 1986.

Vas, P.V.S.M., Eric A., *Without Baggage: A Personal Account of the Jammu & Kashmir Operations, October 1947–January 1949*, Dehra Dun: Natraj Publishers, 2003.

Vaz, Clarice, *Romalina: Goodbye Africa, Adeus Portugal, Namaste Goa,* Goa: self-published, 2022.

Whiteway, R.S., *The Rise of Portuguese Power in India 1497–1550,* New Delhi: Asian Educational Services, third reprint 2007 (first published 1899).

Other Publications

Extract from the official account of the 1961 Goa Ops of the Sikh Light Infantry Regiment as provided by Colonel Harjeet Singh, compiler of the Sikh Light Infantry Regimental History and personal account provided by Brigadier Ravi K. Mehta who, as a young Captain with 4 Sikh LI, participated in the events at Alpalqueiros Hill, Vasco da Gama, on the afternoon of 19 December 1961.

Boletim do Instituto Vasco da Gama (now Institute Menezes Braganza), Goa, of the year 1953.

Central Intelligence Agency (USA), Special National Intelligence Estimate No. 31-61, dated 13 December 1961 (on Goa, declassified and approved for release on 26 March 2014).

Dabolim and TAIP: A Tale of a Goan Airport and Airline, online essay by Gabriel de Figueiredo, 2005, which was available at http://www. colaco.net, now defunct.

Diário da Câmara dos Srs Deputados (parliament proceedings) of the Côrtes, Lisbon.

Eye Witness to the Liberation of Goa by Air Marshal S. Raghavendran (V) available at: https://www.bharat-rakshak.com/IAF/history/1961goa/raghavendran/

Goa Invasion by Bonnie Lubega, at: http://goa-invasion-1961.blogspot.com/2013/04/goa-african-writers-perspective.html

Goa in Retrospect: Colonial Memories Published Recently in Goa and in Portugal, essay by Teotónio R. de Souza, in *Portuguese Literary & Cultural Studies* 17/18, Dartmouth: University of Massachusetts, 2010, pp.141–64.

Goa in Wider Perspective by Margaret W. Fisher, *Asian Survey,* 1962.

Goa's Struggle for Freedom, 1946–1961: The Contribution of National Congress (Goa) and Azad Gomantak Dal, doctoral thesis by Seema Suresh Risbud, Goa University, 2002 (http://library.unigoa.ac.in:8081/xmlui/handle/123456789/224).

De Sousa, Ana Naomi, 'How Portugal Silenced "Centuries of Violence and Trauma"', Al Jazeera, 10 March 2021, at: https://www.aljazeera.com/amp/features/2021/3/10/how-portugal-silenced-centuries-of-violence-and-trauma

Illustrated Weekly of India (Special Issue on Goa), edition LXXXIII.7 of 18 February 1962.

INAS 550: History of the Flying Fish (Commemorative Book of the Golden Jubilee of Indian Naval Air Squadron 550), Kochi: INAS 550, INS Garuda, 2009.

'India: End of an Image', *Time*, 29 December 1961.

Indian Occupation of Portuguese Territories in India–Invasion of Goa, Daman, and Diu–Incorporation in Indian Union, Keesing's Record of World Events (formerly Keesing's Contemporary Archives), volume 8, March 1962, pp. 18, 623 [Keesing's Worldwide, LLC].

International Reactions to Indian Attack on Goa, Keesing's Record of World Events, vol. 8, March 1962, accessed at: https://web.stanford.edu/group/tomzgroup/pmwiki/uploads/1074-1962-03-KS-b-RCW.pdf

O Heraldo, Portuguese-language daily newspaper published from Goa, editions of late 1961 (courtesy: Central Library-Rare Books Section, Panjim, Goa).

Purity of Blood and Caste: Identity Narratives among Early Modern Goan Elites by Ângela Barreto Xavier in *Race and Blood in the Iberian World* Max S. Hering Torres et al. (eds), Zurich and Berlin: Lit Verlag, undated, pp.125–49.

Guha, Ramachandra, 'Recalling the Liberation of Goa', *The Hindu*, 2 September 2007.

Relatório ao Governo, 1956, https://gloriainacselsis.wordpress.com/2008/04/13/goa-em-1956-relatorio-de-orlando-ribeiro/

Pereira, Gerald, *Resources and Potentialities of Goa*, available at: https://medium.com/@larapereiranaik/resources-potentialities-of-goa-during-the-portuguese-regime-c1c6797424be

Dias, Remy, *Some Aspects of the Consumption History of Estado da India: 1900–50*, in *Goa in the Twentieth Century: History and Culture*, edited by Pius Malekandathil and Remy Dias, Goa: Institute Menezes Braganza, 2008.

Sun Sets on Portugal's Asian Empire: Liberation of Goa, Daman and Diu (Indian Navy's official account of the ops).

Albuquerque, Teresa, *The Anglo–Portuguese Treaty of 1878: Impact on Goa*, accessed at https://www.mail-archive.com/goanet@lists.goanet.org/msg98414.html

Bravo, Philip, *The Case of Goa*, Alberta (Canada): Past Imperfect, vol. 7, 1998, https://journals.library.ualberta.ca/pi/index.php/pi/article/view/1400

Welles Hangen, Putnam, *The Dirty Game Played by V.K. Krishna Menon Against Goa* (available at https://portugueseindia.wordpress.com/2011/07/09/the-dirty-game-played-by-v-k-krishna-menon-against-goa/ or http://www.ocnus.net/artman2/publish/Dark_Side_4/THE-DIRTY-GAME-PLAYED-BY-V-K-KRISHNA-MENON-AGAINST-GOA--1961.shtml).

The Grinder, vol. 1/10 (Annual 2010), 26 January 2010.

Adiga, Aravind, 'The Lusitanian in Hind', *Outlook*, 30 September 2021.

Lobo, Sandra Ataide, 'The Return to Indianness: Goan Nationalism in the 1920s', in *Goa 2011: Reviewing and Recovering Fifty Years* (Xavier Centre of Historical Research, Goa, XCHR Studies Series No. 12), New Delhi: Concept Publishing Company Pvt. Ltd, New Delhi, 2014.

The Sun Sets on Portugal's Asian Empire: Liberation of Goa, Daman and Diu, official account of the 1961 Goa Ops of the Indian Navy, Chapter 12, PDF available at: https://www.indiannavy.nic.in/sites/default/themes/indiannavy/images/pdf/chapter12.pdf

Dias, Remy, 'Trials and Turbulences of Goa's Post-colonial Transition to Democracy, 1961–63', *Radix International Journal of Research in Social Science*, vol. 2, issue 6, June 2014.

Cota, Xavier, *Tribute to Felicio Cardoso—the Unassuming Giant* (available at http://konknnifelicio.blogspot.com/2016/07/tribute-to-felicio-cardoso-unassuming_31.html?m=1).

Athale, Anil, *Unsung Heroes VII: The Thinking General: The Chapati Truth* and *A Tribute to Lt Gen Eric Vas, 15 May 1923–18 Aug. 2009*, (https://www.sify.com/news/unsung-heroes-vii-the-thinking-general-imagegallery-0-national-jj4uwKbjihbsi.html).

Visão História, quarterly published in Portugal, volume 14. *A Queda da Índia Portuguesa: O Princípio do Fim do Império* (The Fall of Portuguese India: The Beginning of the End of the Empire), 2011.

When a Dog Bit a General and the 2/Lt the Bullet, article by Lieutenant General and former Vice Chief of Army Staff Vijay Oberoi (https://www.indianpolitics.co.in/when-a-dog-bit-a-general-and-the-2-lt-the-bullet/).

White Tigers on the Prowl (Commemorative Book of the Golden Jubilee of Indian Naval Air Squadron 300), Goa: INAS 300, INS Hansa, 2010.

Viegas, Valentino, *18 de Dezembro de 1961—Uma data histórica*, *Diario de Noticias*, Portugal.

WEBSITES

https://archive.org/stream/newdelhireportth009987mbp/newdelhire
    portth009987mbp_djvu.txt

www.bharat-rakshak.com (for reconfirmation of data and history/opinion)

https://www.artandculture.goa.gov.in/art-culture/konkani-
    literature-of-goa

https://history.state.gov/historicaldocuments/frus1955-57v27/d148

https://www.icj-cij.org/public/files/case-related/32/9113.pdf

http://www.indiandefencereview.com/

https://www.indiannavy.nic.in/sites/default/themes/indiannavy/images/
    pdf/chapter12.pdf

https://knowindia.gov.in/general-information/

https://sites.google.com/site/pequenashistorietas/personalidades/
    jorge-jardim

https://timesofindia.indiatimes.com/city/goa/portuguese-nationality-is-
    fundamental-right-by-law/articleshow/28808047.cms

https://www.sify.com/news/remembering-lt-gen-sagat-singh-on-his-
    birth-centenary-news-columns-thprpwhjbhbdg.html

https://origin-www.sify.com/news/unsung-heroes-vii-the-thinking-
    general-imagegallery-thumbnail-national-jj4uwKbjihbsi.html

https://timesofindia.indiatimes.com/india/john-f-kennedy/
    articleshow/26169547.cms

https://www.indianpolitics.co.in/when-a-dog-bit-a-general-and-the-2-lt-
    the-bullet/

https://en.wikipedia.org/wiki/

And all other websites whose links are provided in the text and footnotes.

NOTES

Chapter 1: The Background

1. For more, the reader may refer to *Oriente Conquistado* by the Portuguese Jesuit Priest-Historian in four volumes, originally published in the seventeenth century, the second edition of which was published by the Examiner Press of Bombay in 1881, and more recent authors like Anant Kakba Priolkar in his book *The Goa Inquistion*, second edition, 2016, and Alan Machado Prabhu in his book, *Goa's Inquisition: Facts, Fiction, Factoids*, 2022.

2. Author Nirad Chaudhuri wrote in his award-winning 1965 book, *The Continent of Circe* (Jaico Books), that half-caste, mestizo Goans supplied Bombay's ayahs, butlers, cooks, fiddlers, maidservants, waiters and whores. The term 'ABC' (ayahs, butlers, cooks) gained currency after that. Robert de Souza, who countered with his book, *Goa and the Continent of Circe*, Bombay: Wilco Publishing House, 1973, asked, 'Wherefrom did he [Nirad] get the information? Did he refer to any statistics?' and went on to quote (pp. 131–36) from a 1931 official report of a fifteen-member Enquiry Committee into the 'Situation of the Indo-Portuguese Emigrants in British India', which was contrary to what Chaudhuri wrote years later in 1965. The foreword to Robert de Souza's book was by journo–author Khushwant Singh, who wrote that Nirad Babu had tried to bait him earlier saying that Sikhs were not Indian.

3. A rather bizarre aside: Lohia Maidan is today bordered by the L-shaped edifice of the Administration of Salcete Comunidades and, adjoining it, a taller private building. The Comunidades building was the last Portuguese governor-general's last public project in Goa. Three petrol pumps existing there were shifted in 1960 to the eastern margin of Margao's old bus stand to make way for this building.

The adjacent building, which came up later, housing an Udupi restaurant on its mezzanine and a hotel on the upper floors, is mute witness to civic misgovernance in the post-1961 era. The then nominated Câmara Municipal de Salcete permitted some businessmen from Margao to construct a multi-storeyed hotel in the Parque Infantil Sua Alteza O Aga Khan (His Highness the Aga Khan Children's Park) in the middle of the municipal garden. A public furore over the private project compelled its relocation. The municipality advised the businessmen to shift to the Lohia Maidan land.

The open ground floor of the aborted hotel project in the middle of the municipal garden—its massive columns and beams give an idea of the height of the proposed monstrosity—exists like an eyesore. But that is Margao, the political, cultural and commercial capital of Goa.

4.   'In India now' because India was once the most prosperous land on earth. Roman Emperor Vespasian (69–79 AD) discouraged Indian imports and Pliny the Elder (23–79 AD) lamented, 'Not a year passed in which India did not take 50 million "*sesterces*" away from Rome' (*Naturalis Historiae* or Natural History).

British economist Angus Maddison (1926–2010) estimated in *The World Economy's: Historical Statistics* (2004) that India enjoyed a staggering 33 per cent share of the world economy in the first century AD, compared to that of entire Europe (21.5 per cent) and China (26 per cent).

India held about 25–30 per cent of the gold ever mined in the world. This attracted invaders and plunderers. Mahmud of Ghazni raided India seventeen times in twenty-five years, between the years 1001 to 1026. Babar wrote, 'Hindustan is a place of little charm ... The one nice aspect of Hindustan is that it is a large country with lots of gold and money' (*Tuzuk-i-Baburi*).

By 1498, when Vasco da Gama arrived, India's share of the world economy stood at 24.5 per cent and, thanks to Great Britain, shrank to 16 per cent by end of the First Industrial Revolution (1820), and to a dismal 4.2 per cent in 1947 (Europe and North America surged to 60 per cent). Between 1765 and 1938, Britain spirited away an estimated £ 45 trillion from India. Post-1947, India's leadership chose not to prosper. The share slid to 3 per cent in 1991 when, under severe circumstances, India, the world's second most populous country, pawned gold with the Union Bank of Switzerland.

Chapter 4: Majestic Menon

5. Lt Gen. Walter A.G. Pinto, when a major general, led 54 Infantry Division (including 47 Basantar Brigade) deep into Pakistan, fought the biggest-ever tank battle, decimated Pak armour and severely depleted her ability to counter-attack, which shocked the western world and catalysed the 1971 war ceasefire. Lt Gen. B.T. Pandit (Engineers), who retired as adjutant general of the Indian Army, wrote of then Maj. Gen. Pinto, 'Operationally our commander was a hard taskmaster and had little time for armchair strategists. On a personal plane, he was brave, kind-hearted and of forgiving nature. Even in stressful situations, he retained and exhibited a unique sense of humour.'

6. The first wave of the Chinese aggression lasted eight days. The second wave was launched from 16 November 1962. Thousands of unprepared but otherwise gallant Indian troops—ill-armed, ill-fed, ill-clothed and bereft of a leader—were sacrificed at the altar of political folly in NEFA. The Chinese overran NEFA. Tawang and Bomdila fell like a pack of cards. The Chinese were everywhere. Panic gripped Assam. Tezpur was deserted. Patients of a local mental hospital were let loose. Railway staff deserted trains and ran away. Civil servants fled. Indian soldiers fought on bravely. When they ran out of ammunition, they fixed bayonets and charged out of their trenches at an infinitely bigger, better equipped and acclimatized enemy. Said *Time* magazine, 'The Indian Army needs almost everything except courage.'

Chapter 5: Mobilizing the War Machine

7. The operational 63 Infantry Brigade was allotted 8 Cavalry (AMX tanks) less two squadrons of 1 Armoured Division under Major Luis Fonseca (later Lieutenant Colonel, from Badem, Salvador do Mundo, Goa), 10 Field Regiment under Major D.C. Noronha, 137 Heavy Mortar Battery, 27 Medical Battery, 377 Field and Bridge Company, a unit of which led by Major Vitalio de Paula Ribeiro Lobo (later Lieutenant Colonel, from Camorlim-Bardez, Goa, who built the Bailey bridge at Borim), 'C' Company 7 Mahar MG, ADS

152 Field Amb (TA) and AWD 210 Field Workshop Company. The 'Black Cat' motorized column was led by Captain Paul Fernandes (later Lieutenant Colonel, from Sarzora, Goa).

50 Indep Para Brigade was given 7 Cavalry (Stuart armoured vehicles and AMX tanks) of 1 Armoured Division under Major S.S. Sidhu (who later died in action at Aguada), the elite medium artillery 17 Parachute Regiment under Major (later Colonel) Peter Mendonca from Moira, Goa, 17 Field Regiment under Major Arjinder Singh, 74 Mountain Battery, P Battery of 24 Medium Regiment, 135 Heavy Mortar Battery, 64/45 Light Anti-aircraft Battery, 380 Field Company (engineers) and one-tonne trucks.

8. Captain (later Rear Admiral) Douglas St John Cameron was skipper of INS *Mysore*, the command ship for surface action in Mormugao and Anjediva.

    The Task Force commander of the assault squadron at Mormugao and skipper of the INS *Betwa* was Commander (later Vice Admiral) Rustom ('Rusi') Khushro Shapoorjee Gandhi, PVSM, VrC, a gallant officer, the only Indian naval officer to command ships in all the naval wars fought by India. Interestingly, he was also the only naval officer who, on his passing, as per his wish, was buried at sea: 'I enjoyed fish all my life, now let the fish enjoy me.'

9. Another marvel dogs the dubious freedom fighter. The freedom movement definitely ended on 18 December 1961. Freedom fighter Dr Suresh Kanekar said in 2011, '...most of the freedom fighters are now dead' (Kanekar, Suresh, *Goa's Liberation and Thereafter: Chronicles of a Fragmented Life*, 2011, p. 255). Yet, their official number as of 31 March 2005—forty-four years after the event—was 1393. Assuming without admitting that the figure was not inflated, their official number as of 31 December 2010, five years later, actually rose: from 1393 to 1501! A strange species that runs contrary to the laws of evolution.

10. Some of those freedom fighters have been named in published accounts, including:

    •   P.D. Gaitonde, *The Liberation of Goa: A Participant's View of History*, Rajhauns Sankalpana, Goa, 2016.

- Suresh Kanekar, *Goa's Liberation and Thereafter: Chronicles of a Fragmented Life*, Goa, 1556, 2011.
- P.P. Shirodkar, *My Life in Exile* (translated into English by Lt Col Pravinkumar P. Shirodkar, Goa, 2012)
- A press statement issued by twelve freedom fighters carried in the Goan daily *oHERALDo* of 2 February 1987 on p. 2 under the title 'Goan Catholics Are Not Anti-Nationals!'.

Chapter 6: Operation Vijay (The Actual Military Ops)

11. This author is grateful to Brig. Ravi K. Mehta (who was a captain with 4 Sikh LI during the Goa ops in 1961 and participated in the events at Alpalqueiros Hill, Vasco da Gama on the afternoon of 19 December 1961) and to Col Harjeet Singh (veteran, ex-2 Sikh LI), compiler of the Sikh Light Infantry Regimental History who clarified certain facts from the official account of the ops and provided some rare photographs. This unearthing of facts after sixty years was possible only because of the gracious help of Maj. Gen. Anil R.Raikar, VSM (veteran, Sikh Light Infantry Regiment) of Siolim, Goa, now in Pune, to this author.

12. For more on the naval operations and the role of Commander A.F. Collaco (he was awarded a M-in-D for the major role he played in mopping up remnants of the Portuguese garrison at Anjediva), see *The Sun Sets on Protugal's Asian Empire: Liberation of Goa, Daman and Diu*, p. 336, of the account, p. 47 onwards of the PDF document available at: https://www.indiannavy.nic.in/sites/default/themes/indiannavy/images/pdf/chapter12.pdf

13. Type 41 frigates were a novelty that used diesel instead of steam turbines for propulsion; only seven such warships were ever made—four for the British Royal Navy and three for India: INS *Brahmaputra*, *Beas* and the *Betwa*.

14. Not many would know that there were at least a score Indian commissioned officers of Goan origin who participated in Operation Vijay 1 to help relieve Goa of her colonial yoke—and at least one

Goan who died fighting on the side of the Portuguese. Here is a list compiled by this author, but which (caveat, caveat!) is by no means claimed to be complete. There could well be additions. The present list:

1.   Air Vice Marshal Erlic Wilmot Pinto, AOC-in-C of the then unified Operational Command, Indian Air Force, responsible for the conduct of air ops throughout India, was naturally in charge of IAF's ops in Goa, Daman and Diu in 1961. Shifting his base from Poona to Belgaum, he planned and directed air ops in the Portuguese enclaves to ensure nil casualties to the civilian population. From Porvorim.

2.   Brig. Donald Viegas, then a colonel at Army HQ, was sent to Goa to assist then Maj. Gen. K.P. Candeth GOC 17 Infantry Division, appointed military governor of Goa, Daman and Diu. Brig. Viegas was father of well-known Doordarshan news anchor Usha Albuquerque and uncle of Lt Col George Viegas (engineers) who participated in the 1971 war in the East Pakistan theatre. From Curtorim.

3.   Colonel Peter Mendonca, then a major, was the lead battery commander of the elite 17 Parachute Field Regiment—one of the only two specialized airborne artillery units in the Indian Army—as part of the 50 Independent Parachute Brigade, the force that spearheaded the operations, entering Goa from Dodamarg in the north in 1961. Units of the brigade were the first to reach Betim and Banastari by the same evening, 18 December 1961. From Moira.

4.   Capt. Patrick Ivor Telles, a seasoned gunner of the Indian Navy, sailed aboard the INS *Dharini* with Capt. H.A. Agate, Naval Officer-in-charge Goa, as his chief staff officer. On 26 December 1961, he was also appointed captain of ports, the first captain of ports in post-1961 Goa. When in Goa, he also served at INS *Angre* (Addl Goa Command) upto 24 February 1963 and as captain of ports Goa up to mid-1963. From Ponda.

5.   Capt. A.F. Collaco, then a commander, was fleet operations officer of the then unified Indian Fleet, aboard the surface action command ship, INS *Mysore*. He went to Anjediva

Island during the ops, re-established radio-telephone contact between the landing parties on the island and the warships, aided in the assault and played a major role in the mopping-up ops for which he was awarded an M-in-D. From Margao (?)

6. Group Capt. Trevor Joseph Fernandes, then a young flight lieutenant, flew one of the six Hawker Hunters of 17 Squadron that disabled the communications and radio centre at Bambolim. He was then part of the escort that provided cover to the second wave of Canberra bombers targeting the Dabolim runway. From Siolim.

7. Lt Col Louis Fonseca, then a major with 1 Armoured Regiment, led 8 Cavalry, a column of AMX battle tanks. He was part of the 17 Infantry Division that entered Goa via Anmod–Molem–Darbandora and then, on account of broken bridges, took a diversion via Sanvordem–Quepem–Margao–Vasco da Gama, together with the artillery and motorized column of the Division. From Badem, Salvador do Mundo.

8. Lt Col Vitalio de Paula Ribeiro Lobo, engineers, then a major, built the bailey bridge across the Zuari River at Borim along with his troops in double quick time. He was married to a Correia-Afonso of Benaulim. From Camorlim–Bardez.

9. Lt Col Paul Baylon Fernandes, then a captain, headed the 'Black Cats' motorized column of the 17 Infantry Division (taking the same route as the artillery and armour as mentioned at 7 above). He was retained in Goa to help in the takeover of the administration. From Sarzora.

10. Surgeon Cdr Joseph G. Rodrigues accompanied the naval Task Force to Goa on board the R Class destroyer INS *Rajput*. From Piedade–Divar.

11. Surgeon Cdr Frederick Nazareth accompanied the naval Task Force to Goa on board the surface action command ship, cruiser INS *Mysore*. From Nachinola.

12. Surgeon Cdr Joel de Sa Cordeiro was onboard the carrier INS *Vikrant* from the time of the carrier's arrival in India from the UK. Goa was her first op. From Piedade–Divar.

13. Wing Cdr Vishwanath Balakrishna Sawardekar participated in Op Vijay-1, but his specific role is not available. From Sanvordem.

14. Wing Cdr Mervyn Jude Pinto ('Top Gun') participated in Op Vijay-1, but his specific role is not available. From Socorro–Porvorim.

15. Wing Cdr Remegius ('Remy') Victor Paul, then a flight sergeant, flew in B-24 Liberator bomber aircraft of 6 Squadron from the Pune airbase. From Tivim.

16. Maj. Gerson R.A. de Souza served as aide to military governor, Maj. Gen. K.P. Candeth, in 1961–62. From Moira.

17. Maj. Cezar P.F. Lobo, a pilot with the Air Observation Post of the Artillery Regiment, was tasked to take charge and look after the VIP POW a day after Maj. Gen. Vassalo e Silva surrendered at Alpalqueiros Hill, Vasco da Gama, as Maj. Lobo was fluent in the Portuguese language. From Aldona.

18. Lt Cdr John Eric Gomes was onboard Frigate No. 2, INS *Cauvery*, one of the three Indian assault warships that disabled the destroyer NRP *Afonso de Albuquerque*, the only Portuguese warship then in Goa. The defending destroyer took a direct hit from a 4-inch shell fired by the INS *Cauvery*. Lt Cdr Gomes was retained in Goa to help in the takeover of the administration. From Margao.

19. Captain Pinto. Dr Suresh Kanekar, freedom fighter, says in his book *Goa's Liberation and Thereafter: Chronicles of a Fragmented Life*, 'Brig. K.S. Dhillon's adjutant was Captain Pinto, a Goan, who naturally knew the language of the natives' (Kanekar, 2011, p. 146). Brig. Dhillon commanded the 63 Infantry Brigade that entered Goa from Anmod on 18 December 1961.

20. Lt Jose de Figueiredo Melo was on the anti-submarine frigate INS *Kirpan*, first deployed at Karwar on 28 November 1961 and was then part of the INS *Vikrant* carrier group. The *Kirpan* was the first Indian warship to enter Goan waters on 15 December 1961. From Saligao.

    There may be other Goans who participated in Op Vijay-1 that the author is presently not aware of.

There were others who were seconded to help run the administration. Lt Cdr (later commander) Cajetan Francis Dias of Ambora–Salcete was sent as the deputy captain of ports in April 1962.

According to Portuguese General Carlos de Azeredo (*Passagem para a Índia* in Portugal's *O Expresso* of 8 December 2001), then twenty-eight-year-old, future general Sunith F. Rodrigues—hailing from a 'remarkable family that provided five priests but only one general'—accompanied the 1961 *Op Vijay-1* forces to Goa, although he did not participate in the ops. Gen. Rodrigues was a pilot at the Air Observation Post of the Artillery in Adampur at the time.

Gen. Rodrigues was nine years old when his father, a journalist with the *Times of India* in Bombay, wrote some scathing articles against the Portuguese and the family was denied entry into Goa until the colonial yoke was unshackled in December 1961. The future chief of the Indian Army did not need a Portuguese visa when entering Goa! His cousin, his father's brother's son, John Rodrigues, a police sub-inspector in Bombay, was deputed to Goa immediately after 19 December 1961.

According to a report quoted by author Shrikant Y. Ramani, fatalities at Anjediva Island on 18 December 1961 included a Goan who fought for the Portuguese, Damuno Vassu Canencar (Damu Vassu Kanekar) (Ramani, *Operation Vijay: The Ultimate Solution*, 2008, p. 342).

Chapter 7: Portuguese Surrender and POW Repatriation

15.   An aside: Konkani, this author's mother tongue, is a versatile language. It changes from state to state. Konkani spoken in south Maharashtra's Konkan region is not the same as that which is spoken in Goa, is not the same as that which is spoken in coastal Karnataka and is certainly not the same as that which is spoken in north coastal Kerala. Why, even within Goa, the language varies from one riverbank to the other (rivers generally demarcate Goa's talukas). Bardesi Konkani differs

from Tiswadi Konkani, which together vary from Ponda's *Antruzi* Konkani, all of which differ from Salcete Konkani. A soft and almost lilting *sheum* (girl) in Bardez morphs into a gruff *cheddum*, in this author's native Salcete. Wailed a Bardesi adage, *naka ghe mai Xashticho ghov, maddak bandun dita fov* (a maiden pleads with her mother that she doesn't want a roughshod husband from Salcete). The language is so versatile that one can judge the geographic origin of its speaker!

16.   There is a story behind the name of Portugal's 1974 revolution. Led by Artillery Colonel Otelo Saraiva Carvalho, the main attack unit passed by Rossio, Lisbon's central square where, by tradition, florists sell the first red carnations of the season. Celeste, a female florist, was keen that her unsold flowers (due to political disturbances) were given away before they wilted. Troops took the carnations from her and stuck them in the barrel-ends of their guns and tank cannons to symbolize a bloodless overthrow. Col Otelo Saraiva Carvalho was of Luso–Goan descent. His mother, Fernanda Áurea Pegado Romão, was a Goan born in Goa and married to a Portuguese who worked either for the railways or for the colonial postal service in Goa.

Chapter 9: The Fallacies

17.   The signatories to the press handout were: George Vaz (trade unionist), Padmashri Lambert Mascarenhas (editor, *Goa Today*), Froilano Machado (former Speaker, Goa Legislative Assembly), Cajetan Lobo (journalist), Dr Jose Francisco Martins (medical practitioner), Antonio Blasio de Souza (retired Civil and Criminal Judge), Dr J. Carvalho (medical practitioner), Roque Santan Fernandes (former MLA), Armando Santan Pereira (advocate), Ilidio Costa (businessman), Enio Pimenta (former MLA) and Fabião Costa (landlord).

18.   The names of a few leaders would suffice to demonstrate how mixed the group was. Among those fighting for Goa's freedom by peaceful means: T.B. Cunha and his myriad followers (Goa National Congress, Goan Youth League, Goa Action Committee), Adv. Ariosto Tovar Dias, Caetano Manuel de Souza, Adv. Cristovam Furtado, Enio Pimenta, Dr Eric D'Melo, Guilherme de Souza Ticlo, Prof. James Fernandes, Dr Jose Francisco Martins, Jaywant Kunde,

Dr Jose Maria Furtado, Laxmanrao Sardesai, Mark Fernandes, Mukund Kamat Dhakankar, Narayan Naik, Nilkanth M. Karapurkar, Dr P.D. Gaitonde, Peter Alvares, P.J. Pinto, P.P. Shirodkar, Rafael A. de Souza, Dr Ram Hegde, S.F. de Melo, Dr Suresh Kanekar, S.S. Carvalho, Vasant Kare, Venkatesh Vaidya, Vinayak N. Mayenkar (National Congress Goa), Prof. Aloysius Soares, Prof. Armando Menezes, Prof. Velingkar, Prof. Francisco Correia Afonso, J.M. Pinto, J.N. Heredia, L.J. de Souza (Goa Liberation Council), John Mariano D'Souza (Goan National Union), Dr Juliao de Menezes (*Gomantak Praja Mandal*), Dr H.C. Denis and Adv. João Cabral (Goan Political Convention/Goan League, London).

In a sub-category of the above were Goan Catholic professionals like Adv. A.X. Gomes Pereira, Dr Álvaro de Loyola Furtado and Dr António Colaço who also favoured integration with India but not hurriedly, as did journalists like Alfred Braganza, Alvaro da Costa, Arsenio Jacques, Berta de Menezes Braganza, Bonifacio Dias, Cajetan Lobo, Evagrio Jorge, Felicio Cardoso, Felix Valois Rodrigues, Flaviano Dias, F.M. Pinto, J.M. Pinto, Lambert Mascarenhas, Massilon de Almeida, Porfirio Silva Lobo and Santana Sebastiao ('SS') Carvalho.

Among those working towards the same end but by militant means: Vishwanath Lawande (Azad Gomantak Dal, which had a large number of Catholics like Albert Fernandes, Anthony Leo Sequeira, Armando Pereira, Chagas da Cunha, Christopher Lobo, Cristovam Gabriel Paulo das Angustias Furtado, Fulgencio Moraes, Dr John Costa Bir, Mussolini Menezes, Rafael Tavares, Roque Santan Fernandes, Sebastiao ('Tony') Fernandes and Zotico de Souza), Augusto Alvares, Balkrishna Bhonsle, Jaysingrao Rane, Shivaji Desai, Urselino Almeida (Goa Liberation Army), George Vaz, Divakar Kakodkar (Goan People's Party), Frank R.P. Andrades, Janardhan Shinkre, John Gilbert Rebello and Libano de Souza (Quit Goa Organisation), Prabhakar Sinari (*Rancour Patriotica*, which also had a large number of Catholics like Antonio Costa Frias, Ernesto Costa Frias, Ilidio Costa, Cruz Viegas, Eusebio Viegas, Inacinho Viegas, Dr Manu Fernandes, Manuelinho Viegas, Polly Silva, Ponciano Pereira and Socorro Costa), Antonio Furtado, Francisco Mascarenhas and Vaman Desai (United Front of Goans).

19.   Known votaries of this group were António Sequeira, Balkrishna
      Sinai Sukhtankar, Bombi Naik, Adv. Fanchu Loyola, Fernando
      Menezes Bragança, Francisco Xavier Furtado, Dr Froilano de
      Melo, Adv. Gopal Apa Kamat, Gopinath Kurade, Adv. Pandurang
      Mulgaokar, Adv. Francisco Paola Ribeiro, Purushottam Kakodkar,
      Shankar Sardesai and Vicente João de Figueiredo.

20.   Prominent Hindus were Anant Palondikar, Adv. Atmaram Poi
      Palondicar, B. Sinai Ramani, Balkrishna Sinai Sukhtankar, Datta
      Fatu Dessai, Gopal Prabhu Nachinolkar, Dr Govind D. Vaidya, Adv.
      Govind Sinai Orti, Jaywant Surya Kandeparkar, Kashinath Sar Desai,
      Krishna Bangui, Adv. Madhav Rao, Madhusudan Desai, Manohar
      Prabhu Tamba, Adv. Mukund Sincró, Narayan Parcenkar Desai,
      Narayan Surya Rau Desai, Dr Ramesh Atmaram Borkar, Sadanand
      Govind Prabhu Desai, Sakharam Gopal Sinai Gude, Dr Vaman
      Naik, Dr Vaman Sinai Xeldenkar, Adv. Vassu Fatu Gauns, Venctexa
      Ananta Pai Raikar, Dr Venkatesh Rau Sar Desai, Adv. Vinayak
      Sinai Kaissare, Vinayak Sinai Neurenkar and Margao businessmen
      Esvonta Poy Raiturcar, Gopal Sinai Borkar, Kashinath Damodar
      Naik, Narayan Virgincar, Narcinva Damodar Naik, Sambari and
      Vissu Sinai Virgincar.

21.   If further proof of a mix of creeds and castes is necessary, peruse
      this list of Goans who signed the 29 March 1952 Memorandum
      in Margao, handed over to visiting Portuguese Overseas Minister,
      Cmde. Manuel Maria Sarmento Rodrigues (due to visit Goa
      20 April to 12 May 1952). It may be noted that each and every
      signatory was against continuance of Portuguese rule in Goa. The
      list totally dispels the myth that each approach to Goa's future was
      divided by caste and creed:
           Abílio Souza (adv.), Aires Gomes (landlord), Aleixo Veloso
      (Dr), Aluísio Colaço (eng.), Álvaro de Loyola Furtado (Dr), Álvaro
      Remédios Furtado (adv.), Anastácio Souza (adv.), António Anastácio
      Bruto da Costa (adv.), António Cândido dos Santos Pereira
      (landlord), António da Costa (adv.), António do Nascimento Colaço
      (Dr), António Gracias (Dr), António João Quadros (adv.), António
      José de Souza (landlord), António José Pais (landlord), Argemiro da
      Gama Barreto (Dr), Ariosto Tovar Dias (adv.), A.T. Prisónio Furtado
      (adv.), Atmarama Xembu Palondicar (adv.), Augusto Barreto

(pharmacist), Aureliano Miranda (Dr), A.X. Gomes Pereira (adv.), Barónio Monteiro (Dr), Basílio Cota (Dr), Bernardo Reis (adv.), Caetano Filipe da Silva (adv.), Caetano Vás (Dr), Camilo Severino Rodrigues (landlord, president of Landlords and Agriculturists Association), Carmino de Santa Rita Lobo (Dr), Carmo Eduardo da Silva (teacher), Casimiro Ribeiro (landlord), Cipriano da Cunha Gomes (adv., president of Advocates Association), Emérico Martins (Dr), Esvonta Poi Raiturcar (businessman), Francisco Correia (Dr), Francisco da Paula Ribeiro (adv.), Francisco Figueiredo (landlord), Francisco Pinto de Menezes (adv.), Francisco Xavier Furtado (agriculturist), Francisco Xavier Valles (adv.), Gambeta da Costa (Dr), Govind D. Vaidya (Dr), Govind Sinai Orti (adv.), Joaquim da Cunha (landlord), Joaquim Filipe Álvares (priest), José Francisco Furtado (landlord), José Martinho Cordeiro (Adv.), José Sebastião da Piedade Colaço (landlord), Kashinath Damodar Naik (businessman), Baltazar Fernandes (landlord), Lázaro de Souza (landlord), Lázaro Gonzaga Faleiro (adv.), Lino Souza (landlord), Luís Colaço (landlord), Luís da Costa (landlord), Luís José Lourenço (eng.), Madhusudan Desai (landlord), Mário Cardoso (adv.), Mário da Silva Coelho (adv.), Mukund Sincró (adv.), Narayan Parcenkar Desai (landlord), Narcinva Damodar Naik (businessman), Nicolau Menezes (teacher), Nicolau Noronha (priest, editor, *A Vida*), Pascoal Menezes (Dr), Roldão de Souza (landlord), Roque Azaredo (adv.), Salvador J.J. de Souza (adv.), Vaman Naik (Dr), Vaman Sinai Xeldencar (Dr), Vassu Fatu Gauns (adv.), Venctexa Ananta Poi Raikar (writer), Venctexa V. Sardesai (pharmacist), Vinayak Sinai Kaissare (adv.) and Vissu Sinai Virgincar (businessman).

The list above is borrowed from Adv. Mário Bruto da Costa, *Goa: A terceira corrente*, 2013, pp. 6–8, also reproduced by Filipa Alexandra Carvalho Sousa Lopes, *As vozes da oposição ao estado novo e a questão de Goa (1950–1961)*, University of Porto, 2017, in Chapter 2 ('A viagem ministerial a Goa'), footnote no. 258, p. 153.